Aslı Gürer
Information Structure Within Interfaces

Interface Explorations

Edited by
Artemis Alexiadou
T. Alan Hall

Volume 32

Aslı Gürer
Information Structure Within Interfaces

Consequences for the Phrase Structure

DE GRUYTER
MOUTON

ISBN 978-1-5015-2671-8
e-ISBN (PDF) 978-1-5015-0558-4
e-ISBN (EPUB) 978-1-5015-0556-0
ISSN 1861-4167

Library of Congress Control Number: 2019950537

Bibliographic information published by the Deutsche Nationalbibliothek
The Deutsche Nationalbibliothek lists this publication in the Deutsche Nationalbibliografie;
detailed bibliographic data are available on the Internet at http://dnb.dnb.de.

© 2021 Walter de Gruyter Inc., Boston/Berlin
This volume is text- and page-identical with the hardback published in 2020.
Typesetting: Integra Software Services Pvt. Ltd.
Printing and binding: CPI books GmbH, Leck

www.degruyter.com

Contents

Chapter 1
Information structure within interfaces —— 1
1.1 Introduction —— 1
1.2 Theoretical framework —— 5
1.2.1 The phases as the building blocks —— 5
1.2.2 Discourse features as formal features —— 7
1.3 A brief note on information structural notions: "a terminological minefield" —— 10
1.4 Word order variation in a discourse-configurational language: Turkish —— 14
1.5 Layout of the book —— 19

Chapter 2
Semantic and pragmatic marking of information structure —— 20
2.1 Introduction —— 20
2.2 Different approaches to information structuring —— 21
2.3 Information structural units in Turkish —— 24
2.3.1 Focus —— 24
2.3.2 Topic —— 37
2.3.3 Contrast —— 52
2.3.4 Discourse anaphoric constituents —— 53
2.4 Overt particles with contrastive topic and focus phrases —— 56
2.4.1 Sadece/yalnızca, bile —— 56
2.4.2 dA —— 58
2.4.3 ise —— 60
2.5 Distribution of information structural units in Turkish —— 60
2.5.1 Focus phrases —— 60
2.5.2 Topic phrases —— 72
2.5.3 Discourse anaphoric constituents —— 80
2.6 Conclusion —— 81

Chapter 3
Prosodic marking of focus —— 83
3.1 Introduction —— 83
3.2 Prosodic realization of focus —— 84
3.3 Prosodic properties of Turkish —— 88
3.4 First study —— 96
3.4.1 The stimuli —— 97

3.4.2	Participants and the recording procedure —— 100	
3.4.3	Measurement points —— 100	
3.4.4	Results —— 101	
3.4.5	Discussion —— 104	
3.5	Second study —— 106	
3.5.1	The stimuli —— 106	
3.5.2	Participants and the recording procedure —— 108	
3.5.3	Measurement points —— 109	
3.5.4	Results —— 111	
3.5.5	GCG pitch tracks with a different pattern —— 115	
3.5.6	Post focal fall pattern —— 117	
3.5.7	Interim summary —— 120	
3.5.8	Discussion —— 120	
3.6	Phase driven sentential stress and focal stress —— 131	
3.7	One-word level propositions —— 136	
3.8	Conclusion —— 138	

Chapter 4
Syntactic marking of information structural units —— 140

4.1	Introduction —— 140	
4.2	Left peripheral or IP internal functional projections —— 141	
4.3	The interaction of information structural units with negation —— 142	
4.3.1	Position of contrastive topic —— 152	
4.4	The interaction of information structural units with quantifier scope and binding —— 157	
4.4.1	First study —— 159	
4.4.2	Second study —— 167	
4.4.3	Third study —— 173	
4.5	The syntactic mechanism —— 176	
4.5.1	Quantifier scope and binding in SOV with indefinite-universal quantifier order —— 176	
4.5.2	Quantifier scope and binding in OSV with universal-indefinite quantifier order —— 186	
4.5.3	Quantifier scope in OSV with indefinite-universal quantifier order —— 193	
4.6	Scope domain of focus —— 198	
4.7	Derivation of information structural units at LF —— 208	

4.8	Multiple focus projections —— 213
4.8.1	Focus and wh-features —— 219
4.9	Conclusion —— 222

Chapter 5
Revisiting the phrase structure of Turkish —— 224

5.1	Introduction —— 224
5.2	CP/DP parallelism —— 225
5.3	Determiner phrase in Turkish —— 227
5.3.1	Arguments against DP —— 227
5.3.2	Arguments for DP —— 237
5.4	Complementizer phrase in Turkish —— 242
5.4.1	Binding data and the CP domain —— 244
5.4.2	ECM clauses and the CP domain —— 251
5.4.3	Bounding nodes and the CP domain —— 257
5.5	Tense phrase in Turkish —— 259
5.5.1	Alternative heads for case checking and temporal interpretation —— 259
5.5.2	Verbal inflectional morphology and the status of TP —— 263
5.5.3	No DP no TP —— 272
5.6	Concluding Remarks —— 281

Appendix A —— 283

Appendix B —— 285

Appendix C —— 287

Bibliography —— 295

Index —— 307

Chapter 1
Information structure within interfaces

1.1 Introduction

The investigation of information structural units has been a central issue in understanding the structure of grammar. Semantic, pragmatic, syntactic and prosodic factors are intertwined in the expression of information packaging, which in turn provides insight, not only, into the interfaces of these components, but also, into how diverse languages encode such information. The present work establishes a three-way classification for information structural units as (i) topic, which is further classified as aboutness topic and contrastive topic, (ii) focus, which is realized as discourse-new and contrastive focus and (iii) discourse anaphoric, given constituents. The investigation of information packaging becomes more complex but all the more intriguing, as some languages encode information structural units in several domains, use the same tools in the expression of further linguistic operations or do not mark them at all.

Gungbe (Aboh 2007), Chickasaw (Büring 2009), West Chadic languages Bole, Hausa and Tangale (Zimmerman 2011), Somali (Frascarelli 2012) mark focus with overt morphological markers. However, variation is observed even within a single language. In Gungbe, there is a difference between subject and object focus phrases in that in-situ object phrases are not marked overtly (1b).

(1) a. Été wὲ Kòfí ḍù?
 what FOC Kofi eat
 'What did Kofi eat?'
 b. É ḍù lésì
 3SG eat rice
 'He ate rice.'
 c. Lésì wὲ é ḍù (bò bέ àwútù)
 rice FOC 3SG eat and start sickness
 'He ate rice (and became sick).'
 (adapted from Aboh 2007: 291)

Some languages encode information structure through prosodic strategies. In English, the distinction between discourse-new constituents and contrastive focus is reflected in prosody in that contrastive focus has a higher pitch height and duration than discourse-new constituents (Katz and Selkirk 2011). In Italian, if a constituent in a sentence is marked with [F], it restructures and enlarges its phonological phrase but this is not the case in constructions with all-new sentences (Frascarelli 1997). In Japanese and German, focus and givenness have an effect on pitch register while syntactic structure has an effect on prosodic structure (Féry and Ishihara 2009). In Tangale, a phrase boundary is inserted before the focused phrase (Zimmerman 2011).

Syntactic reordering is another strategy used to mark information packaging. In Italian, shifting (aboutness), contrastive and familiar topic phrases surface in a sentence in this hierarchical order (Frascarelli and Hinterhölzl 2007). In Romanian, Catalan and Hungarian, the immediately preverbal position has been suggested to be the identificational, contrastive focus position (Kiss 1998).

(2) a. *Tegnap este Marinak mutattam be Pétert.*
 last night Mary.DAT introduced.I PERF Peter.ACC
 'It was to Mary that I introduced Peter last night.'
 b. *Tegnap este be mutattam Pétert Marinak.*
 'Last night I introduced Peter to Mary.'
 (adapted from Kiss 1998: 247)

In (2a), the preverbal dative marked constituent bears identificational focus in Hungarian. It is the sentence final position that is reserved for this purpose in Russian (Dyakonova 2009) and Spanish (Zubizarretta 1998) or sentence initial position in Finnish (Vallduví and Vilkuna 1998) and Hausa (Zimmermann 2011). In Bole, a Bantu language, focused subjects undergo movement to the postverbal position and in that case, morphological marking becomes optional (Zimmermann 2011).

A language can also use mixed strategies and encode the information status of the constituent in different domains of the grammar. In Hungarian, narrow focus phrases undergo movement to the immediate preverbal position as in (2a). Genzel, Ishihara and Surányi (2014) note that in the prosodic domain, narrow focus phrases have higher f0 values and longer duration when compared to the constituents in the same position in broad focus sentences. Additionally, contrastive focus phrases yield more pre-focal and post-focal prominence reduction than non-contrastive focus phrases.

The prosodic, syntactic or morphological strategies used to realize information structural units can be used for certain other constructions as well. In Gungbe and Somali, the morphological marker used with focus phrases is also used with wh-phrases (Aboh 2007; Frascarelli 2012). In Somali, question formation requires the question marker *ma* and the focus marker *baa* as illustrated below.

(3) *Cali muxuu (ma+wax+baa+uu) cunay?*
     Cali QM.thing.FM.3SGM   eat.PAST.1SG
     'What did Cali eat?'
     (Frascarelli 2012: 184)

Hence, the investigation of information structural encoding is not an easy task as it is not possible to restrict the investigation to a single domain.

This book aims to offer an in-depth investigation of information structural units by taking semantic, syntactic, prosodic domains and their interactions into consideration. Bringing data from different domains is advantageous in gaining new insights into the model of grammar. The novelty and main contribution of the present work also rests on exploring interfaces via experimental studies.

The language that the current study focuses on is Turkish and Turkish has been cited as a free word order language, as definite arguments allow six word order permutations (Erkü 1982; Erguvanlı 1984; Kural 1992; Göksel and Kerslake 2005; Şener 2010; among many others). However, the same researchers have concluded that this variation is not fully free in the sense that each word order serves special discourse-related purposes. Word order variation is used to express a different information structuring and hence it is not possible to propose an analysis of movement operations in Turkish without recourse to the semantic properties of these units, which in turn have an effect on prosody.

Taking into account the above-mentioned dimensions of grammar, the central findings of the book are that:

(i) Within the semantic domain, a ternary classification captures information packaging: topic as aboutness topic and contrastive topic, focus as discourse-new and contrastive focus, and finally discourse anaphoric or given constituents. The investigation within this study sheds new light on word order restrictions in Turkish. Neither contrastive nor discourse-new focus phrases are restricted to a designated syntactic position, both focus types can surface in-situ optionally followed by discourse anaphoric constituents. It is not contrast but exhaustive identification that differentiates contrastive focus phrases from discourse-new focus in that only with contrastive focus phrases is the constituent exhaustively identified as the correct answer to the exclusion of the other alternatives. Another major contribution of this study is to show the dependency between focus and contrastive topic phrases. The dependency of contrastive topics on focus phrases and the ordering restrictions are due to the semantic compositionality of contrastive topics. Contrastive topic phrases build up on focus phrases in the sense that while focus is a set of alternative propositions, contrastive topic is a set of sets of alternative propositions. The ordering restriction of contrastive topic over contrastive focus cannot be explained via a nested-foci analysis in line with Wagner (2007, 2008) as contrastive topic phrases can surface in the postverbal domain which is not possible for focus phrases in Turkish. The so-called double foci constructions in Turkish are reanalyzed as contrastive topic-focus order and arbitrary results for Turkish intervention effects are explained (Kesen 2010).

(ii) In the prosodic domain, experimental studies reveal that in SOV order, discourse-new and contrastive focus phrases in the immediately preverbal position do not differ from the constituents in broad focus sentences in the same position or from each other with respect to f0 height or duration. Phonologically, the phonological phrase including the focus phrase necessitates alignment as the rightmost phonological phrase. Phonetically, focus prominence is realized as IP level stress. F marking strategy is the driving force behind IP level stress assignment. The other option is to resort to phase domains to determine stress assignment. According to this line of argument, the highest constituent in the lower *v*P phase domain attracts IP level stress (Üntak-Tarhan 2006). However, this analysis cannot account for the optional phrasing possibilities of unergative and unaccusative structures in Turkish. If stress assignment is due to phase domains which maps strictly onto phonological phrases, optionality is not expected.

(iii) In the syntactic domain, experimental tests have been run to reveal the interaction of information structural notions with negation and quantifier scope. Based on the findings of these various tests and including binding data by Şener (2010), a parsimonious syntactic mechanism is proposed that can fully capture the data. In contrast to the cartographic approach (Rizzi 1997), IP internal CP projections above *v*P are proposed. IP internal FocP captures the tendency of focus phrases to appear in the immediate preverbal position in Turkish. Scope judgments for SOV and OSV order in Turkish with all possible information structural encodings illustrate that movement operations in Turkish are driven only by discourse-related purposes. The binding and quantifier scope data further indicates that reconstruction possibilities for the first merge position are not the same for constituents with different discourse functions. Hence, the discussion in this chapter also casts doubt on the diagnostics of phasehood.

(iv) The book takes a novel look at Turkish phrase structure based on the empirical findings regarding semantic, prosodic and syntactic domains. The interfaces of these domains lead to implications for movement operations, the inventory of functional categories, and phase theory which are central to syntactic theory. Firstly, *v*P as a phase cannot determine stress assignment, reconstruction to the complement domain of the *v*P phase shows variation with respect to information structural units. Secondly, Turkish data reveals that binding is possible across two CP boundaries which gives empirical support for the questionable phasehood status of *v*P. Building also on the diagnostics of the presence of TP projection proposed by Bošković (2010, 2012), the status of these projections is questioned.

Before going into the details of the present study, the next section briefly summarizes the theoretical framework relevant to the discussion of information packaging with a special focus on phase domains as propositional units, phase edges for restrictions on movement operations and reconstruction sites.

1.2 Theoretical framework

1.2.1 The phases as the building blocks

The analysis of the structures in this book is carried out in reference to the Minimalist Program (MP). The structures are built via Merge. Merge is further classified as External Merge (EM) and Internal Merge (IM). Chomsky (2008: 140) suggests that "(...) EM yields generalized argument structure (theta roles, the 'cartographic' hierarchies, and similar properties); and IM yields discourse-related properties such as old information and specificity, along with scopal effects." In a sense, phases, the heads of which are the locus of all features, are derived through external merge. Chomsky (2000) suggests two criteria for phasehood. Phases are propositional in that these syntactic units can be judged as true or false and independent in the sense that *v*P displays full argument structure while CP has tense and force properties. Legate (2003) suggests the following criteria in applying the diagnostics for phasehood:

i. Phase edges are possible quantifier raising targets in antecedent contained deletion (ACD).
ii. Phase edges are possible reconstruction sites.
iii. Parasitic gaps are licensed by a wh-trace at the V phase edge.

Note that the diagnostics depend heavily on the edge positions of a phase. The edge position of a phase serves as an escape hatch for movement which is carried out through internal merge. Once the complement domain of a phase is sent to LF and PF, the complement domain of a phase is no longer available for computation. However, the edge can still be within the search domain of a probe in the higher phase. This restriction is labeled as Phase Impenetrability Condition (PIC): in phase α with head H, the domain of H is not accessible to operations outside α, but only H and its edge (Chomsky 2000: 108).

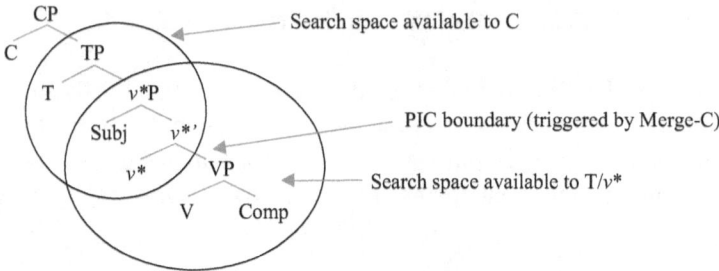

Figure 1: Search domain of probes (Richards 2012: 137).

As shown above, the complement domain of vP is not sent to Spell-Out until the merge of CP and hence VP is within the search domain of the T head. Note that according to this representation once CP is merged, only v and the edge of vP are available as an escape hatch for movement.

Phases have not been exempt from controversy. Chomsky (2001) distinguishes phases as strong and weak phases and suggests that unaccusative and passive vPs are weak phases. Legate (2003) opposes this view and argues that unaccusative and passive vPs display phasehood properties relying on the above-mentioned tests. Butler (2004) argues that if vP and CP are phases then they should have an equal amount of semantic and syntactic structures and proposes IP internal CP level projections in the middle field. With this adjustment to the phase system, quantificational heads such as FocP, NegP, which are generated at the left periphery within the cartographic approach (Rizzi 1997), can surface above the lower phase. These additional functional projections above the lower phase evaluate the quantificational relations and make the domain of the phase a referential unit to be used in higher phases. Based on the CP/DP parallelism, Hiraiwa (2005) suggests not only CP but also DP as a phase. Öztürk (2005) argues that in Turkish the vP phase does not exist. Grohmann (2003), on the other hand, suggests prolific domains of vP, IP, and CP as spell-out units similar to phase theory. However, in Grohmann's work, instead of phase impenetrability condition, restriction on movement and reconstruction is dealt with through restrictions on successive cyclic movement. Hence, phase edges do not have a special status within his analysis. Based on binding and movement data, Bošković (2016) suggests that only the outmost specifier position of a phase serves as a basis for further operations and the spell-out domain excludes only this outmost specifier position. To sum up, the status or spell-out domain of a phase is far from resolved from a theoretical and cross-linguistic perspective.

Turkish is a good testing ground for understanding phrase structure and phases because movement operations are triggered for discourse-related purposes. This book is an attempt to shed new light on the architecture of grammar from the perspective of a discourse-configurational language.

1.2.2 Discourse features as formal features

As noted in the preceding section, internal merge yields discourse-related properties. A natural question arises at this point concerning the motivation of merge operations. As is well known, the formal features such as phi features are part of the lexical item coming from the lexicon. A feature checking operation occurs between a probe and a goal through Agree and if the probe has an edge feature the goal is attracted to its specifier position. Can this analysis be extended to discourse features? If the answer is yes, this amounts to saying that discourse features are encoded in syntax. This is the line of argument pursued in this book and it is assumed that the constituents marked with focus, topic or discourse anaphoric functions enter the derivation with the relevant discourse features, as is the case with formal features.

Adopting discourse features as formal features has been questioned based on the distinction between the two. A constituent can be focus, topic or discourse anaphoric based on context so information structure is more of a relational concept when compared to formal features. This raises a problem for the Inclusiveness Condition which states that the output of a system does not contain anything beyond its input (Slioussar 2007). As for movement operations that seem to be triggered for discourse-related purposes, operational movements have been proposed (Horvath 2005). This point is further supported by the observation that so-called focus and topic movements are not morphologically marked. Formal features, in contrast, are generally marked.

Frascarelli (2012) argues against this analysis, based on languages that mark focus or topic with overt morphological markers such as Bole (Zimmerman 2008), Chickasaw (Büring 2009), Gungbe (Dyakonova 2009) and Somali (Frascarelli 2012). Similar to formal features, a feature checking mechanism occurs between a probe and a goal, and overt morphological markers surface on the constituents.

There is also a close relationship between the wh-feature which is an unquestioned formal feature and focus. In Gungbe, wh-questions also bear a focus marker as illustrated in (1). Somali is similar to Gungbe in that both wh-phrases and focus phrases are marked with the same morphological marker

(Frascarelli 2012). For Turkish, Şener (2010) also suggests that non-discourse linked wh-phrases are focus phrases marked with [F] feature similar to non-wh-focus phrases. Hence, an [F] feature must be a part of the syntax.

The other proposal for discourse features to be encoded in syntax comes from consideration of the differences between root and embedded CPs with respect to information structuring. Frascarelli (2012) suggests that as root and embedded CPs do not have the same array of functional projections some of the discourse-related features are available only in main clauses. If syntax were blind to discourse features, the parallelism between the lack of some functional projections in embedded CPs and the lack of some information structural units could not be explained. Dyakonova (2009: 18) further suggests that, even sentences without a context, undergo information structure partitioning. Hence, information structuring is rooted in syntax and not fully dependent on context.

In Turkish, there is no morphological marker that surfaces obligatorily with focus and topic phrases. However, there are optional discourse particles that surface with contrastive focus, discourse-new focus, and contrastive topic phrases. In (5A), *ise* 'as for' follows the contrastive topic. Now, consider the following Turkish data. In (4A), the accusative case marked constituent undergoes movement. It is possible for the same constituent to remain in its base generated position as in (4B). In (5A), again, the accusative marked constituent undergoes movement but it cannot remain in its base generated position as illustrated in (5B).

(4) *Kitab-ı   Ahmet mi yoksa Mehmet mi oku-muş?*
    book-ACC Ahmet QP or   Mehmet QP read-PERF
    bir fikr-in   var mı
    a   idea-2SG.POSS exist QP
    'Did Ahmet or Mehmet read the book? Do you have any ideas?'
    A: *Kitab-ı   Ahmet oku-muş.*
       book-ACC Ahmet read-PERF
       'Ahmet read the book.'
    B: *Ahmet   kitab-ı oku-muş.*

(5) *Kitab-ı   Ahmet mi yoksa Mehmet mi oku-muş?*
    book-ACC Ahmet QP or   Mehmet QP read-PERF
    bir fikr-in   var mı
    a   idea-2SG.POSS exist QP
    'Did Ahmet or Mehmet read the book? Do you have any ideas?'

A: *Ahmet kitab-ı oku-muş.*
    Ahmet book-ACC read-PERF
    Dergi-yi ise Mehmet oku-muş.
    magazine-ACC as for Mehmet read-PERF
    'Ahmet read the book. As for the magazine, Mehmet read it.'
B: *Ahmet kitab-ı oku-muş.*
    Ahmet book-ACC read-PERF
    #Mehmet dergi-yi ise oku-muş.
    Mehmet magazine-ACC as for read-PERF

If syntax cannot make reference to discourse features, movement operations can only be triggered by the edge features of the probes. If it were only the edge feature that attracts these constituents to specifier positions, it would not be possible to account for the difference between the two examples. In (4A), the dislocated constituent is an aboutness topic while in (5A) a contrastive topic is evidenced. While discourse anaphoric constituents can follow focus phrases, contrastive topic phrases cannot, and hence there is an obligatory movement operation for contrastive topic phrases. In order to capture these differences, syntax must have recourse to discourse features.

Additionally, the discussion in Chapter 3 indicates that the phrase that includes the [F] marked constituent always aligns with the rightmost phonological phrase. The focus phrase can appear in sentence initial, medial or final domains. As the focused constituent is not restricted to a syntactic position, if focus is not encoded in syntax, how does prosody make the alignment? The alternative analysis is that PF works in tandem with syntax and movement operations are triggered by PF driven motivations which is in line with the Contiguity Theory of Richards (2016). Prosody of information structural units will function similarly to formal features triggering movement operations.[1] This also captures the observation of Dyakonova (2009: 18) that we tend to apply information structural partition even for out of the blue sentences. Both lines of arguments can be captured by the data in this book and

---

[1] Gürer and Göksel (2019) note that prosody does not build up on the syntactic output but works in tandem with syntax. The argument is based on forward and backward gapping constructions in Turkish, which are found to be unacceptable if associated with a particular intonational phrasing pattern. Prosody has a direct effect on syntax forcing constituents to appear in certain positions in the structure, thus yielding the otherwise infelicitous utterances felicitous.

more investigation is needed before conclusive evidence supporting one analysis over the other can be determined. Hence, it is assumed, in accordance with the mainstream approach, that focus and topic features are encoded in syntax as features to be interpretable at LF and PF. Whether through PF driven motivations or information structural features in syntax, what is suggested in this book is that information structuring, similar to formal features, is encoded in syntax.

1.3 A brief note on information structural notions: "a terminological minefield"[2]

Information packaging is multifaceted. The referential status of being given or new, being contrastive with another constituent or not and, if contrastive, being exhaustive or not, being a part of the vehicular or newsy part of the utterance or ordering restrictions in a sentence, all play a crucial role in the identification of information structural notions. As illustrated in the introduction, languages can also differ in the way they mark these constituents. Hence, it is difficult to give an unequivocal definition for information structural terms. The same term explicated in different studies may not refer to the same concept, or the same concept may conflate different terms. The semantic and pragmatic discussion of information packaging is dealt with in Chapter 2. In this section, the terminology used in the literature is outlined.[3]

A focused constituent evokes alternatives as illustrated below (Rooth 1996). A set of propositions is triggered in the form of sentences with alternatives replacing the focus phrase.

(6) A: *Who finished the book?*
    B: *Mary$_F$ finished the book.*[4]
    Focus semantic value *{Mary, John, Tim finished the book}*

---

[2] Vallduví and Engdahl (1996) use the phrase terminological minefield to indicate how risky it is to use the terms interchangeably.
[3] This is not an exhaustive list of the studies on information packaging but demonstrates how packaging is labeled for various languages from different perspectives and the way in which these terms are used in this book.
[4] Throughout the book, the information structural status of the constituents are indicated with subscripts. The same subscripts are also used with quoted examples.

1.3 A brief note on information structural notions: "a terminological minefield"

The terms "presentational focus" or "informational focus" (Krifka 2006), "information focus" (Ishihara and Surányi 2014), "regular focus" (Neeleman and Vermeulen 2012) have been used to refer to focus phrases that are not given and that evoke alternatives in the context of overt or covert questions. Katz and Selkirk (2011), on the other hand, use the term "contrastive focus" for exactly the same discourse function. They use the term "discourse-new" to refer to constituents that are not [F] marked and hence incapable of evoking alternatives. Although discourse-new constituents and presentational/information focus phrases are newly introduced into the discourse, the two terms are not interchangeable because presentational/information focus evokes alternatives.

The terms "identificational (exhaustive) focus" (Krifka 2006) and "identificational (contrastive) focus" (Kiss 1998) refer to a focus constituent that exclusively makes the proposition true from a number of possible alternatives. Kiss (1998) further notes that an identificational focus is also contrastive if the set of alternative propositions are closed. Note that mention of contrast does not make the focus phrases the same in the studies of Katz and Selkirk (2011) and (Kiss 1998).

(7) A: *Did John or Mary finish the book?*
     B: *Mary$_{CF}$ finished the book.*
     Focus semantic value {Mary finished the book, John finished the book}

There is another term that is closely related with focus: "rheme". Rheme, defined as "(...) the actual update potential of an utterance (...)" (Vallduví 2014: 7), is proposed as part of focus together with "kontrast" (Vallduví and Vilkuna 1998). In a similar line, Steedman (2014) suggests that the rheme of an utterance updates the common ground while theme is that part of the utterance that is already in the common ground. Steedman (2014) further suggests that discourse-new and contrastive focus in Katz and Selkirk (2011) can be interpreted as rheme and theme respectively in the context of his study.

In addition to focus sub-types, variation in usage is observed with the terms "narrow focus", "broad focus", "wide focus", "all-new" or "all-rheme". Broad focus (Jackendoff 1972; Ladd 1980; Genzel, Ishihara and Surányi 2014: 3), all-focus (Vallduví 1990: 63; Vallduví and Engdahl 1993: 471), all-rheme (Steedman 2014: 14; Vallduví 2014: 13), and all-new (Katz and Selkirk 2011: 771) refers to cases where the whole utterance is marked as focused.

(8) A: *What is new?*
     B: *[Mary finished the book]$_F$*

However, for Ladd (2008: 215), when a phrase is contrasted with its alternatives which are unlimited in nature, it is marked as broad focus as illustrated below.[5] Hence, being a broad focus is dependent on the nature of the alternative sets.

(9)　*I didn't give him　a dollar　　　I gave him 5 francs.*
　　　　　　　　　　　fifty centimes
　　　　　　　　　　　my notebook
　　　　　　　　　　　your camera
　　　　　　　　　　　the car keys
　　　　　　　　　　　a sandwich
　　　　　　　　　　　a lot of money

The terms referring to topic phrases are not exempt from imprecision. A topic phrase is an entry under which propositions are classified (Reinhart 1981), or "organizational pivots for information" (Vallduví 2014: 21)

(10)　A:　*What about Mary?*
　　　　B:　*[Mary]$_{TOP}$ finished the book.*

In (10) above, it is the sentence initial subject under which the new information is given. Determining the status of a constituent as a topic phrase based on its being a subject or being given in the previous discourse (Chafe 1976) is too permissive.

Contrastive topic phrases differ from (aboutness) topic phrases in that they evoke sets of alternatives. The usage of a contrastive topic phrase indicates a discourse strategy. As illustrated below, the maximum question under discussion is composed of possible questions under discussion and the speaker refrains from giving a complete answer, or shifts the topic from a sub-question to another sub-question (Büring 2003, 2013; Krifka 2008; Wagner 2007, 2008; Dyakonova 2009; Tomioka 2010; Neeleman and Vermeulen 2012; Constant 2014).

(11)　A:　*Who read what?*
　　　　B:　*Mary read the book.*

---

5 Ladd (2008) argues that the structure is ambiguous in that the same phrase can also be taken as narrow focus if one or both of the words in a phrase are contrasted to other possible words from a limited set of possibilities.

1.3 A brief note on information structural notions: "a terminological minefield" — 13

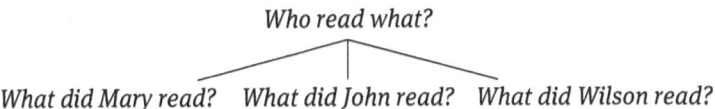

Who read what?

What did Mary read?   What did John read?   What did Wilson read?

At this point, it can be seen that the terms "theme" and "topic" cannot be used interchangeably. While rheme is "(...) the actual update potential of an utterance (...)" (Vallduví 2014: 7), theme is a preparation or elaboration for the update as in (12) and (13). For the expression of theme, some parts of the maximum question under discussion can be copied as illustrated below. Themes can also be used in preparation for implicit questions under discussion as in (14).

(12) A: *What are we having for dinner?*
     B: *[We are having]$_{THEME}$ [mutton-bird]$_{RHEME}$ [for dinner]$_{THEME}$*

(13) A: *Will Anna marry Manny?*
     B: *[Anna]$_{THEME}$ [adores/hates]$_{RHEME}$ [Manny]$_{THEME}$*

(14) A: *How was Lorde's concert?*
     B: *[The band]$_{THEME}$ [played very well]$_{RHEME}$*
     (adapted from Vallduví 2014: 8 and 11)

Note that theme in (14) can easily be identified as a contrastive topic in that the answer is not a thorough one for the maximum question under discussion. Indeed, Steedman (2014: 11) argues that themes with contrast can be interpretable as contrastive topics in a similar vein to Büring (2003) and Neeleman and Vermeulen (2012).

Finally, a discourse anaphoric constituent can be defined as a familiar topic which is discourse-linked, a given or salient constituent (Frascarelli and Hinterhölzl 2007) or an unaccented theme (Steedman 2014).

In this study, the terms "discourse-new focus" and "contrastive focus" are used as focus phrases evoking alternatives as in (6) and (7) respectively, but contrastive focus is exhaustively identified as the correct answer. Although the term "discourse-new" is used, a discourse-new focus phrase that evokes alternatives is assumed in the current study in contrast to Katz and Selkirk (2011). Broad focus is an utterance with all-new constituents as in (8). A topic is what the sentence is about as in (10) and, a contrastive topic evokes alternatives for the maximum question under discussion. Finally, for given constituents that do not evoke alternatives or function as the pivot for information, the term "discourse anaphoric" is used.

1.4 Word order variation in a discourse-configurational language: Turkish

In Turkish, with definite noun phrases, six word order variations are possible resulting in different discourse interpretational effects.[6]

(15) a. *Ali   ev-i   sat-tı.*   SOV
     Ali   house-ACC sell-PERF
     'Ali sold the house.'
  b. *Ev-i Ali   sat-tı.*   OSV
     Ali   sat-tı   ev-i.   SVO
     Ev-i sat-tı   Ali.   OVS
     Sat-tı Ali   ev-i.   VSO
     Sat-tı ev-i   Ali.   VOS
    (Göksel and Kerslake 2005: 395)

For non-specific bare nominals, the immediate preverbal position has been suggested as the canonical position (Kornfilt 2003a; Aydemir 2004). The following examples clearly indicate that a bare nominal does not have to surface in the immediate preverbal position (Sezer 1996; Göksel 1998, 2013; Uygun 2006; Öztürk 2009; Gračanin-Yüksek and İşsever 2011).

(16) a. *[Kahve] Ali de   iste-miş-ti.*
     coffee Ali also want-EVID-PAST
     'Ali too wanted coffee.'
     (Uygun 2006)
  b. *[Kitap] Ali çok   oku-yor.*
     book   Ali a lot read-IMPF
     'Ali reads books a lot.'
     'Ali does a lot of book reading.'
     (Gračanin-Yüksek and İşsever 2011: 5)
  c. *Gör-dü-n   mü hayat-ın-da   hiç [film]?*
     see-PERF-2SG QP life-2SG.POSS-LOC ever film
     'Have you ever seen a film/films in your life?'
     (Göksel 2013: 10)

---

[6] The adult speech corpus of Slobin and Bever (1982) which consists of 500 utterances in Turkish shows that nearly half of the data is in SOV order (48%). İkizoğlu (2010), on the other hand, reports that more than half of the data in the spoken corpus on quotatives was VO.

1.4 Word order variation in a discourse-configurational language: Turkish — 15

Based on this flexibility, Turkish is classified as a free word order language. This is seen to be a misnomer because each word order variation is felicitous in certain contexts. In other words, it is information packaging that determines the acceptable word order.

Non-contrastive (aboutness) topic phrases are pivots for the upcoming information and they surface in the sentence initial position (Erkü 1982; Erguvanlı 1984; Hoffman 1995).

(17) A: *Ayşe'den n'aber? Uzun süredir görmüyorum onu.*
'What is new with Ayşe? I have not seen her for a long time.'
B: [Ayşe]$_{TOP}$ iş-in-den ayrıl-dı.
Ayşe job-3SG.POSS-ABL leave-PERF
'Ayşe left her job.'

When there is an additional contrastive topic, the aboutness topic phrase precedes the contrastive topic.

(18) *Ayşe gives some New Year gifts to her office mates. Aysel was not there and she asks Bülent what Ayşe bought for each of her mates.*
A: *Ayşe kime ne almış?*
'What did Ayşe buy for whom?'
B: [Ayşe]$_{TOP}$ [Ahmet-e]$_{CT}$ [saat]$_F$ [al-mış]$_{DA}$
Ayşe Ahmet-DAT watch buy-PERF
'Ayşe bought a watch for Ahmet.'

The first constituent serves as the entry under which the proposition is given and hence it is the (aboutness) topic phrase. The maximum question triggers a pair-list answer; however, the speaker does not give a comprehensive answer to this question. While the beneficiary is the contrastive topic phrase, the object evokes a set of alternative gifts and hence it is the focus phrase. The verb is given in the previous discourse and it is a discourse anaphoric constituent.

In Turkish linguistics literature, it is unequivocally accepted that focus phrases are not possible in the postverbal position as illustrated below.

(19) A: *Saat-i kim al-mış?*
watch who buy-PERF
'Who bought the watch?'

B: *Saat-i   al-mış   [Ahmet]_F
   watch-ACC buy-PERF   Ahmet
   'Ahmet bought the watch.'
B': [Ahmet]_F   al-mış   saat-i.

However, different views exist regarding the positions in which focus phrases can surface. The studies form a continuum with researchers at one end arguing that all focus phrases must be in the immediate preverbal position (Şener 2010) while at the other end some argue that all focus types can appear in the preverbal domain without being restricted to the immediate preverbal position (Göksel and Özsoy 2000; Kılıçaslan 2004). Erguvanlı (1984) and İşsever (2003) suggest that contrastive focus does not have to appear in the preverbal domain. İşsever (2003) further notes that in presentational focus sentences, the focused constituent must be in the preverbal position. Based on the examples similar to the one in (20), it is proposed that all focus types can surface in-situ, without having to be in the immediate preverbal position.

(20) A: *Sabah Ayşe'ye çiçek geldi.*
        'They brought flowers to Ayşe this morning.'
     B: *Hadi ya! Üzerinde kart var mıydı?*
        'Don't say that! Was there a card on it?'
        Kim   Ayşe-ye   çiçek   gönder-miş?
        who   Ayşe-DAT   flower   send-PERF
        'Who has sent the flowers to Ayşe?'
     A: *Ahmet Ayşe-ye   çiçek   gönder-miş.*
        Ahmet   Ayşe-DAT flower   send-PERF
        'Ahmet sent the flowers to Ayşe.'

The discussion so far indicates that syntax plays a crucial role in information packaging in Turkish. However, the felicity of a sentence is not always dependent on ordering restrictions. An utterance with an otherwise acceptable order can be infelicitous with a certain intonation pattern. For the question given in (21), VSO, VOS, SVO, SOV are all possible answers.

(21)   Ali   ev-i   yap-tı   mı   yık-tı   mı?
        Ali   house-ACC   do-PERF   QP   demolish-PERF   QP
        'Did Ali build or demolish the house?'
    a. *Yık-tı Ali*   *ev-i.*   VSO
    b. *Yık-tı ev-i*   *Ali.*   VOS

c.	Ali	yık-tı	ev-i.	SVO
d.	Ali	ev-i	yık-tı.	SOV

However, the answers in (21c-d) are not acceptable when prominence is realized on a constituent other than the verb. This is also the case in the following examples.

(22) A: *Kim ev-i sat-tı?*
   who house-ACC sell-PERF
   'Who sold the house?'
   B: #Ali [ev-i]_F sat-tı.   SOV

(23) A: *Ali ev-i yap-tı mı yık-tı mı?*
   Ali house-ACC do-PERF QP demolish-PERF QP
   'Did Ali build or demolish the house?'
   B: #[Ali]_F yık-tı ev-i.   SVO

Pure word order by itself cannot account for the well formedness of sentences. The intonation pattern of sentences, a reflection of information packaging, also plays a crucial role.

Now, consider movement operations in Turkish. For Turkish, two main lines of analysis have been suggested to account for movement operations: (i) movement for case purposes (Kornfilt 2001, 2003; Özsoy 2001) or EPP purposes (Aygen 2002a)[7], (ii) movement to an A' position for discourse-related purposes (Kural 1992), movement for discourse-related purposes showing both A and A' target position properties (Öztürk 2005), topic movement to an A position, specifically to Spec TP (Jiménez-Fernandez and İşsever 2012).[8]

In this study, we propose that all movement operations are triggered for discourse-related purposes. The ordering restrictions and the syntactic mechanism proposed for word order variation are radically different from those in

---

7 Öztürk (2005) and Şener (2010) suggest that in Turkish the external argument does not move up to Spec TP position for case or EPP purposes. Some other researchers (Özsoy 2001; Kelepir 2001; Gürer 2010), on the other hand, suggest that EPP exists in Turkish and subjects leave their base generated positions and move to Spec TP. See Chapter 5 for the discussion of EPP in Turkish.

8 The studies cited in this section are of course not an exhaustive list of studies on Turkish syntax but only the ones that are directly related to this study are cited, namely those relating to movement operations for interpretive purposes. For a detailed discussion of these analyses, the interested reader is referred to the relevant studies cited in the text.

previous studies. The discussion on semantic, prosodic and syntactic marking of information structural units in Turkish has led to the phrase structure given in Figure 2 below.

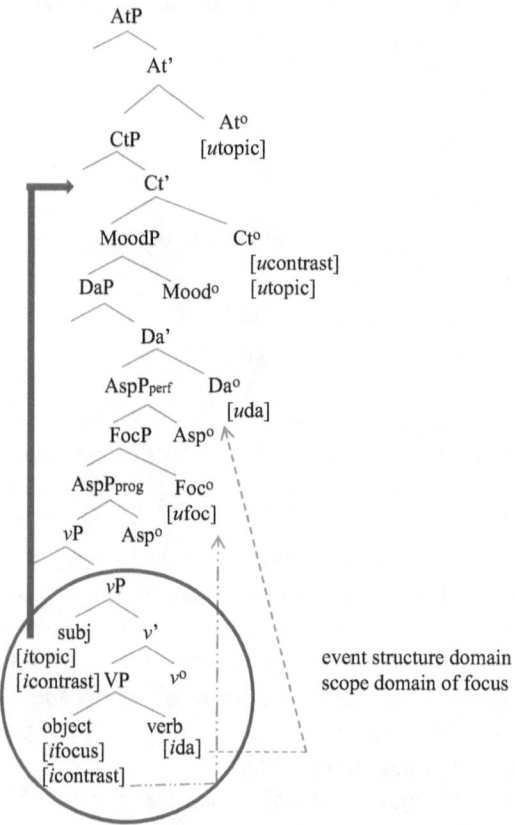

Figure 2: Phrase structure of Turkish.

To summarize, FocP and DaP project above the *v*P domain. However, TopP is in the left periphery, being the target positions for topic phrases, in the speech act domain. This explains (i) the tendency in Turkish to put focus on the immediate preverbal position and the interaction of FocP with different aspectual markers, (ii) the generalization that topic is an utterance level constituent, while focus is a propositional level constituent.

There are no semantically vacuous movement operations. The scope domain of focus maps onto the first merge positions of the constituents in *v*P and reconstruction to this domain is restricted. In the middle domain, TP is lacking and Aspect and Mood projections encode temporal interpretation. The motivation for all these arguments will be elaborated in the following chapters. A brief outline of the book is set out in the following section.

1.5 Layout of the book

In Chapter 2, the information structural units of topic, focus and discourse anaphoric constituents and the subtypes of topic and focus are explicated. Ordering restrictions and the semantic composition of information structural units are investigated in this chapter, which will shed light on the syntactic marking of these units in Turkish.

Chapter 3 deals with how focus subtypes are encoded prosodically in SOV order. The results of two experimental studies conducted to find out how focus prominence is realized in the immediate preverbal position are discussed. The studies also reveal how Turkish marks focus in initial, medial and final domains. The chapter concludes with a comparison of focal prominence assignment determined by [F] marking versus phase domains.

Chapter 4 focuses on the syntactic mechanism behind movement operations that are all triggered for discourse-related purposes. The discussion is based on the interaction of information structural units with negation, quantifier scope, and binding. The chapter offers a unified analysis for the movement operations in Turkish drawing on the binding data of Şener (2010) and quantifier scope data based on three experimental studies. The shortcomings of LF movement analysis are explicated with the interaction of discourse anaphoric constituents with topic and focus phrases. The chapter concludes with a discussion on focus and wh-features.

Based on the findings within the domains of semantics, prosody and syntax, Chapter 5 investigates the phrase structure of Turkish building on the CP/DP parallelism. The phasehood properties of *v*P and CP and the existence of DP/TP in Turkish are questioned. Finally, the phrase structure that derives from information structuring is discussed with implications for further research.

Chapter 2
Semantic and pragmatic marking of information structure

2.1 Introduction

Communication can be thought of as the mutual organization or structuring of the informational content of the message between the speaker and the hearer. The speaker structures the knowledge as a unit composed of an informative part and an anchoring part. The informative part adds new information to the knowledge store of the hearer. The anchoring part helps the hearer organize new information based on that pre-existing body of knowledge. This dynamic, continuous structuring of the knowledge store has been labeled as information packaging (Chafe 1976). Chafe (1976: 28) notes that the term information packaging refers to "(...) how the message is sent and only secondarily with the message itself, just as the packaging of toothpaste can affect sales in partial independence of the quality of the toothpaste inside." Hence, sentences with the same semantic content can have different information structural organizations. Consider the following sentences.

(24) Haber-ler-i   duy-du-n   mu? Ayşe bu   yaz
      news-PL-ACC   hear-PERF-2SG QP   Ayşe this summer
      [evlen-iyor-muş]$_F$.
      marry-IMPF-HS
      'Did you hear the news? Ayşe will get married this summer.'

(25) Haber-ler-i duy-du-n mu? Ayşe [bu yaz]$_F$ evlen-iyor-muş.

Although they have the same content, the new information and vehicular parts differ in both sentences. Different parts of the sentence bear prominence in each case. The focus marked constituents are the informative parts and the remainder forms the anchoring part of the clauses. The sentence in (24) is felicitous in a context in which both the speaker and the hearer have the information within their knowledge store that Ayşe is preparing for something during the following summer. The contribution of the speaker is the information that Ayşe will get married. The sentence in (25) on the other hand is felicitous in a context in which the shared information between the speaker and the hearer is that Ayşe will get married at some time in the future. The speaker updates the hearer's knowledge store with the new information that the marriage will take place the following summer.

https://doi.org/10.1515/9781501505584-002

In this chapter, possible information structural organizations in Turkish will be investigated building on (i) focus, (ii) topic, and (iii) discourse anaphoric classification. The first part of the chapter is an elaboration on how focus, topic and discourse anaphoric constituents are explicated in this study. In the second half, the ordering restrictions of information structural units are discussed which paves the way for a syntactic analysis. The next section illustrates different accounts for the organization of information packaging.

2.2 Different approaches to information structuring

In the literature, many different analyses have been proposed for the partitioning of utterances but the methods of partitioning can be summarized as three fundamental types. The information structural units have been analyzed by applying (i) a file system in which the hearer evaluates and updates the cards based on utterances, (ii) bipartition or tripartition in which the newsy and vehicular parts are determined based on order, and (iii) contexts in which the newsy and vehicular parts are determined based on triggering conditions.

Firstly, the file system is considered. Speaking within the terms expounded by Reinhart (1981) and Heim (1982), discourse is composed of a set of utterances which function as instructions given by the speaker to the hearer to update the relevant file. The rules are outlined as follows (Erteschik-Shir 1997: 18):

I. TOPIC instructs the hearer to locate on the top of his file an existing card (or an existing set of cards) with the relevant heading and index.
II. FOCUS instructs the hearer to either
    (i) open a new card and put it on the top of the file. Assign it a *heading* and a new index (in the case of an indefinite) or
    (ii) locate an existing card and put it on top of the file (in the case of a definite)
III. PREDICATION instructs the hearer to evaluate the predicate with respect to the topic where the predicate is taken to be the complement of the topic.
    If the result of the evaluation is TRUE the UPDATE rule applies:
IV. UPDATE instructs the hearer to enter the focus on the topic card and then to copy all entries to all cards activated by the focus rule.

Taking the utterance in (24) as an example, the speaker starts the sentence with a shared constituent and guides the hearer to the card bearing the name of *Ayşe* as a heading. This heading functions as the topic and signals the subject matter of the rest of the sentence. On that card, the fact that she will get married is also written as part of the shared information. The hearer evaluates the predicate (the complement of the topic) with respect to the heading and moves to the next step. With the focused phrase, the speaker adds further information to the card. The hearer updates the existing card and enters the new information on the card. Vallduví (1990) criticizes this metaphor, based on the redundancy the cards are likely to cause. Following an utterance, the cards that share the given information in the utterance will be activated and new information will be entered on all the activated cards. For example, in (24) not only the card for *Ayşe* but also the card for *bu yaz* 'this summer' will be activated. The new information will be entered to these existing cards in the same manner which results in redundancy in the system.

In agreeing with Vallduví (1990), it is further suggested that this mechanism cannot capture the finer distinctions between different focus and topic types nor can it shed light on their semantic compositionality. By relating topics with already existing cards, the system equates topichood with givenness and this is evaluated and criticized in section 2.3.2. Additionally, in the following sections relating to Turkish data, it can be seen that there are some ordering restrictions for the position of information structural units within a sentence and also in relation to each other. The card system does not have sufficient mechanisms to explain these finer restrictions.

Bipartite or tripartite analyses proposed for information structuring are now considered. Vallduví (1990: 36) details the following analyses, with our addition of the tripartite analysis of Erguvanlı (1984), Vallduví's own analysis and the analyses for Turkish:

I. Theme-Rheme (Ammann 1928; Danes 1968 (1957); Firbas 1964, 1971, 1975; Halliday 1967; Contreras 1976)
II. Topic-Comment (Mathesius 1915; Hockett 1958; Strawson 1964; Gundel 1974, 1988; Dahl 1974; Li and Thompson 1976; Kuno 1980; Reinhart 1982; Davison 1984)
III. Topic-Focus (Sgall and Hajicova 1977, 1978; von Stechow 1981)
IV. Focus- Presupposition or Focus/Open-Proposition (Akmajian 1970 (1979); Chomsky 1971; Jackendoff 1972; Dahl 1974; Rochemont 1978, 1986; Wilson and Sperber 1979; Williams 1981; Prince 1981, 1984, 1986; Selkirk 1984; Ward 1985; Lambrecht 1987, 1988; Välimaa-Blum 1988)
V. Dominance (Erteschik-Shir 1973, 1979, 1986; Erteschik-Shir and Lappin 1979, 1983)
VI. Topic - Focus - Background (Erguvanlı 1984)
VII. S = Focus, Ground Ground = Link, Tail (Vallduví 1990)
VIII. S = Topic, Comment Comment = Focus, Ground (Hoffman 1995)
IX. S = Focus, Ground Ground = Topic, Tail (İşsever 2003)

The analyses in (i-v) offer a bipartite structuring of the utterance. However, from Section 1.3 it should be remembered that even if the same terms are used to encode information packaging, they may not have the same connotation.[9] Erguvanlı (1984) makes the first tripartite structuring marking sentence initial constituents as topic, immediate preverbal constituents as focus and postverbal constituents as background as illustrated below.

(26) [Ayşe]$_{TOPIC}$ [elma-yı]$_{FOCUS}$ [ye-di]$_{BACKGROUND}$
Ayşe   apple-ACC   eat-PERF
'Ayşe ate the apple.'

Based on examples from Dahl (1974: 2), Vallduví (1993: 7–8) suggests that for the same utterance binomial approaches result in different partitionings. In (27), the partitioning is the same for Topic-Comment and Ground-Focus analyses. However, this is not the case in (28).

(27) A: *What about John? What does he do?*
B: *John drinks beer.*
[John]$_{Topic}$ [drinks beer]$_{Comment}$
[John]$_{Ground}$ [drinks beer]$_{Focus}$

(28) A: *What about John? What does he drink?*
B: *John drinks beer.*
[John]$_{Topic}$ [drinks beer]$_{Comment}$
[John drinks]$_{Ground}$ [beer]$_{Focus}$

Consider how a tripartite analysis can capture the data in (28).

(29) a. [[John]$_{Link}$ drinks]$_{Ground}$ [beer]$_{Focus}$
b. [[John]$_{Topic}$ drinks]$_{Background}$ [beer]$_{Focus}$

It is clear from the discussion that tripartite analyses are more advantageous than binominal ones. However, with tripartite analyses it is still not possible to create finer distinctions between topic and focus phrases nor to explain ordering restrictions. As mentioned in section 2.1, communication is dynamic in

---

9 For example, although given under the same partitioning, Vallduví (1990: 37) suggests that "Interestingly, a Firbas-theme is more or less analogous to the topic in the topic-focus framework, while a Halliday-theme is almost equivalent to the topic in the topic-comment framework."

nature and contexts can capture this dynamicity. Note that information packaging in (24) and (25), which have exactly the same ordering, can only be explained when embedded in a context. The bipartite and tripartite analyses reflect the end result of this dynamicity. In this study, contexts will be used to trigger information structural units and there will be an opportunity to capture all ordering possibilities in Turkish.

2.3 Information structural units in Turkish

This section focuses on the notions of information structure and how they are explicated within this study. Section 2.3.1 discusses focus phrases, section 2.3.2 topic phrases and section 2.3.4 discourse anaphoric phrases.

2.3.1 Focus

In the literature on Turkish linguistics, within the information structural notions, focus has been the most widely studied concept from syntactic (Emre 1931; Erguvanlı 1984; Kural 1993; Demircan 1996; Kennelly 1999, 2003; Göksel and Özsoy 2000; İşsever 2003; Şener 2010), semantic (Erguvanlı 1984; Göksel 1998; Göksel and Özsoy 2003; Şener 2010) and prosodic (Göksel and Özsoy 2003; İşsever 2003; Özge and Bozşahin 2010; Ipek 2011; Güneş 2012; İvoşeviç and Bekâr 2015) perspectives. In the following sub-sections, focus will discussed within a semantic/pragmatic perspective. First, the literature will be reviewed to see how focus is defined.

Focus can be defined as the most prominent constituent in an utterance. A focused constituent is not part of the shared information between the speaker and the hearer and so pushes the conversation forward. Krifka (2006) suggests that taking focus as the most important part of the utterance is insufficiently explanatory as illustrated in (30).

(30) *It wasn't JOHN who stole the cookie.*
     (Krifka 2006: 122)

The most important thing in this utterance is the fact that someone stole the cookie. The fact that, that person was not John is not so important. Hence, the function of focus cannot be reduced solely to bearing prominence. Additionally, being prominent can be rather elusive.

Jackendoff (1972: 230) defines focus as "(....) the information in the sentence that is assumed by the speaker not to be shared by him and the hearer (....)" within the Structured Meaning Approach. The presupposition on the other hand denotes "(....) the information in the sentence that is assumed to be shared by him and the hearer (....)" (Jackendoff 1972: 230)[10]

(31) a. *John introduced [Bill]$_F$ to Sue.*
 b. *John introduced Bill to [Sue]$_F$.*

(32) a. $< \lambda x \, [introduce \, (j, x, s)], b >$
 b. $< \lambda y \, [introduce \, (j, b, y)], s >$
 (Rooth 1996: 274)

The lambda operator entails the presupposition that in (32a) there is someone whom John introduced to Sue and that person is Bill. In (32b), there is someone to whom John introduced Bill and that person is Sue.[11]

Rooth (1996) suggests that as an existential presupposition can be cancelled within context, an existential presupposition cannot form a part of focus semantics as illustrated in (33) below.

(33) A: *Did anyone win the football pool this week?*
 B: *Probably not, because it is unlikely that [[Mary$_F$ won it] ~ C], and I know that nobody else did.*

---

10 The definition of presupposition has been taken as shared information or common ground (Stalnaker 1974, 2002; Karttunen 1974).

"A proposition P is a pragmatic presupposition of a speaker in a given context just in case the speaker assumes or believes that P, assumes or believes that his addressee assumes or believes that P, and assumes or believes that his addressee recognizes that he is making these assumptions, or has these beliefs." (Stalnaker 1974: 473)

As cited in Horn (1996), Burton-Roberts (1989) suggest that presupposition cannot be purely defined as shared assumption between speaker and hearer.

"If I were to say to you, "My sister is coming to lunch tomorrow", I do presuppose that I have a sister but in presupposing it I do not necessarily assume that you have a prior assumption or belief that I have a sister. (Burton-Roberts 1989: 26)"

Stalnaker (2002: 701) in turn claims that "to presuppose something is to take it for granted or at least to act as if one takes it for granted, as background information-as common ground among the participants in the conversation.' In line with Stalnaker (2002), presupposition is taken as background information that is taken as granted even if it is not shared.

11 Zimmermann and Onea (2011) mention that this partitioning is compatible with syntactic analyses which assume focus movement. The semantic partitioning decomposes the structure as focus and background. In syntax, this partitioning is observed as focus movement to the left periphery.

(34) A: *Did anyone win the football pool this week?*
B: *#I doubt it, because it is unlikely that it's [Mary]$_F$ who won it, and I know that nobody else did.*
(Rooth 1996: 287)

The focused phrase in (33) evokes a set of alternatives in the form of "*x won the pool*" where *x* ranges over a set of people. The existential presupposition triggered by the alternative set of propositions is that someone won the pool but the following sentence cancels this presupposition. This is further illustrated in (34) with a cleft construction which already evokes an existential presupposition that there is someone who won the pool. As the existential presupposition is cancelled with the sentence following the cleft sentence, the whole structure sounds odd. The discussion so far indicates that focus cannot be defined as the most prominent constituent or as a constituent triggering an existential presupposition.

Within the assumptions of Alternative Semantics, Rooth (1985, 1992, 1996) suggests that the function of focus is to evoke alternatives. In this approach, the focus-presupposition partition is replaced by a set of alternative propositions. The proposition of the sentence constitutes the ordinary semantic value as illustrated below. The focus semantic value is derived by making a substitution in the position corresponding to the focus phrase. The alternative propositions differ only with respect to the focused phrase.

(35) *Does Ede want tea or coffee?*
Ede wants [coffee]$_F$
ordinary semantic value
{Ede wants coffee, Ede wants tea}
focus semantic value
{Ede wants coffee, Ede wants tea}

(36) *Who wants coffee?*
[Ede]$_F$ wants coffee.
ordinary semantic value
{Ede wants coffee}
focus semantic value
{Ede wants coffee, Mary wants coffee, John wants coffee...}
(adapted from Rooth 1996: 271)

Rooth (1996) further adds that questions determine the alternative sets in answers with focus phrases. The question serves as the antecedent for the variable and the focus evokes the alternative propositions. The question in (35) is an alternative question and the ordinary semantic value of the question already includes two propositions as {Ede wants coffee, Ede wants tea}. In (36), the question evokes an open set of alternative propositions as its focus semantic value.

This analysis can be extended to interrogatives to capture their semantic properties (Rooth 1985; Roberts 1996; Abusch 2010).

(37) *[Who took Mary's bike] (=Q)*
Q is a set of propositions of the form 'x took Mary's bike', where x ranges over a set of relevant people.
(Abusch 2010: 54)

As is the case with focus phrases, the wh-phrase evokes a set of propositions. Note that the propositions are in the form of answers. There is question-answer congruence as the set of alternative propositions of the question is a subset of the set of propositions of the focus phrase.[12]

In the alternative semantics approach, presuppositions that accompany focus constructions are analyzed as the secondary effects of alternative sets in that there is a default process that generates presuppositions from alternative sets. In (36), for instance, the focus phrase evokes a set of alternative propositions in the form of "x wants coffee" and the assumption is that one of these propositions is true. It is the alternative set of propositions that triggers this existential presupposition. Additionally, Krifka (2006) suggests that focus is defined as highlighted, the most important constituent due to the presence of the alternatives evoked by the focus phrases. As illustrated in (35) and (36) above, one of the propositions is chosen in contrast to other alternatives which results in the chosen focus phrase being highlighted and important. It is due to the presence of these alternatives that creates a tendency to interpret focus phrases as the most important constituents.

The discussion in this section has shown that the existential presuppositions, being highlighted or prominent do not form an essential part of the semantics of focus phrases. All these interpretations arise due to the alternatives evoked by the focus phrase. Hence, within this study, there will be an analysis of focus phrases as indicators of the presence of alternatives within the assumptions offered by alternative semantics.

In the literature, a further distinction is made for focus phrases as (i) discourse-new/presentational focus and, (ii) contrastive focus/identificational focus.

---

12 As indicated in Zimmerman and Onea (2011) in order to avoid an unconstrained set of alternatives which can result in incorrect predictions, the focus operator mediates between the context variables for which the question serves as the antecedent and the focus alternatives and ensures that C is a subset of the set of alternatives evoked by the focus phrase.

There is also some empirical evidence for this distinction. Katz and Selkirk (2011) note that this distinction is reflected in prosody, in that in English, contrastive focus has a higher pitch height and duration than non-contrastive, discourse-new constituents which are not F marked. Additionally, there are some languages such as the West Chadic languages (Zimmermann 2011) which mark contrastive and informational focus with a special morphological marker that is obligatory for contrastive focus phrases but not for informational focus phrases. In the next sub-sections, how this distinction is reflected in Turkish from a semantic/pragmatic point of view will be investigated.

2.3.1.1 Discourse-new constituents

As the name of this focus type suggests, these phrases introduce constituents to the discourse that is not shared between the speaker and the hearer. Discourse-new constituents are triggered by wh-questions as illustrated in (38) and (39) below and evoke a set of alternatives.[13]

(38) *When you saw Mete leaving the house*
    A: *Mete nere-ye git-ti?*
       Mete where-DAT go-PERF
       'Where did Mete go?'
    B: *Mete [sinema-ya]$_F$ git-ti.*
       Mete cinema-DAT go-PERF
       'Mete went to the cinema.'
       ordinary semantic value
       {Mete sinema-ya git-ti}
       'Mete went to the cinema.'
       focus semantic value
       {Mete sinema-ya git-ti, Mete tiyatro-ya git-ti, Mete spor-a git-ti......)
       'Mete went to the cinema, Mete went to the theatre, Mete went to the gym......'

(39) *When you cannot see or understand the thing that Mete gave to the students......*
    A: *Mete öğrenci-ler-e ne ver-di?*
       Mete student-PL-DAT what give-PERF
       'What did Mete give to the students?'

---

[13] Note that the nature of discourse-new constituents in this study is different from discourse-new constituents in Katz and Selkirk (2011).

B: *Mete öğrenci-ler-e   [izin kağıd-ı]$_F$ ver-di.*
    Mete student-PL-DAT   permission slip-CM give-PERF
    'Mete gave the students a permission slip.'
    ordinary semantic value
    {Mete öğrenci-ler-e izin kağıd-ı ver-di}
    'Mete gave the students a permission slip.'
    focus semantic value
    {Mete öğrenci-ler-e izin kağıd-ı ver-di, Mete öğrenci-ler-e karne ver-di, Mete öğrenci-ler-e elma ver-di...}
    'Mete gave the students a permission slip, Mete gave the students the reports, Mete gave the students apples....'

In (38), the focus phrase evokes a set of alternatives and the alternatives range over a set of places or activities. In (39), the focus phrase evokes a set of alternatives which range over a set of things that can be given to someone. Note that the alternatives triggered by the discourse-new focus are not given in the previous context (See section 2.4.2 for further contexts triggering discourse-new focus).[14]

---

14 Not every wh-question triggers focus as already indicated by Şener (2010) who makes a distinction between discourse-linked and non-discourse linked wh-phrases. With non-discourse linked wh-phrases the antecedent of the wh-phrase is not existentially presupposed and so they are like focus phrases. Discourse linked wh-phrases have an antecedent in the given discourse. For the following wh-question given in a context, Şener (2010) suggests that the discourse linked wh-phrase moves to contrastive DaP at the left periphery.

(1) *Mete and Pelin are invited to Suna's wedding. They see at the wedding ceremony that Suna has kissed at least 10 well-wishers so far, and her husband, Selim, has kissed as many people as Suna has. Thinking that Pelin has been a better observer of all that than he has, Mete asks Pelin:*
    kim(-ler)-i   yalnızca Suna   öp-tü?
    who(-PL)-ACC only   Suna-NOM kiss-PAST
    'Who did only Suna kiss?'
    (Şener 2010: 213)

The discussion in section 2.3.2.2 shows that the discourse linked wh-phrase in this example is actually a contrastive topic as the big question of "who kissed whom?" is narrowed to the question in this example, triggering a partial answer. The important point here is that without putting the sentence in a rich context, one cannot conclude that each wh-phrase triggers discourse-new information. (See section 2.5.1 for further discussion)

2.3.1.2 Contrastive focus phrases

Contrastive focus phrases also evoke a set of alternatives. Alternative questions and corrective statements trigger contrastive focus phrases as exemplified in (40) and (41) respectively.

(40) A: *Mete sinema-ya mı yoksa tiyatro-ya mı git-ti?*
Mete cinema-DAT QP or theatre-DAT QP go-PERF
'Did Mete go the cinema or to the theatre?'

B: *Mete [sinema-ya]$_{CF}$ git-ti.*
Mete cinema-DAT go-PERF
'Mete went to the cinema.'
ordinary semantic value
{Mete sinema-ya git-ti, Mete tiyatro-ya git-ti}
'Mete went to the cinema, Mete went to the theatre'
focus semantic value
{Mete sinema-ya git-ti, Mete tiyatro-ya git-ti)
'Mete went to the cinema, Mete went to the theatre'

(41) A: *Mete tiyatro-ya git-ti.*
Mete theatre-DAT go-PERF
'Mete went to the theatre.'

B: *Hayır, Mete [sinema-ya]$_{CF}$ git-ti.*
No, Mete cinema-DAT go-PERF
'No, Mete went to the cinema.'
ordinary semantic value
{Mete sinema-ya git-ti}
'Mete went to the cinema'
focus semantic value
{Mete sinema-ya git-ti, Mete tiyatro-ya git-ti, Mete spor-a git-ti)
'Mete went to the cinema, Mete went to the theatre, Mete went to the gym......'

Note that in contrast to the alternative sets of discourse-new focus, with contrastive focus phrases at least one of the constituents in the alternative set is explicitly given in the previous context.[15]

---

[15] Based on similar examples, Krifka (2006) suggests that focus cannot be taken as new information that is not shared between the speaker and the hearer.

Additionally, yes/no questions can trigger contrastive focus phrases in Turkish as illustrated in (42) and (43) below. Note that the position of the question particle signals the focus phrase in the answer, in that, in (42) it is the object phrase, and in (43) it is the verb that bear focus.[16]

(42) A: *Yurt dışında çalışmaya giden Alanya ve Anamurlular çalışmalarıyla büyük beğeni toplamış. Şimdi de bir Alman kanalında teşekkür konuşması yapılıyor.*
'The guest worker groups from Alanya and Anamur who went abroad won recognition with their work. Now, a vote of thanks is delivered on a German TV channel.'
B: *Almanyalılar Alanyalıları mı övüyor?*
'Do the German people praise the people from Alanya?'
A: *Hayır, Almanyalı-lar [Anamurlu-lar-ı]$_{CF}$ öv-üyor.*
No, German-PL people of Anamur-PL-ACC praise-IMPF
'No, the German people praise the people from Anamur.'

(43) A: *Almanya'ya giden Alanyalı bir grup hakkında televizyonda bir konuşma var.*
'There is a program on the television about a group of people from Alanya who went to Germany.'
B: *Almanyalılar Alanyalıları övüyor mu?*
'Do the German people praise the people from Alanya?'

---

16 Truckenbrodt (2009) notes a similar property of yes/no questions in German with a falling intonation pattern. He suggests that alternative questions (a) and yes/no questions which have a falling intonation (b) have an assertive salient proposition. The yes/no question in (c) differs from the one in (b) in that it ends with a rising intonation and the most salient proposition is not asserted.

a. *Hat Peter einen Hund [/] oder eine Katze? [\] L%*
   'Does Peter have a dog or a cat?'
   Most salient proposition: Peter has a dog or a cat.
b. *Hat Peter einen Hund? [\] L%*
   'Does Peter have a dog?'
   Salient proposition: Peter has a dog or he doesn't.
c. *Hat Peter einen Hund? [/] H%*
   'Does Peter have a dog?'
   Most salient proposition: Peter has a dog.
   (Truckenbrodt 2009: 36–37)

A: *Hayır, Almanyalı-lar Alanyalı-lar-ı*   *[yer-iyor]$_{CF}$*
    No,   German-PL   people of Alanya-PL-ACC   criticize-IMPF
    'No, the German people criticize the people from Alanya.'

Note that yes/no questions can easily be paraphrased as alternative questions. In (42), the implicit alternative is "Do the German people praise the people from Alanya or Anamur?" In (43), it is "Do the German people praise people from Alanya or not?" Based on this similarity, it is suggested that yes/no questions in Turkish trigger contrastive focus phrases.

Note that both contrastive focus and discourse-new focus evoke a set of alternatives triggered by different contexts. Additionally, with both discourse-new and contrastive focus constituents one of the alternatives is chosen as the correct answer in contrast to other alternatives. Hence, both focus types are contrastive in nature. A natural question to ask is how the difference is marked between the two focus types if being contrastive is not conclusive. Krifka (2006) defines contrastive focus not based on the feature contrast but based on the nature of the alternative set, suggesting that contrastive focus phrases have a restricted alternative set which is labeled as closed focus. He defines discourse-new focus (presentational focus in his terms) as a focus phrase with an open set of alternatives which is labeled as open focus. For instance, the alternative set of the alternative question in (44) is composed of only two alternatives, while the alternative sets of discourse-new focus in (45) has more alternatives.

(44)   A: *What do you want to drink, tea or coffee?*
        B: *I want [tea]$_F$*
            focus semantic value *{I want tea, I want coffee}*

(45)   A: *What do you want to drink?*
        B: *I want [tea]$_F$*
            focus semantic value *{I want tea, I want coffee, I want water, I want lemonade...}*

In both (44) and (45), one of the alternatives is chosen as the correct answer in contrast to the other alternatives in the set. However, note that the alternative set of contrastive focus in (41) is as open as the alternative set of discourse-new focus in (38). Hence, it is argued that it is not possible to make a distinction between contrastive focus and discourse-new focus based on the open vs. closed nature of the alternative sets either.

Neeleman and Vermeulen (2012) make the distinction between contrastive focus and discourse-new focus based on the presence of a negation operator with contrastive focus phrases. This is illustrated with contrastive focus triggered by a corrective statement in (46).

(46) A: *John read The Extended Phenotype.*
B: *(No, you are wrong.) He read [The Selfish Gene]$_{CF}$.*

(47) a. < λx [John read x], The Selfish Gene, {The Blind Watchmaker,
　　　　　　　　　　　　　　　　　　　　The Ancestor's Tale,
　　　　　　　　　　　　　　　　　　　　The Extended Phenotype,....}>
　　b ∃y [y ϵ {The Blind Watchmaker, The Ancestor's Tale, The Extended Phenotype,....}& ¬ [John read y]]
　　(Neeleman and Vermeulen 2012: 8–12)

The lambda operator in (47) entails that John read something. The ordinary value of the focus is given as the "The Selfish Gene" which is followed by the alternative phrases that can replace the focused phrase. Note that up to this point, this line of argument is not different from the alternative semantics approach. However, this is not the end of the representation for the contrastive focus phrase. In (47b), the negation operator asserts that the alternative propositions are not correct and John did not read these books. The negative statement is suggested to be a part of the semantics of contrast which in turn differentiates contrastive focus from discourse-new focus as a quantificational force. Before reaching a conclusion, another possible distinction between the two focus types is analyzed.

Kiss (1998, 2002) makes the distinction between contrastive focus and discourse-new focus in Hungarian based on exhaustive identification using the tests proposed by Szabolcsi (1981) and Donka Farkas (cited in Kiss 1998: 250). Contrastive focus which surfaces ex-situ in the immediate preverbal position expresses exhaustive identification. In-situ informational focus does not express exhaustive identification based on which Kiss concludes that contrastive focus constituents are quantificational in nature.

Now, the question arises as to whether Turkish contrastive focus and discourse-new focus show different properties with respect to exhaustive identification. Szabolcsi (1981) suggests that an answer to an alternative question as in (48A) may include focus phrases composed of two individuals or entities as in (48B). However, a following sentence which drops one of the constituents and includes only one of the entities is not possible in the case of contrastive focus phrases as in (48C), if it is not a logical consequence of the first sentence.

(48) A: *Ahmet   Ayşe-ye   [Büşra ve Sevgi-yi]$_{CF}$ mi yoksa*
Ahmet   Ayşe-DAT Büşra and Sevgi-ACC QP or
[Ali ve Veli-yi]$_{CF}$ mi tanıt-tı?
Ali and Veli-ACC QP introduce-PERF
'Did Ahmet introduce Büşra and Sevgi or Ali and Veli to Ayşe?'
B: *Ahmet   Ayşe-ye   [Ali ve Veli-yi]$_{CF}$ tanıt-tı*
Ahmet   Ayşe-DAT   Ali and Veli-ACC   introduce-PERF
'Ahmet introduced Ali and Veli to Ayşe.'
C: #*Ahmet   Ayşe-ye   [Ali-yi]$_{CF}$ tanıt-tı*

The answer in (48C) is licit only when uttered as a corrective statement for (48B) or as an answer in the absence of (48B), but not as a subsequent confirmation sentence of (48B). Now, a closer look at the alternative sets of the focus phrase will assist in understanding the reason behind the unacceptability of the sentence in (48C).

(49) ordinary semantic value
{Ahmet Ayşe-ye Büşra ve Sevgi-yi tanıt-tı, Ahmet Ayşe-ye Ali ve Veli-yi tanıt-tı}
'Ahmet introduced Büşra and Sevgi to Ayşe, Ahmet introduced Ali and Veli to Ayşe.'
focus semantic value
{Ahmet Ayşe-ye Ali ve Veli-yi tanıt-tı, Ahmet Ayşe-ye Büşra ve Sevgi-yi tanıt-tı, Ahmet Ayşe-ye Ali-yi tanıt-tı, Ahmet Ayşe-ye Veli-yi tanıt-tı...}
'Ahmet introduced Ali and Veli to Ayşe, Ahmet introduced Büşra and Sevgi to Ayşe, Ahmet introduced Ali to Ayşe, Ahmet introduced Veli to Ayşe......'

The answer in (48B) identifies *Ali ve Veli* as the correct answer in contrast to the other alternatives given in (49). The unacceptability of the sentence in (48C) indicates that the sentence includes an alternative already excluded by the focus phrase in (48B). Note that *Ali* as a single unit is already a part of the alternative set and *Ali ve Veli* as the correct answer exhaustively excludes this unit as the correct answer.

A similar context with the discourse-new counterpart in the follow-up sentence is not unacceptable as exemplified in (50) below.[17]

---

[17] Göksel and Özsoy (2003) suggest that this test is not applicable in Turkish. They suggest that with both informational focus (1) and contrastive focus (2), the follow-up sentence is a logical consequence of the preceding sentence.

(50) *You see that Ahmet introduces someone to Ayşe, but you cannot see or recognize the person...*
   A: *Ahmet Ayşe-ye   kim-i   tanıt-tı?*
      Ahmet Ayşe-DAT whom-ACC introduce-PERF
      'Whom did Ali introduce to Ayşe?'
   B: *Ahmet Ayşe-ye   [Ali ve Veli-yi]$_{DN}$ tanıt-tı?*
      Ahmet Ayşe-DAT Ali and Veli-ACC introduce-PERF
      'Ali introduced Ali and Veli to Ayşe.'
   C: *Ahmet Ayşe-ye   [Ali-yi]$_{DN}$ tanıt-tı?*

(50C) can follow in the conversation as a felicitous sentence in this context. (50C) is a logical consequence of (50B). Note that *Ali ve Veli* is chosen as the correct answer in contrast to the alternatives among which *Ali* as a single unit is a member. However, as (50C) is a possible follow-up of (50B), it is clear that the answer is not exhaustively identified as the correct answer.

---

(1) A: *Deniz-de her   gün [bir adam ve   bir kadın]$_{DN}$ yüz-üyor-du.*
       sea-LOC every day a   man and a   woman swim-PROG-PAST
       'A man and a woman used to swim in the sea every day.'
    B: *Deniz-de her   gün [bir kadın]$_{DN}$ yüz-üyor-du.*
       sea-LOC every day a   woman swim-PROG-PAST
       'A woman used to swim in the sea every day.'

(2) A: *[Bir adam ve   bir kadın]$_{CF}$ her   gün deniz-de yüz-üyor-du.*
       a   man and a   woman every day sea-LOC swim-PROG-PAST
       'A man and a woman used to swim in the sea every day.'
    B: *[Bir kadın]$_{CF}$ her   gün deniz-de yüz-üyor-du.*
       a   woman every day sea-LOC swim-PROG-PAST
       (Göksel and Özsoy 2003: 1155)

Note that the so called contrastive focus is not triggered by context in (2), and hence it cannot be determined whether it is contrastive focus or not. As the sentences are not triggered by the contrastive focus eliciting context, it is suggested that both sentences are acceptable because they are interpreted as discourse-new focus. When the sentences are placed in the triggering contexts, the difference between the two focus types as illustrated in (48) and (50) in the text above can be seen. In line with Göksel and Özsoy (2002), one of the reviewers suggests that in (48) and (50), the propositions given in (C) are in contradiction with the ones in (B) and hence there seems no difference between contrastive and discourse-new focus with respect to exhaustivity. However, the other test presented in (51), (52) and (53) which is a follow-up of this test, further shows that contrastive focus differs from discourse-new focus with respect to exhaustive identification.

Donka Farkas (as cited in Kiss, 1998: 251) suggests another test to differentiate contrastive focus from discourse-new focus with respect to exhaustive identification. In (51A), the speaker asks an alternative question. In (51B), another speaker answers the question with a contrastive focus excluding the explicitly given alternative in the question in (51A). Adding a further focus constituent as an answer with a sentence initial opposition does not result in a contradiction with the previous answer in (51C).

(51) A: *Ahmet Ayşe-ye [Ali-yi]$_{CF}$ mi yoksa [Mehmet-i]$_{CF}$*
       Ahmet Ayşe-DAT Ali-ACC QP or Mehmet-ACC
       mi   tanıt-tı?
       QP   introduce-PERF
       'Did Ahmet introduce Ali or Mehmet to Ayşe?'
   B: *Ahmet Ayşe-ye [Ali-yi]$_{CF}$ tanıt-tı.*
       Ahmet Ayşe-DAT Ali-ACC introduce-PERF
       'Ahmet introduced Ali to Ayşe.'
   C: *Hayır, Ahmet Ayşe-ye Veli-yi de tanıt-tı.*
       No   Ahmet Ayşe-DAT Veli-ACC too introduce-PERF
       'No, Ahmet also introduced Veli to Ayşe.'

It is important to take a closer look at the alternative set of contrastive focus to see what makes the answer in (51C) felicitous with sentence initial opposition.

(52) ordinary semantic value
    {Ahmet Ayşe-ye Ali-yi tanıt-tı, Ahmet Ayşe-ye Mehmet-i tanıt-tı}
    'Ahmet introduced Ali to Ayşe, Ahmet introduced Mehmet to Ayşe'
    focus semantic value
    {Ahmet Ayşe-ye Ali-yi tanıt-tı Ahmet Ayşe-ye Mehmet-i tanıt-tı}

The addition of a further constituent requires a contradiction of the previous sentence which indicates that the contrastive focus constituent in (51B) excludes all other possible answers given in (52). In a sense, the alternative set has to be triggered anew with (51C).

In (53), with a discourse-new focus, on the other hand, contradicting the previous answer by adding a further constituent as an answer results in degradation.

(53) A: *Ahmet Ayşe-ye [kim-i]$_{DN}$ tanıt-tı?*
       Ahmet Ayşe-DAT whom-ACC introduce-PERF
       'Whom did Ahmet introduce to Ayşe?'

B: *Ahmet   Ayşe-ye   [Ali-yi]$_{DN}$ tanıt-tı.*
   Ahmet Ayşe-DAT   Ali-ACC   introduce-PERF
   'Ahmet introduced Ali to Ayşe.'
C: *#Hayır, Ahmet Ayşe-ye Veli-yi de   tanıt-tı.*
   'No, Ahmet also introduced Veli to Ayşe.'

The answer with sentence initial opposition in (53C) is not felicitous. Based on these tests, it can be concluded that it is exhaustive identification that differentiates contrastive focus from discourse-new focus. Both discourse-new and contrastive focus phrases evoke alternatives and one of the propositions in the alternative set is chosen in contrast to other alternatives. The nature of the alternative sets also cannot constitute the criteria to differentiate contrastive focus and discourse-new focus as contrastive focus constituents may have an open set of alternative propositions. However, only contrastive focus phrases encode exhaustive identification. Discourse-new focus constituents evoke an alternative set of propositions without exhaustive identification while contrastive focus constituents evoke an alternative set of propositions and involve exhaustive identification. Without appealing to negation as an operator (Neeleman and Vermeulen 2012), the distinction between the two focus types is captured.[18] The next section turns to the investigation of topic.

2.3.2 Topic

It is not so easy to identify topic phrases as is the case with focus phrases. Topichood is associated with the information status of being "old" or "given" or alternatively as the sentence initial position which is taken to be the subject position (Chafe 1976). Within this analysis, information status is a property of

---

18 Note that this line of argument does not differ much from the analysis of Neeleman and Vermeulen (2012) according to which contrastive focus differs from discourse-new focus in the presence of a negative statement. The negative statement is quantificational in nature and it is a part of the semantics of contrast. However, the current analysis does not take contrast as a primitive semantic notion as discussed in section 2.3.3. Additionally, the discussion in Chapter 5 will show that contrastive focus in Turkish is devoid of any quantificational force in the absence of an accompanying quantifier. To put it more precisely, contrastive focus cannot take scope over contrastive topic phrases without an accompanying quantifier which is not the case for some other languages such as Dutch and English as indicated by Neeleman and Vermeulen (2012). Hence, the current analysis diverges from the analysis of Neeleman and Vermeulen (2012). Additionally, exhaustive identification captures the semantic extension of the negative statement without appealing to an operator.

the referents. Reinhart (1981) notes that topichood cannot be defined based on the property of the referents as illustrated in (54) and (55).

(54) A: *Who did Felix praise?*
    B: *Felix praised HIMSELF.*
    (Reinhart 1981: 72)

(55) A: *I can't find broccoli anywhere.*
    B: *Crack they sell at every corner but broccoli it is like they don't grow it anymore.*
    (Vallduví 1990: 25)

In (54B), the subject and the object refers to the same person. Hence, the referent denotes new and old information at the same time. In (55B), the sentence initial topic is not given and is not part of the previous discourse. Hence, topichood cannot be defined based on the referential status of referents as given/new. The criterion of subjecthood also fails as a conclusive test for topichood as illustrated in the following example.

(56) *Max saw Rosa yesterday.*
    (Reinhart 1981: 56)

Reinhart (1981) indicates that "Max" can be labeled as topic if this sentence is given as an answer to the question of "Who did Max see yesterday?", and "Rosa" if the same sentence is an answer to the question of "Has anybody seen Rosa yesterday?" Hence, the sentence initial position cannot always be associated with topichood.

Reinhart (1981: 80) suggests that topics are "(....) referential entries under which we classify propositions in the context set and the propositions under such entries in the context set represent what we know about them in this set." Reinhart (1981) uses "as for", "what about", and "said about" paraphrases to identify topics in an utterance. Taking the example in (56) as the testing ground, it is possible to apply these paraphrasing options to determine whether they can provide a method for a clear-cut classification. As illustrated in (57), "Max" can easily be identified as the topic of this utterance.

(57) a. *As for Max, he saw Rosa yesterday.*
    b. *What about Max? Max saw Rosa yesterday.*
    c. *I said about Max that he saw Rosa yesterday.*

However, note that "Rosa" can also be identified as the topic of the sentence as illustrated below.

(58) a. *As for Rosa, Max saw her yesterday.*
   b. *What about Rosa? Max saw her yesterday.*
   c. *I said about Rosa that Max saw her yesterday.*

These tests are too permissive and identify both the subject and the object as the topic of the utterance. This confusion with the tests reveals that a finer classification method for information packaging is needed. Depending solely on order in the sentence or paraphrasing the sentence with certain expressions are not conclusive tests for determining topic phrases as shown in (57) and (58). However, these tests have also been criticized as being too strong to identify aboutness topics as illustrated below (Vallduví 1990: 41).

(59) She told me I needed a change in my life, like getting a new job. It was to no avail. Linguistics fascinated me. Wall Street would have to wait.
   a. I said about linguistics that it fascinated me.
   b. (?) As for linguistics, it fascinated me.
   c. What about linguistics? It fascinated me.

"Linguistics" as the topic of the sentence fails the test in (59b). Now, consider the reason behind this infelicity. Remember that, an aboutness topic phrase is an entry under which propositions are made. However, "as for" and "what about" phrases mark a shift for the topic under discussion. As is clear from the discussion so far, aboutness topics can be new or given in the previous discourse and they mark only what the rest of the sentence is about without marking a shift in the conversation. Hence, infelicity is seen in (59b).

The discussion so far indicates that paraphrasing sentences as diagnostic tests for topic phrases cannot be free of problems. Finer distinctions and more tools are required. The following sub-sections elaborate on what is meant by aboutness topic and contrastive topics within this study.

2.3.2.1 Aboutness topic

For Turkish, Erkü (1982) and Erguvanlı (1984) suggest that sentence initial constituents are topics. The sentence initial subject, as the aboutness topic, marks what the rest of the sentence is about.

(60) A: *Ahmet   ne   oku-du?*
       Ahmet   what   read-PAST
       'What did Ahmet read?'
   B: *[Ahmet]$_{AT}$ kitab-ı   oku-du*
       Ahmet   book-ACC read-PAST
       'Ahmet read the book.'
       (Erkü 1982: 30)

Now, the topichood diagnostic tests can be applied to see whether they capture the Turkish data.

(61) *[Ahmet]$_{AT}$ kitab-ı   oku-du*
     Ahmet   book-ACC read-PERF
     'Ahmet read the book.'
   a. *Ahmet ile ilgili, Ahmet'in kitabı okuduğunu söyledim.*
      'I said about Ahmet that Ahmet read the book.'
   b. *Ahmet'e gelince, Ahmet'in kitabı okuduğunu söyledim.*
      'As for Ahmet, I said that Ahmet read the book.'
   c. *Peki ya Ahmet? Ahmet kitabı okudu.*
      'What about Ahmet? Ahmet read the book.'

(61a) is a natural follow-up sentence for the target sentence in (61), which is further illustrated in (62a) below. However, (62b) and (62c) are more natural in the following contexts.

(62) a. *Ben ne dediğimi gayet iyi hatırlıyorum.*
        'I remember exactly what I said.'
        Ahmet ile ilgili, Ahmet'in kitabı okuduğunu söyledim.
        'I said about Ahmet that Ahmet had read the book.'
   b. *Ben ne dediğimi gayet iyi hatırlıyorum. Mehmet'in dergiyi okuduğunu söyledim.*
      'I remember exactly what I said. I said that Mehmet read the magazine'
      Ahmet'e gelince, Ahmet'in kitabı okuduğunu söyledim.
      'As for Ahmet, I said that Ahmet read the book.'
   c. *Kimin ne yaptığını gayet iyi hatırlıyorum. Mehmet dergiyi okudu.*
      'I remember exactly who did what. Mehmet read the magazine.'
      Peki ya Ahmet? Ahmet kitabı okudu.
      'What about Ahmet? Ahmet read the book.'

Note that (62b) and (62c), *Ahmet* encodes what the rest of the sentence is about but additionally there is a clear contrast with *Mehmet* in the preceding sentence. Based on this example, it is suggested that paraphrases as a topichood diagnostic test is inconclusive. This diagnostic test is too permissive in that (62a) has different information packaging than (62b) and (62c) as the contexts clearly indicate but they are used to trigger the same information structural notion.

Additionally, as illustrated in (63) below, not only the sentence initial subject phrase, but also the object phrase can pass this topichood test.

(63) *Ayşe ile ilgili yeni bir şey var mı?*
Ayşe with about new anything exist QP
'Is there anything new about Ayşe?'
   a. *Ayşe-yi [Ahmet]$_F$ gör-müş.*
      Ayşe-ACC Ahmet see-PERF
      'Ahmet saw Ayşe.'
   b. *Ahmet Ayşe-yi [gör-müş]$_F$*
   c. #*[Ahmet]$_F$ Ayşe-yi gör-müş.*

In (63), the preposed object with the focus marked subject in (63a) is the most natural answer. The in-situ answer is acceptable only when the focus is on the verb (63b). In SOV order, when the focus is on the subject and the object is the aboutness topic, the sentence is not felicitous as in (63c).[19]

Aboutness topic phrases are entries under which propositions are encoded. If Erkü (1982) and Erguvanlı (1984) are on the right track and it is the sentence initial constituent that defines the aboutness topic, what is the function of the object in (63b)? According to the paraphrasing diagnostic test, the accusative case marked object is the aboutness topic but it is not in sentence initial position. The in-situ answer is also possible when there is a referential relationship between the subject and the object as illustrated below.

---

19 One of the reviewers suggests that (63a) and (63c) are both felicitous in this context and asks how it is possible for a constituent to be a DA constituent or an AT at different positions within the same context. The delusion has to do with the question under discussion in that it can be embedded in two different contexts. If the question is a general query about *Ayşe*, (63a) is the most felicitous answer to this question and the sentence initial subject is the AT. However, if we all know that something bad happened to *Ayşe* and someone saw her, (63c) becomes a felicitous answer in this particular context. In this context, *Ayşe* is the discourse anaphoric constituent, namely it is not the pivot of the discourse. The same question is embedded under different contexts. Hence, the information structural function of the same consituent changes according to context, not based on pure word order.

(64) *Ayşe ile ilgili yeni bir şey var mı?*
Ayşe with about new anything exist QP
'Is there anything new about Ayşe?'
  a. *Hoca-sı   Ayşe-yi   sınıf-tan   at-mış.*
     teacher-3SG.POSS Ayşe-ACC class-LOC take out-PERF
     'Ayşe's teacher took her out of the class.'
  b. *Köpek Ayşe-yi   ısır-mış.*
     dog   Ayşe-ACC bite-PERF
     'The dog bit Ayşe.'

These answers are acceptable and a relationship between the subject and the object is predicted. There is a tendency to interpret the subjects of these sentences as the teacher of Ayşe (64a), the dog of Ayşe or a dog both the speaker and the hearer know (64b). One can suggest that the subject forms a semantic unit with the object and the whole utterance is interpreted as a proposition about this compact unit but the following example contradicts this suggestion.

In (65), it is not possible to suggest a semantic relationship between the sentence initial subject and object constituents as illustrated below.

(65) A: *Istakoz-dan ne   haber? O-na   ne   ol-du?*
        lobster-ABL what news   it-DAT what happen-PAST
        'What about the lobster? What happened to it?'
     B: *[Hasan] [ıstakoz-u] [Ali-ye]$_F$ ver-di*
        Hasan   lobster-ACC Ali-DAT   give-PAST
        'Hasan gave the lobster to Ali.'
        (adapted from Kılıçaslan 2004: 730)[20]

This example differs from the ones given in (64) in that it is not possible to make a relational bond between the subject and the object. Hence, it cannot be suggested that the relational bond makes the whole unit an aboutness topic phrase. As the discussion so far indicates, paraphrasing tests are actually inconclusive. Hence, these sentences should be placed in a rich context to determine the information structural role of the sentence initial and medial constituents.

---

[20] Kılıçaslan (2004) suggests that the object constituent is actually the aboutness topic phrase and aboutness topic phrases do not have to be sentence initial constituents.

(66) Dünkü yemeğe, beklediğinizden daha az misafir gelince yemeklerin çoğu yenmemiş diye duydum. Ahmet pastayı almış getirmiş. Istakozdan n'aber? Ona ne oldu?
'I heard that fewer guests came to dinner yesterday and most of the dishes were not eaten. Ahmet brought the cake with him. What about the lobster? What happened to it?'

a. [Hasan]   [ıstakoz-u]   [Ali-ye]   [ver-di]
   Hasan   lobster-ACC   Ali-DAT   give-PERF
   'Hasan gave the lobster to Ali.'
b. [Hasan]   [o-nu]   [Ali-ye]   [ver-di]
   Hasan   it-ACC   Ali-DAT   give-PERF
c. [Hasan]   [Ali-ye]   [ver-di]   [o-nu]
   Hasan   Ali-DAT   give-PERF it-ACC
d. [Hasan]   [Ali-ye]   [ver-di]
   Hasan   Ali-DAT   give-PERF
e. #[O]   [ıstakoz-u]   [Ali-ye]   [ver-di]
   he   lobster-ACC   Ali-DAT   give-PERF
f. #[O-nu]   [Ali-ye]   [ver-di]
   it-ACC   Ali-DAT   give-PERF

Note that it is possible to replace the accusative case marked object that is given in the previous discourse with a pronoun as in (66b), to dislocate the pronoun to the postverbal domain as in (66c), or not to use it at all as in (66d). Note that it is not possible to put a pronominal expression into the subject position as in (66e), or delete the subject as in (66f). Based on different restrictions for the subject and the object, it is suggested that they have different information structural functions and they do not form a compact unit. As the object (i) is overtly given in the previous context, (ii) can be pronominalized, (iii) can be deleted or dislocated to the postverbal domain, it is the discourse-given, discourse anaphoric constituent which is discussed in detail in section 2.3.4. As the initial constituent cannot be pronominalized or deleted in this context, it is the aboutness topic under which new propositions are stacked.[21]

---

[21] One of the reviewers suggests that the distinction between a discourse anaphoric and an aboutness topic phrase with respect to pronominalization, deletion and dislocation to the postverbal domain has to do with the given or new status of the constituents. In pro-drop languages, these properties are expected for given constituents. This is actually, what the current study aims to show. Although aboutness topic and discourse anaphoric constituents share many properties such as being expressed with a pronominal expression or a constituent given in the previous context, aboutness topic phrases differ from discourse anaphoric constituents in that they are

Note that aboutness topic phrases in (64) and (66) are not given but new in discourse and this sets them apart from discourse anaphoric constituents which have to be given in discourse. The next section investigates contrastive topic phrases.

2.3.2.2 Contrastive topic

Within the cartographic approach (Rizzi 1997), TopP projection is assumed for topic phrases. In contrast to FocP, which is unique in the tree structure, a recursive TopP projection is assumed surfacing above and below FocP. Recursive Topic projections in the cartographic approach are criticized in that recursive topic projections are regarded as a reflection of the need for a finer distinction for the topic phrases (Frascarelli and Hinterhölzl 2007; Neeleman and Vermeulen 2012).

Frascarelli and Hinterhölzl (2007) make a three-way distinction for topic phrases as: (i) aboutness topic; (ii) contrastive topic; and (iii) familiar topic. The definition of an aboutness topic is in line with the definition of Reinhart's sentence topic in that an aboutness topic is newly introduced or marks a shift in the conversation. Familiar topics are constituents that are given or salient in discourse, which are analyzed as discourse anaphoric constituents within this study, and they will be discussed in the next section. Contrastive topics evoke alternatives that contrast with other topics. Neeleman and Vermeulen (2012) make a bipartite classification for topic phrases as (i) aboutness topic and (ii) contrastive topic. While aboutness topic phrases bear only a topic feature, contrastive topic phrases bear the additional contrast feature. Contrastive topics differ from aboutness topics in that contrastive topics evoke alternatives, as illustrated below.

(67) A: *Tell me about Bill. Was he invited to a party when he went to New York?*
 B: *Well, I don't know about Bill, but Maxine$_{CT}$ was invited to a party on her first trip to New York by Claire.*

(68) a. $< \lambda x$ ASSERT [x was invited by Claire to a party in New York], Maxine, {Susan, Bill,......}>
 b. $\exists y$ [$y \in$ {Susan, Bill,......}& ¬ASSERT [x was invited by Claire to a party in New York](y)]
 (Neeleman and Vermeulen 2012: 20–21)

---

sentence initial constituents that can also be discourse-new in the context. Whether given or new, aboutness topic phrases surface at the sentence initial position as the pivot of the upcoming proposition.

Note that the answer in (67B) marks a shift in the conversation and indicates the presence of alternatives. However, in contrast to contrastive focus phrases, the alternatives in the set are not excluded with contrastive topic phrases. While the contrastive topic is asserted as the answer, the other alternatives are left unresolved by the speaker.

Büring (2013) briefly summarizes the functions of contrastive topics under five headings, illustrated by the following examples:

i. A sense of incompleteness with the functions of addition, possibility and openness

(69) A: *Ayşe ile   kaç-ta   buluş-acak-sın?*
       Ayşe with   what time-LOC   meet-FUT-2SG
       'When will you meet with Ayşe?'
    B: *[Ayşe]$_{CT}$ ile   [üç-te]$_F$ buluş-uyor-uz   ama   bir-de*
       Ayşe   with   three-LOC   meet-IMPF-1PL   but   one-LOC
       toplantı-ya   gid-eceğ-im.
       meeting-DAT   go-FUT-1SG
       'I will meet Ayşe at 3, but I will go to the meeting at 1 o'clock.'

The answer signals that it is not an exhaustive answer and adds another alternative to the list without excluding the first alternative.

ii. Partial topics

(70) A: *Doğum gün-ün-de   kim   ne   getir-miş?*
       birthday-2SG.POSS-LOC   who   what   bring-PERF
       'Who brought what for your birthday?'
    B: *[Abi-m]$_{CT}$ [küpe]$_F$ al-mış.*
       brother-1SG.POSS   earring   buy-PERF
       'My brother bought earrings.'

The speaker in B gives only a partial answer to the question which triggers a pair/list answer and refrains from giving a complete answer. The question under discussion namely the immediate topic of discussion (Roberts 1996) is not fully resolved.

iii. Shifting topics

(71) A: *Doğum gün-ün-e   Ahmet   gel-ecek   mi?*
       birthday-2SG.POSS-DAT   Ahmet   come-FUT   QP
       'Will Ahmet come to your birthday party?'

B: *Ahmet-i bil-mi-yor-um ama [abi-m]$_{CT}$ [gel-ecek]$_F$.*
   Ahmet-ACC know-NEG-IMPF-1SG but brother-1SG.POSS come-FUT
   'I don't know about Ahmet but my brother will come.'

Similar to the case in (67), the issue under discussion is not resolved and the speaker gives an answer shifting the topic of the previous utterance.

iv. Purely implicational topics

(72) A: *Dün bütün gün nere-de-ydi-n?*
   yesterday whole day where-LOC-COP-2SG
   'Where were you the whole day yesterday?'
   B: *[Ben]$_{CT}$ [ev-de-ydi-m]$_F$, ya sen?*
   I home-LOC-COP-1SG how about you
   'I was at home, how about you?'

The question puts the referent of the question at the center of the discussion but the answer shifts the topic. Even in the absence of the tag question, it is clear that the speaker in B directs the same question to the other speaker.

v. Scope Fixing

(73) A: *Parti-ye kim-ler gel-di?*
   party-DAT who-PL come-PERF
   'Who came to the party?'
   B: *[Davet et-tik-ler-im]$_{CT}$ [gel-di]$_F$.*
   invite-REL-PL-1SG.POSS come-PERF
   'Those I invited came.'
   B': #*[Herkes]$_{CT}$ [gel-di]$_F$.*
   everybody come-PERF
   'Everybody came.'

Similar to the example in (70) the speaker does not give a satisfactory answer to the question. Note that a quantifier which resolves the question under discussion is not felicitous in the same context and this is expected, as utterances with contrastive topic phrases "(...) can never be (...) thoroughly exhaustive answers" (Constant 2014: 50).[22]

---

[22] One of the reviewers suggests that the answer in (73B') is acceptable and hence it is not valid to suggest that some quantifiers cannot be CT phrases. Actually, the answer in (73B') can be interpreted in two different patterns following this question: (i) the quantifier is CT and the speaker refrains from giving a complete answer; (ii) the quantifier is F and the speaker asserts

All the functions listed above clearly indicate that answers with contrastive topic phrases narrow down the question into sub-questions and answer only one of them, refrain from giving an exhaustive answer, or make a shift in the current discussion. The speaker does not give a thorough answer to the question either because she does not know the complete answer or because she is unwilling to do so. Hence, the usage of contrastive topic is a kind of discourse strategy as indicated in the literature (Büring 2003; Krifka 2008; Wagner 2007, 2008; Dyakonova 2009; Tomioka 2010; Neeleman and Vermeulen 2012; Constant 2014).

The discussion in section 2.3.1.2 indicated that, in Turkish, yes/no questions trigger contrastive focus phrases. Additionally, based on the position of the question particle, yes/no questions also trigger contrastive topic phrases as already noted by Kamali and Büring (2011).

(74) A: *Almanya ve Hollanda'ya çalışmaya giden Alanyalılar büyük beğeni toplamışlar. Hollandalılar da onları öven bir konuşma yapıyor.*
'One of the groups that went from Alanya to Holland and Germany won recognition with their work. Now the Dutch people give a vote of thanks.'
B: $[Almanyalı\text{-}lar]_{CT}$ Alanyalı-lar-ı $[öv\text{-}üyor]_F$ mu?
German-PL people of Alanya-PL-ACC praise-IMPF QP
'Do the German people praise the people from Alanya?'

(75) A: *Yurt dışına çalışmaya giden Alanya ve Anamurlular çalışmalarıyla büyük beğeni toplamış. Şimdi de bir Alman kanalında Anamurlulara teşekkür konuşması yapılıyor.*
'The guest worker groups from Alanya and Anamur who went abroad won recognition with their work. Now, a vote of thanks is delivered to the people from Anamur on a German TV channel.'
B: $[Almanyalı\text{-}lar]_{AT}$ $[Alanyalı\text{-}lar\text{-}ı]_{CT}$ $[övü\text{-}yor]_F$ mu?
German-PL people of Alanya-PL-ACC praise-IMPF QP
'Do the German people praise the people from Alanya?'

Both of the questions mark a shift in the topic under discussion. The comparison between (42) and (74) indicates that the question particle can directly

---

that in contrast to all the other alternatives this one is chosen as the correct answer. It is suggested that this sentence is felicitous when the quantifier is interpreted as an F marked constituent. When the quantifier bears focus, the verb is interpreted as a DA constituent. However, the same sentence is infelicitous when the quantifier is interpreted and uttered with the intonation pattern of a CT. Then the verb bears focus. See footnote 34 for a discussion on how a CT/F shift is possible in certain constructions.

follow the focused constituent even if it is not the verb. In both (43) and (75), the question particle is in its canonical sentence final position and it follows the focus phrase. In these examples, the difference is marked only by intonation.

Now, the alternatives induced by contrastive topic phrases will be investigated by comparing them with the alternatives evoked by contrastive focus phrases at each step. Remember that within alternative semantics, the function of focus is taken as evoking alternatives (Rooth 1985, 1992). The alternative propositions differ with respect to the constituent in the focus position and so the focus value of the sentence is obtained.

(76) *What did Ayşe fly?*
 ordinary semantic value
 {Ayşe flew the kite}
 focus semantic value
 {Ayşe flew the kite, Ayşe flew the balloon, Ayşe flew the plane......}

As for the focus semantic value of a question, remember that the question has a set of possible answers. Question-answer congruence can be found because the set of alternative propositions of the question is a subset of the set of alternative propositions of the focus phrase as illustrated in (76) and (77).

(77) *What did Ayşe fly?*
 {Ayşe flew the kite, Ayşe flew the balloon, Ayşe flew the plane......}

Contrastive topics evoke alternatives through a set of questions. Hence, the semantic value of contrastive topics denotes a set of sets of alternative propositions as shown in (78) below.

This is illustrated below in line with the discourse tree representation of Büring (2003).[23]

(78) A: *Hava   rüzgarlı-ydı, kim ne   uçur-muş?*
 weather windy-COP who what fly-PERF
 'The weather was windy, who flew what?'

---

[23] Adopting the analysis of Roberts (1996), Büring (2003) develops a hierarchical discourse tree in which discourse is represented as questions which are further decomposed into subquestions and answers. In the tree, each node represents a sentence with a focus and a contrastive topic which is labeled as CTF pattern.

B: [Ayşe]_CT [uçurtma]_F uçur-muş.
   Ayşe   kite   flew-PERF
   'Ayşe flew a kite.'

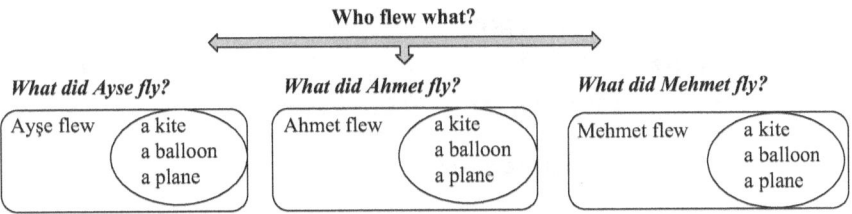

Figure 3: The discourse tree representation.

The big question (Roberts 1996) is narrowed down to sub-questions which evoke a set of possible answers as alternatives; hence the contrastive topic is a set of questions or set of sets of alternative propositions. The answer with contrastive topic in (78B) leaves some questions unresolved.

Note that the semantic value of the focus phrase in (76) which is defined as the semantic value of a question or a set of alternative propositions is only a sub-part of the semantic representation of the contrastive topic. The semantic value of the focus phrase is used in the semantic computation of the contrastive topic. Hence, there is a close relationship between a focus and a contrastive topic phrase.

Now, some data taken as focus phrases in the literature can be considered anew. Göksel and Özsoy (2000) take the sentence initial constituents in (80) as focus phrases. For the contrast between (79) and (80), they suggest that wh-phrases can follow focus phrases but not vice versa.[24]

---

[24] The construction in (80) in the text can also be used in the following context. Within this context, the sentence initial constituent is not a contrastive topic.

(1) A: Ne zaman gid-ecek-sin?
       when   go-FUT-2SG
       'When will you go?'

    B: Ev-e   mi?
       house-DAT QP
       'To the house?'

    A: Ev-e   değil OKUL-A   ne zaman gid-ecek-sin.
       house-DAT not   school-DAT when   go-FUT-2SG
       'Not to the house, when will you go to the school.'

Note that the construction has the intonational properties of a declarative clause, not an interrogative clause.

(79) a. *Ne zaman [okul-a]_F gid-ecek-sin?
       when   school-DAT go-FUT-2SG
       'When will you go to school?'
    b. *Kim [sen-i]_F sev-iyor?
       who you-ACC   love-PROG
       'Who loves you?'
    c. *Kim-i   [sinema-da]_F gör-ecek-sin?
       who-ACC cinema-LOC   see-FUT-2SG
       'Who will you see at the cinema?'

(80) a. [Okul-a]_F   ne zaman gid-ecek-sin?
       school-DAT   when   go-FUT-2SG
    b. [Sen-i]_F   kim   sev-iyor?
       you-ACC   who   love-PROG
    c. [Sinema-da]_F   kim-i   gör-ecek-sin?
       cinema-LOC   who-ACC   see-FUT-2SG
       (adapted from Göksel and Özsoy 2000: 2)

We suggest that the sentences in (79) are out as there are two focus phrases within the same sentence. As for the examples in (80), in this study it is proposed that the sentence initial constituents are in fact contrastive topic phrases followed by focused wh-phrases based on their function within the sentence.[25] The utterances in (80a), (80b) and (80c) are exemplified below in a context.

(81) A: Ev-e   saat   2-de   gid-eceğ-im.
       home-DAT   hour   two-LOC   go-FUT-1SG
       'I will go home at 2 o'clock.'
    B: Peki,   okul-a   ne zaman gid-ecek-sin?
       OK,   school-DAT   when   go-FUT-2SG
       'OK, when will you go to school?'

(82) A: Ahmet Ayşe-yi   sev-iyor.
       Ahmet Ayşe-ACC   love-IMPF
       'Ahmet loves Ayşe.'

---

[25] In the next chapter, it will be shown in detail why two independent focus phrases are not possible within a single sentence. To briefly note, focus phrases attract the highest prominence within their domains. Hence, two prominent focus phrases within a sentence result in a clash.

B: *Peki, ya sen, sen-i   kim   sev-iyor?*
   OK   you   you-ACC who love-IMPF
   'OK, what about you, who loves you?'

(83) A: *Yarın   okul-da   İpek-i   gör-eceğ-im.*
        tomorrow school-DAT İpek-ACC see-FUT-1SG
        'Tomorrow I will see İpek at school.'
     B: *Peki sinema-da   kim-i   gör-ecek-sin?*
        OK   cinema-LOC who-ACC see-FUT-2SG
        'OK, whom will you see at the cinema?'

Similar to the example in (71), the constituents preceding the wh-phrases in (81), (82) and (83) mark a shift in topic.[26] Kılıçaslan (2004) also suggests a multiple foci analysis for Turkish based on the example given below.

(84) A: *Kim   kim-le   evlen-di?*
        who   who-COM marry-PAST
        'Who married whom?'

---

26 Analyzing the sentence initial phrases in (80) as contrastive topic phrases also provides more ideas with respect to the analysis of intervention effects in Turkish. Kesen (2010) notes that although focus phrases with overt particles and negative polarity items induce intervention effects for wh-phrases (1a) and (2a), focus phrases without focus particles do not (3b).

(1) a. **Kimse   kim-i   gör-me-di?*   b. *Kim-i   kimse   gör-me-di?*
       anyone   who-ACC see-NEG-PERF   'Whom nobody saw?'

(2) a. **Sadece Ali kim-i   ara-dı?*   b. *Kim-i   sadece Ali ara-dı?*
       Only   Ali who-ACC call-PERF   'Whom Ali called only?'
       (Kesen 2010: 82)

(3) a. **Ne zaman okul-a   gid-ecek-sin?* b. *Okul-a ne zaman gid-ecek-sin?*
       when   school-DAT go-FUT-2SG   'When will you go to school?'

Based on three judgment tests Kesen (2010) concludes that interveners in Turkish do not form a homogeneous class and in contrast to Korean, the interveners cannot be grouped as focus phrases. However, as illustrated above, the sentence initial constituents are in fact contrastive topic phrases not focus phrases. Hence, Turkish does not present an exceptional case with respect to intervention effects.

B: [Oya]_F [Kaya-yla]_F evlen-di.
   Oya   Kaya-COM   marry-PAST
   '[Oya] married [Kaya].
   (Kılıçaslan 2004: 720)

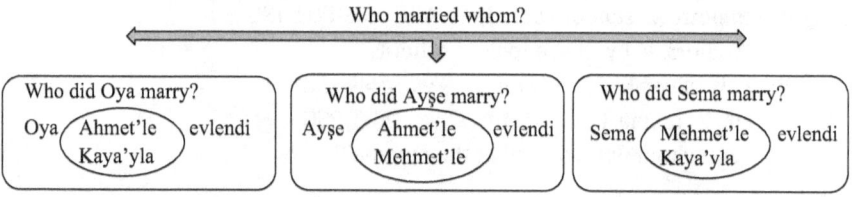

Figure 4: A discourse tree in Turkish.

Note that the question in (84) triggers a contrastive topic. The big question under discussion includes many sub-questions. It is suggested that the answer in (84), given to the question triggering a pair list answer, has a sense of incompleteness or openness. It gives a partial answer to the question similar to the answers in (69) and (70) and hence while the first wh-phrase is a contrastive topic, the second wh-phrase is a focus phrase. In the next section, the focus will be on contrast.

2.3.3 Contrast

The status of contrast has been a controversial issue being regarded as (i) a primitive feature not as a part of topic or focus (Neeleman and Vermeulen 2012) or (ii) a dependent feature of topic and focus (Büring 2003; Krifka 2008; Wagner 2007, 2008; Dyakonova 2009; Tomioka 2010; Constant 2014).

Neeleman and Vermeulen (2012) regard contrast as a primitive feature because based on the feature contrast, they can make some generalizations about contrastive topic and contrastive focus. For example, in some languages only contrastive topic and focus can undergo A' scrambling while this is not possible with non-contrastive topic and focus phrases.

In Turkish, there is no overt focus movement, so this cannot be a common property of contrastive topic and focus in Turkish. Additionally, there are some generalizations that extend to not only contrastive topic and focus but also to discourse-new focus. For example, not only contrastive topic and contrastive focus but also discourse-new focus evoke alternatives. With contrastive focus, other alternatives are excluded; with contrastive topic, the speaker refrains from talking about the other alternatives and the answer does not resolve the issue under discussion. Finally, with discourse-new focus, the other alternatives are not excluded and the answer is not an exhaustive answer. It is possible to generalize the property of evoking alternatives over contrastive topic, focus and discourse-new focus. Additionally, when the alternative sets of these constituents are compared, it can readily be seen that the alternative sets of discourse-new focus and contrastive topic phrases are more closely related, as the answer is not an exhaustive answer with these constituents in contrast to contrastive focus phrases. Hence, there is no syntactic or semantic property that can be generalized only for contrastive topic and focus.

Dyakonova (2009) suggests that topic and focus are absolute in nature while contrast is gradable in the sense that contrast depends on different factors such as the explicitness, or the range of the alternative sets. There is a tendency to interpret contrastive focus as more contrastive as it has a closed set of alternatives when compared to discourse-new focus with an open set of alternatives. Additionally, contrast can be cancelled out with contrastive focus (85a) and contrastive topic (85b).

(85) a. *Manuel slapped his daughter$_{CF}$.*
Implicature: not his wife, or any of his other kids.
Cancellation: and not only her, his wife got a couple of boxes in the ear as well.
b. *Mary$_{CT}$ sent Daniel a birthday card.*
Implicature: there were other people who congratulated him.
Cancellation: in fact, she was the only one who happened to remember about his birthday.
(Dyakonova 2009: 18)

This calls into question the status of contrast as a primitive semantic notion. Hence, it can be concluded that contrast is not a primitive notion and does not occupy a specific position in the structure.

2.3.4 Discourse anaphoric constituents

Discourse anaphoric expressions are information structural units that are salient or given in discourse such as pronominals. Neeleman and Vermeulen (2012) suggest that the notion of topic used by Rizzi (1997) actually covers discourse anaphoric expressions, as topic is defined as a discourse constituent "(….) normally expressing old information somehow available and salient in previous discourse (….)" (Rizzi, 1997: 285).

Discourse anaphoric expressions in this study are aligned with the notion of familiar topic defined by Frascarelli and Hinterhölzl (2007: 2) as a "(....) given or accessible (Chafe 1987) constituent, which is typically destressed and realized in a pronominal form (Pesetsky 1987) (....)" In the following example, it is "the check", which is given in the discourse and serves as the continuing topic.

(86) B: *io dovevo studiare le regole qui e li fare solo esercizio, invece mi aspettvo di trovare dei punti a cui far riferimento ogni volta per vedere la regola, questo mi e mancato praticamento per avare la conferma di ricodare tutto insomma; A: comunque quelle domande ti davano la conferma che avevi capito; B: ma... magari non me la-* <u>non riesco a darmela da sola la conferma.</u>
'I was supposed to study rules here and do the exercises there, while I expected to find some outlines I could refer to, at any point, to check the relevant rule, this is what I missed, to check that I could remember everything. A: however those questions gave you the possibility to check your understanding; B; well, maybe <u>I cannot make this check on my own.</u>'
(Frascarelli and Hinterhölzl 2007: 93)

Discourse anaphoric constituents do not evoke alternatives or mark a contrast with another constituent in the previous context. In the following example, it is the dative marked constituent in the answer that functions as the discourse anaphoric constituent.

(87) A: *İzmir'de düzenlenecek konferans için Ankara'dan bakanlar gelmiş. İstanbul ve Ankara'dan getirilen 10 kişilik güvenlik ekibi yoğun güvenlik önlemleri almış. Duyduğum kadarıyla, İstanbullu güvenlik görevlileri bakanlara hiç yardımcı olmamışlar.*
'For the conference that will be held in İzmir, some ministers came from Ankara. The security guard crew who came from İstanbul and Ankara took precautionary security measures. As far as I have heard, the security guards from İstanbul did not help the ministers.'

B: *İstanbullu   güvenlik   görevli-ler-in-i*
   person from İstanbul   security   guard-PL-CM-ACC
   bil-mi-yor-um   ama   [Ankaralı   güvenlik
   know-NEG-IMPF-1SG   but   person from Ankara   security
   görevli-ler-i]$_{CT}$ [bakan-lar-a]$_{DA}$ [eskortluk   et-miş-ler]$_{FOC}$
   guard-PL-CM   minister-PL-DAT   escort   do-PERF-3PL
   'I don't know about the security guards from İstanbul but the security guards from Ankara escorted the ministers.'

Prosodic or syntactic strategies can be used to mark discourse anaphoric constituents in a sentence. Krifka (2006) lists three strategies used to signal given information as: (i) deaccentuation; (ii) deletion; and (iii) word order change. The first strategy will be considered in the next chapter. Turkish widely uses the other strategies. Discourse anaphoric expressions as continuing or familiar topics can be omitted (88a) or dislocated to the postverbal position (88b).

(88) *Arabayı aldın mı?*
 'Did you take the car?'
 a. ~~O-nu~~ yarın al-acağ-ım.
    it-ACC tomorrow take-FUT-1SG
    'I will take (it) tomorrow.'
 b. *Yarın al-acağ-ım o-nu.*
    tomorrow take-FUT-1SG it-ACC

Based on the observation that contrastive topic and focus phrases cannot appear in the postverbal position in Turkish, Şener (2010) assumes that discourse anaphoric expressions in the left periphery have an additional contrast feature which postverbal discourse anaphoric constituents lack. The postverbal position is also illicit for discourse-new focus constituents, which are not contrastive and contrastive topic phrases may surface in the postverbal domain (see also section 2.5.2). Hence, an additional contrast feature to make a distinction between discourse anaphoric expressions in the right or left periphery will not be assumed in the current study.[27]

At this point, it is a natural question to ask whether discourse anaphoric constituents can be a subtype of topic phrases given that they do not bear focus. Taking discourse anaphoric constituents as a topic type will not change the current analysis and a parsimonious classification for information structural units may be assumed. However, this option will not be adopted due to the fact that: (i) more than one discourse anaphoric constituent can surface in a sentence while this is not the case with aboutness topic phrases; (ii) discourse anaphoric constituents have different ordering restrictions than aboutness topic phrases in that only discourse anaphoric constituents can follow focus phrases; and (iii) the referential status of discourse anaphoric constituents are always given but this is not the case for aboutness topic phrases. Hence, in this

---

[27] In the syntax chapter, only preverbal discourse anaphoric constituents will be dealt with as the data is restricted to SOV and OSV orders in Turkish.

study, discourse anaphoric constituents are analyzed as distinct information structural units serving as vehicular parts of the sentence.[28]

2.4 Overt particles with contrastive topic and focus phrases

It has been suggested in the literature that focus phrases with overt particles have a truth conditional effect and a semantic dimension (Rooth 1996; Krifka 2006). Answers to wh-questions, corrections, confirmations have been suggested to be pragmatic purposes of focus (Krifka 2006).

(89) a. *John only showed Mary [the PICTures]$_F$.*
   b. *John only showed [MARy]$_F$ the pictures.*

(90) A: *What did John show Mary?*
   B: *John showed Mary [the PICTures]$_F$.*

(91) A: *Who did John show the pictures?*
   B: *John showed [MARy]$_F$ the pictures.*
   (Krifka 2006: 14–15)

The difference is that while the focus status of the constituents in (90) and (91) is dependent on the context as shown in (90B) and (91B), the focus status of the constituents in (89) is not. In the following sections, discourse particles that follow contrastive topic and focus phrases are considered.

2.4.1 Sadece/yalnızca, bile

The particles *sadece/yalnızca* 'only' surface in contrastive focus phrases. This is expected as contrastive focus is identified with exhaustive identification.

---

28 One of the reviewers suggests that it is problematic to define discourse anaphoric constituents as a unit of information structure just based on the feature of being given in discourse. It is true that the discourse anaphoric constituents always bear the status of being given in discourse. However, as the discussion so far illustrates, discourse anaphoric constituents serve as the linkage within the discourse and they are part of focus semantic value namely the alternative propositions. Hence, within this study they are taken as an information structural notion.

(92) A: *Ahmet tiyatro-ya git-ti.*
Ahmet theatre-DAT go-PERF
'Ahmet went to the theatre.'
B: *Hayır, [sadece Mete]$_{CF}$ tiyatro-ya git-ti.*
No, only Mete theatre-DAT go-PERF
'No, only Mete went to the theatre.'

In (92) above, the focus phrase evokes alternatives ranging over a set of the names of people. However, only one of the answers is exhaustively identified as the correct answer to the exclusion of the alternatives in the set.

The other particle that surfaces with focus phrases is *bile*, which has the meaning of 'even'. In fact, the type of the focus constituent that this particle attaches to is controversial. Kerslake (1992: 92) explains this controversy in the following way: "(...) although it does sometimes have an additive function its primary meaning is not 'in addition x' but 'as an extreme case, x', and this does not depend upon a specific 'non-extreme' case being having been mentioned or implied in the preceding discourse." Consider the following example.

(93) A: *Gid-eceğ-imiz film güzel mi?*
go-REL-1PL.POSS film good QP
'Is the film that we will see good?'
B: *Mete bile o film-i izle-miş.*
Mete even that film-ACC watch-PERF
'Even Mete has seen that film.'
Daha ne olsun?
'What else do you expect?'

In this example, the host subject phrase evokes a set of alternatives. The particle *bile* 'even' signals that there are some additional alternatives of people that saw the film. One of the alternatives is chosen as an extreme case of the alternative set to the exclusion of the other alternatives. The other alternatives are excluded, as they are not as surprising or unexpected as the chosen focus phrase. The following example further illustrates that *bile* 'even' does not just signal the addition of an alternative to the set of alternatives.

(94) A: *Ahmet tiyatro-ya git-miş. Başka kim git-miş?*
Ahmet theatre-DAT go-PERF else who go-PERF
'Ahmet went to the theatre. Who else went to the theatre?'

B: *Mete bile   tiyatro-ya   git-miş.*
   Mete even   theatre-DAT go-PERF
   'Even Mete went to the theatre.'

The answer is fully acceptable only when the fact that Mete's going to the theatre is taken as an exceptional case when compared to the other alternatives in the set. Hence, it is suggested that the host phrase of the particle is a contrastive focus phrase and not a discourse-new focus.[29]

2.4.2 dA

Erguvanlı (1984) is the first to note that *dA* surfaces with strong topics. Kerslake (1992) identifies two functions for this particle as (i) non-focused *dA* marking a change of subject as topic marker and (ii) focused *dA* signaling the focused phrase making an addition to the preceding context. Göksel and Özsoy (2003) suggest that *dA* either marks the focus phrase as in (95a) or attaches to a non-focused constituent as in (95b). Kesen (2010) also suggests that *dA* surfaces with focus phrases in examples similar to the one in (95a).

(95) a. *[Ahmet]$_F$ de   sinema-ya   gid-iyor.*
        Ahmet   dA   cinema-DAT   go-PROG
        'Ahmet, too, is going to the cinema.'
     b. *Ahmet   de   [sinema-ya]$_F$ gid-iyor.*
        Ahmet   dA   cinema-DAT   go-PROG
        'As for Ahmet, he is going to the cinema.'
        'Ahmet, on the other hand, is going to the cinema.'
        (Göksel and Özsoy 2003: 1147)

Göksel and Özsoy (2003) suggest that in (95a) the focused phrase together with the clitic *dA* evoke a set of alternatives and *dA* asserts that one of the alternatives is true. In (95b), on the other hand, both the clitic and focused phrase evoke alternatives and *dA* forces one of these alternatives to be true.

Firstly, the example in (95b) is examined. As Kerslake (1992) points out, the host marks a shift in conversation as illustrated below.[30] In (96B), the speaker

---

[29] Kiss (1998) suggests that "even" in Hungarian surfaces with information focus, but not with identificational focus (except in special contexts).
[30] Erguvanlı (1984) analyzes topic phrases marked with this particle as strong topics.

shifts the topic under discussion from *Mete* to *Ahmet* which is signaled with the particle *dA*.

(96) A: *Mete tiyatro-ya   gid-iyor.*
      Mete   theatre-DAT go-IMPF
      'Mete is going to the theatre.
   B: *[Ahmet]$_{CT}$ de   [sinema-ya]$_F$ gid-iyor.*
      Ahmet   dA   cinema-DAT   go-IMPF
      'As for Ahmet, he is going to the cinema.'

The big question of "Who went where?" is decomposed into the sub-questions as "Who went to the cinema?, Who went to the theatre?, Who went to the market?" In this example, the first speaker was talking about a specific node of the tree about *Mete* when the other speaker moves to another node to talk about *Ahmet*. This is similar to the utterance in (71) under the labeling of shifting topics. Hence, the host in (96b) can be taken as a contrastive topic phrase.[31]

The additive function of this clitic is exemplified below. The host of the particle is triggered by a wh-question, triggering alternatives.

---

(1)   *Bir gömlek san-a   bir gömlek de kardeş-in-e   al-dı-m.*
      one shirt   you-DAT one shirt   too brother-2SG.POSS-DAT get-PAST-1SG
      'I got a shirt for you and a shirt for your brother.'
      (Erguvanlı 1984: 38)

[31] Note that the intonational properties of the structures in (81) and (96), which are illustrated below as (1–2) for ease of exposition, differ although the same ordering exists, namely contrastive topic followed by focus phrase.

(1) A: *Mete tiyatro-ya   gid-iyor.*   B: *Ahmet$_{CT}$ de   sinema-ya$_F$ gid-iyor.*
       Mete   theatre-DA   go-IMPF   Ahmet   dA   cinema-DAT   go-IMPF
       'Mete is going to the theatre.'   'As for Ahmet, he is going to the cinema.'

(2) A: *Ev-e   saat   2-de   gid-eceğ-im.*
       home-DAT hour   two-LOC go-FUT-1SG
       'I will go home at 2 o'clock.'
    B: *Peki, okul-a$_{CT}$ ne zaman$_F$ gid-ecek-sin?*
       OK,   school-DAT   when   go-FUT-2SG
       'OK, when will you go to school?'

It is suggested that this difference is due to the interaction of contrastive topic and focus phrases with the intonational patterns of questions and declaratives in Turkish which require a controlled prosodic analysis that is left for further research.

(97) A: *Mete   sinema-ya   git-miş.   Başka   kim   git-miş?*
     Mete   cinema-DAT   go-PERF   else   who   go-PERF
     'Mete went to the cinema. Who else went to the cinema?'
   B: *Ahmet   de   sinema-ya   git-miş.*
     Ahmet   dA   cinema-DAT   go-PERF
     'Ahmet, too, went to the cinema.'
   C: *Ayşe   de.*
     'Ayşe, too.'

The addition of another constituent does not result in unacceptability, which indicates that the alternative is not exhaustively identified as the correct answer. Hence, it is proposed that the clitic *dA* signals discourse-new focus constituents.

2.4.3 ise

Finally, the particle *ise* 'as for' should be examined. Kerslake (1992) suggests that this particle shifts the attention to a new topic in a more marked way than *dA*.

(98) A: *Mete   tiyatro-ya   gid-iyor.*
     Mete   theatre-DAT   go-IMPF
     'Mete is going to the theatre.'
   B: *[Ahmet]$_{CT}$ ise   [sinema-ya]$_F$ gid-iyor.*
     Ahmet   ise   cinema-DA   go-IMPF
     'As for Ahmet, he is going to the cinema.'

As the example illustrates, the host of this particle marks a shift in the topic under discussion as in (96). Hence, the host will be analyzed as a contrastive topic with the function of topic shifting.

2.5 Distribution of information structural units in Turkish

2.5.1 Focus phrases

As already pointed out in section 1.3, the following analyses have been suggested in Turkish with respect to the position of focus (i) all types of focus must be left adjacent to the verb (Erguvanlı 1984; Şener 2010); (ii) presentational focus must be left adjacent to the verb but contrastive focus can appear in the preverbal domain (İşsever 2003); (iii) all focus types can appear in the preverbal domain (Göksel and Özsoy 2000; Kılıçaslan 2004).

The position of focus phrases will be addressed in more detail in the following commentary. What is meant by in-situ focus is not akin to Hungarian in which identificational focus moves to the immediate preverbal position while informational focus remains in-situ. In Turkish, focused constituents do not move at all as illustrated below.

(99) A: *Ahmet sınav öncesi tutmuş defterini vermiş başka birine. Nasıl çalışacak şimdi defteri olmadan?*
'Ahmet gave his notebook to someone before the exam. How is he going to study for the exam now without his notebook?'
B: *[Mehmet]$_F$ [defter-in-i]$_{DA}$ [ver-miş]$_{DA}$, Ahmet değil.*
Mehmet notebook-3SG.POSS-ACC give-PERF Ahmet not
'Mehmet gave his book to someone not Ahmet.'
C: *[Defter-in-i]$_{AT}$ [Mehmet]$_F$ [ver-miş]$_{DA}$, Ahmet değil.*

In (99B), the focused constituent remains in-situ with a following discourse-anaphoric constituent in the immediate preverbal domain. In (99C), a non-focused constituent surfaces in a position preceding the focused phrase leaving the focused phrase in the immediate preverbal position.[32] Göksel and Özsoy (2003: 1153) also suggest that "(....) the generalization that Turkish is a focus-in-situ language holds in all instances". An in-situ focus in Turkish means the constituents following the focus phrase move to another position leaving the focus phrase in the immediately preverbal position. To evaluate this claim, first

---

[32] The other question is whether there is focus movement to the immediate preverbal position or not in Turkish. Vallduví and Engdahl (1996: 489) suggest that Turkish immediate preverbal focus differs from Hungarian immediate preverbal focus with respect to projection possibilities. In Hungarian, focus projection of the immediate preverbal focus phrase is to the right, while it is to the left in Turkish which indicates that the syntactic make up is different.

(1) *Bir hizmetçi [$_F$ masa-nın üzer-in-e [$_F$ yemek-ten önce*
a servant table-GEN on-POSS-DAT lunch-ABL before
[$_F$ [not-u]$_F$ bırak-tı]]].
note-ACC leave-PAST
A. *What did a servant leave on the table before lunch?*
B. *What did a servant do before lunch having to do with the table?*
C. *What did a servant do before lunch?*
D. *What did a servant do?*

contrastive focus phrases triggered by alternative questions or corrective statements should be considered.

(100) *Okulumuz öğretmenlerinden bazıları öğrencileriyle birlikte ders çıkışı pikniğe gitmişler. Rüzgârı fırsat bilen öğrenciler yanlarında uçurmak için uçurtma götürmüşler. Öğretmenler de öğrenciler gibi eğlenmişler. Sen biliyor musun, piknikten sonra öğretmenler mi yoksa öğrenciler mi uçurtmaları uçurmuşlar?*
'Some of the teachers from our school went on a picnic with their students after school. The students brought with them some kites to fly. The teachers also had fun. Do you know whether the teachers or the students flew the kites after the picnic?'

A: [Öğrenci-ler]$_{CF}$ [uçurtma-lar-ı]$_{DA}$ [uçur-muş-lar]$_{DA}$ SOV
    student-PL   kite-PL-ACC   fly-PERF-3PL
   'The students flew the kites.'
B: [Öğrenci-ler]$_{CF}$ [uçur-muş-lar]$_{DA}$ [uçurtma-lar-ı]$_{DA}$ SVO
C: [Öğrenci-ler]$_{CF}$ [uçur-muş-lar]$_{DA}$ SV

(101) *Ayşe'nin dolabına sınav kağıtlarını bırakmıştım. Toplantıda velilere dağıtacaktı. Dolapta sınav kağıdı kalmadığına göre velilere vermiş.*
'I had left the exam papers in Ayşe's cupboard. She was going to give them to the parents at the meeting. As there were no exam result papers in the cupboard, Ayşe gave them to the parents.'

A: Yoo, hayır. [Ayşe]$_{AT}$ [öğrenci-ler-e]$_{CF}$
   No.   Ayşe   student-PL-DAT
   [sınav kağıt-lar-ın-ı]$_{DA}$ [ver-di]$_{DA}$ (veli-ler-e   değil).
   exam paper-PL-3SG.POSS-ACC give-PERF parents-PL-DAT not
   'No. Ayşe gave the exam papers to the students (not to the parents)'
B: Yoo, hayır. [Ayşe]$_{AT}$ [sınav kağıt-lar-ın-ı]$_{DA}$ [öğrenci-ler-e]$_{CF}$
   [ver-di]$_{DA}$ (veli-ler-e değil).
C: Yoo, hayır. [Ayşe]$_{AT}$ [öğrenci-ler-e]$_{CF}$ [ver-di]$_{DA}$
   [sınav kağıt-lar-ın-ı]$_{DA}$ (veli-ler-e değil).
D: Yoo, hayır. [Ayşe]$_{AT}$ [öğrenci-ler-e]$_{CF}$ [verdi]$_{DA}$
   (veli-ler-e değil).

As exemplified above, the subject in (100) or the dative marked constituent in (101) can bear contrastive focus in their base generated positions in the presence of discourse anaphoric constituents in the immediate preverbal domain. Additionally, a contrastive focus phrase can appear in the immediate preverbal

2.5 Distribution of information structural units in Turkish — 63

position and the discourse anaphoric constituents can either move to an ex-situ position as in (100B), (101B) and (101C) or get deleted as in (100C) and (101D).

There are similar analyses suggesting that contrastive focus can appear in the preverbal domain without restricting it to the immediately preverbal domain (Göksel and Özsoy 2000; İşsever 2003; Kılıçaslan 2004). However, İşsever (2003) suggests that this optionality is only restricted to contrastive focus phrases and discourse-new focus can only appear in the immediate preverbal position. Now, whether the optionality of appearing in-situ is possible for discourse-new focus constituents or not needs to be investigated.

İşsever (2003) gives the following example as evidence that discourse-new focus, presentational focus, applying his terminology, cannot surface in-situ.

(102) A: *Fatma-yı   kim   arı-yor?*
       Fatma-ACC   who   look for-PROG
       'Who is looking for Fatma?'
   B: #*Ali   Fatma-yı   arı-yor.*
       Ali   Fatma-ACC   look for-PROG
       'Ali is looking for Fatma.'
       (İşsever 2003: 1034)

There is question and answer congruence in that the alternatives of the question given in (103a) are a subset of the alternative propositions of the focus phrase in (103b).

(103)   ordinary semantic value
     a. *{Fatma-yı   Ali   arı-yor}*
        Fatma-ACC   Ali   look for-IMPF
        'Ali is looking for Fatma'
        focus semantic value
        {Fatma-yı Ali arıyor, Fatma-yı Ayşe arı-yor......}
        ordinary semantic value
     b. *{Ali   Fatma-yı   arı-yor}*
        Ali   Fatma-ACC   look for-IMPF
        'Ali is looking for Fatma'
        focus semantic value
        {Ali Fatma-yı arı-yor, Ayşe Fatma-yı arı-yor......}

However, the position of the focus phrase differs in the question and the answer above. The unacceptability of this sentence can be due to a mismatch between the melody of the question and the answer due to the difference in the position of the focus phrase.

Whether it is the difference in the position of the focus phrase in the question and answer that makes the sentence unacceptable should now be tested. Three types of questions are detailed: (i) subject wh-in-situ and discourse-new focus in-situ in the answer (104); (ii) immediate preverbal subject wh-phrase and in-situ discourse-new focus in the answer (105); and (iii) immediate preverbal subject wh-phrase and in-situ discourse-new focus with preceding additional information (106).

(104) A: *Kapı-nın   zil-i   tüm   gün   çal-dı.*
       door-GEN bell-POSS whole day   ring-PERF
       'The doorbell rang the whole day.'
       Kim   Ayşe- yi   sor-uyor?
       Who   Ayşe-ACC ask-IMPF
       'Who is asking for Ayşe?'
   B: *[Ali]$_{DN}$ Ayşe-yi   sor-uyor.*
      Ali   Ayşe-ACC ask-IMPF
      'Ali is asking for Ayşe.'

(105) A: *Ayşe-nin   telefon-u   tüm   gün   çal-dı.*
       Ayşe-GEN   phone-POSS whole day   ring-PERF
       'Ayşe's phone rang the whole day.'
       Ayşe-yi   kim   arı-yor?
       Ayşe-ACC   who   call-IMPF
       'Who is calling Ayşe?'
   B: #*[Ali]$_{DN}$ Ayşe-yi   arı-yor.*
      Ali   Ayşe-ACC call-IMPF
      'Ali is calling Ayşe.'

(106) A: *Ayşe-nin   telefon-u   tüm   gün   çal-dı.*
       Ayşe-GEN   phone-POSS whole day   ring-PERF
       'Ayşe's phone rang the whole day.'
       Ayşe-yi   kim   arı-yor?
       Ayşe-ACC   who   call-IMPF
       'Who is calling Ayşe?'
   B: *Herkes   de   bu   soru-yu   sor-uyor.*
      everybody dA   this   question-ACC   ask-IMPF
      'Everybody is asking this question.'
      [Ali]$_{DN}$ Ayşe-yi   arı-yor.
      Ali   Ayşe-ACC call-IMPF
      'Ali is calling Ayşe.'

As the examples in (104), (105) and (106) illustrate, the acceptability decreases when the position of the wh-phrase and the focus phrase do not match. However, when additional information is given so that this mismatch in the melody is disguised, the structure is more acceptable as in (106). Hence, these examples show that similar to contrastive focus phrases, discourse-new focus constituents can appear in-situ.

Based on the data discussed in Vallduví and Engdahl (1996), İşsever (2003) further adds that in the following examples the answers in (107a), (108a) and (109a) can be interpreted in contrastive and non-contrastive contexts while the answers in (107b), (108b) and (109b) can only be interpreted in a contrastive context. Following from this, he suggests that in-situ focus can only be contrastive focus.

(107)   When did a servant put a note on the table?
  a. Bir hizmetçi masa-nın üzer-in-e not-u
   a servant table-GEN on-3SG.POSS-DAT note-ACC
   [yemek-ten önce]$_F$ bırak-tı.
   lunch-ABL before leave-PAST
  b. Bir hizmetçi [yemek-ten önce]$_F$ masa-nın üzer-in-e
   not-u bırak-tı.
   'A servant left the note on the table before lunch.'

(108)   Where did a servant put a note before lunch?
  a. Bir hizmetçi not-u yemek-ten önce [masa-nın
   a servant note-ACC lunch-ABL before table-GEN
   üzer-in-e]$_F$ bırak-tı.
   on-3SG.POSS-DAT leave-PAST
  b. Bir hizmetçi yemek-ten önce [masa-nın üzer-in-e]$_F$
   not-u bırak-tı.
   'A servant left the note on the table before lunch.'

(109)   Who put a note on the table before lunch?
  a. Yemek-ten önce not-u masa-nın üzer-in-e
   lunch-ABL before note-ACC table-GEN on-3SG.POSS-DAT
   [bir hizmetçi]$_F$ bırak-tı.
   a servant leave-PAST
  b. [Bir hizmetçi]$_F$ yemek-ten önce not-u masa-nın
   üzer-in-e bırak-tı.
   'A servant left the note on the table before lunch.'
   (Vallduví and Engdahl 1996: 489)

İşsever (2003) suggests that the answers in (107b), (108b) and (109b) are contrastive in the sense that there is at least one other alternative under discussion that contrasts with the focus phrase. However, it is still possible to analyze the focus phrases in (107b), (108b) and (109b) as discourse-new focus constituents triggered by wh-phrases as none of the alternatives are explicitly given in the previous context. Additionally, this explanation is not explanatory enough conceptually because for all the contexts triggering discourse-new focus, there is a set of implicit contrastive alternatives as discussed in sections 2.3.1.1 and 2.3.1.2. There is contrast as soon as there are alternatives in that, in contrast to the alternatives in the set, one is chosen as the answer with both discourse-new and contrastive focus phrases. If it is suggested that with contrastive focus phrases there is an implicit contrasting alternative, then there is no way to make a distinction between discourse-new constituents and contrastive focus phrases. The difference between the two focus types is that only contrastive focus phrases are exhaustively identified as the correct answer to the exclusion of other alternatives. Hence, the examples in (107b), (108b) and (109b) cannot be taken as evidence that discourse-new focus constituents must occur in the immediate preverbal position.

Now, it is important to look at other examples, the answers of which are triggered by wh-phrases, to shed further light on the distribution of discourse-new constituents.

(110) A: *Bu tür silahların yapımında uranyum kullanımı onaylanmadığı halde kullanıldığını biliyoruz.*
'Although the usage of uranium in these kinds of weapons is not approved, we know that it is used.'
B: *Peki kim uranyum-u onaylı-yor?*
then who uranium-ACC approve-IMPF
'Then, who approves the usage of uranium.'
A: *Romanyalı-lar uranyum-u onaylı-yor.*
Rumanian-PL uranium-ACC approve-IMPF
'The Rumanians approve of uranium.'

The subject is the answer to the wh-phrase in the question, the alternatives are not explicitly given in the question but a problem remains. The question can be analyzed as triggering a contrastive topic. In the preceding context, it is clear that there are two groups of countries, those who approve the usage of uranium and those who do not. Hence, the question denotes a subset of the topic introduced in the context. How about the following example?

(111) A: *Anamurdan yurt dışına giden bir grup çalışmalarıyla büyük beğeni toplamış. Şimdi de misafir ülke onları öven bir konuşma yapıyor ama anlayamadım.*
'The guest worker groups from Anamur who went abroad won recognition with their work. Now the host country makes a speech that praises them but I couldn't understand.'

Kim	Anamurlu-lar-ı	öv-üyor?
who	people of Anamur-PL-ACC	praise-IMPF

'Who praise the people of Anamur?'

B: *Almanyalı-lar Anamurlu-lar-ı öv-üyor.*
German-PL people of Anamur-PL-ACC praise-IMPF
'The German people praise the people of Anamur.'

There is no topic shift in that the previous discourse topic continues without partitioning it into sub-questions. However, it is still possible to interpret the question as triggering a contrastive topic. In the context, it is pointed out that these workers went abroad and the question is, out of a set of possible countries, which country praised the people of Anamur. Now, consider the following example.

(112) A: *Ayşe'nin dolabına sınav kağıtlarını bırakmıştım. Toplantıda velilere dağıtacaktı. Veliler sınav kağıtlarını almamışlar ama dolapta da yok kağıtlar.*
'I had left the exam papers in Ayşe's cupboard. She was going to give them to the parents at the meeting. The parents didn't take the papers but the papers are also not in the cupboard.'

Ayşe kim-e sınav kağıt-lar-ın-ı ver-di?
Ayşe who-DAT exam paper-PL-CM-ACC give-PERF
'To whom did Ayşe give the exam papers?'

B: *Ayşe öğrenci-ler-e sınav kağıt-lar-ın-ı ver-di.*
Ayşe student-PL-DAT exam paper-PL-CM-ACC give-PERF
'Ayşe gave the exam papers to the students.'

Although the answer is triggered by a wh-question, the focused phrase can readily be analyzed as contrastive focus in that the set of students is contrasted with the set of parents which is similar to a corrective statement.[33]

---

[33] For some speakers the answer in (112B) is judged to be better when accompanied by the other alternative in the postverbal domain.

The problem is that the answer of the wh-question can be interpreted as either a contrastive topic or focus phrase. One of the strategies to discard 'contrast', as a confounding variable within these contexts, is to use wh-questions which ask for discourse-new and additional information as illustrated below.

(113) A: *Bu programda her ili temsilen gelen yarışmacılar hünerlerini gösteriyor. Örneğin Yalovalılar elektronik cihaz onarıyorlar. Oldukça da yetenekliler.*
'In this program contestants who represent towns show their skills. For instance, the people of Yalova repair electrical devices. They are very skillful.'
B: *Yalovalı-lar   başka ne   onar-ıyor-lar?*
people of Yalova-PL else   what repair-IMPF-3PL
'What else do the people of Yalova repair?'
A: *Yalovalı-lar   mobilya-lar-ı   onar-ıyor-lar.*
people of Yalova-PL furniture-PL-ACC repair-IMPF-3PL
'The people of Yalova repair furniture.'

(114) A: *Bu programda her ili temsilen gelen yarışmacılar hünerlerini gösteriyor. Örneğin Yalovalılar elektronik cihaz onarıyorlar. Oldukça da yetenekliler.*
'In this program contestants who represent towns show their skills. For instance, the people of Yalova repair electrical devices. They are very skillful.'
B: *Başka kim elektronik cihaz-lar-ı   onar-ıyor?*
else   who electrical device-PL-ACC repair-IMPF
'Who else repair electrical devices?'
A: *Gümüşhaneli-ler   elektronik cihaz-lar-ı   onar-ıyor.*
people of Gümüşhane-PL electrical device-PL-ACC repair-IMPF
'The people of Gümüşhane repair electrical devices.'

(115) A: *Duydun mu, Hale Ayşe'ye yılbaşı hediyesi almış*
'Have you heard that Hale bought a Christmas gift for Ayşe?'
B: *Peki Hale başka kim-e   yılbaşı   hediye-si al-mış?*
well Hale else who-DAT Christmas gift-CM buy-PERF
'Well, for whom else did Hale buy a Christmas gift?'

---

(1) *Ayşe   öğrenci-ler-e   sınav kağıt-lar-ın-ı   ver-di*
Ayşe   student-PL-DAT exam paper-PL-POSS-ACC give-PERF
veli-ler-e   değil.
parent-PL-DAT not
'Ayşe gave the exam papers to the students, not to the parents'

A: *Hale Ahmet-e   de yılbaşı   hediye-si al-mış.*
   Hale Ahmet-DAT   dA Christmas gift-CM   buy-PERF
   'Hale bought a gift for Ahmet too.'

In (113), it is the object phrase; in (114), it is the subject phrase; in (115), it is the indirect object phrase that serves as the discourse-new focus providing additional information not available in the preceding context. Remember that answers with contrastive topic are partial in nature and they do not resolve the issue under discussion or create a shift for the topic under discussion. In (113–115), the constituents providing additional information cannot be analyzed as a contrastive topic as the answer resolves the issue under discussion. The other point is that in these sentences the constituents providing discourse-new information are not uttered similarly to the contrastive topic constituents given in (69–73). There is an additional focus phrase in (69–73) that bears the main prominence in the sentence. However, in (113–115) it is the discourse-new constituent that bears main prominence. The discussion in 4.2 on contrastive topic phrases will further show that there is a crucial difference between contrastive topic phrases asking for additional information and discourse-new constituents providing additional information. As the questions elicit additional information, one cannot analyze the questions as triggering contrastive focus phrases. Based on the discussion so far it is possible to conclude that, as is the case with contrastive focus phrases, discourse-new focus phrases are not restricted to the immediate preverbal position.

The question raised at this point is: why is it difficult to form a sentence with discourse-new focus constituents not surfacing in the immediate preverbal position? When it is not explicitly indicated with additional constituents that the in-situ constituent is a discourse-new focus as in (113–115), the sentence initial position is interpreted to be the position of the contrastive topic or aboutness topic. This is indicated in examples (110) and (111). As is the case with contrastive focus phrases, discourse-new constituents are not restricted to the immediate preverbal position but as the sentence initial position is mostly occupied by topic phrases, discourse-new constituents must be accompanied by expressions indicating that the information is purely discourse-new and additional. Maybe that is why in (112), the addition of contrastive alternatives in the postverbal domain marking contrast explicitly makes the structure more acceptable indicating that the in-situ constituent is a contrastive focus.

Finally, in this section, the restriction on movement of focus phrases to the postverbal domain will be discussed. As already noted in the literature, focus phrases cannot surface in the postverbal domain (Erguvanlı 1984; Kural 1993;

Demircan 1996; Kennelly 1999; Göksel and Özsoy 2000; İşsever 2003; Şener 2010) as this domain is not a discourse prominent domain.

(116) A: *Romanyalı-lar uranyum-u onay-lıyor.*
Rumanian-PL uranium-ACC approve-IMPF
'The Rumanians approve of uranium.'
B: *#Hayır, Romanyalı-lar onay-lıyor [magnezyum-u]$_{CF}$.*
No Rumanian-PL approve-IMPF magnesium-ACC
Intended reading: 'No, the Rumanians approve of magnesium.'

(117) A: *İyonyalı-lar nere-ye yayıl-ıyor?*
Ionian-PL where-DAT move-IMPF
'Where do the Ionians move towards?'
B: *#İyonyalı-lar yayıl-ıyor [Menemen-e]$_{DN}$.*
Ionian-PL move-IMPF Menemen-DAT
'The Ionians move towards Menemen.'

However, with focus phrases marked with overt particles the particle can surface in the postverbal domain but prominence cannot be on the particle.

(118) a. *[Sadece Romanyalı-lar]$_{CF}$ uranyum-u onaylı-yor.*
only Rumanian-PL uranium-ACC approve-IMPF
'Only the Rumanians approve of uranium.'
b. *#Uranyum-u onaylı-yor [sadece Romanyalı-lar]$_{CF}$.*
Intended reading: 'Only the Rumanians approve of uranium.'
c. *[Romanyalı-lar]$_{CF}$ uranyum-u onaylı-yor sadece.*

The difference between (118a) and (118c) is that in (118c), it is necessary to put the main prominence on the subject otherwise; the particle can be interpreted as being attached to the object or the verb. The next section takes a look at how focus phrases are categorized.

2.5.1.1 Focus categorization
The final issue to be resolved regarding focus phrases is the semantic/pragmatic distinctions between contrastive and discourse-new focus. The discussions in section 2.3.1.1 and 2.3.1.2 have shown that both discourse-new and contrastive focus phrases evoke a set of alternatives. One of the alternatives is chosen as the answer in contrast to the other alternatives with discourse-new and contrastive focus constituents. Hence, contrast seems to be a side effect of the presence of alternatives that are not chosen. It is not possible to take

contrast as a feature to distinguish the focus subtypes as both discourse-new and contrastive focus are contrastive. Krifka (2006) also suggests that the distinction between the two focus types is not due to the feature of contrast but due to the nature of the alternative sets, one being closed and the other open. This is similar to the analysis of contrast by Kiss (1998: 267) who suggests that identificational focus is contrastive "(....) if it operates on a closed set of entities whose members are known to the participants of the discourse." Note that this property of contrastive focus is closely related to the triggering contexts. With alternative questions, triggering contrastive focus, the set members are known to the participants of the discourse but this is not the case with corrective sentences which trigger contrastive focus. Remember that with corrective statements, contrastive focus can also evoke an open set of alternatives. Hence, the distinction between the two focus types cannot be contrast or the nature of the triggered sets as these factors are context dependent.

The other option is to take the syntactic position of discourse-new and contrastive focus phrases as marking the difference. The contrastive focus has also been suggested as a subtype of focus due to the possibilities of movement in that they move to a designated position to be marked as contrastive focus which is not possible with discourse-new focus. In Finish, contrast is identified by the sentence initial position. Vallduví and Vilkuna (1998) make a distinction as rheme and kontrast. Rheme refers to new information while kontrast is the equivalent of identificational/exhaustive focus.

(119) A: *What things did Anna get for her birthday?*
     B: *Anna   sai   [kukkia]$_R$*
         Anna   got   flowers

(120) A: *What is it that Anna got for her birthday?*
     B: *[kukkia]$_R$ Anna   sai*
    (Vallduví and Vilkuna 1998: 90–91)

Vallduví and Vilkuna (1998) suggest that in (119) and (120), the accented phrase is rheme, but in addition in (120) it is contrastive. Therefore, it is contrast which determines the position of the focus phrase. However, Zimmermann and Onea (2011) suggest that in some languages contrastive focus phrases which appear ex-situ can optionally surface in-situ. Additionally in Hausa, for instance, the ex-situ focus position occupied by contrastive focus can also be occupied by discourse-new focus.

Remember the discussion in section 2.5.1 on the distributional properties of focus phrases in Turkish. When contrastive or additional discourse-new functions of focus phrases are marked in context, contrastive and discourse-new focus constituents can surface in-situ followed by discourse anaphoric constituents. Hence, the syntactic position also does not also make a distinction between the two focus types as it is suggested to be the case in Turkish (İşsever 2003).

To recap, if contrast is taken as a side effect of alternatives and the closed or open nature of the alternative set is taken as a side effect of context, the distinction between contrastive focus and discourse-new focus remains to be exhaustive identification. Within terms of Kiss' view (1998), the predicate phrase exhaustively holds for the contrastive focus, but not for the discourse-new focus.

2.5.2 Topic phrases

First, the distributional properties of contrastive topic phrases will be discussed. Contrastive topic phrases cannot surface following the focus phrase as illustrated below.[34]

(121) A: *Can'dan n'aber? O ne yedi partide?*
'What about John? What did he eat at the party?'
B: *Valla   Can-ı   bil-mi-yor-um   ama   [Aylin]$_{CT}$*
frankly   Can-ACC   know-NEG-IMPF-1SG   but   Aylin
[dolma-lar-dan]$_F$ ye-di.
dolma-PL-ABL   eat-PAST
'Frankly, I don't know about John, but Aylin ate from dolmas.'
#*[Dolma-lar-dan]$_F$ [Aylin]$_{CT}$ ye-di.*
(Şener 2010: 19–20)

The following examples indicate infelicitous utterances with contrastive topic. The sentence in (122B) is grammatical only when focus is placed on the verb. In (122C), the elliptical part includes the focused part and hence the sentence is unacceptable with a single contrastive topic in the absence of a focus phrase.

---

[34] Wagner (cited in Neeleman and Vermeulen 2012: 31) argues that the questions for which the answers require a contrastive topic and a focus phrase can be analyzed as a pair list question. The question in (121) in the text above can be thought of as "Who ate what at the party?" The reader can easily interchange the positions of contrastive topic and focus in the answer and find the answer acceptable. Hence, in order to understand the unacceptability of the answer in (121) it is also necessary to read the target sentence with the correct intonation.

The construction becomes acceptable when the focused part is included as in (122D). Hence, it is proposed that contrastive topic phrases cannot surface in the absence of a focus phrase in the same sentence.[35]

(122) A: *Toplantı-dan sonra çalışan-lar istifa mektub-un-u*
meeting-ABL after worker-PL resignation letter-CM-ACC
ver-miş-ler.
give-PERF-3PL
'After the meeting the workers gave the resignation letters.'

B: #*Valla, çalışan-lar-ı bil-me-m ama* [*patron*]$_{CT}$
well worker-PL-ACC know-NEG-1SG but boss
istifa mektub-un-u ver-miş.
resignation letter-CM-ACC give-PERF
Intended reading: 'Well, I don't know about the workers but the boss gave the resignation letter.'

C: #*Çalışan-lar istifa mektub-un-u ver-miş-ler,*
worker-PL resignation letter-CM-ACC give-PERF-3PL
[*patron*]$_{CT}$ *da.*[36]
boss as for

D: *Çalışan-lar istifa mektub-un-u ver-miş-ler,*
worker-PL resignation letter-CM-ACC give-PERF-3PL
[*patron*]$_{CT}$ *da* [*rapor-u*]$_F$
boss as for report-ACC
'The workers gave the resignation letter, as for the boss (he gave) the report.'

---

35 Neeleman and Van de Koot (2012) indicate that, in Dutch, contrastive topic can surface following an in-situ focus phrase. This is possible because, at LF, contrastive topic which is an utterance level constituent extends its scope domain over the focus phrase which is a propositional level constituent. Within the current study, it is suggested that contrastive topic phrases cannot surface within the scope domain of focus phrases. Both approaches can account for the distribution of contrastive topic and focus phrases. However, reconstruction differences between contrastive topic and aboutness topic phrases indicate that, although aboutness topic is also an utterance level constituent, it can surface within the scope domain of focus while this is not possible for contrastive topic phrases (See Chapter 4 for details). Hence, it is suggested that the ordering restrictions of contrastive topic and focus cannot be reduced to utterance versus propositional level differences. Otherwise, the same ordering restrictions for aboutness topic and contrastive topic phrases would be expected.

36 The structure in (122C) is acceptable only when *dA* is interpreted to be attached to a discourse-new constituent encoding additional information.

This suggestion is in contradiction to an observation regarding contrastive topic phrases. In the literature, it is suggested that in some languages such as Dutch (Neeleman and Van de Koot 2012) and English (Constant 2014), contrastive topic phrases can surface without a following focus phrase which are labeled as lone contrastive topic phrases (Constant 2014).

Now, it is useful to take a closer look at the Turkish equivalents of those examples. There appears to be a lone contrastive topic in (123).

(123) A: *Ahmet CD-yi Ayşe-ye ver-di mi?*
Ahmet CD-ACC Ayşe-DAT give-PERF QP
'Did Ahmet give the CD to Ayşe?'
B: *Valla CD-yi bil-mi-yor-um ama, [kitab-ı]$_{CT}$ ver-di.*
well CD-ACC know-NEG-IMPF-1SG but book-ACC give-PERF
'Well, I don't know about the CD but (he) gave the book.'

However, it is easy to analyze yes/no questions in Turkish as alternative questions with an implicit and negated coordinate as shown in (124). Remember that alternative questions are analyzed as a sub-type of contrastive focus (Götze et al. 2007).[37]

(124) A: *Ahmet CD-yi Ayşe-ye ver-di mi yoksa ver-me-di mi?*
Ahmet CD-ACC Ayşe-DAT give-PERF QP or give-NEG-PERF QP
'Did Ahmet give the CD to Ayşe or not?'
B: *Valla CD-yi bil-mi-yor-um ama, [kitab-ı]$_{CT}$ [ver-di]$_F$.*
well CD-ACC know-NEG-IMPF-1SG but book-ACC give-PERF
'Well, I don't know about the CD but (he) gave the book.'

The other example which can be analyzed as a case of lone contrastive topic is given in (125) below. The subject of the answer is analyzed to be a contrastive topic because it is not an exhaustive answer to the question under discussion. The issue is not resolved completely with the given answer.

---

37 Kelepir (2001) notes that in Turkish negative polarity items are licensed either in the presence of negation or in yes/no questions. In this study, it is suggested that it is the presence of the implicit negation that licenses negative polarity items in yes/no questions.

(125) A: *Zararları bilindiği halde uranyum kullanımı devam ediyormuş. Hangi ülkeler uranyumu onaylıyor?*
'Although its damage is known, the usage of uranium continues. Which countries approve of uranium?'
B: *Valla, bildiğim kadarıyla, [Romanyalı-lar]$_{CT}$ uranyum-u*
well   as far as I know   Rumanian-PL   uranium-ACC
onaylı- yor.
approve-IMPF
'Well, as far as I know, the Rumanians approve of uranium.'

This is not a yes/no question and the verb in the answer is the same as the verb in the question. Note that the same answer can be given to this question with focus on the subject which makes the answer an exhaustive answer and does not leave the issue unresolved as exemplified in (126).

(126) A: *Zararları bilindiği halde uranyum kullanımı devam ediyormuş. Hangi ülkeler uranyumu onaylıyor?*
'Although its damage is known, the usage of uranium continues. Which countries approve of uranium?'
B: *[Romanyalı-lar]$_F$ uranyum-u   onaylı-yor.*
Rumanian-PL   uranium-ACC   approve-IMPF
'The Rumanians approve of uranium.'

In order to make sure that there is really no focus phrase and that there is a lone contrastive topic in the answer in (125), the pitch track of the same sentence was compared with focus on the subject in (126).[38]

---

[38] With the aim of having a non-perturbated pitch track and a pitch track with a prenuclear, nuclear and postnuclear domains dialogues with words composed of sonorants and sentences composed of at least three constituents were presented. Hence, the contextual difference between (125) and (126) may not be so clear, so the following dialogue is given as a further example to better illustrate the difference.

(1) A: *Parti-ye   kaç   kişi   gel-ecek?*
party-DAT how many   person   come-FUT
'How many people will come to the party?'
B: *Bildiğim kadarıyla, [üç   kişi]$_{CT}$ gel-ecek,   diğer-ler-in-den*
As far as I know,   three   person   come-FUT   other-PL-POSS-ABL
haber-im   yok.
news-POSS   absent
'As far as I know, three people will come, I don't know anything about the others.'

In Figure 5, when the subject is the contrastive topic, the verb bears focus and shows the prosodic properties of the nuclear and postnuclear domain in that there is a bump with the accented syllable of the verb and the fall starts only after the accented syllable of the verb (see Chapter 3 for details).[39] The non-final domains show the properties of the prenuclear domain in that there is a H-boundary tone at the right edge of these domains. In Figure 6, on the other hand, the initial domain shows the prosodic properties of the nuclear domain in that there is a bump with the accented syllable of the subject which is followed by a low reference height until the end of the utterance. Hence, it can be safely concluded that contrastive topic in Turkish cannot surface within the scope of focus (121) and in the absence of focus (122C).

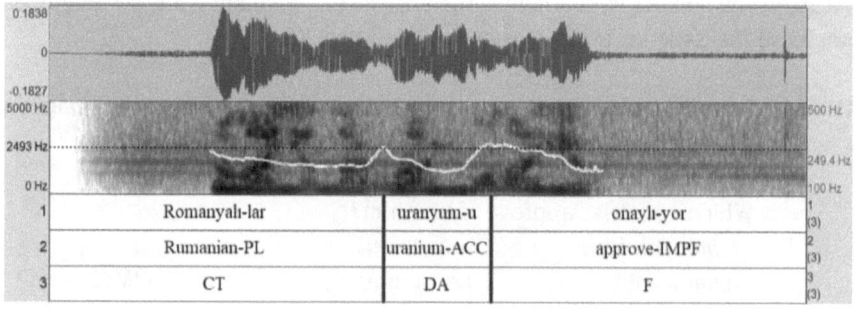

Figure 5: Answer with the subject as the contrastive topic.

As for the distribution of aboutness and contrastive topic, the data given in (75) repeated below as (127) for ease of exposition illustrates that aboutness topics precede contrastive topics.

(2)   A: *Partiye kaç kişi gel-ecek?*
            'How many people will come to the party?'
      B: *[Üç kişi]$_F$ gel-ecek, başka kimse ism-in-i liste-ye*
            three person come-FUT else anyone name-POSS-ACC list-DAT
            yaz-ma-mış.
            write-NEG-PERF
            'Three people will come; no one else wrote his/her name on the list.'

While the answer in (2) resolves the issue under discussion, the answer in (1) can only be regarded as a partial answer.

[39] When the truth value of the whole proposition is emphasized it is called verum focus (Götze et. al 2007). The emphasized part is not only the semantic content of the constituent bearing focus but the whole proposition. This construction is an example of verum focus.

2.5 Distribution of information structural units in Turkish — 77

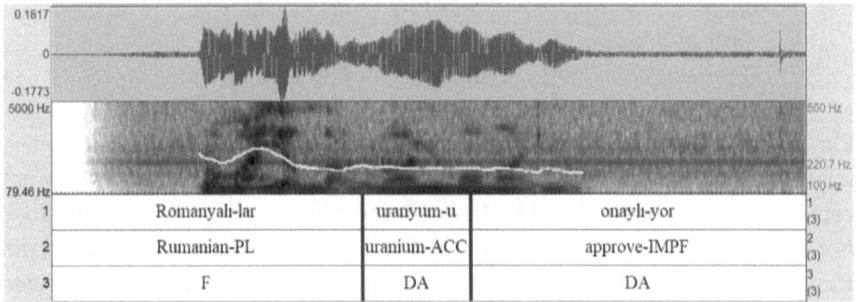

Figure 6: Answer with the subject as the focus.

(127) A: *Yurt dışına çalışmaya giden Alanya ve Anamurlular çalışmalarıyla büyük beğeni toplamış. Şimdi de bir Alman kanalında Anamurlulara teşekkür konuşması yapılıyor.*
'The guest worker groups from Alanya and Anamur who went abroad won recognition with their work. Now, a vote of thanks is delivered to the people from Anamur on a German TV channel.'

B: [*Almanyalı-lar*]$_{AT}$ [*Alanyalı-lar-ı*]$_{CT}$ [*övü-yor*]$_F$ *mu?*
German-PL   people of Alanya-PL-ACC   praise-IMPF   QP
'Do the German people praise the people from Alanya?'

B': #[*Alanyalı-lar-ı*]$_{CT}$ [*Almanyalı-lar*]$_{AT}$ [*övü-yor*]$_F$ *mu?*

Note that in (127B), the sentence initial constituent is salient but not explicitly given in discourse. Hence, in sentence initial position, it marks what the rest of the sentence is about without marking a contrast with another constituent in the context. When a contrastive topic precedes an aboutness topic as in (127B'), the sentence is not felicitous.[40]

Finally, the question of whether contrastive topic phrases can appear in the postverbal domain will be investigated with an example from Şener (2010: 28) which is suggested to be unacceptable.

(128) A: *Can'dan n'aber? O ne yedi partide?*
'What about John? What did he eat at the party?'

B: *Valla   Can-ı   bil-mi-yor-um   ama [dolma-lar-dan]$_F$*
frankly   Can-ACC   know-NEG-IMPF-1SG   but   dolma-PL-ABL

---

[40] A discourse anaphoric constituent following a contrastive topic is possible. In order to make sure that the aboutness topic is not interpreted as a discourse anaphoric constituent in (127), the information status of the topic constituent is not marked as given. Although it is salient in the context, it is not explicitly given in the previous discourse.

ye-di   *[Aylin]$_{CT}$*
eat-PAST Aylin
'Frankly, I don't know about John, but Aylin ate from dolmas.'

The first observation is that although the intonational property of this sentence is not the same as the ones given in (124) and (125), the sentence is totally acceptable. Göksel and Özsoy (2003: 1149) note that when *dA* is attached to a non-focused phrase, the host and the clitic cannot appear to the right of the focus phrase with the exception of answers echoing questions. This provides evidence for the argument that the non-focused host with *dA* clitic is in fact a contrastive topic phrase. Göksel and Özsoy (2003) further note that when *dA* is not attached to the focus phrase, the host of this clitic, which is a contrastive topic, can appear in the postverbal domain.

(129) a. *Anne-si-yle*   *de Ahmet bu günlerde [hiç]$_F$*
       mother-3SG.POSS-COM dA Ahmet nowadays   at all
       anlaş-a-mı-yor-muş.
       get along-AB-NEG-PROG-EVID
       'As for his mother, Ahmet can't along at all with her nowadays.'
    b. *Ahmet bu günlerde [hiç]$_F$ anlaş-a-mı-yor-muş anne-si-yle de.*
    c. *Ahmet bu günlerde [hiç]$_F$ anlaş-a-mı-yor-muş o-nun-la   da.*
       (adapted from Göksel and Özsoy 2003: 1148)

Note that in (129c), it is possible to replace the postverbal constituent with a pronoun. Hence, it is similar to a discourse anaphoric constituent. However, postverbal constituents in (128) and (129) are not taken as discourse anaphoric constituent because a postverbal constituent continues to preserve the function of shifting the discussion under question. In contrast to another possible topic under discussion, this topic is chosen, but this information packaging is not possible with a discourse anaphoric constituent. Additionally, it is not possible to delete the postverbal constituent without a loss of meaning in (128) and (129). Remember that this is possible with a discourse anaphoric constituent. The data shows that in contrast to focus phrases, contrastive topic phrases can surface in the postverbal domain thus losing their intonational properties which are observed when they occur in the preverbal domain. This poses a challenge in relation to the analysis of Wagner (2007, 2008) who takes contrastive topic and focus phrases as nested focus phrases. If contrastive topics are taken as focus phrases, the restriction on F phrases to appear in the postverbal domain, which does not hold for contrastive topic phrases as illustrated above, cannot be explained. As indicated in the previous sections, contrastive topic phrases cannot surface following focus phrases. Movement of the contrastive topic to the postverbal position is not a problem for this requirement as postverbal constituents are observed to be able to take scope over preverbal constituents in Turkish (Kural 1997; Göksel 1998).[41]

Now, it is time to focus on aboutness topic phrases. As the discussion so far indicates, aboutness topic phrases serve as the milestone for the upcoming propositions. They can be confused with discourse anaphoric constituents as aboutness topic phrases can also be given. However, discourse anaphoric constituents can never be new in discourse which is possible with aboutness topic phrases. Aboutness topic phrases surface in the sentence initial position as in (130a). As the examples illustrate, deletion (130b) or dislocation of the aboutness topic (130c) results in infelicity. It is suggested that deletion of the constituent is not possible because it is new in the discourse.

(130) *Her şeyi anlattın ama asıl meseleye girmedin. Yeni kız arkadaşından bahsetsene biraz. Adını bile bilmiyoruz.*
'You talked about everything but said nothing about the real issue. Tell me a bit about your new girlfriend. We don't know even her name.'

---

[41] It has already been noted in Turkish linguistics literature that postverbal domain is not accessible for focus phrases (Erguvanlı 1984; Kural 1993; Demircan 1996; Kennelly 1997; Göksel and Özsoy 2000; İşsever 2003; Şener 2010). However, the discussion so far indicates that this domain is not restricted to non-contrastive, given, salient constituents as is claimed by Şener (2010). Contrastive topic phrases can but aboutness topic phrases, and focus phrases cannot appear in this domain. In this study, it is suggested that the restriction on aboutness topic phrases depends on semantic incompatibility in that as pointed out earlier, aboutness topic phrases mark what the rest of the sentence is about. Hence, sentence final position is not relevant for this function. As for focus phrases, the discussion on the prosody of focus phrases indicates that focus phrases attract IP level stress. IP stress is not possible in the postverbal domain and focus phrases are not expected to appear in this domain. As already pointed out by Göksel (2013), the restriction on the appearance of focus phrases in the postverbal domain can be due to the copula which seems to act like a pivot dividing the sentence into two parts. Focus phrases attract IP level stress and appear in the rightmost phonological phrase. As an anonymous reviewer notes a natural question is raised at this point: If a contrastive topic can surface in the postverbal domain devoid of its intonational properties, why isn't it possible for a focus phrase? A possible hypothesis is that each sentence must receive IP level stress and when a focus phrase is devoid of its properties, this becomes impossible. This is possible with a contrastive topic because there remains a focus phrase in the preverbal domain. Then the following question is raised: why is not focus prominence realized in the postverbal domain? In fact, there are languages which mark focus in the postverbal domain. What hinders postverbal focus in Turkish needs further investigation which is beyond the scope of this study.

a. *Gökçe-yi   ilk kez okul-da   gör-dü-m.*
   Gökçe-ACC first   school-LOC see-PERF-1SG
   'I saw Gökçe at school for the first time.'
b. *#okul-da gör-dü-m.*
c. *#ilk kez okul-da gör-dü-m Gökçe-yi.*

This contrasts with discourse anaphoric constituents which can be deleted or dislocated to the postverbal domain. The next section focuses on discourse anaphoric constituents.

2.5.3 Discourse anaphoric constituents

As the discussion on focus phrases has already shown, discourse anaphoric constituents can optionally follow in-situ focus phrases as in (131) and (132). Note that it is possible to delete discourse anaphoric constituents as in (131b).

(131) *Ahmet sınav öncesi tutmuş defterini vermiş başka birine. Nasıl çalışacak şimdi defteri olmadan?*
'Ahmet gave his notebook to someone before the exam. How is he going to study for the exam now without his notebook?'
a. *[Mehmet]$_F$ [defter-in-i]$_{DA}$ [ver-miş]$_{DA}$,*
   Mehmet   notebook-3SG.POSS-ACC give-PERF
   Ahmet   değil.
   Ahmet   not
   'Mehmet gave his notebook to someone, not Ahmet.'
b. *[Mehmet,   Mehmet]$_F$,   Ahmet   değil.*

(132) A: *Duy-du-n   mu, Ayşe yılbaşı   hediye-si al-mış.*
       hear-PERF-2SG QP   Ayşe Christmas gift-CM   buy-PERF
       'Have you heard that Ayşe bought a Christmas gift?'
    B: *Peki, başka kim yılbaşı   hediye-si al-mış?*
       well else   who Christmas gift-CM   buy-PERF
       'Well, who else bought a Christmas gift?'
    A: *[Ahmet de]$_F$ [yılbaşı   hediye-si]$_{DA}$ [al-mış]$_{DA}$*
       Ahmet dA   Christmas gift-CM   buy-PERF
       'Ahmet, too, bought a gift.'

However, these sentences are not acceptable for some speakers who place focus phrases in the immediate preverbal position. The discussion of this issue will be dealt with in the next chapter.

Now, the ordering restrictions between a discourse anaphoric constituent and a contrastive topic will be considered.

(133) A: *Hayatımda bu fabrikanın patronu kadar cömert bir insan daha tanımadım. İşçilerini öylesine çok seviyordu ki ölümünden önce arabalarını işçilere bırakmış.*
'I never met another person as generous a man as the boss of this factory. She loved her workers so much that before she died she left all her cars to the workers.'

B: *Valla   araba-lar-ın-ı   bil-mi-yor-um   ama*
frankly   car-PL-3SG.POSS-ACC   know-NEG-IMPF-1SG   but
[patron]$_{AT}$ [işçi-ler-e]$_{DA}$ [fabrika-yı]$_{CT}$ [bırak-mış]$_F$
boss   worker-PL-DAT   factory-ACC   leave-PERF
'Well, I don't know about her cars but the boss has left the factory to the workers.'

As illustrated in a rich context above, the sentence initial constituent is discourse-given and it indicates what the rest of the sentence is about. With the accusative marked object the topic under discussion is changed and hence it marks contrastive topic in the presence of focus on the predicate. The discourse anaphoric constituent is felicitous in this context preceding the contrastive topic. Based on the discussion so far it can be safely concluded that discourse anaphoric constituents can surface following or preceding contrastive topics and focus phrases. As mentioned before, they are the vehicular parts of the sentence that serve as fillers.

2.6 Conclusion

In this chapter, how Turkish encodes focus, topic and discourse anaphoric constituents has been investigated. The main findings of this chapter are that: (i) focus phrases are distinguished not with respect to contrast, or the size of the alternative sets but by exhaustive identification and both discourse-new and contrastive focus phrases do not have to surface in the immediate preverbal position when they are placed in appropriate contexts specifying their function; (ii) contrastive topics cannot surface in the absence of focus phrases but neither can they do so following the focus phrase due to the semantic composition of the contrastive topic; (iii) contrast is not a primitive notion; (iv) contrastive topic-focus order cannot be analyzed as nested foci because contrastive topic phrases have distinctive distributional properties; (v) aboutness topics are taken to be sentence initial constituents indicating what the rest of the sentence is about without marking a contrast or making a shift in the topic under discussion; and (vi) discourse anaphoric constituents are salient constituents, given in the previous context, that do not mark a topic shift or contrast and they can surface between the focus phrase and the verb.

Chapter 3
Prosodic marking of focus

3.1 Introduction

The investigation of prosodic realization of focus phrases has been an intriguing issue, as languages opt for different phonological or phonetic strategies to mark focus phrases.[42] In this chapter, the prosodic marking of focus phrases is investigated within the assumptions of the focus prominence rule (Truckenbrodt 1995: 11) according to which "if F is a focus and domain of focus (DF) is its domain, then the highest prominence in DF will be within F."

The way prominence is realized varies across languages. Focus has an effect on phonological rephrasing in Italian (Frascarelli 1997, 2000) and Tangale (Zimmerman 2011), on tonal height in Japanese and German (Féry and Ishihara 2009), on f0 and duration in Hungarian (Genzel, Ishihara and Surányi 2014) and on f0, duration, intensity and pitch excursion in English (Katz and Selkirk 2011).[43]

For Turkish focus marking and stress assignment, the following suggestions have been made: (i) focus phrases are marked distinctively with a H*L pitch accent (Özge and Bozşahin 2010); (ii) only contrastive focus is marked through prosody while discourse-new/presentational focus is marked through its syntactic position (İşsever 2003); and (iii) stress assignment can be captured through phase domains (Üntak-Tarhan 2006).

The first observation is not based on a systematic experimental study. As for the second suggestion, from the discussion in Chapter 2, it can be seen that there is not a distinctive position in syntax for contrastive and discourse-new focus. Additionally, the suggestion that contrastive focus is marked differently

---

[42] The book is based on my dissertation and the earlier version of this chapter was published as Gürer (2014).
[43] f0, fundamental frequency is the lowest frequency component of a sound signal. Ladefoged (2010: 24) defines frequency as "(....) a technical term for an acoustic property of a sound – namely, the number of complete repetitions (cycles) of variations in air pressure occurring in a second." The pitch on the other hand is "(....) an auditory property that enables a listener to place it on a scale going from low to high, without considering its acoustic properties" (Ladefoged 2010: 23). Although they are not the same, as their up and down movements coincide, measuring f0 is equated as measuring the pitch of a sound signal in the literature.
Pitch excursion is the difference between the minimum and maximum f0 in the target syllable.

https://doi.org/10.1515/9781501505584-003

than discourse-new focus in the prosodic domain is not based on a prosodic study. The last suggestion needs to be checked with additional data. The issue of how focus shapes prosody is far from resolved in Turkish. That is why systematic experimental studies have been carried out in conducting this research.

Turkish is similar to Hungarian in that the immediate preverbal position is the default nuclear prominence position (Emre 1931; Erkü 1983; Erguvanlı 1984; Göksel and Özsoy 2000; Kılıçaslan 2004). The experimental studies conducted in this chapter reveal that, unlike Hungarian (Genzel, Ishihara and Surányi 2014), a narrow focus constituent in the immediate preverbal position in Turkish does not differ from the constituent in the same position in broad focus condition with regard to f0 and duration measurements. Additionally, contrastive and discourse-new focus is not marked in the prosody in a distinct way. However, when focus is in the initial or final domains, the [F] marked constituents attract IP level stress which indicates that focus prominence is realized as IP stress in Turkish. Finally, it will be shown that a phase based stress assignment analysis (Üntak-Tarhan 2006) cannot capture the Turkish data.

3.2 Prosodic realization of focus

The phonological representation of syntactic structures is composed of prosodic domains. The post-syntactic hierarchical prosodic domains (Selkirk 1983, 1995, 2005; Truckenbrodt 1995) can be illustrated in the following way.[44]

(134) Utterance (Utt):   Utterance
      Intonational Phrase (IP): Root clause
      Phonological Phrase (PPh): XP
      Prosodic Word (PWd):   X°

---

[44] For Japanese, phonological phrase is further analyzed as the minor (MiP) and major phrase (MaP). There are some phonological and phonetic properties which indicate hierarchical organization of prosodic domains of languages in general. The pitch reset at the MaP is found to be stronger than the reset at the MiP edge (Selkirk and Tateishi 1991), prosodic breaks are observed following IPs but obligatory pauses are not observed after MaP (Kawahara and Shinya 2008; Kan 2009), at IP edges vowels are found to be longer (Kan 2009) or more creaky (Kawahara and Shinya 2008), the initial rises and final lowering is suggested to be stronger at the Utt level (Kawahara and Shinya 2008).

In Italian, some phonological rules apply taking phonological phrases as the domain of application.[45] Frascarelli (1997) compares structures with an [+F] marked constituent and structures with broad focus with all-new constituents as illustrated in (135) below.

(135) a. new   new   new
      b. new   contrastive   new

Frascarelli (1997, 2000) uses (i) the phonological phrase domain rule *Raddoppiamento Sintattico* (RS) which applies between two words and lengthens the initial consonant of the second word under certain conditions and (ii) the intonational phrase domain rule *Gorgia Toscana* (GT) which changes the voiceless stops into corresponding fricatives between two vowels within and across words.

In an all-new sentence, as in (136a), phonological phrase domain rules do not apply as the words belong to different phrases as indicated with the brackets.

(136) a. *[portero]   [tre   [b:]assotti]*
         bring-will-1SG three dachshunds
         '(I) will bring three dachshunds.'
      b. *[portero   [t:]RE [b:]assotti]*
         (Frascarelli 1997: 231)

In (136b), the F-marked constituent *tre* 'three' enlarges its phonological phrase domain, *RS* applies and the initial consonant of *tre* 'three' is lengthened. In (137a), all the constituents are in the same IP domain. *GT*, which changes voiceless stops into fricatives between two vowels and across words, applies and [k] of *kon* 'with' turns into [h] between two vowels across words.

---

45 Phonological rules for a phonological phrase are summarized below:

(i)   Wrap XP: for every XP, XP a projection of a lexical category, there is a phonological phrase Ø, such that all terminal elements that are dominated by XP are also dominated by Ø
(ii) Stress XP: Each lexically headed XP must contain a phrasal stress.
(iii) Align (PPh, R/L): align the right/left edge of every phonological phrase with the right/left edge of phrasal stress (Truckenbrodt 1995).

While the Wrap XP rule maps syntactic constituents onto prosodic constituents, the Stress XP rule in (i) determines the prominence at the level of phonological phrase making sure that each phonological phrase has a phrasal stress. The last rule in (iii) determines the direction of the edge-most prominence for the phonological phrases which can be rightmost or leftmost.

(137) a. [[Andro]_Φ [al cinema]_Φ [[h]on Luigi]Φ]_I
go-will-1SG to-the cinema with Luigi
'(I) will go to the cinema with Luigi.'
b. [[Andro]_Φ [al CINEMA]_Φ]_I [[k]on Luigi]_I
(Frascarelli 1997: 236)

In (137b), on the other hand, *al cinema* 'to the cinema' is focused and an IP boundary is inserted to the right edge of the focused constituent which blocks the application of GT as a result of which the voiceless stop surfaces as [k]. Hence, in Italian focus has an effect on phonological phrasing.

Féry and Ishihara (2009) indicate that in Japanese and German, focus and givenness keep phonological phrasing the same and have an impact on the pitch accent and boundary tone height.[46] In Japanese, downstep applies within a phonological phrase and the reference height of the prosodic words undergoes lowering as illustrated in Figure 7 below. Downstep is blocked at the beginning of the adverbial phrase *ímademo* 'still' as it forms a separate phrase.

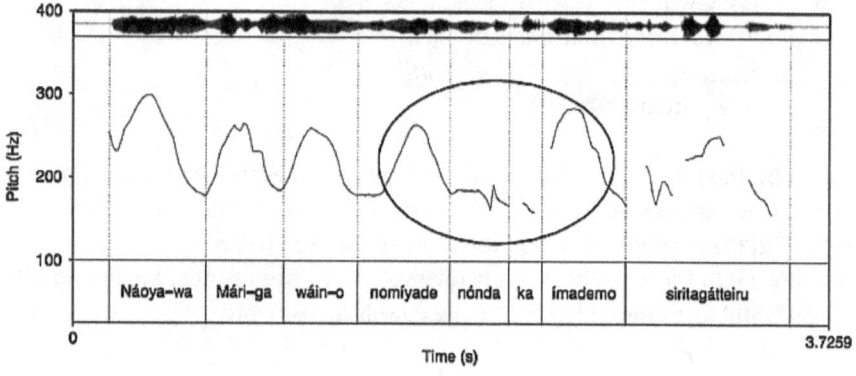

Figure 7: Pitch track of an all-new declarative sentence in Japanese. (Féry and Ishihara 2009: 56).

(138) Náoya-wa [CP Mári-ga wain-o_i [VP nomíya-de t_i nónda]
Náoya-TOP Mári-NOM wine-ACC bar-LOC drank
to] ímademo omótteru
that still think
'Naoya still thought that Mari drank something at the bar.'

---

[46] Pitch accents mark the prominent syllable and boundary tones mark the edge of a phonological phrase.

In the presence of a sentence initial focus phrase as in (139), post-focal compression is observed.[47]

(139) *dáre-ga   [CP Mári-ga   wáin-o$_i$ [VP nomíya-de t$_i$ nónda]*
     who-NOM   Mári-NOM wine-ACC   bar-LOC   drank
     to]   ímademo omótteru o?
     that still   think   Q
     'Who still thinks that Mari drank wine at the bar?'

However, phonological phrasing remains the same as illustrated in Figure 8.

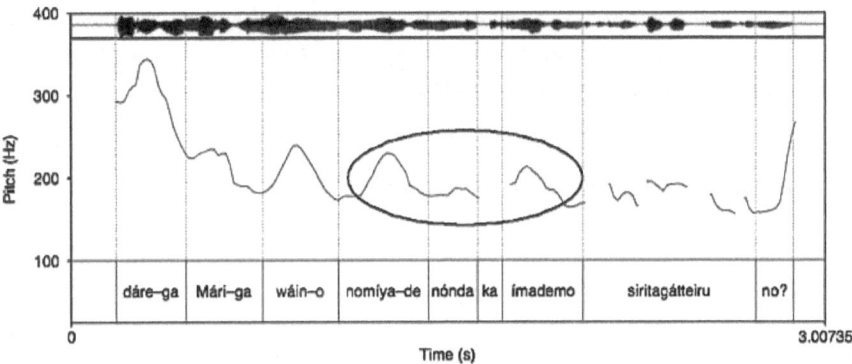

Figure 8: Pitch track of a wh-question in Japanese. (Féry and Ishihara 2009: 57).

For English, Katz and Selkirk (2011) investigate the prosodic properties of contrastive focus and discourse-new constituents based on the following set.

(140) a. Focus-new: [..... [...]Focus   [...] Discourse-New]
      b. new-Focus: [..... [...]Discourse-New [...] Focus]
      c. new-new: [..... [...]Discourse-New [...] Discourse-New]

Katz and Selkirk (2011) suggest that contrastive focus and discourse-new constituents do not differ with respect to types of pitch accents or prosodic phrasing. Pitch accents are marked with H* preceding a phrase final L tone. However, contrastive focus differs from discourse-new information in that the pitch accented

---

[47] Post-focal compression refers to compression of the pitch height of the post-focal constituents or deaccenting.

syllable of contrastive focus has an increased duration, larger pitch excursion and greater intensity.

Finally, for Hungarian, Genzel, Ishihara and Surányi (2014) suggest that syntactic focus marking is not the only strategy and narrow focus phrases in the immediate preverbal position also have a higher pitch height and longer duration than in broad focus sentences. As for the distinction between contrastive and non-contrastive focus distinction, they find out that there is not a distinction with the focus phrase itself but contrastive focus reduces the prominence of the post-focal background domain more than the non-contrastive focus.

To recap, phonetic or phonological means are used to encode focus prosodically and the aim of this chapter is to determine the prosodic mechanisms used in Turkish. Before a discussion of the experimental studies that have been conducted, it is appropriate to review the prosodic properties of focus neutral utterances in Turkish as discussed in the literature.

3.3 Prosodic properties of Turkish

Kabak and Vogel (2001) organize the prosodic domains of Turkish as a Phonological Phrase (PPh), a Clitic Group (CG) and a Phonological Word (PW) to explain the stress domains in Turkish. PW is the domain of word stress and the final syllable of the phonological word is stressed. CG is the domain of clitic group stress and the first word in this domain is promoted in stress. PPh is the domain of phrasal stress and the first word in this domain is promoted in stress.

(141) Phrase
 $[[[sǘt\,]_{PW}]_{CG}\,\,[[beyáz]_{PW}\text{-}dır]_{CG}]$
 milk white-EP COP
 'Milk is white.'

(142) Compound
 $[[[sǘt\,]_{PW}\,\,[beyaz]_{PW}\text{-}dır\,]_{CG}]$
 '(It) is milk-white.'
 (Kabak & Vogel 2001: 339)

In (141), word stress is assigned to the PW *süt* 'milk' and to the final syllable of *beyaz* 'white'. In (142), only the leftmost PW *'süt* 'milk' receives stress as the whole compound is within a CG. Kabak and Vogel (2001) make a distinction between phrase and compound stress based on the assumption that the constituents of a compound are under a single CG while the constituents of a phrase are under separate CGs. Charette, Göksel and Şener (2007) and İkizoğlu and Kamali (2015), on the other hand, suggest that the distinction between phrase and compound stress based on CGs is not well motivated. İkizoğlu and Kamali (2015) argue that in (141) *süt* 'milk' is the syntactic subject even the topic of the clause and hence separate phrasing is expected. As phonological phrasing distinction can explain the different stress patterns in (141) and (142), in this study CG is not taken as a hierarchical prosodic domain of Turkish.

Kan (2009) works on the tonal representation of Turkish and lists the following accents for Turkish. Pitch accents which mark the prominent syllable are realized as H*, !H*, L+H* and L+!H*. They are in free variation as nuclear accents, the starred tone indicating the prominent syllable. Boundary tones mark the edge of phrases and L%, H% are boundary tones marking IP in Turkish. Finally, phrase accents surface between the last pitch accent and the boundary tone. L-, H- and bitonal L+H- and L+!H- are possible phrase accents marking the PPh boundary in Turkish.

Kan (2009) further adds that in addition to the prosodic domains suggested by Kabak and Vogel (2001), there is an Intonational Phrase (IP) as a higher prosodic domain above PPh in Turkish. Kan (2009) bases her arguments on: (i) boundary tone placement; (ii) linguistic pause distribution; (iii) head prominence; and (iv) phrase-final lengthening of vowels.

(143)   L+H*   L+H*   L- H%
   [[Ayla]$_{PPh}$ [muz-lar-ı   soy-uyo]$_{PPh}$]$_{IP}$
   Ayla   banana-PL-ACC peel-PROG
        L+H*   L+H*   L- H%
   [[Numan]$_{PPh}$ [elma-lar-ı   yıkı-yo]$_{PPh}$]$_{IP}$
   Numan   apple-PL-ACC   wash-PROG
        L+H*   L+!H*   L- L%
   [[Miray]$_{PPh}$ [ayva-lar-ı   dilimli-yo]$_{PPh}$]$_{IP}$
   Miray   quince-PL-ACC slice-PROG
   'Ayla is peeling the bananas, Numan is washing the apples, and Miray is slicing the quinces.'
   (Kan 2009: 93)

The first piece of evidence for a distinct level of IP in Turkish is that there is a rapid rise in IP final position as illustrated in Figure 9 below. Kan (2009) suggests that this L-H% boundary tone marks the end of IP. The second piece of evidence comes from linguistic pauses. Although there is no obligatory pause at PPh level, there is a pause IP finally as illustrated below. The third piece of

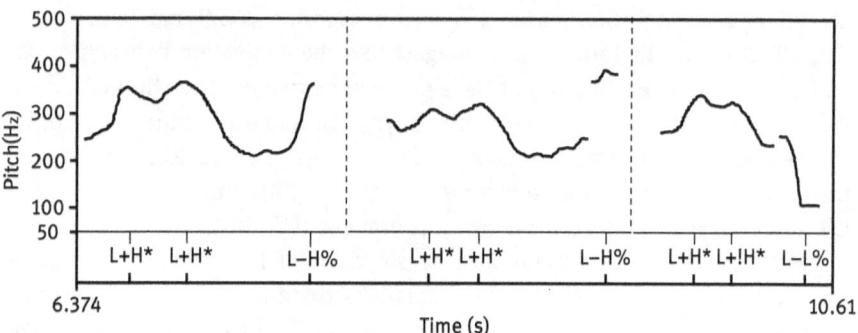

Figure 9: Pitch track of conjoined IPs. (Kan 2009: 93).

evidence is that IP final vowels are lengthened even if no pause follows in fast speech rates.

Based on all-new, broad focus sentences, Kan (2009) suggests that prominence realization at PPh and IP levels differs. At PPh domain, prominence is realized on the leftmost constituent. Kan (2009: 81) suggests that "The head of a phonological phrase requires an intonational pitch accent" which is labeled as Pitch Accent Placement Rule. According to this rule, pitch accent is anchored to the stress bearing syllable of the head in the PPh. This is illustrated in (144) below.

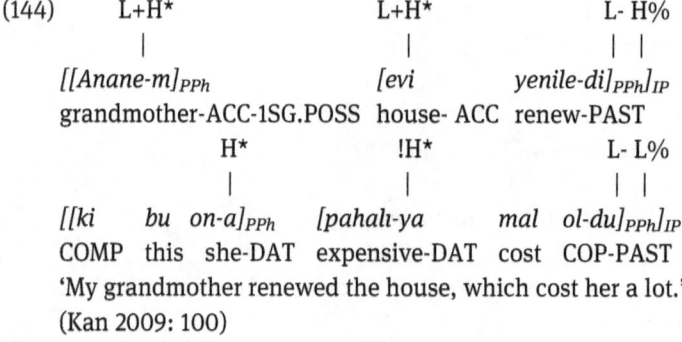

(144)   L+H*   L+H*   L- H%
            | | | |
      [[Anane-m]$_{PPh}$ [evi   yenile-di]$_{PPh}$]$_{IP}$
      grandmother-ACC-1SG.POSS house- ACC renew-PAST
                        H*   !H*   L- L%
                         | | | |
      [[ki   bu   on-a]$_{PPh}$ [pahalı-ya   mal   ol-du]$_{PPh}$]$_{IP}$
      COMP   this   she-DAT   expensive-DAT cost COP-PAST
      'My grandmother renewed the house, which cost her a lot.'
      (Kan 2009: 100)

Each pitch accent is anchored to the stress bearing syllable of the head of the PPhs. At IP level, on the other hand, the prominence is on the rightmost PPh within the IP. There are two IPs and hence IP stress is on the rightmost PPh in each case. *Evi* 'house' and *pahalıya* 'expensive' bear IP stress being the head of the rightmost PPh within the IPs.

Özge & Bozşahin (2010) investigate prosody of focus phrases in Turkish and claim that prosody is the only strategy that signals focus and it is marked with H*L- pitch contour in Turkish. Özge & Bozşahin (2010) suggest that there is no semantic distinction between contrastive focus and presentational focus. The difference is due to the fact that contrastive focus is more restricted with regard to projection possibilities and it is followed by a de-accentuated domain while presentational focus can project focus and include the verb in the same phrase as well.

(145) A: *Berlin seyahat-iniz nasıl geç-ti?*
         Berlin trip-2PL.POSS how pass-PAST
         'How was your trip to Berlin?'
    B: *AYNUR Berlin-e   gitti.   O-na   sor.*
         Aynur Berlin-DAT go-PAST s/he-DAT ask
         'Aynur has been to Berlin; ask her.'
         (Özge & Bozşahin 2010: 158)

(146) a. *Ali kim-i   gör-dü?*
          Ali who-ACC see-PAST
          'Whom did Ali see?'
     b. *Ali ne   yap-tı?*
          Ali what do-PAST
          'What did Ali do?'

(147) a. rheme[48]   theme   b.   rheme
         ...(AYNUR-U gör-dü)....   ...(AYNUR-U gör-dü)...
              H*   L-L%   H*   L-L%
         (Özge & Bozşahin 2010: 154–155)

In (145B), the contrastive focus is on a narrow argument. The answers in (147a) and (147b) with H* L-L% tones, on the other hand, are potential answers to the questions in (146a) and (146b) respectively which trigger presentational focus. As (147b) indicates, focus can project to the whole VP.[49] In (147a), the object

---

[48] For Özge and Bozşahin (2010), rheme is interchangeable with focus.
[49] Özge and Bozşahin (2010) suggest that there is no semantic distinction between contrastive focus and presentational focus based on the following example in which the answer is not necessarily contrastive.
(1) A: *Daha önce   Berlin-e   git-miş biri-ler-inin   yardım-ın-a*
        more before Berlin-DAT go-REL   one-PL-GEN   help-3SG.POSS-DAT
       ihtiyac-ımız   var
        need-1PL.POSS   exist
        'We need help from someone who has been to Berlin before.'

phrase is triggered as the focus phrase while in (147b) the whole VP is triggered. However, the verb surfaces in the same PPh with the object in (147a), too. The verb does not bear focus and surfaces in the same PPh with the object. Within each PPh, it is the leftmost constituent that gets PPh level prominence and hence (147a) and (147b) are both potential answers to (146a) and (146b), consequently, ambiguity is found. Özge and Bozşahin (2010) claim that two distinct focus strategies are not available, instead the difference between contrastive and presentational focus is marked through projection possibilities.

Note that the examples given above do not necessarily illustrate the difference in the projection possibilities of contrastive and presentational focus phrases. In (146a) and (146b), even if there were alternative questions or corrective statements triggering contrastive focus on the object, the projection possibilities would be the same as in (147a) and (147b), namely, the object would bear main prominence and the verb would be in the same PPh with the object. Hence, the difference cannot be interpreted as a distinction between the two focus types.

As for the tonal representations, Kamali (2011) refines the tonal representation of Turkish in the following way. The boundary tones are restricted to a H- boundary tone at the right edge of the utterance initial domain and L- at the right edge of the non-initial domains. As for pitch accents, in line with Levi (2005), Kamali suggests H*L for the lexically accented words with stress on the non-final syllable.[50] Kamali (2011) does not suggest a pitch accent for non-lexically accented words.[51] Now, it is time to go over the prosodic properties of the prenuclear,

---

B: *(AYNUR) (Berlin-e   git-ti)   o-ndan   sor-abil-ir-im)*
    Aynur   Berlin-DAT go-PAST s/he-ABL ask-ABL-PRES-1SG
'Aynur has been to Berlin. I can ask her.'
(Özge and Bozşahin 2010: 158)

Contrastive focus interpretation is not likely to be available in this sentence because the subject given in capital letters is in fact a contrastive topic phrase. The implicit big question under discussion is "Among us, who has been to Berlin?" and this question is answered for only one person and hence the answer is partial but not exhaustive. That is why the answer is not taken as contrastive.

50 See also Özge (2003), Levi (2005) and Özge and Bozşahin (2010), Ipek and Jun (2013) for the tonal representations of Turkish. As the labeling of the tonal properties of the constituents does not make a difference to this study, the tonal representation of Kamali (2011) is used.

51 In Turkish the majority of the words have stress on the final syllable, labeled as non-lexically accented words. Stress shifts when affixes are added to the stem.

(1)   a.   *ele<u>man</u>*   b. *eleman-<u>lar</u>*
           'personnel'   personnel-PL
                              'personnels'

nuclear and postnuclear domains in Turkish under neutral intonation based on the findings of Kamali (2011).

(i) Prenuclear Domain: Under neutral intonation, the subject in an SOV sentence surfaces in the prenuclear domain.

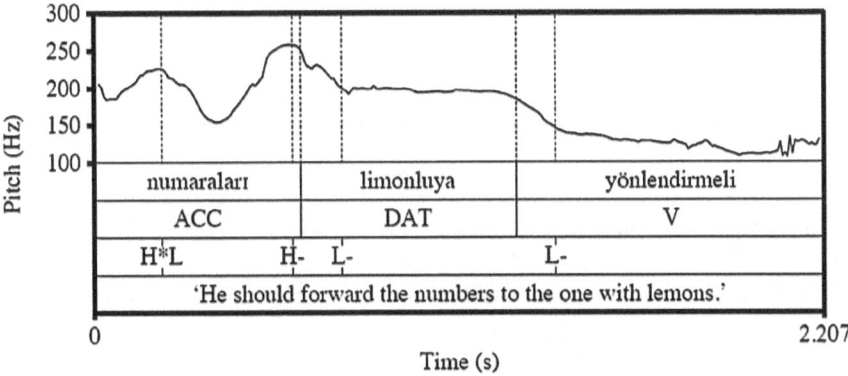

Figure 10: Prenuclear domain. (Kamali 2011: 70).

The pitch accent of the subject is realized as H*L. A H- boundary tone surfaces at the right edge of this domain with both lexically accented and finally stressed words.

(ii) Nuclear Domain: In SOV order, this is the domain where object surfaces under neutral intonation and gets nuclear prominence. There is a different pattern between lexically accented words and finally stressed words in this domain. When there is a finally stressed word a plateau is observed followed by a fall starting with the onset of the verb as in Figure 11 below.

With lexically accented words, the fall starts earlier with the L of the H*L pitch accent of the lexically accented syllable as in Figure 12 below.

Some of the words are stressed on a non-final syllable and stress does not shift when affixes are added to the stem. These words are lexically accented words.

(2) a. İyonya b. İyonya-da
    'Ionia' Ionian-LOC
              'in Ionia'

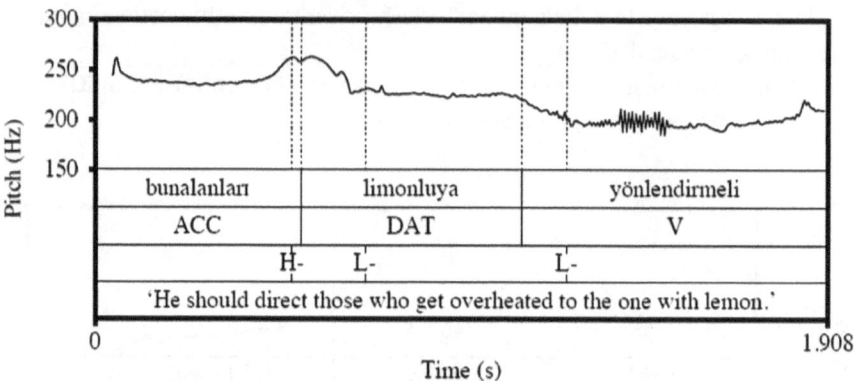

Figure 11: Nuclear domain with a finally stressed word. (Kamali 2011: 74).

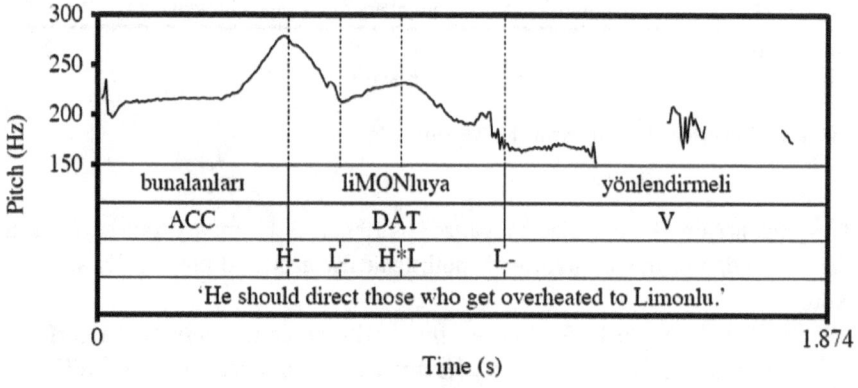

Figure 12: Nuclear domain with a lexically accented word. (Kamali 2011: 75).

(iii) Postnuclear Domain: In the postnuclear domain, the reference height of the nuclear domain is not preserved and a lower height is retained until the end of the utterance as illustrated in Figure 13 below.

Before moving on to the current study, it is helpful to review two studies on prosodic realization of focus in Turkish. Ipek (2011) measures f0, duration and intensity of focus phrases in medial, initial and final domains based on the following target sentences.

(148) a. *Tuna baba-m-ı döv-müş*
    Tuna father-1SG.POSS-ACC beat-PERF
    'Tuna beat my dad.'

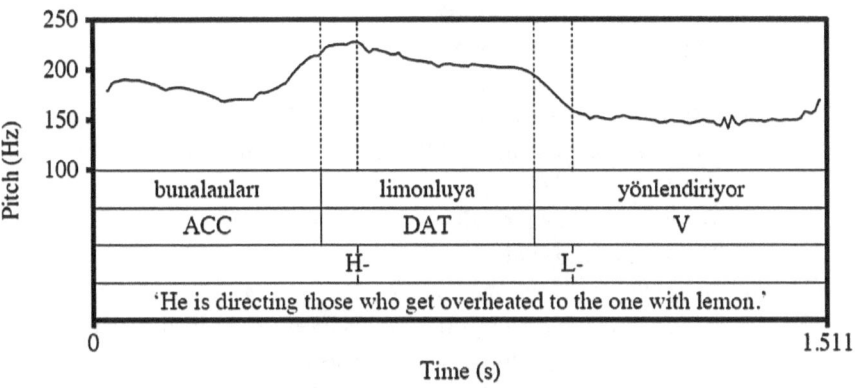

Figure 13: Postnuclear domain. (Kamali 2011: 79).

    b. *Lale   duvar-ı   boya-mış*
       Lale   wall-ACC paint-PERF
       'Lale painted the wall.'
    c. *Döne   dede-m-i   kov-muş.*
       Döne   grandpa-1SG.POSS-ACC send away-PERF
       'Döne sent away my grandpa.'
    d. *Mine   burn-un-u   yıka-mış.*
       Mine   nose-2SG.POSS-ACC wash-PERF
       'Mine washed her nose.'
       (adapted from Ipek 2011: 140)

As for the results of the study, Ipek (2011) notes that: (i) medial focus does not differ from broad focus with regard to f0, duration or intensity; (ii) initial focus has a higher duration; and (iii) final focus has greater intensity. Ipek (2011) suggests these sentences were triggered by questions to trigger right information structure but the triggering questions are not included in the paper. Hence, it is not known whether the focus phrases are contrastive or discourse-new focus in this work. İvoşeviç and Bekâr (2015) conduct a similar experimental study to determine phonetic correlates of immediate preverbal focus phrases. A three-way classification is made for focus phrases as: (i) broad focus (149a); (ii) informational focus (149b); and (iii) contrastive focus (149c). The following examples indicate how each type of focus is triggered.

(149) a. A: *Gezi nasıl geçti?*
              'How was the trip?'

B: *Gizem [yılan-ı]$_F$ gör-dü.*
Gizem snake-ACC see-PERF
'Gizem saw the snake.'
b. A: *Gizem'in gözünden hiç bir şey kaçmaz. Bu sefer neyi görmüş?*
'Nothing escapes Gizem. What did she see this time?'
B: *Gizem [yılan-ı]$_{INF}$ gör-dü.*
Gizem snake-ACC see-PERF
'Gizem saw the snake.'
c. A: *Bu ormanda çok sevimli bir sincap var. Gizem onu gördü mü?*
'There is a very cute squirrel in this forest. Did Gizem see it?'
B: *Gizem [yılan-ı]$_{CF}$ gör-dü.*
Gizem snake-ACC see-PERF
'Gizem saw the snake.'
(adapted from İvoşeviç and Bekar 2015: 21–22)

Similar to Ipek (2011), İvoşeviç and Bekâr (2015) find out that focus types do not differ from each other with respect to f0 height or intensity. However, they note a significant difference between broad focus and informational focus with respect to the duration of focus bearing words.

The studies of Kan (2009) and Kamali (2011) are based on focus neutral sentences. Hence, it is not possible to see prosodic marking of focus phrases in these studies. Özge and Bozşahin (2010) work on focus phrases but their study is not a strictly controlled study in that contrastive focus and presentational focus do not appear on the same constituent in the same environment. The study of Ipek (2011) is more controlled in that focus in initial, medial and final domains are investigated based on the same set of sentences. However, as pointed out earlier, not much is known about the nature of the focus phrase as sentences are given out of context. The experimental study of İvoşeviç and Bekâr (2015) is a controlled study with target sentences triggered through contexts and they note a difference between broad and informational focus with respect to word duration, which was found to be insignificant in the study of Ipek (2011). Hence, a further controlled experimental study needed to be conducted. The next section is the investigation of the current study.

3.4 First study

In the first study, the aim was to find an answer to the research questions raised at the beginning of the chapter, namely, the prosodic realization of (i) broad focus and narrow focus sentences; and (ii) contrastive focus and discourse-new focus and possible differences among these conditions.

3.4.1 The stimuli

The target (a–b–e) and control sentences (c–d) included the following information structural ordering in SOV order.

Table 1: The Order of the Structures Used in the First Study.

		S	O	V
(a)	GNG	given	discourse-new	given
(b)	GCG	given	contrastive focus	given
(c)	Broad Focus	discourse-new	discourse-new	discourse-new
(d)	GGG	given	given	given
(e)	CGG	contrastive focus	given	given

In target structures (a) and (b), contrastive focus and discourse-new information is in the medial position, given constituents surfacing in the initial and final positions. Given constituents explicitly surface in the preceding context. As Katz and Selkirk (2011) indicate, comparing the context in (b) with the context in (c) has some drawbacks in that a contrastive focus constituent can be found to have greater phonetic prominence than a discourse-new constituent as they are not in the same minimal context. In (c), a discourse-new constituent is preceded and followed by new information and downstep is expected following the prenuclear domain. In (b), on the other hand, the contrastive focus constituent is surrounded by given material which is expected to be phonetically non-prominent (Féry and Samek-Lodovici 2006). Hence, a downstep pattern will not have the same effect in this structure and the contrastive focus constituent can be found to have greater phonetic prominence. In this study, this is controlled as discourse-new and contrastive focus is presented in the same minimal context surrounded by given information in both cases as in (a) and (b). The comparison of (a) and (b) will indicate whether there is a difference between the two narrow focus types which is one of the major research questions in this study. The comparison of (a) and (b) with (c) and (d) will also show whether contrastive focus and discourse-new object phrases are realized in a different way than the object in the same position in all-new or all-given conditions. With the final order in (e), the aim was to determine whether focus phrases show different prosodic properties with respect to pitch register and phonological phrasing in sentence initial and medial positions.

For each condition, the same 4 target sentences were used. Three of these sentences were composed of lexically accented words and one of them was composed of finally stressed words. With the aim of avoiding perturbations in the pitch track due to sounds in the obstruent category, sonorants and voiced obstruents were used in all sentences. The sentences were set in a dialogue to ensure that the correct information structural notions were triggered. It was also the objective to make the reading process as natural as possible (See Appendix A for examples of the structures in the first study).

Contrastive focus was triggered by corrective statements (150) or alternative questions (151) in medial and initial domains (152).

(150) A: *İyonyalı-lar Ömerli-ye   yayıl-ıyor-lar.*
Ionian-PL   Ömerli-DAT   move-IMPF-3PL
'The Ionians move towards Ömerli.'

B: *Hayır yanılıyorsun, İyonyalı-lar [Menemen-e]$_{CF}$ yayıl-ıyor-lar.*
No, you are wrong, Ionian-PL   Menemen-DAT   move-IMPF-3PL
'No, you are wrong, the Ionians move towards Menemen.'

(151) A: *İyonyalı-lar Menemen-e   mi   yoksa Ömerli-ye*
Ionian-PL   Menemen-DAT QP   or   Ömerli-DAT
mi   yayıl-ıyor-lar?
QP   move-IMPF-3PL
'Do the Ionians move towards Menemen or Ömerli?'

B: *İyonyalı-lar [Ömerli-ye]$_{CF}$ yayıl-ıyor-lar.*
Ionian-PL   Ömerli-DAT   move-IMPF-3PL
'The Ionians move towards Ömerli.'

(152) A: *Pek çok ülke bu tür silahların yapımında uranyum kullanımını onaylıyor. Bunlardan biri de Yunanlılar.*
'Many of the countries approve the usage of uranium in these kinds of weapons. The Greeks are one of these.'

B: *Hayır yanılıyorsun   Yunanlı-lar   değil.*
No, you are wrong   Greek-PL   not
[Romanyalı-lar]$_{CF}$ uranyum-u   onaylı-yor.
Rumanian-PL   uranium-ACC   approve-IMPF
'No you are wrong. It is not the Greeks. The Rumanians approve of uranium.'

Discourse-new focus was triggered by wh-questions (153).

(153) A: *İyonyalı-lar nereye yayıl-ıyor-lar?*
Ionian-PL where move-IMPF-3PL
'Where do the Ionians move?'
B: *İyonyalı-lar [Menemen-e]$_{DN}$ yayıl-ıyor-lar.*
Ionian-PL Menemen-DAT move-IMPF-3PL
'The Ionians move towards Menemen.'

Broad focus sentences (154), and all-given sentences (155) were triggered in dialogues similar to the one exemplified below.

(154) A: *Ne izliyorsun, ne var televizyonda?*
'What are you watching, what is on TV?'
B: *[Almanyalı-lar Anamurlu-lar-ı öv-üyor-lar]*
German-PL people of Anamur-PL-ACC praise-IMPF-3PL
Belli ki Anamurlu-lar iyi çalış-ıyor-lar.
apparently people of Anamur-PL good work-IMPF-3PL
'The German people praise the people from Anamur. Apparently, the people from Anamur work hard.'

(155) A: *Biliyor musun, şu anda bir televizyon programı izliyorum ve Almanyalılar Anamurluları övüyorlar.*
'You know what, I am watching a TV program now and the German people praise the people from Anamur.'
B: *Bil-iyor-um, biliyorum. [Almanyalı-lar*
know-IMPF-1SG German-PL
Anamurlu-lar-ı öv-üyor-lar]
people of Anamur-PL-ACC praise-IMPF-3PL
Ben de şu an aynı programı izliyorum. Bir Anamurlu olarak çok mutlu-yum.
'I know, I know. The German people praise the people of Anamur. I am also watching the same program now. As a person from Anamur, I am very happy.'

In total, there were 20 sentences, four sentences for each condition, and six fillers. The next section focuses on the elicitation process and the participants.

3.4.2 Participants and the recording procedure

Three female speakers (AD, ET, Nİ) and three male speakers (İG, OG, ST) with an age span between 26 and 58 participated in the first study. All the participants were native speakers of Turkish living in İstanbul. None were linguists and they were all naïve to the purpose of the study.

The recording was done in a quiet setting and in three sessions. The target and control dialogues were given to the informants in a paper in random order. The dialogues were rehearsed with the researcher and the participant in order to make the conversation as natural as possible. For each dialogue, the researcher read the triggering context and the participant read the target structures. Repetition of the structures was done only in cases of mispronunciation and hesitation pauses. Each session was recorded with the recording function of the software program Praat (Boersma and Weenink 2018) without a break and then the target and control sentences were extracted for analysis in Praat.

3.4.3 Measurement points

The sentences were annotated manually by the researcher taking the syllables as intervals. The annotation was done listening to the sound file and focusing on the characteristic formants of the vowels in the spectrogram as a cue for the boundaries (Ladefoged 2010).

In the prenuclear domain, in which the subject surfaces, the (i) maximum height of the accented syllable of the subject, abbreviated as (subj_max_pitch_accent) for ease of exposition in the graph and (ii) the peak of the boundary tone (H_boundary_tone) were measured. The aim was to determine whether focus in the nuclear domain has an effect in the initial domain. The measurements in this domain would also offer ideas as to how discourse-given, discourse-new distinction is marked in Turkish. In broad focus sentences, discourse-new constituents and in narrow focus sentences, discourse-given constituents surface in this domain. In the nuclear domain, the measurement points are (i) the maximum height of the accented syllable of the object (max_pitch_accent), and (ii) the minimum pitch value of the preceding (rise_min_pitch) and succeeding syllable (fall_min_pitch). The minimum pitch value of the preceding and succeeding syllable were measured to ascertain whether there was pitch excursion or not. With finally stressed words, the fall following the accented syllable is measured as the minimum pitch value at the end of the final syllable. In the postnuclear domain the minimum pitch value at the first syllable of the verb (verb_min_pitch)

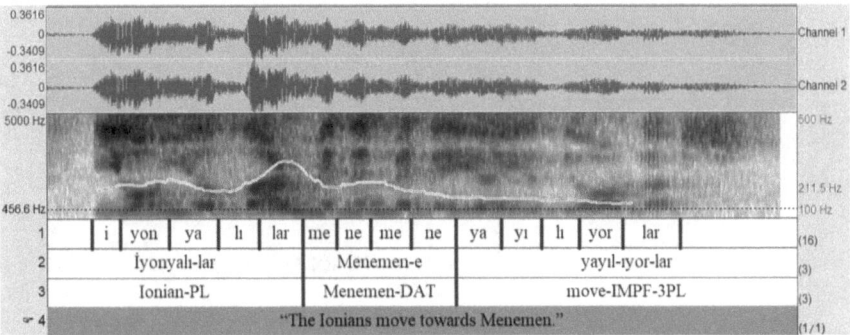

Figure 14: Measurement points in the first study, GNG sentence, speaker Nİ.

is the measurement point. The aim was to find out whether there is post-focal compression or not. The sentences in the CGG condition were annotated without doing measurements.

Based on the syllable intervals, the minimum and maximum f0 measurements were extracted manually using the get maximum pitch and get minimum pitch commands of Praat. The f0 values were then entered in an excel sheet which was used for statistical analysis.

3.4.4 Results

First, it is beneficial to review the pitch tracks of the structures with narrow focus and broad focus cases to see whether there is a difference with respect to pitch accents or phonological phrasing.

As illustrated in Figure 15, 16 and 17 for the same sentence, in the prenuclear domain there is a bump with the accented syllable of the subject and the right edge of the prenuclear domain is marked with a H- boundary tone. In the nuclear domain, there is a slight bump with the pitch accent of the object. Finally, in the postnuclear domain a lower reference height is retained.

Hence, it can be concluded that focus in the immediate preverbal position does not have an effect on pitch accents or phonological phrasing. Now, consider the sentences with contrastive focus in the initial domain in Figure 18.

Note that the pitch track of this sentence is different from the ones in Figures 15–17. There is a bump with the accented syllable of the subject followed by a low reference height until the end of the sentence. The CGG sentences have not been included for the statistical analysis as the same measurements points do not surface and so the discussion of these structures has been kept to

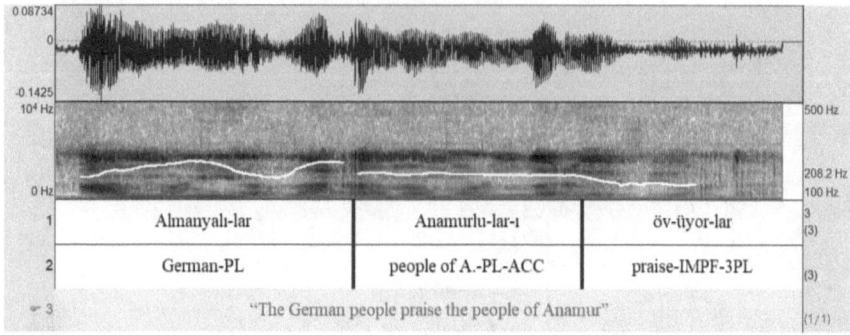

Figure 15: Broad focus condition, speaker Nİ.

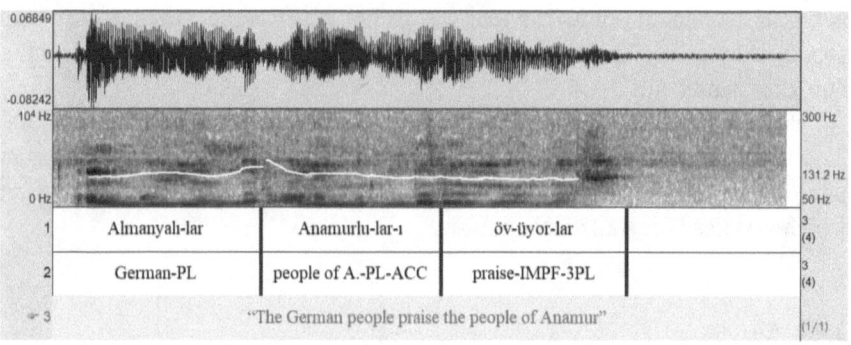

Figure 16: GCG condition, speaker OG.

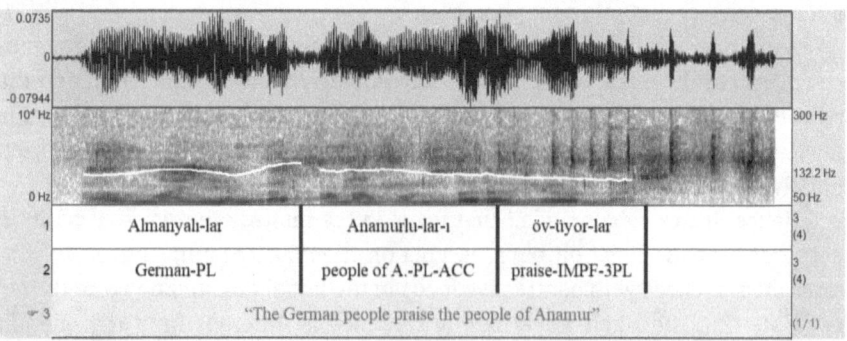

Figure 17: GNG condition, speaker OG.

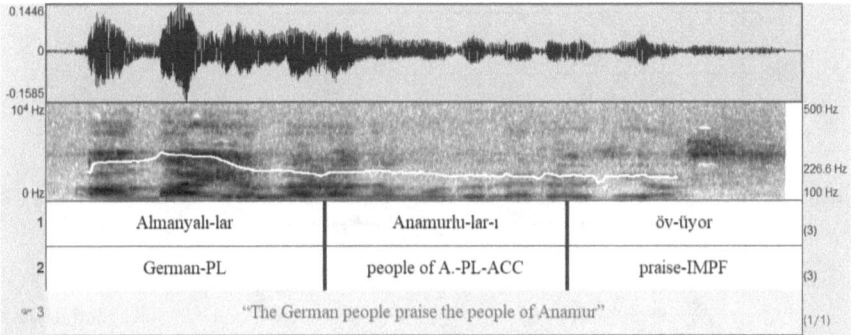

Figure 18: CGG condition, speaker AD.

section 3.5.8.2. Now, the question is whether focus makes a difference for the tonal height of pitch accents or boundary tones. Some of the speakers have a pitch span between 100 Hz and 300 Hz while others have a pitch range between 75 Hz and 275 Hz. Although the lowest and the highest pitch values differ, the speakers have the same pitch range.[52] After the extraction of the f0 values for the target measurement points, with the aim of excluding the variation not due to focus condition but due to speaker pitch range variation, the measured f0 values for each speaker were normalized. The transformed value is measured based on the mean value of the lowest value in the postnuclear domain and the highest value in the prenuclear domain.[53] The following plot for the 6 speakers based on these measurement points was extrapolated.

Given constituents are prosodically non-prominent and they are destressed (Féry and Samek-Lodovici 2006). With greater speaker involvement wider pitch ranges are expected (Bolinger 1986) and hence structures with discourse-new and contrastive focus phrases are predicted to have higher values than the other conditions. However, as illustrated in Figure 19 below, the structures with contrastive focus have the lowest values while the all-given structures have the highest values at all measurement points which is puzzling. Even all-new sentences have lower values than all-given sentences.

---

[52] Pitch span refers to the highest and lowest values for the pitch range.
[53] For each speaker the mean minimum value in the postnuclear domain for GCG, GNG and broad cases is found, which is taken as the baseline. The mean maximum value is also measured for GCG, GNG and broad focus cases based on the highest value of the boundary tone. The following formula is used to obtain the transformed results.
   Transformed value = measured f0 - baseline ÷ mean of maximum height - baseline

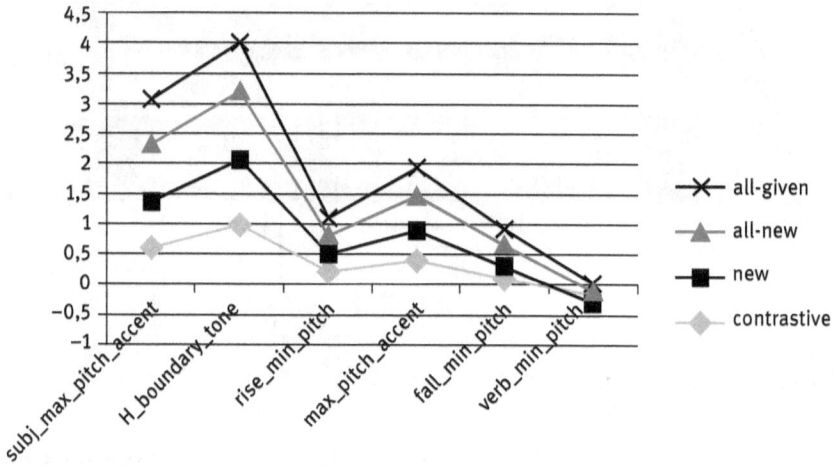

Figure 19: Plot of the four conditions based on the transformed values of 6 speakers.

3.4.5 Discussion

There were a few issues that made the results of the first study inconclusive. Note that in the plot given in Figure 19, all-given and broad focus structures have higher values than GNG and GCG condition. A closer look at the pitch tracks of all-given and broad focus structures revealed that some of these sentences did not surface with prominence on the object but on the verb. This is illustrated in Figure 20 for a broad focus sentence and in Figure 21 for an all-given sentence.

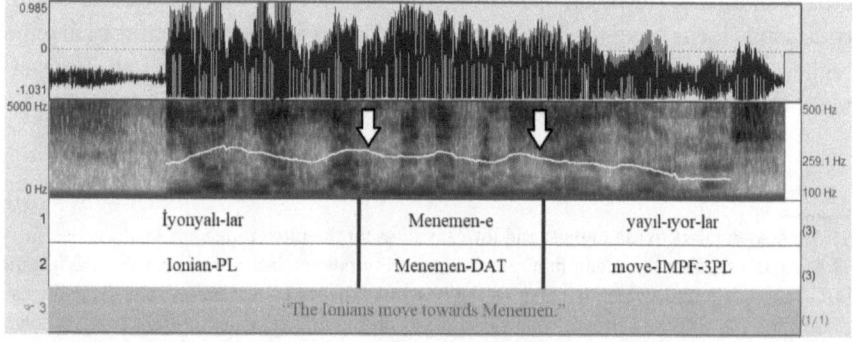

Figure 20: Pitch track of a broad focus sentence, speaker ET.

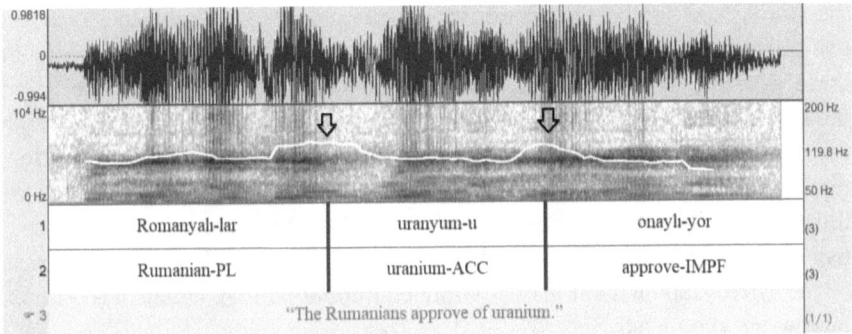

Figure 21: Pitch track of an all-given structure, speaker ST.

Note that in both pitch tracks, the H-boundary tone which marks the end of the prenuclear domain surfaces not only at the end of the initial domain but also at the end of the medial domain (shown with arrows). In the final domain, the fall starts after the accented syllable of the verb which indicates that the verb forms both the nuclear and the postnuclear domain. The initial and medial domains show the properties of the prenuclear domain with a H-boundary tone marking the end of these domains.

Out of 24 all-new sentences, 13 sentences surface with prominence on the verb and not on the immediate preverbal object. A possible explanation for the tendency to place prominence on the verb comes from Nakipoğlu (2009) who suggests that unaccented accusative objects trigger pragmatic presupposition rendering discourse-given status to the constituent while accented accusative objects trigger only existential presupposition rendering discourse-new status to the constituent. For the current study, it is suggested that in the data with all-new sentences, accusative or dative marked objects were uttered by the speakers as part of the background information, triggering pragmatic presupposition, and focus surfacing on the verb. As for all-given conditions, out of 24 all-given sentences, 15 sentences surfaced with focus on the verb not on the immediate preverbal object. It is most likely that these sentences were not uttered as a mere repetition of the previous sentence but as an assertion of the previous sentence with focus on the verb. These structures were not omitted in the statistical analysis when comparing all-given and broad focus conditions with GNG and GCG cases and hence the higher values for all-new and all-given conditions can be misleading in Figure 19.

For the lower value of contrastive focus and discourse-new constituents, the puzzling result could be due to the nature of the target structures used in the study.[54] Remember that contrastive focus phrases were elicited by corrective statements as in (150) but in each structure that was used in the experiment there were the expressions *hayır* 'no', *yanlıyorsun* 'you are wrong' preceding the target sentence. The problem is that as contrast is already signaled through these expressions, it may not only be intonation that marks focus in the structure but the expressions of denial. Similarly with the alternative questions as illustrated in (151), the speakers already know from the question which alternative is excluded by way of contrastive focus in the answer. Hence, as is the case in corrective statements it may not only be intonation that signals the contrast but the question itself.[55]

As for the discourse-new constituents elicited through wh-questions, Hubert Truckenbrodt (p.c) notes that one cannot be certain that they are not exhaustive answers. The speakers can utter the answer as an exhaustive answer to the preceding wh-question excluding the implicit alternatives although alternatives are not given in the question. To recap, there were some confounding properties with respect to the stimuli which led to the second experimental study the details of which are investigated in the following section.

3.5 Second study

In the second study, the data was restricted to GNG, GCG and broad focus sentences and target sentences were composed taking into consideration the above mentioned confounding facts.

3.5.1 The stimuli

The structures used in the second phase of the study are illustrated in Table 2.

In order to avoid perturbation and distortion in the pitch track due to obstruent sounds, lexically accented words with sonorants and voiced obstruents were chosen. For each condition, 6 target structures were identified all of which were composed of lexically accented words. There were 24 fillers included in this

---

[54] Gratitude is due to Hubert Truckenbrodt for pointing this out.
[55] Caroline Féry (p.c) suggests that the other possible reason for the lower values of contrastive focus can be due to downstepping. As illustrated in (152) for contrastive focus condition, there are two sentences in the same utterance. After the expressions of denial there can be a downstep with the ongoing sentence with contrastive focus constituent.

Table 2: The Order of the Structures Used in the Second Study.

		S	O	V
(a)	GNG	given	discourse-new	given
(b)	GCG	given	contrastive focus	given
(c)	Broad Focus	discourse-new	discourse-new	discourse-new

phase of the study which could be grouped into three main categories. The first two groups were given as answers to the questions of "what kind of" and "how" and the final group was composed of additional comments to the previous context without triggering questions (See Appendix B for examples of structures in the second study).

Contrastive focus constituents in GCG order were triggered by corrective statements embedded in dialogues. With the aim of leaving intonation as the only cue to mark focus phrase, expressions of denial were not used in the target sentences as exemplified in (156).

(156) A: *Bu programda her ili temsilen gelen yarışmacılar hünerlerini gösteriyor. Örneğin Yalovalılar elektronik cihaz onarıyorlar. Oldukça da yetenekliler.*
 'In this program, the contestants who represent each city show their skills. For instance, the people of Yalova repair electrical devices. They are very skillful.'
 B: *Yalovalı-lar [mobilya]$_{CF}$ onar-ıyor-lar.*
 people of Yalova-PL furniture repair-IMPF-3PL
 'The people of Yalova repair furniture.'

The contrastive focus constituent in the answer excludes the explicitly mentioned alternative in the preceding context. The exclusion of the alternative can be signaled only with intonation as the expressions of overt denial such as *hayır* 'no', *yanılıyorsun* 'you are wrong' are not included in the answer. In this study, alternative questions are not used as one of the alternatives is explicitly given in the previous discourse, and the speaker knows which alternative is excluded.

As for discourse-new constituents, with the aim of ensuring that the answer to the question is not interpreted as an exhaustive answer, discourse-new constituents are elicited with wh-questions asking for additional information (See the discussion in section 2.5.1).

(157) A: *Bu programda her ili temsilen gelen yarışmacılar hünerlerini gösteriyor. Örneğin Yalovalılar elektronik cihaz onarıyorlar. Oldukça da yetenekliler.*
'In this program, the contestants who represent a city show their skills. For instance, the people of Yalova repair electrical devices. They are very skillful.'
B: *Yalovalılar başka ne onarıyorlar?*
'What else do the people of Yalova repair?'
A: *Yalovalı-lar [mobilya]$_{DN}$ onar-ıyor-lar.*
people of Yalova-PL furniture repair-IMPF-3PL
'The people of Yalova repair furniture.'

The question elicits an additional answer which does not exclude the alternative given in the previous discourse.

Finally, broad focus sentences are elicited in the following context by way of "what else?" question type.

(158) A: *Neler oluyor?*
'What is happening?'
B: *Öğrenciler okula başlıyor.*
'Students are starting school.'
A: *Başka?*
'What else?'
B: *[Yalovalı-lar mobilya onar-ıyor-lar]$_{BF}$*
people of Yalova-PL furniture repair-IMPF-3PL
'The people of Yalova repair furniture.'

In the first study, speakers tended to interpret a broad focus sentence as part of shared information and in nearly half of the structures prominence was realized on the verb not on the object. With the aim of avoiding this possibility, the target sentence was expressed as an answer asking for additional information which was not related to the first question. The next section focuses on the participants and the elicitation procedure for the second phase of the study.

3.5.2 Participants and the recording procedure

Five female speakers (BB, CT, EE, HT, KÇ) and three male speakers (EK, MA, ÜE) with the age span between 20 and 29 participated in the study. All the participants were native speakers of Turkish and had been living in Germany for between 2 weeks to 6 months at the time of the recording and none of them was fluent in German as a second language. None of them was a linguist and they were all naïve to the purpose of the study.

The recording was undertaken in a quiet setting and in single sessions with a portable recorder (TASCAM DR-05) with 48 kHz sampling rate and 16 bit solution. The dialogues were given to the participants on paper. Two randomization processes were applied with respect to the presentation of the data. With the aim of avoiding researcher bias, the researcher did not take active part in the elicitation process and the participants were randomly matched to rehearse the dialogues. In the first phase of the recording session, the target and control dialogues were given to the participants on paper in random order and the dialogues were rehearsed by two of the participants. One of the participants uttered the triggering contexts and the other participant uttered the target sentences. In the second phase of the study, the same speakers were given another paper in which the order of the dialogues was again randomized. During this phase, the participant, who uttered the triggering contexts in the first phase of the recording procedure, uttered the target sentences. Repetition of the structures was done only in cases of mispronunciation and hesitation pauses. The entire session was recorded with only a short break after the first phase and then the target and control sentences were extracted for analysis in Praat (Boersma and Weenink 2018).

3.5.3 Measurement points

The target sentences were annotated manually taking syllables as the intervals as illustrated in Figure 22 below. The syllables were labeled based on the sound

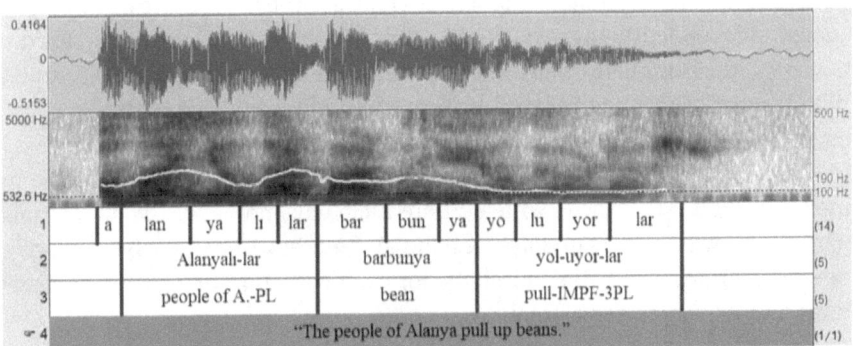

Figure 22: Measurement points in the second study, broad focus sentence, speaker KÇ.

file and the spectrogram, taking the characteristic location of formants of vowels as cues (Ladefoged 2010) as in the first study.

In the prenuclear domain, the maximum pitch value of the accented syllable of the subject, the maximum pitch value of the boundary tone marking the end of the prenuclear domain and the minimum pitch value in between these points were measured. The measurement points in the nuclear domain were the maximum pitch value of the accented syllable of the object and the maximum pitch value of the final syllable of the object. Finally, in the postnuclear domain, the minimum pitch value at the first syllable of the verb and the minimum pitch value at the postnuclear domain were measured.

The measurement points in the initial domain were chosen to test the effect of focus in this domain. The peak of the accented syllable of the object was measured to find out whether focus was marked as focal boost, namely, with a higher pitch height. The peak in the final syllable of the object and the minimum value at the final domain was chosen to ascertain whether there was post-focal compression namely whether the pitch register of the verb was compressed following the focus phrase in the nuclear domain. In this study, the duration of the focus phrases was also measured. The duration measurement was undertaken for the subject in the prenuclear domain, and the object in the nuclear domain.

Remember that for each condition, the same 6 sentences were embedded in different contexts and there were 8 participants. Hence, in total there were 48 stimuli for each condition. However, in broad focus condition out of 48 structures, 3 structures were excluded from statistical analysis as the prominence did not surface on the object but on the verb. For the 48 GCG sentences, as the majority of the sentences of two speakers (EE and HT) had a different tonal melody from the other speakers, 11 of the sentences of these speakers were excluded from the main statistical analysis. These sentences will be discussed independently in section 3.5.5. Hence, there were 37 sentences for the GCG condition and there were 48 sentences to be analyzed for the GNG order. With the aim of having the same amount of data for each condition, the counterparts of the omitted structures in broad focus and contrastive focus cases in the discourse-new cases were omitted. The whole GCG data elicited from the participant HT surfaced with a different melody and hence the data of this participant was also completely excluded from statistical analysis for the other conditions. After the omissions, for each condition there were 35 structures and 105 structures in total.

In the first study, the minimum and maximum pitch heights were measured manually. In this study, they were extracted from the structures via ProsodyPro (Xu 2013) semi-automatically. The script takes the syllables as the domains of the measurement and lists the minimum and maximum f0 value within the syllable for each speaker. This data was entered in an excel sheet for further statistical analysis.

A pitch range between 75–500 Hz was taken. However, for the octave errors, namely uneven jumps or falls in the pitch tracks, the pitch range was changed and a speaker based measurement was taken for the speaker CT with a range between 75–200 Hz. The other pitch tracks were also checked for possible octave errors. In the postnuclear domain, the minimum f0 value was measured but creaky and breathy voice was realized at the end of some of the sentences. Hence, the last two syllables of the verb were discarded from the measurement domain. The minimum value before the uneven jump or fall due to creaky and breathy voices was taken as the minimum value of the postnuclear domain.

ProsodyPro was also used to elicit the duration measurements for each structure. The measurement domain was chosen as the word interval in this case.

3.5.4 Results

The pitch tracks of the sentences in GCG, GNG will first be considered along with broad focus cases to determine whether there is a change in pitch accent or phonological phrasing. As is the case in the first study, there was no difference between the three conditions with respect to phonological phrasing or pitch accents.

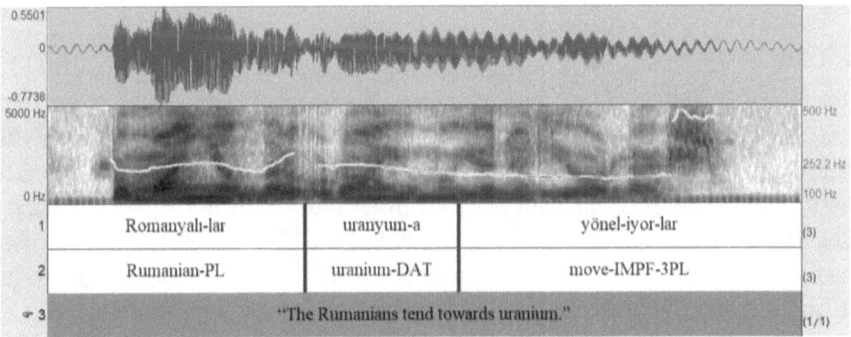

Figure 23: Pitch track of a broad focus sentence, speaker EE.

In all pitch tracks, there is a bump with the accented syllable of the subject in the prenuclear domain and the object in the nuclear domain. At the right edge of

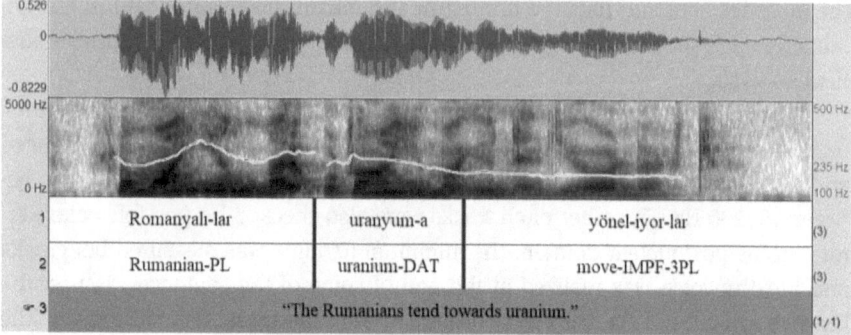

Figure 24: Pitch track of a GNG sentence, speaker EE.

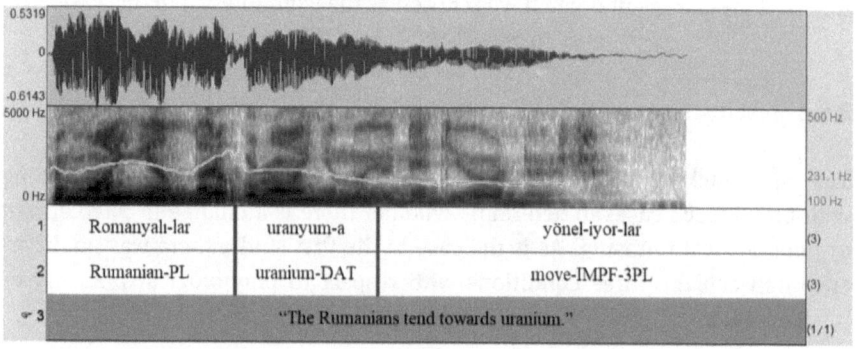

Figure 25: Pitch track of a GCG sentence, speaker EE.

the prenuclear domain, a H- boundary tone surfaces. In order to check whether the three focus conditions differ with respect to pitch and boundary tone height and duration, an analysis was conducted. Following the extraction of the f0 values for the target measurement points with ProsodyPro, with the aim of excluding the variation not due to focus condition but due to speaker pitch span variation, the raw f0 values were normalised based on the model suggested in Pierrehumbert (1980). Based on these transformed values, it was possible to generate the plot in Figure 26 for GCG, GNG and broad focus conditions.[56]

---

[56] For each speaker the mean minimum value in the postnuclear domain for GCG, GNG and broad cases was found which is taken as the baseline. The following formula was used to obtain the transformed values for all measurement points for each sentence: Transformed value = measured f0-baseline ÷ baseline

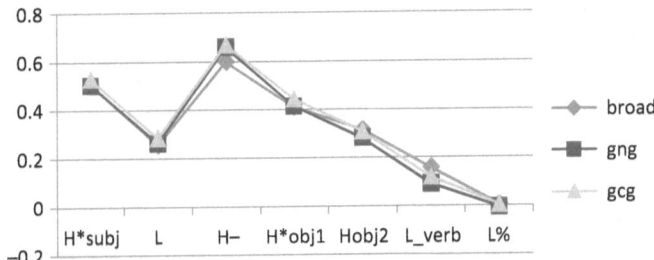

Figure 26: Plot of the target sentences for the 7 participants, 35 structures for each condition.

The first point in the plot refers to the pitch height of the accented syllable of the subject abbreviated as (H*subj) for ease of exposition in the plot. The second point is the minimum pitch value between the accented syllable of the subject and the H- boundary tone (L). The third point is the maximum height of the H- boundary tone (H-) at the right edge of the prenuclear domain. The fourth point represents the pitch height of the accented syllable of the object (H*obj1) and the fifth point is the maximum pitch value of the last syllable of the object (Hobj2). At the sixth point, there is the minimum pitch value at the beginning of the verb (L_verb) and in the last point the minimum pitch value in the entire postnuclear domain (L%).

As illustrated in Figure 26 above, the values for the three conditions seem to group together and a similar pitch track for the conditions was obtained. One initial observation is that the pitch track for the GCG condition has higher values than the pitch track for broad focus and GNG conditions almost at all measurement points with the exception of the postnuclear domain. The second observation is that the minimum pitch value at the beginning of the verb is higher with broad focus condition than GCG and GNG conditions. However, all three conditions reach a similar point at the end of the postnuclear domain.

With the aim of ascertaining whether there is a significant difference between the measurement points within each focus condition and whether there is a significant difference between GCG and the other conditions illustrated in Figure 26, the within-subjects repeated measures ANOVA was conducted.[57] For the difference between measurement points within each focus condition, Mauchly's test of sphericity indicated that the assumption of sphericity had been violated, chi square (20) = 130,376, p = 000) therefore degrees of freedom were corrected

---

[57] Thanks to Süleyman S. Taşçı for his help with the statistical analysis.

using the Greenhouse estimates of sphericity (ϵ = .39) The results indicate that, overall, different measurement points have a significant effect on f0 $F_{(20, 80)}$ = 175,986, p = .000, η_p^2 = .838). The result shows that within a focus condition each measurement point is significantly different from the other points.

However, a pairwise comparison between the three focus conditions did not reveal a significant difference in that the three focus conditions do not differ from each other with respect to the seven measurement points. The results of the study clearly indicate that focus in the immediate preverbal position is not realized as focal boost in Turkish, and hence one cannot assume that focus phrases are marked with a distinctive pitch accent in Turkish. Remember that lexically accented words are realized with H*L pitch accent irrespective of their information structural status. Moreover, no post-focal compression is observed following the contrastive focus phrases or discourse-new constituents and hence deaccentuated post-focal domain is not a distinctive property of contrastive focus phrases. The results of the study illustrate that contrastive focus and discourse-new phrases are not marked distinctively with respect to f0 measurements and additionally they do not differ from broad focus sentences. Turkish is in contrast with English (Katz and Selkirk 2011) in which focus is not restricted to a specific position and prosody distinctively marks (i) the contrastive focus and discourse-new constituents from a broad focus condition and (ii) contrastive focus phrases from discourse-new phrases. Turkish also differs from Hungarian (Genzel, Ishihara and Surányi 2014) in which narrow focus in the immediate preverbal position is realized with extended height of the fundamental frequency (f0) and longer duration when compared to broad focus sentences. In Turkish, focus phrases are not restricted to the immediate preverbal position but narrow focus structures do not differ prosodically from a broad focus condition in the immediate preverbal domain.

The duration of the subject in the prenuclear domain, and the object focus phrase in the nuclear domain were measured. The duration measurements were extracted from the pitch tracks via ProsodyPro (Xu 2013); however, for the pitch tracks with breaks following the prenuclear domain the duration measurements were carried out manually. Following the extraction of the duration measurements, another within-subjects repeated measures ANOVA was conducted. Contrary to İvoşeviç and Bekâr (2015), no significant difference was noted for the pairwise comparisons of focus conditions. This finding further indicates that the three focus conditions do not differ from each other with respect to the criteria of duration as is the case with f0 measurements.

The results of this study provide answers to the research questions put forward at the beginning of the discussion in that (i) in SOV order with the object as the focus marked constituent, focus phrases are not marked with a distinctive pitch accent nor do they show phrasing that differs from constituents in the same position in broad focus sentences, and (ii) contrastive focus is not marked with a prosodic strategy that differs from discourse-new focus phrases.

3.5.5 GCG pitch tracks with a different pattern

As indicated in the preceding section, the majority of the GCG patterns of two speakers surfaced with different tonal properties from the others. These sentences were excluded from the main analysis to be discussed separately. After the extraction of the values, with the aim of excluding the variation due to speaker pitch span variation, the raw f0 values were normalised based on the model suggested in Pierrehumbert (1980) and the plot in Figure 27 was generated.

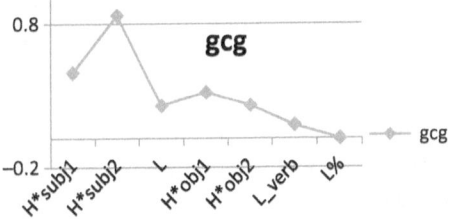

Figure 27: Plot of the 11 GCG sentences for the speakers EE and HT.

The first point in the plot refers to the pitch height of the accented syllable of the subject abbreviated as (H*subj1). The second point is the maximum height following the accented syllable of the subject given as (H*subj2) in the plot. The lowest value between the highest point in the prenuclear domain and the highest value of the accented syllable of the object in the nuclear domain are labeled as (L) in the plot. The fourth point represents the pitch height of the accented syllable of the object (H*obj1) and the fifth point is the maximum pitch value of the last syllable of the object (Hobj2). In the sixth point, the minimum pitch value is at the beginning of the verb (L_verb). The last point is the minimum pitch value in the whole postnuclear domain (L%).

The first difference to be noted between the plots in Figure 26 and Figure 27 is that the highest value in the prenuclear domain in Figure 26, which surfaces with the boundary tone, is realized earlier in Figure 27 with a non-final syllable of the subject. Note that the height of the non-final syllable in Figure 27 is higher than the pitch height of the accented syllable and even higher than the peak of the boundary tone in Figure 26. The other difference observed is that the accented syllable in the nuclear domain and the height of the accented syllable of the focus phrase is higher in Figure 26. It is suggested that the higher values observed in Figure 27 in contrast to Figure 26 can be due to higher degree of speaker involvement. Bolinger (1986) suggests that a wider pitch range is an indication of a greater degree of involvement while a narrower pitch range indicates a lesser degree of speaker involvement. Note that this different pattern is observed only with contrastive focus phrases which may include speaker involvement.

Gussenhoven (2004) also proposes paralinguistic intonational meaning based on 3 universal biological codes: (i) frequency code; (ii) effort code; and (iii) production (phase) codes which are signaled by pitch variation as illustrated in Table 3 below. When the paralinguistic intonational meaning concerns the message itself, it is informational. When it is about the speaker, it is affective. Of the three codes, effort code is closely related to the expression of contrastive focus as the speakers assert the importance of their message and, by excluding the other alternatives, they exhaustively identify a contrastive focus constituent as the correct answer. Hence, the message is more emphatic. The

Table 3: Universal Codes (Gussenhoven 2004: 95).

Physiological sources	Biological Codes	Universal Interpretations Linguistic Interpretations	Linguistic Interpretations
SIZE	Frequency Code small~big → high~low	submissive~authoritative vulnerable~protective friendly~not friendly *Informational* uncertain~certain	? Question vs. Statement (e.g. H% /L%)
ENERGY (phasing)	Production Code beginning~end → high~low	*Informational* At beginning: new topic~continued topic At end: continuation~finality	 Continuation rise vs. final low (H%/L%)
ENERGY (level)	Effort Code less effort~more effort → smaller excursion~greater excursion	*Affective* less surprised~more surprised less helpful ~more helpful *Informational* Less urgent ~more urgent	Polar onset tone (%T) Focus

speakers are predicted to use a higher pitch range or pitch excursion to emphasize the importance of the message.

The difference between Figure 26 and Figure 27 further indicates that focus in the nuclear domain may have an effect on the prenuclear domain. The H-boundary tone that surfaces with the last syllable of the constituent in the prenuclear domain does not surface. Instead, the highest pitch value surfaces on one of the non-final syllables of the subject. It is proposed that this difference is particular to exhaustive identification as this pattern surfaces only with contrastive focus phrases and shows not only inter-speaker but also intra-speaker variation.

3.5.6 Post focal fall pattern

Before entering into a general discussion on the findings of the study, it is necessary to take a closer look at the fall pattern following the accented syllable of the focus phrase in the nuclear domain. Although there is no significant difference between the three focus conditions in the prenuclear, nuclear and postnuclear domains from a statistical point of view, a difference between narrow focus and broad focus cases was observed with respect to the fall pattern in the nuclear and postnuclear domains. Kamali (2011) notes that if there is a lexically accented word in the nuclear domain, the fall starts earlier with the L of the H*L pitch accent of the lexically accented syllable but when there is a non-lexically accented word, a plateau is observed followed by a fall starting with the onset of the verb. However, in the current study the fall pattern in the nuclear domain shows some variation for each focus condition. With the aim of establishing whether these tendencies are categorical or gradient, the time normalized pitch tracks extracted via ProsodyPro (Xu 2013) were reviewed. Each pitch track has 10 interval points for the subject and the object but only 4 interval points for the verb were included due to creaky or breathy voices at the end of some utterances. In the plot "s" refers to the subject, "o1" represents the accented syllable and the preceding syllable(s), while "o2" refers to the remaining syllable(s) following the accented syllable and "v" refers to the verb.

A pattern was found in which (i) the fall starts immediately after the accented syllable in the nuclear domain and a low reference height is retained until the end of the postnuclear domain which was labeled as early fall, and (ii) the fall starts immediately after the accented syllable in the nuclear domain but a steeper fall is observed in the postnuclear domain which was labeled as late fall. These are illustrated in Figure 28, 29 and 30.

The distribution of these patterns across focus conditions has revealed the graph illustrated below.

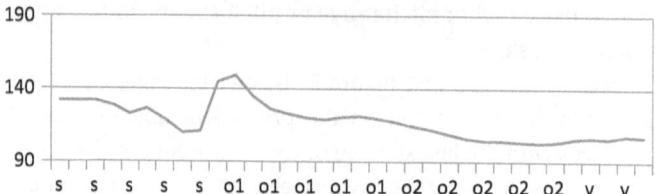

Figure 28: Early fall, speaker CT, GCG condition.

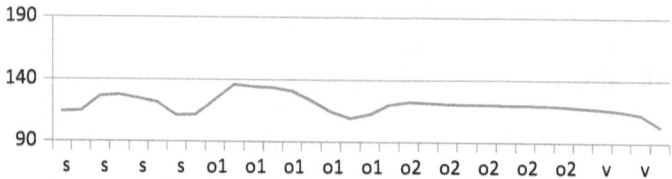

Figure 29: Late fall, speaker ÜE, GNG condition.

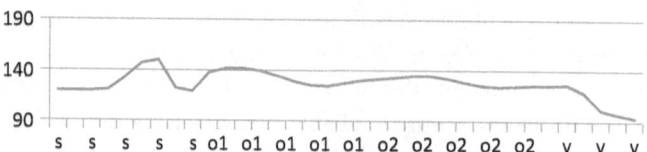

Figure 30: Late fall speaker ÜE, broad focus condition.

As shown in Figure 31, a late fall pattern is mostly observed with a broad focus condition. Early fall immediately after the accented syllable is mostly observed with a GCG condition, with a GNG condition being the second one. Hence, it is suggested that narrow focus has a tendency towards the early fall pattern.

Note that in Figure 26, for the maximum value at the final syllable of the object and the minimum value at the first syllable of the verb, a broad focus condition has the highest value. At the final syllable of the object all the focus conditions tend to group together but diverge at the measurement point at the beginning of the verb indicated as L-verb in Figure 26. This distinction can be due to the early fall pattern after the accented syllable with the narrow focus conditions which is carried over to the beginning of the verb.

An alternative analysis is that the difference in the final domain is due to the information structural status of the constituents in the final domain. In broad focus conditions, a discourse-new constituent occupies the postnuclear

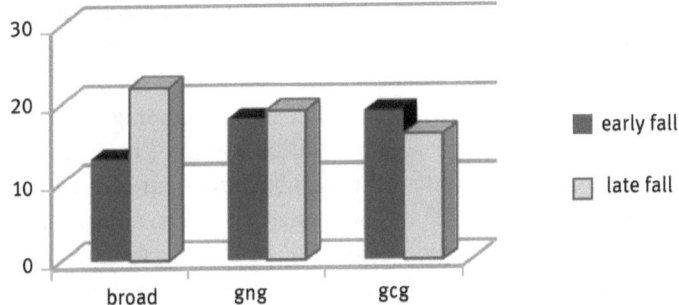

Figure 31: Fall pattern after the accented syllable of the focus phrase in 3 focus conditions.

domain. However, given constituents, occupy the postnuclear domain in narrow focus conditions and hence the constituent in the postnuclear domain of broad focus condition has higher values. In line with the destress given rule (Féry and Samek-Lodovici 2006) according to which a given phrase is prosodically non-prominent, discourse-given constituents are expected to have lower values than discourse-new constituents.

The early fall pattern can be due to the given status of the constituents in the postnuclear domain. The same distinction is also observed in the initial domain in that in narrow focus conditions, given constituents surface in the prenuclear domain while discourse-new constituents surface in this position in broad focus conditions. However, the measurement points in this domain for the broad focus condition group together with the measurement points of the narrow focus conditions as illustrated in Figure 26. Additionally, statistically there is no significant difference between the focus conditions which poses a challenge for the analysis suggesting that different fall patterns are due to the different information structural status of the sentence final constituents in broad focus and narrow focus conditions.

However, one can still argue that the difference between the given constituents in the prenuclear and postnuclear domain can be due to being at the beginning or at the end of the utterance. At the beginning of the utterance, the speaker starts with a higher level of energy. Although in broad focus condition there is a discourse-new constituent in the initial domain and in narrow focus condition there is a given constituent, the higher level of energy at the beginning of the sentence may reduce the difference in this domain. Hence, the given or discourse-new distinction observed at the end of the utterance can be missing in the initial domain. However, as all focus conditions tend to group together at the measurement point of the highest value in the final syllable of the object and the difference is not statistically significant, it is suggested that this distinction is only gradient.

The difference cannot be analyzed as post-focal compression when focus is in the immediate preverbal position and the difference can be due to discourse-given, discourse-new distinctions in the final domain.

Recall the focus prominence rule (Truckenbrodt 1995) according to which the highest prominence in the domain of focus will be within F. If discourse-new and contrastive focus phrases do not differ significantly from broad focus conditions, how is prominence realized? It is suggested that focus phrases bear the highest prominence which is followed by a fall that, in some form, signals the prominence bearing constituent in the sentence. This is also the default strategy in broad focus condition hence; any difference between these two conditions when focus is on the immediate preverbal constituent will not be found. A post-focal compression strategy is reflected more clearly when focus is on the subject in that following the subject focus phrase, a low reference height is observed until the end of the utterance as illustrated in Figure 18. This discussion will be elaborated in section 3.5.8.

3.5.7 Interim summary

The experimental studies conducted in this chapter illustrate that in Turkish SOV order, when f0 height and duration are the comparison points: (i) broad focus, discourse-new and contrastive focus phrases do not differ significantly with respect to any of the measurement points in the prenuclear, nuclear and postnuclear domains which is in clear contrast with English (Katz and Selkirk 2011) and Hungarian (Genzel, Ishihara and Surányi 2014); (ii) discourse-new and contrastive focus phrases do not differ significantly with respect to any of the measurement points in contrast to English (Katz and Selkirk 2011); and (iii) it cannot safely be concluded that there is a post-focal compression difference between broad focus and narrow focus conditions when the immediately preverbal constituent bears focus. The latter difference can also be due to the different information structural status of the constituent in the final domain. The next section discusses the reflections on these findings for syntax-prosody interaction.

3.5.8 Discussion

In this section, how focus is marked in the grammar will be investigated; specifically the mechanism that maps syntax onto prosody will be discussed. First, the theoretical discussion in section 3.5.8.1 will be reviewed, followed by a discussion of facts relating to Turkish in 3.5.8.2.

3.5.8.1 How focus affects prosody

The Italian data in section 3.2 has shown that some phonological rules make reference to syntactic constituency which indicates the presence of an intermediary prosodic level. At this level, the syntactic hierarchy from head to clause level is mapped onto a prosodic hierarchy (Pierrehumbert 1980; Inkelas 1989; Truckenbrodt 1995; Kabagema-Bilan, López-Jiménez, Truckenbrodt 2011).

The question raised at this point is how F marking is reflected between syntax and phonetics. There are two lines of analyses. According to the direct reference hypothesis F(ocus) and G(ivenness) features have a direct effect on the phonetic realization which is encoded in the grammar (Kaisse 1985; Odden 1995). According to the indirect effect hypothesis (Inkelas 1989), elaborated as the extended indirect reference hypothesis in Kabagema-Bilan et al. (2011), F and G features are syntactic features and they cannot have direct phonetic effects. The phonetic effects of F and G are mediated through the intermediary prosodic level as illustrated below.[58]

(159)

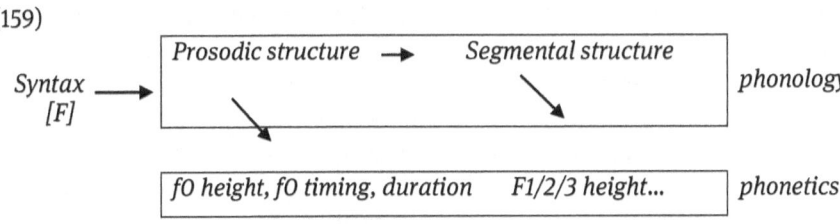

(Kabagema-Bilan et al., 2011: 1891)

Kabagema-Bilan et al. (2011) provide empirical support for the indirect reference hypothesis based on double focus constructions in Mandarin Chinese. Their arguments will be briefly reviewed here. Based on an experimental study on the prosodic properties of single focus phrases in Mandarin Chinese, Xu (1999) suggests that focus is realized as focal boost and post-focal compression. As illustrated in Figure 32, when the sentence initial subject is focused, there is a bump with the focused subject followed by compression.

Kabagema-Bilan et al. (2011) on the other hand suggest that F marking in syntax cannot be directly connected to phonetics; instead, an F feature attracts

---

[58] If these features are not assumed to be marked at syntax, phonological and phonetic rules cannot be explained. If languages had designated positions for each information structural unit and there were direct mappings between syntactic hierarchies and prosodic hierarchies, these features would be redundant. However, in most of the languages, including Turkish, the surface ordering of information structural units shows variation and there is not a direct map between syntactic and prosodic domains.

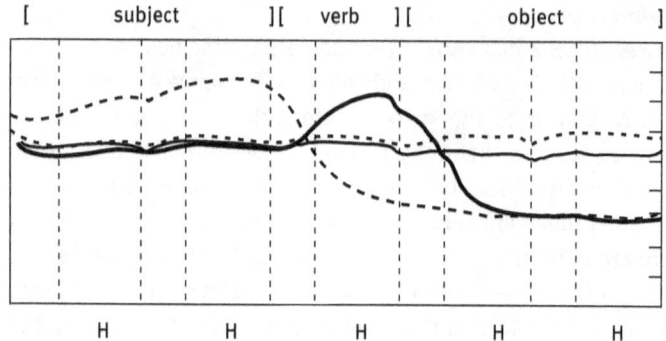

Figure 32: No narrow focus (thin sold line), narrow focus on the subject (thick dotted line), narrow focus on the verb (thick solid line), and narrow focus on the object (thin dotted line). (Xu 1999: 64).

stress and the stress raises the tonal height. Truckenbrodt (2013b) suggests that syntactic F and G features have an effect on the grid-marks in the prosody as grid mark attraction or rejection which is reflected as tonal height in the phonetics. According to the extended indirect reference hypothesis (Kabagema-Bilan et al., 2011: 1893) "each F marked constituent must carry stress at the level of the phonological phrase and each domain of focus must carry stress at the level of the intonation phrase on some F marked constituent"[59] The prediction of these rules

---

[59] Jackendoff (1972: 237) suggests that "if a phrase P is chosen as the focus of a sentence S, the highest stress in S will be on the syllable of P that is assigned highest stress by the regular stress rules." Truckenbrodt (1995: 161–162) indicates that the domain of focus is not necessarily the clause or the sentence. This is indicated with the contrast in the following examples. In (2), the domain of focus maps onto the whole clause while in (1), it does not.

$$\begin{array}{ccc} & & x \\ x & x & x \end{array}$$
(1) [[John's]$_F$ sister]$_{DF}$ and [[Bill's]$_F$ sister]$_{DF}$ get along well

(2) Who gets along well?
$$\begin{array}{cc} & x \\ x & x \end{array}$$
[[John and Bill]$_F$ get along well]$_{DF}$

Truckenbrodt (1995) further notes that scope domain of focus in phonology is the same as the domain of focus in semantics. In this study, what is taken as scope domain of focus is the domain at which background is encoded in line with Rooth (1985, 1996), which generally maps onto a sentence.

is that if there are multiple foci in the structure, the phonetic effects of F marking in the grammar can only be observed on one of the focus phrases as intonational phrase level prominence is assigned to only one constituent in the intonational phrase. The direct reference hypothesis on the other hand predicts the phonetic effects of F marking in syntax to be realized on both focus phrases as the tonal height is not mediated through prosody. Kabagema-Bilan et al. (2011) test the predictions of the rules based on multiple foci constructions in Mandarin Chinese. In the following example, both the subject and the modifier bear focus. If the assumptions of the extended indirect reference hypothesis are correct, intonational phrase level prominence will only be realized on one of the focus phrases. If not, as indicated by the direct reference hypothesis, syntax has a direct effect on phonetics and both will attract stress.

(160)   intonation phrase level stress
                x   x   phonological phrase level stress
        [Subject]$_F$ verb [[modifier]$_F$ noun]$_{object}$

Now, consider the plot below showing the results for the sentence, the order of which is given above. In conditions of multiple focus on the subject and the modifier indicated as (F-SU-M-q) and (F-SU-M-c), the focused subject and the modifier are triggered by wh-questions (q) and by corrective statements (c) respectively. In these conditions, only the rightmost focus phrase, the modifier, shows focal raising and post-focal lowering and not the subject. This is similar to the condition in which only the modifier is focused (F-M).

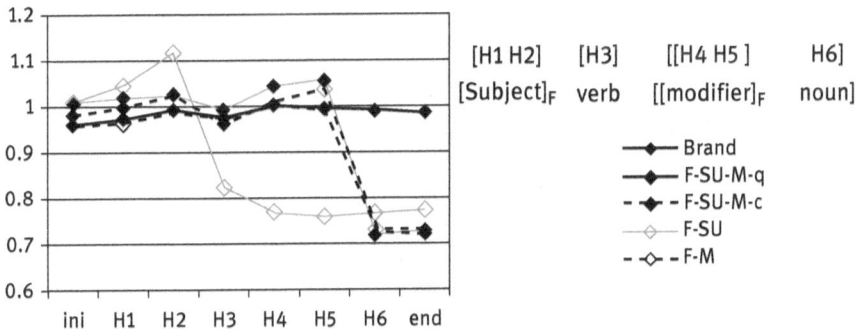

Figure 33: Rightmost focus attracts IP level stress. (Kabagema-Bilan et al., 2011: 1898).

The findings of this study provide clear evidence for the extended indirect reference hypothesis. A focus phrase attracts intonation phrase stress and this stress cannot be carried by two foci. It is the rightmost focus phrase that wins and takes intonation phrase level stress.⁶⁰

Another study that provides experimental evidence for the indirect reference hypothesis with a different perspective is that conducted by Katz and Selkirk (2011), the details of which were discussed in section 3.1. Remember that Katz and Selkirk (2011) establish that contrastive focus constituents are more prominent than discourse-new constituents with respect to pitch range, duration and intensity based on which they suggest that contrastive focus and discourse-new constituents are marked distinctively in the grammar. In this section, how they account for these findings will be considered.

Katz and Selkirk (2011) suggest that discourse-new constituents bear only default prosodic prominence at phonological phrase level as is the case in all-new sentences. Only contrastive focus phrases bear prosodic prominence at intonation phrase level as illustrated in (161–163).

(161) Foc-new

```
(                    x                              )  IP
(                    x        ) (    x              )  PPh
  (x)   (x)   ( x        )        ( x               )  PWd
  [He   even  took [Minnie]_Foc  to a [Mariners game ] ]
   H*    H*    L-              H*              L-
```

---

60 Güneş (2013) suggests a similar argument for Turkish. She argues that in Turkish double focus constructions it is only the rightmost one that reveals the properties of the nucleus and bears IP level stress. Güneş (2013) bases her arguments on the following example.

A: To whom did Emre give what?

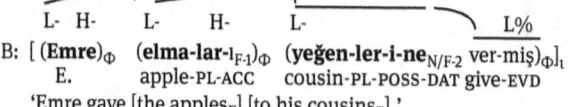

B: [((**Emre**)_Φ   (**elma-lar**-ı_F-1)_Φ   (**yeğen-ler-i-ne**_N/F-2 ver-miş)_Φ]_ı
  E.   apple-PL-ACC   cousin-PL-POSS-DAT give-EVD
'Emre gave [the apples_F] [to his cousins_F].'

(Güneş 2013: 39)

As discussed in the previous chapter, the answers of pair list questions are taken as partial answers. Hence, in the answer above, the accusative marked object is the contrastive topic phrase while the dative marked constituent is the focus phrase. As the structure is not a double focus construction, this data will not be taken as evidence for the extended indirect reference hypothesis for Turkish. One can still argue in line with Wagner (2007, 2008) that contrastive topic phrases are in fact focus phrases and in the representation above it is the rightmost focus phrase that receives the IP stress. However, recall that in Turkish while contrastive topic phrases can occur in the postverbal domain, focus phrases cannot and this indicates that they are not the same.

(162) New-Foc
```
    (                         x              )   IP
    (          x     )  (     x              )   PPh
      (x) (x)  ( x    )      ( x             )   PWd
     [He even took [Minnie] to a [Mariners game ] Foc]
       H*   H*    L-       H*              L-
```

(163) New-New
```
    (                                  )   IP
    (          x     )  (     x        )   PPh
      (   ) ( x    )        ( x        )   PWd
     [He   took  [Minnie] to a [Mariners game ]]
                 H*   L-     H*           L-
```
(Katz and Selkirk 2011: 796)

Katz and Selkirk (2011: 797) suggest that contrastive focus is marked with F in the grammar but discourse-new constituents are not and hence "(...) the phonological representation of discourse-new constituents is a matter of default phonology (...)" as is the case in broad focus constructions. They take phonological phrase level prominence as a requirement of a phonological phrase to be prosodically headed. Based on the discussion on Mandarin Chinese (Kabagema Bilan et.al. 2011) and English (Katz and Selkirk 2011), in this study the extended indirect reference hypothesis is adopted, according to which the phonetic effects of focus phrases are mediated by prosody.[61] The next section is a discussion of the facts relating to Turkish.

3.5.8.2 Focus marking and prosody interaction in Turkish
The syntax-prosody interface model given in (159) assumes an indirect relation between syntax and phonetics mediated through prosody. The focus prominence

---

[61] A similar analysis is proposed for German all-new sentences. In their experimental study on German given, new and focus phrases, Féry and Kügler (2008) find out downstep and upstep patterns for the all-new sentences. There is either downstep and each tone is lower than a preceding one, or there is upstep on the preverbal argument or on the verb. In narrow focus condition, on the other hand, upstep is observed consistently. Truckenbrodt (2013b) explains this data by way of optional i-stress assignment in that, when rightmost strengthening does not apply and the rightmost phonological phrase does not project up to intonational phrase level and downstep is observed; when rightmost strengthening applies upstep is observed. When there is a narrow focus phrase on the other hand the rightmost strengthening applies and the F marked constituent receives intonational phrase level stress.

rule requires each F marked constituent to bear PPh level prominence and in the domain of focus it is the F marked constituent that attracts IP level prominence. When all these assumptions are put together, the following order is seen.

(164) Syntax   (F marking)
      ↓
      Prosody   (IP level prominence)
      ↓
      Phonetics (IP stress)

It is time to look at some Turkish data within these assumptions. In the representation in (164), the heads of the PPhs attract PPh level prominence as indicated by the grid marks. As there is no significant difference between the two focus types, as explained in section 3.5.4, the same F marking strategy for contrastive focus and discourse-new constituents is assumed. It is the F marked object phrase in the rightmost PPh that attracts the IP level prominence. This is reflected in phonetics as IP stress.

(165) (x   ) IP
      (x   ) (x   ) PPh
      (x   ) (x   ) (x   ) PWd
      [Alanyalı-lar   barbunya$_{Foc}$ yol-uyor-lar]
      people of Alanya-PL bean   pull-IMPF-3PL
      'The people of Alanya pull up the kidney beans.'

Let's assume that in broad focus condition default phonology applies and only PPh level prominence is assigned.

(166) (   ) IP
      (x   ) (x   ) PPh
      (x   ) (x   ) (x   ) PWd
      [Alanyalı-lar   barbunya yol-uyor-lar]
      people of Alanya-PL bean   pull-IMPF-3PL
      'The people of Alanya pull up the kidney beans.'

This line of argument predicts a phonetic difference to be found between the broad focus condition in (166), and narrow focus condition in (165). However, the experimental study has shown that there is no significant difference with regard to pitch height and duration between the focus conditions. In line with the focus prominence rules, the Turkish data clearly shows that, when the object is marked with an F feature in syntax, the focus phrase attracts IP level prominence which is reflected in the phonetics as IP stress. As for broad focus conditions, first the leftmost constituents in the PPhs attract PPh level prominence. Then the head of the rightmost PPh attracts IP level prominence which is realized as IP stress as in (167). Actually, IP stress on the preverbal constituent in broad focus conditions is a matter of default phonology in Turkish.

(167) (x   ) IP
      (x   )   (x   ) PPh
      (x   )   (x) (x   ) PWd
      [Alanyalı-lar   barbunya yol-uyor-lar]
      people of Alanya-PL bean   pull-IMPF-3PL
      'The people of Alanya pull up the kidney beans.'

In narrow focus conditions, an F marked constituent attracts the highest level of prominence which is realized as IP level stress. Hence, no difference is detected between narrow and broad focus conditions when focus is on the immediate preverbal constituent. The question raised at this point is what happens when focus is on the sentence initial constituent, as illustrated by the different pitch track in Figure 34 below.

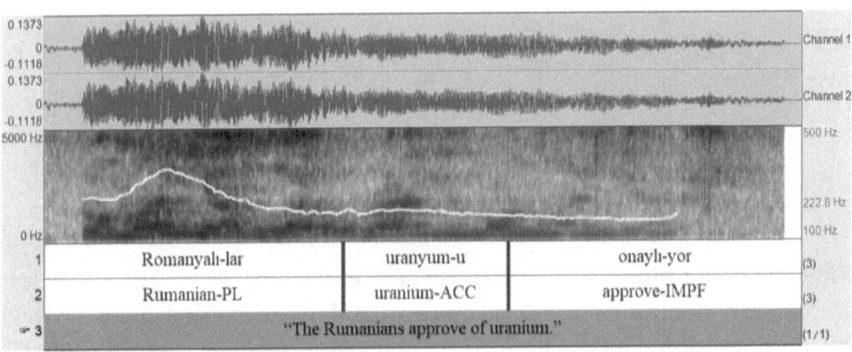

Figure 34: CGG condition, speaker ET.

According to the first hypothesis, the phonological phrasing pattern in (166) is also retained for this pattern in that the subject forms a separate PPh which carries IP level prominence while the object and the verb form another PPh. As the F marked constituent is expected to attract IP level prominence, the default phonology is overridden by the F rule and it is not the rightmost PPh that bears

IP stress but the PPh that includes an F marked constituent as illustrated in (168) below.

(168) (x   )   IP
      (x   ) (x   )   PPh
      (x   ) (x   ) (x   )   PWd
      [Romanyalı-lar]$_{Foc}$ [uranyum-u   onaylı-yor-lar]
      Rumanian-PL   uranium-ACC approve-IMPF-3PL
      'The Rumanians approve of uranium.'

Truckenbrodt (2013b) suggests a height subordination rule that also explains the Japanese post-focal compression that was discussed in section 3.2. According to this rule (Truckenbrodt 2013b: 9) "a grid mark on prosodic level L lowers and compresses the tonal space for following tones; the effect carries on until a tone associated to a higher prosodic level than L is reached." The grid mark attracted by a focused subject on the prosodic IP level lowers and compresses the tonal space for the following PPh level tones.

According to the second hypothesis, the default stress assignment rule on the rightmost PPh is not overridden by the focus assignment rule. The boundary tones following the initial domain are deleted at the PPh level. Hence, as there is only a single PPh, in the end the F marked subject gets IP level prominence.

(169) (x   )   IP
      (x   x   )   PPh
      (x   ) (x   ) (x   )   PWd
      [Romanyalı-lar]$_{Foc}$ [uranyum-u   onaylı-yor-lar]
      Rumanian-PL   uranium-ACC approve-IMPF-3PL
      'The Rumanians approve of uranium.'

The third option takes the directionality of head prominence for PPh and IP levels into account. Kan (2009) suggests that IP level displays a different head prominence pattern than PPh level. In PPh, the leftmost constituent attracts PPh level prominence. In IP, the rightmost PPh attracts IP level prominence. Note that, this is violated in (168) in that IP level prominence is on the leftmost PPh. The third option makes use of this directionality difference. According to the focus prominence rules, an F marked constituent bears PPh level prominence and attracts IP level prominence. Güneş (2013: 120) suggests that "all intonational phrases in Turkish display a nucleus" and that the "nucleus must be inside the (rightmost) narrow focus." In line with Güneş (2013), in the current study it is suggested that F marked constituents not only attract PPh level prominence but need to be within the rightmost PPh. Hence, the subject, the object and the verb form a single PPh. Then, the subject attracts IP level prominence as the head of the rightmost PPh as illustrated below.

(170) (x   )   IP
     (x   )   PPh
     (x   ) (x   ) (x   )   PWd
     [Romanyalı-lar]$_{Foc}$ [uranyum-u   onaylı-yor-lar]
     Rumanian-PL   uranium-ACC approve-IMPF-3PL
     'The Rumanians approve of uranium.'

From the three options, the third one is chosen because it takes head directionality of Turkish into account and does not create a look back problem to delete the already existing phrase boundaries as in (169). The height of the pitch accent or the duration of the F marked subject were not measured or compared with the F marked object in SOV order and hence at this point it is not known whether they are marked with different phonetic properties. However, the representation in (170) suggests that in Turkish, focus is marked phonologically and requires its right edge to be aligned as the rightmost PPh even when it is the leftmost prosodic word in the structure. As indicated in the previous chapter, some speakers do not accept in-situ focus phrases as in (170). The reason behind this variation can be due to this exceptional phonological phrasing option. The prosodic heaviness of the phonological phrase with three prosodic words may yield unacceptability with these speakers. These speakers prefer dislocation of the object phrase which naturally allows the dislocated object phrase to form an independent PPh. The [F] marked subject and the verb forms another PPh. The subject will be the head of the rightmost PPh then without resulting in a heavy phrasing.

Now, the pitch tracks in which focus surfaces on the verb as discussed in section 3.4.4 will be considered and repeated below for ease of exposition. Remember that the non-final domains show the prosodic properties of the prenuclear domain in that at the right edge of these domains H- boundary tones surface.

Now, the syntax-phonology interface for this structure can be examined.

(171) (x   )   IP
     (x   ) (x   ) (x   )   PPh
     (x   ) (x   ) (x   )   PWd
     Romanyalı-lar   [uranyum-u   [onaylı-yor-lar]$_{Foc}$
     Rumanian-PL   uranium-ACC approve-IMPF-3PL
     'The Rumanians approve of uranium.'

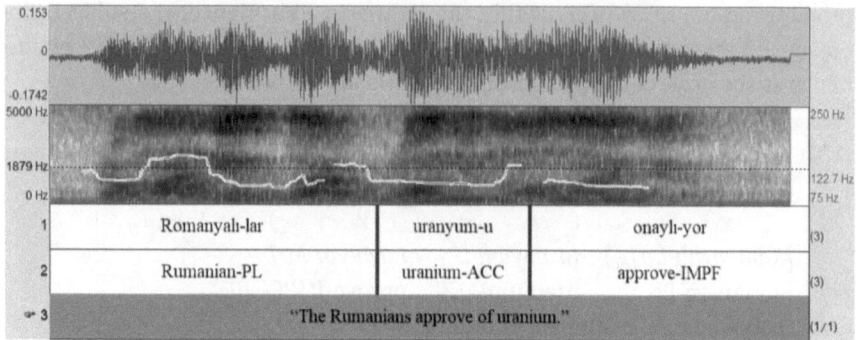

Figure 35: Pitch track of a structure with focus on the verb, speaker ST.

In line with the assumptions of the focus prominence rule, the verb which bears F marking attracts PPh level prominence. It is proposed that it forms an independent PPh as the rightmost PPh. Finally, the F marked verb bears IP level prominence reflected as IP stress. The H- boundary tone at the right edge of non-final domains is also captured with this analysis. Being independent PPhs, their right edge is marked with a H- boundary tone.

Based on this data and the results, it is suggested that in Turkish sentential stress and focus stress are not in fact distinct operations in the sense that they have the same phonetic correlates. Sentential stress refers to IP level stress and focus prominence is realized as IP level stress. That is why in Turkish when focus is on the preverbal object, there is no significant difference between broad focus and narrow focus conditions with regard to f0 height and duration.[62] Based on

---

[62] Kan (2009) shows that taking sentence stress as 'clause' stress is problematic as the domain that assigned IP level stress does not always map onto a 'clause' as illustrated below. The first IP cannot be taken as a clause but it receives IP level stress.

(1) [[Alanyalı-lar]$_{PPh}$ [ki genelde muz yetiştir-ir-ler]$_{PPh}$]$_{IP}$
     people of Alanya-PL COMP generally banana grow-AOR-3PL

   [[mango-yu deni-yo-lar-mış]$_{PPh}$]$_{IP}$
   mango-ACC try-PROG-3PL-EVID

   'The people of Alanya, who generally grow bananas, are trying (growing) bananas now.'

With some embedded clauses on the other hand, the embedded clause does not get IP level stress as in (2).

(2) [[Leman]$_{PPh}$ [sen]$_{PPh}$ [uyu-du-n san-mış]$_{PPh}$]$_{IP}$
     Leman you fall asleep-PAST-2SG think-EVID
     'Leman thought (that) you fell asleep.'
     (Kan 2009: 99, 101)

its position in the sentence, focus attracts IP level stress by way of grid marks in the prosody.⁶³

3.6 Phase driven sentential stress and focal stress

Üntak-Tarhan (2006) explains sentential stress assignment in Turkish taking complement domains of *v*P and CP phases as stress domains. She incorporates the discourse anaphora rule of Neeleman and Reinhart (1998) with the sentential stress rule (SSR) of Kahnemuyipour (2004). According to the discourse anaphora rule (Neeleman and Reinhart 1998: 338) "a DP is stressed if and only if it is D-linked to an accessible discourse entity". According to the sentential stress rule (Kahnemuyipour 2004), sentential stress is assigned to the highest element in the spell out (or stress domain).

Both of these rules operate in tandem at PF. First sentential stress rule applies and the highest constituent in the first stress domain is assigned sentential stress. If this constituent is given, namely, if it bears a D-linked feature then the stress domain is narrowed down and another constituent bears sentential stress. Now, consider the stress assignment for the following sentence. The underlined constituent is the non-D-linked one in the sentence.

(172) A: *Neden yemek ye-mi-yor-uz?*
    why   food   eat-NEG-PROG-1PL
    'Why aren't we eating any food?'
 B: *Çünkü, Ayşe yemeğ-i   yak-mış.*
    because Ayşe food-ACC burn-EVID
    'Because Ayşe burnt the food.'
    (Üntak-Tarhan 2006: 90)

As illustrated in the tree structure in (173), sentential stress rule applies to the stress domain which maps onto the complement domain of the *v*P phase.

---

63 A bottom-up approach for IP stress is assumed, namely, the prominent syllable of the leftmost prosodic word receives PPh level stress and the rightmost PPh is marked with IP level stress. A top-to-bottom analysis could also be assumed, namely, it is suggested that the F marked constituent receives IP level prominence and forms the rightmost PPh putting a boundary to its left edge. As both approaches can capture the data, the mainstream, bottom-up approach is maintained in this study.

(173)

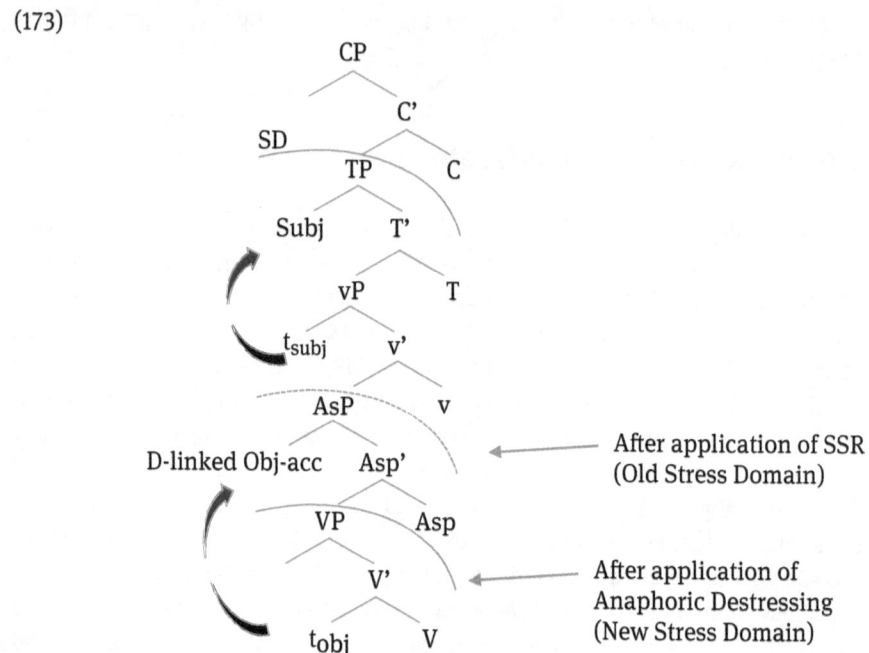

(Üntak-Tarhan 2006: 151)

The highest constituent in this domain is the object phrase; however, it is D-linked. The discourse anaphora rule makes sentential stress assignment impossible and hence the stress domain is narrowed down and the next highest constituent in the stress domain is assigned sentential stress. Note that it is the verb in this example and it receives sentential stress. The subject moves to Spec TP, which is part of the second stress domain, it also receives stress but the prominence on the higher stress domain is not as high as the prominence on the lower stress domain.

For sentential stress assignment in the presence of a focus phrase, Üntak-Tarhan (2006: 208) suggests that "at the phase HP, mark a focussed subconstituent C to receive focus stress. At PF, the constituent marked for focus stress receives the highest prominence of the sentence." Now, the stress assignment within the assumptions of focus stress rule can be seen.

(174) A: Ali musluğ-u değiştir-iyor mu?
       Ali tap-ACC change-PROG QP
       'Is Ali changing the tap?'

3.6 Phase driven sentential stress and focal stress — 133

B: *Hayır, (Ali) (musluğ-u) [vonar-ıyor]$_F$*
No   Ali   tap-ACC   repair-PROG
'Ali is repairing the tap.'
(Üntak-Tarhan 2006: 208)

In line with the sentential stress rule, in the lower stress domain, the object is expected to bear sentential stress. However, as the verb is marked as a focused constituent, at PF the verb receives the stress.

First of all, the sentential stress rule, the discourse anaphora rule and the focus stress rule of Üntak-Tarhan (2006: 208) result in redundancy in the system as already observed with the derivations of (172) and (174). In (172), the verb receives sentential stress due to the discourse anaphora generalization rule. In (174), the sentential stress rule is predicted to assign stress to the object but the verb bears sentential stress due to the focus stress rule.

In the current analysis, a single F marking can account for both of the derivations as discussed in the previous section. It is not the position of the F marked constituent in the complement domain of the phase that determines stress rule assignment. The F marked constituent, be it the object or the verb, receives IP level prominence and IP stress. Within this analysis, there is no separate rule for default IP stress assignment, F marking and G marking. The IP level prominence is always assigned to the rightmost phonological phrase.

The other question raised at this point is: Do we need phase domains to account for stress assignment in Turkish? Within the phase-based analysis, it is assumed that the subject moves to Spec TP and the object which is the highest constituent of the *v*P phase receives sentential stress. As illustrated in the previous section, in an all-new sentence default phonology already assigns IP level stress to the object. The subject forms an independent phonological phrase and as each phonological phrase must be headed, it receives phonological phrase level stress. The object and the verb form a single phonological phrase and the leftmost constituent receives phonological phrase level stress. Finally, IP stress is assigned to the head of the rightmost phonological phrase and hence it is realized on the object. This analysis also reaches the same conclusion without appealing to phase domains.

Now, a new set of data that will lead to the correct analysis will be reviewed. Üntak-Tarhan (2006) investigates stress pattern of unaccusatives, passives and unergatives. She does not take unaccusatives and passives as phases but only unergatives in line with Chomsky (2000). Üntak-Tarhan (2006) goes over stress patterns of these structures and argues that these structures provide empirical evidence for the phase based analysis of stress assignment. Üntak-Tarhan (2006) notes that with unaccusatives and passives it is only the argument of the verb that bears stress as in (175) and (176), with unergatives it is the verb that bears stress as in (177).

(175) A: Çok mutlu görün-üyor-sun. Ne ol-du?
very happy look-PROG-2SG what happen-PAST
'You look very happy. What happened?'
B: <u>Ali</u> gel-di.
Ali come-PAST
'Ali came.'

(176) A: Çok üzgün görün-üyor-sun. Ne ol-du?
very sad look-PROG-2SG what happen-PAST
'You look very sad. What happened?'
B: <u>Cüzdan-ım</u> çal-ın-dı.
wallet-1SG.POSS steal-PASS-PAST
'My wallet was stolen.'

(177) A: Sabah ne ol-du?
morning what happen-PAST
'What happened in the morning?'
B: Ali <u>koş-tu</u>.
Ali run-PAST
'Ali ran.'
(Üntak-Tarhan 2006: 49–53)

The derivations of these two different stress patters are given in the following way. In (178), with unaccusatives and passives the lower *v*P is not a phase. Following the movement of the single argument to Spec TP, sentential stress is assigned to this constituent in the higher stress domain, namely in the higher phase domain. In (179), on the other hand, the lower *v*P is a phase. Following the movement of the subject to Spec TP, sentential stress is assigned to the verb in the lower *v*P phase via sentential stress rule.

(178) (179)

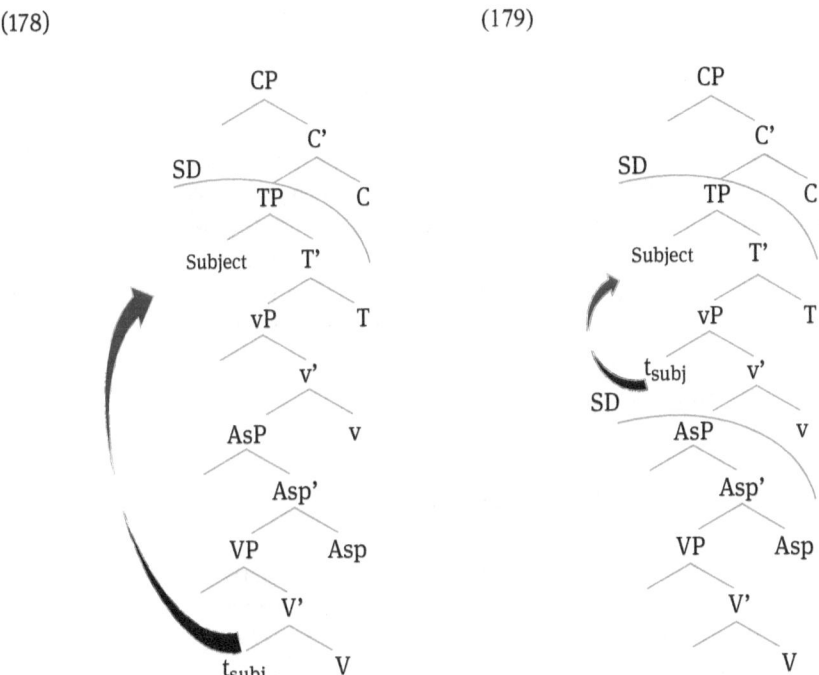

(Üntak-Tarhan 2006: 55–56)

However, this analysis of stress assignment based on phases runs into problems when the findings of further studies on the prosody of Turkish are taken into account. Kan (2009) investigates the prosodic properties of unaccusatives and unergatives and finds that in nearly all cases with unaccusatives, single phrasing is induced namely the argument and the verb forms a single phonological phrase. The IP level stress is realized on the argument. This is in line with the derivation in (178). This is also in line with the current analysis in that within a single phonological phrase, the prominence is realized on the leftmost constituent which in turn also bears IP level stress.

Kan (2009) further notes that with unergatives, nearly half of the data induces multiple phrasing in which both the argument and the verb receive phonological phrase level stress and the verb bears IP level stress, being the rightmost phonological phrase. This is also within the predictions of the derivation in (179). However, in the other half of the data, single phrasing is observed and both the argument and the verb surface in the same phonological phrase. In contrast to the derivation in (179), it is the argument not the verb that bears stress in this case. The derivation in (179) cannot predict this stress pattern. The lower stress domain is not defective and hence there is no need to move up to the higher phase for stress assignment as is the case with unaccusatives. Additionally, the structures triggered in the study of Kan (2009) are focus neutral and hence focus stress rule cannot apply either.

Within the current analysis on the other hand, although optional phrasing is not captured, the IP level stress assignment is captured. When the argument and the verb form independent phonological phrases, the rightmost phonological phrase is expected to bear IP level stress. When there is a single phrasing on the other hand, it is the leftmost constituent in the rightmost phonological phrase that attracts IP level stress. Hence, a phase-based account for sentential stress assignment will not be pursued in this study as it falls short of capturing the data in Turkish.

3.7 One-word level propositions

Göksel (2010) notes that utterances in Turkish can surface as one-word-level propositional utterances (180) or sentence-level utterances (181). In one-word propositions, when the suffix that immediately precedes the copula bears prominence, the proposition is interpreted as presentational or contrastive focus as in (180a). When it is not the immediate pre-copula suffix that bears prominence, the proposition is interpreted as contrastive focus. Göksel (2010) suggests that this is also the case with sentence-level utterances in that only when a constituent that is not immediately preverbal bears prominence, it is interpreted as contrastive focus as in (180b).[64]

(180)   L-   H*L   L%
   a. *gid- ecek- ler- Ø- di.*
      go   FUT 3PL COP PAST
      'They were going to go.'
      'They WERE going to go.'
      L- H*L   L%
   b. *gid- ecek- ler- Ø- di.*

---

[64] Recall from the previous chapter that discourse-new constituents can also appear in the sentence initial position followed by discourse anaphoric constituents as long as it is explicitly marked in the structure as additional information.

3.7 One-word level propositions — 137

(181)   L-   H*L   L%
   a. *Semra-lar*   *dün*   *Ankara-ya*   *gid-ecek-ler- Ø-di*
     Semra-family   yesterday   Ankara-DAT   go-FUT-3PL-COP-PAST
     'Semras were going to Ankara yesterday.'
   L-   H*L   L%
   b. *Semra-lar*   *dün*   *Ankara-ya*   *gid-ecek-ler- Ø-di*
     (adapted from Göksel 2010: 105)

The other similarity is that focus can only appear in the pre-copula domain. In this section, how one-word utterances can be represented within the assumed model will be illustrated.

In (182), at the prosodic word level, it is the agreement marker that bears prominence. At the PPh level, the prominence is anchored to the prominent syllable of the leftmost constituent. As illustrated in (182), the proposition is a single word; hence, the same syllable bears PPh level prominence and IP level prominence.

(182)   (x   ) IP
       (x   ) PPh
       (x   ) PWd
     gid-   *ecek-*   *ler$_{Foc}$-*   *Ø-*   *di*
     go   FUT   3PL   COP   PAST
     'They were going to go.'

Now, consider the following representation. Similar to (182), at the prosodic word level, the F marked affix bears prominence. At the PPh level, the prominence is anchored to the prominent syllable of the leftmost constituent. The proposition is a single word; and again the same syllable bears PPh level prominence and IP level prominence.

(183)   (x   ) IP
       (x   ) PPh
       (x   ) PWd
     gid-   *ecek$_{Foc}$-*   *ler-*   *Ø-*   *di*
     go   FUT   3PL   COP   PAST
     'They were going to go.'

The other option is to assume that one word level propositions compose a domain including the stressed affix (underlined affixes) and the remaining affixes form another domain.[65] This line of argument is pursued in Kabak and Vogel (2001) and they call the non-stress bearing affixes prosodic word adjoiners (PWA).

(184) a. [sev- il- di- niz]_PW
      love- PASS- PAST- 2PL
      'You were loved.'
  b. [[sev- il]_PW- me_(PWA)- di- niz]
      love- PASS- NEG- PAST- 2PL
      'You were not loved.'
      (Kabak and Vogel 2001: 327)

Based on the parallelism between one-word propositions and sentence level utterances, it is suggested that the non-stress bearing affixes belong to the same domain as the F marked affix. Recall that the verb in a broad focus sentence does not bear PPh level stress but it is still in the same domain with the object which does bear PPh and IP level prominence. In a sense, the stray affixes surface in the same PPh with the F marked affix and hence the F marked phrase is the rightmost PPh.

3.8 Conclusion

In this chapter, the prosodic realization of contrastive focus, discourse-new and broad focus constructions in Turkish have been investigated based on f0 and duration measurements. It was found that: (i) in contrast to previous analyses which suggest a distinctive prosodic marking for focus phrases in Turkish (Özge and Bozşahin 2010) or distinctive marking strategies for discourse-new and contrastive focus phrases (İşsever 2003), the statistical analysis has shown that there is no significant difference between the three focus conditions with regard to f0 or duration at any of the measurement points in the prenuclear, nuclear and postnuclear domains; (ii) the lack of a distinction between the three conditions is explained based on the focus prominence rule which requires focus phrases to bear PPh level prominence and attract IP level prominence within their domain of focus; (iii) the focus phrases in initial and final

---

65 See Güneş and Göksel (2016) for an alternative analysis on variable prominence on one-word level utterances.

domains have further shown that F marked constituents attract IP level stress; (iv) phase based stress assignment analysis of Üntak-Tarhan (2006) falls short of explaining the unergative structures when the findings of Kan (2009) on phrasing of unergatives are taken into account; and (v) the constituents that are F marked at syntax require IP level prominence in prosody and IP stress in phonetics whether the utterance is word or sentence level.

The next chapter discusses the syntactic marking of information structural units in Turkish.

Chapter 4
Syntactic marking of information structural units

4.1 Introduction

For the question of how information structuring is encoded in syntax, many different analyses have been put forth which form a continuum as to how discourse notions are encoded in syntax. Within the strong modularity hypothesis (Horvath 2005, 2010), information structural notions cannot be encoded in syntax and what is taken as focus movement is suggested to be exhaustive identificational operator movement which is quantificational in nature. On the other side of the continuum, within the cartographic approach (Rizzi 1997) information structural categories are represented as ordered functional projections in the left periphery. In Turkish linguistics literature, word order permutations have been observed to be related to discourse-pragmatics (Erguvanlı 1984; Kural 1992; Göksel 1998, 2013; Göksel and Özsoy 2000; İşsever 2003; Şener 2010; to cite a few). Şener (2010) takes this a further step and suggests that in Turkish, word order permutations are fully determined by discourse-pragmatic motives and proposes a phrase structure for Turkish in line with the cartographic approach.

The question addressed in this chapter is how information structure and syntax are related. The investigation builds on the interaction of information structural categories having regard to variable binding data, negation and quantifier scope. Whether information structural categories are encoded in syntax through formal features or whether the word order variations can be derived as quantificational operations taking place at the LF domain will be discussed (Bobaljik and Wurmbrand 2012; Neeleman and Van de Koot 2012). The central findings of the chapter show that: (i) IP internal FocP analysis not only captures the tendency of Turkish focus phrases to surface in the immediate preverbal position but also the interaction of focus with different aspectual markers and negation; (ii) the eventual domain in which external and internal arguments are base generated (Ramchand and Svenonius 2013), excluding the outmost specifier of vP, maps onto scope domain of focus but not to the complement domain of vP phase; (iii) contrastive topic, the semantic compositionality of which depends on focus, cannot reconstruct back to the scope domain of focus; (iv) in SOV order, semantically vacuous movement operations do not apply and aboutness topic and discourse anaphoric phrases remain in their first merge position as data on negation indicates; (v) focus does not have a direct effect on scope; in most of the cases, scope can be read off the surface order but inverse scope is possible in a few information structural orderings which are captured by intermediary reconstruction sites; and (vii) binding and scope data can be captured by way of information structural features to be checked, while LF based analysis falls short of explaining the whole data.

4.2 Left peripheral or IP internal functional projections

The cartographic approach (Rizzi 1997) is advantageous in explaining the movement operations triggered by information structuring as semantic/pragmatic notions are directly mapped onto syntactic structure by dedicated functional projections which are rigidly ordered, as illustrated below.

(185)

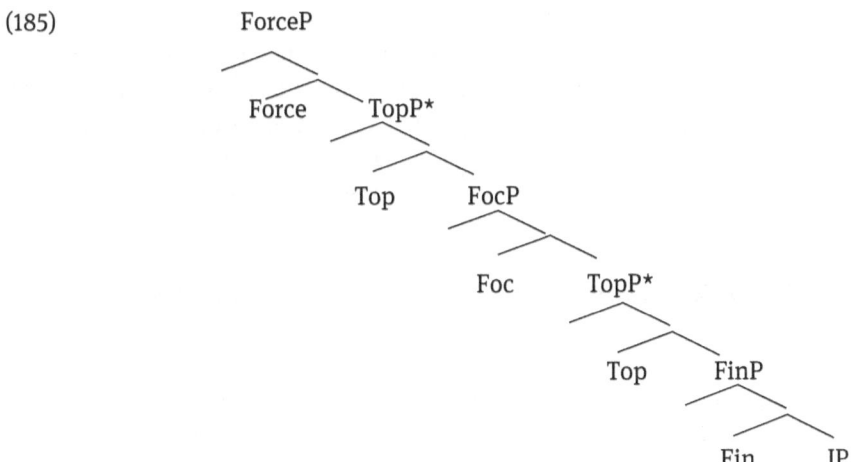

(Rizzi 1997: 297)

This influential study led to many other proposals for the functional projections at the left periphery. Recursive TopP projections have been replaced by peculiar TopP projections (Frascarelli and Hinterhölzl 2007; Neeleman and Vermeulen 2012).

Additionally, IP internal CP projections have been proposed for different languages such as Malayalam and English (Jayaseelan 2001), Italian (Belletti 2003), and Russian (Dyakonova 2009) to account for topic and focus constructions. Jayaseelan (2001) suggests that wh-phrases appear left adjacent to the verb in Malayalam due to the FocP projection above the verbal domain and extends this analysis to English gapping and cleft structures. In Russian, the verb moves to Asp and focus phrases appear to the right of the verb. Based on this property, Dyakonova (2009) proposes an IP internal focus and topic phrase above vP domain for Russian. The verb moves to AspP and the focus phrase moves to FocP above the vP projection. In addition to this lower FocP projection, there is a higher FocP projection in the left periphery. The higher FocP is occupied by D-linked focus phrases. The lower FocP is also motivated by the scope properties of quantifiers in Russian.

In Turkish, there is tendency for the focus phrases to appear in the preverbal position optionally followed by the movement of the constituents to the higher projections. From a theoretical perspective, assuming IP internal functional projections, instead of extra-sentential, left peripheral projections do not make a big difference to an analysis. However, in addition to capturing the reason behind the tendency of the focus phrase to appear in the preverbal position, IP internal focus and discourse anaphoric projections can also better explain the Turkish data from an empirical point of view. This point will be elaborated in sections 4.5 and 4.6 with a discussion of quantifier scope data and the interaction of focus with different aspectual markers respectively. IP internal focus projection can also explain the semantic difference between topic and focus phrases in that topic phrases are utterance level constituents while focus phrases are propositional level constituents. Hence, within this study it is proposed that FocP does not surface at the left periphery but above the vP domain in Turkish.

4.3 The interaction of information structural units with negation

The interaction of negation with information structural constituents is a fruitful testing ground for the phrase structure because the interaction of negation with quantifiers and indefinites yields coherent results. Kelepir (2001) suggests that accusative marked indefinites can have a wide scope over negation as in (186) but in a denial context the indefinite falls within the scope of negation as in (187).

(186) *Hasan iki kapı-yı cilala-ma-dı.*
Hasan two door-ACC polish-NEG-PAST
'Hasan didn't polish two doors.' (Hasan didn't polish two of the doors)

(187) A: *Hasan iki kapıyı cilalamış, sen hala oturuyorsun.*
'Hasan polished two of the doors, you are still sitting (here).'
B: *Hasan iki kapı-yı cilala-ma-dı*
Hasan two door-ACC polish-NEG-PAST
sadece bir kapıyı cilaladı.
'Hasan didn't polish two of the doors, (he) only polished one of the doors.'
(Kelepir 2001: 85–86)

4.3 The interaction of information structural units with negation

What is clear from the context given in (187) is that focus is on the verb which is indicated by the denial context explanation. In (186), on the other hand, focus is on the object. This becomes clearer when this sentence is placed in a context.

(188) A: *Hasan'a cilalaması için 5 tane kapı bırakmıştım. Sadece birini cilalamamış.*
'I had left Hasan 5 doors to be polished. He hasn't polished only one of them.'
B: *Yo, hayır. Hasan iki kapı-yı$_F$ cilala-ma-mış.*
No Hasan two door-ACC polish-NEG-PAST
'No, Hasan didn't polish two of the doors.'

In (188), the interpretation that there are two doors that Hasan did not polish is seen. In a sense, in both (187) and (188) there is a denial of the previous context. In (187), the proposition that Hasan polished two of the doors is denied; in (188) the proposition that Hasan did not polish one of the doors is denied. Öztürk (2005) also suggests that scope possibilities may change in the presence of negation, within the investigation of the position of subjects.

(189) a. [$_{TP}$ [$_{NEG}$ [$_{AgentP}$ *bütün çocuklar* [$_{ThemeP}$ *o test-e*   neg > all, *all > neg
                     all   children   that   test-DAT
[$_{VP}$ *gir-me-di*]]]
take-NEG-PAST
'All children did not take that test.'

                                                           all > neg, *neg > all
b. [$_{TP}$ *bütün çocuklar$_i$* [$_{NEG}$ [$_{AgentP}$ t_i [$_{ThemeP}$ *o test-e*
          all children   that   test-DAT
[$_{VP}$ *gir-me-di-ler*]]]
take-NEG-PAST
'All children did not take that test.'
(Öztürk 2005: 139)

Öztürk suggests that in (189a), the subject does not move up to Spec TP and the movement of V to the T head checks the EPP feature of the T head. Negation is above the subject. In (189b), on the other hand, the subject moves to Spec TP, which is also indicated by the overt agreement marker on the verb. The negation is below TP projection and the subject quantifier takes wide scope over negation.

The contrast in (186), (187) and (188) indicates that the scope possibilities depend on where focus is positioned. Now, consider the structures in (189a) and (189b) by placing them within a context that will force certain information structural interpretations for the constituents. Öztürk (2005) already gives a context for the structure in (189b) as in (191). A context is provided for (189a) in (190) below.

not > all

(190) A: *Dershanede yapılan teste yoğun bir ilgi vardı. Bütün çocuklar girmişler teste.*
'The test at the training center drew intense interest. All children took the test.'

B: *Yanlış   duy-muş-sun,   bütün   çocuk-lar   o   test-e*
wrong   hear-PERF-2SG   all   child-PL   that   test-DAT
[gir-me-di-ler]$_F$[66]
take-NEG-PERF-3PL
'You have misheard; all children did not take that test.'

all > not

(191) *O   test-e   [bütün   çocuklar]$_F$ gir-me-di,*
that   test-DAT   all   children   take-NEG-PAST
[bütün   büyükler]$_F$ gir-di[67]
all   adults   take-PAST
'It was not all the children who took the test, but it was all the adults.'
(Öztürk 2005: 178)

As the structures in (190) and (191) illustrate, the position of the focus has an effect on the interpretation. When the verb bears focus, negation takes wide scope, when the non-verbal constituents bear focus the focused constituent has wide scope. Note that the structures in (190) and (191) gave the same result as in (186), (187) and (188). Now, scope interaction of negation with information structural units will be tested. There are four sets of data: (i) universal quantifier with the focus phrase; (ii) universal quantifier with the contrastive topic;

---

[66] Öztürk (2005) takes overt agreement markers on the verb as an indication of V to T movement and gives a different interpretation. It is suggested that instead of the agreement markers it is the placement of focus, namely the information structural status of the constituents that makes a difference in the position of the subject.

[67] When this sentence is interpreted as "not….but" instead of a coordinated clause as in (191) in the text, interpretation of scope changes and negation takes scope over the universal quantifier. Thanks to Meltem Kelepir and Balkız Öztürk for pointing this out.

(iii) universal quantifier with the aboutness topic; and (iv) universal quantifier with the discourse anaphoric constituent. In all cases, the verb bears perfect marker *–mIş* and negation. The tricky issue with this test is that the scope interpretation in the preceding context can be easily transferred to the target sentence. In order to minimize this effect, short contexts were prepared to trigger the correct information structure in the target sentence and scope ambiguity was also retained in the preceding context.[68]

I. Focus phrase with the universal quantifier
In the first set, argument focus phrases surface with the universal quantifier. Although in (193) and (194) the same order of information structural units is used, in (193) the focus is on the restriction of the focus phrase while in (194) it is on the quantifier itself.

$\forall > \text{neg}$

(192) A: *Yetişkinlerin hepsi o sınava girmemişler.*
 'All the adults did not take that exam.'
 B: *Bütün yetişkin-ler değil, [bütün çocuk-lar]$_F$*
 all adult-PL not all child-PL
 [o sınav-a]$_{DA}$ [gir-me-miş-ler]$_{DA}$
 that exam-DAT take-NEG-PERF-3PL
 'It is not all the adults, all the children did not take that exam.'

$\forall > \text{neg}$

(193) A: *Dershanede yapılan yarışmaların hepsini boykot eden yetişkinler yarışmalara girmemişler.*
 'The adults who protested all the competitions at the training center did not enter the competitions.'
 B: *Valla, yetişkin-ler-i bil-mi-yor-um ama,*
 well adult-PL-ACC know-NEG-IMPF-1SG but
 [çocuk-lar]$_{CT}$ [bütün sınav-lar-a]$_F$ [gir-me-miş-ler]$_{DA}$
 child-PL all exam-PL-DAT take-NEG-PERF-3PL
 'Well, I do not know about the adults, but the children did not take all the exams.'

---

68 The judgments were checked with two other native speakers of Turkish.

∀> neg
(194) A: *Dershanede yapılan sınavları boykot eden yetişkinler bazı sınavlara girmemişler.*
'The adults who protested the exams at the training center did not take some of the exams.'

B: *Valla, yetişkin-ler-i   bil-mi-yor-um   ama,*
well   adult-PL-ACC   know-NEG-IMPF-1SG   but
[çocuk-lar]$_{CT}$ [bütün sınav-lar-a]$_F$ [gir-me-miş-ler]$_{DA}$
child-PL   all   exam-PL-DAT   take-NEG-PERF-3PL
'Well, I do not know about the adults, but the children did not take all the exams.'

II. Contrastive topic with the universal quantifier

In the second set, contrastive topic phrases surface with the universal quantifier. Remember that contrastive topics can be given only as partial answers and hence they cannot be used with quantifiers resisting partial interpretation (see section 2.3.2.2). That is why in (195–197), the contrast is placed not on the quantifier but on the restriction. Hence, in these structures, the topic under discussion is shifted and the group *bütün çocuklar* 'all the children' is contrasted with the group *bütün yetişkinler* 'all the adults'.

neg > ∀
(195) A: *Dershanede yapılan sınava bütün yetişkinler girmemişler galiba, değil mi?*
'All the adults did not take the exam done at the training center, did they?'

B: *Valla,   yetişkin-ler-i   bil-mi-yor-um   ama,*
well   adult-PL-ACC   know-NEG-IMPF-1SG   but
[bütün   çocuk-lar]$_{CT}$ [sınav-a]$_{DA}$ [gir-me-miş-ler]$_F$
all   child-PL   exam-DAT   take-NEG-PERF-3PL
'Well, I do not know about the adults, but all the children did not take the exam.'

∀ > neg
(196) A: *Dershanede yapılan yarışmaya yetişkinlerin hepsi girmemişler.*
'All the adults did not enter the competitions at the training center.'

B: *Valla,   yetişkin-ler-i   bil-mi-yor-um   ama,*
well   adult-PL-ACC   know-NEG-IMPF-1SG   but
[bütün   çocuk-lar]$_{CT}$ [sınav-a]$_F$ [gir-me-miş-ler]$_{DA}$
all   child-PL   exam-DAT   take-NEG-PERF-3PL
'Well, I do not know about the adults, but all the children did not take the exam.'

4.3 The interaction of information structural units with negation — 147

$\exists >$ neg

(197) A: *Annen partiye Fatih'in gelmesini istemediği için onu davet etmemiş.*
'Your mother has not invited Fatih to the party as she does not want him to come to the party.'

B: *Valla, Fatih-i   bil-mi-yor-um   ama,*
well   Fatih-ACC know-NEG-IMPF-1SG   but
[bir arkadaş-ım-ı]$_{CT}$ [kimse]$_F$ davet et-me-miş.
a   friend-1SG.POSS-ACC anybody invite-NEG-PERF
'Well, I don't know about Fatih, but no one has invited a friend of mine to the party.'

III. Aboutness Topic Phrases with the Universal Quantifier
In the third set, aboutness topic phrases occur in sentence initial position as the object in (198) or the subject of the sentence in (199) and (200).

$\forall >$ neg

(198) A: *Dershanedeki yetişkinler bütün sınavlara girmemişler.*
'The adults at the training center did not take all the exams.'

B: *[bütün sınav-lar-a]$_{AT}$ [çocuk-lar]$_F$ [gir-me-miş-ler]$_{DA}$,*
all   exam-PL-DAT   child-PL   take-NEG-PERF-3PL
yetişkin-ler değil
adult-PL   not
'It is the children, not the adults, that did not take all the exams.'

neg $> \forall$

(199) A: *Dershanedeki bütün yetişkinler yarışmalara katılmamışlar.*
'All the adults at the training center did not enter the competitions.'

B: *[Bütün yetişkin-ler]$_{AT}$ [sınav-lar-a]$_F$ [katıl-ma-mış]$_{DA}$,*
all   adult-PL   exam-PL-DAT   participate-NEG-PERF
yarışma-lar-a   değil.
competition-PL-DAT not
'It is the exams, not the competitions, that all the adults did not participate in.'

neg $> \forall$

(200) A: *Dershanede yapılan sınava bütün çocuklar girmişler.*
'All the children took the exam done at the training center.'

B: *Yoo, hayır, [bütün çocuk-lar]$_{AT}$ [sınav-a]$_{DA}$*
no   all   child-PL   exam-DAT

[gir-me-miş-ler]$_F$
   take-NEG-PERF-3PL
   'No, all the children did not take the exam.'

IV. Discourse anaphoric constituent with the universal quantifier
In the final set, discourse anaphoric constituents surface with the universal quantifier.

neg > ∀
(201) A: *Dershanede yapılan bütün sınavlara yetişkinler girmişler, yoğun bir katılım olmuş, değil mi?*
   'The adults took all the exams at the training center, there was a broad participation, wasn't there?'
   B: *Valla, yetişkin-ler-i   bil-mi-yor-um   ama,*
      well   adult-PL-ACC know-NEG-IMPF-1SG but
      [*çocuk-lar*]$_{CT}$ [*bütün sınav-lar-a*]$_{DA}$ [*gir-me-miş-ler*]$_F$
      child-PL   all   exam-PL-DAT take-NEG-PERF-3PL
      'Well, I don't know about the adults, but the children did not take all the exams.'

neg > ∀
(202) A: *Dershanedeki yetişkinler bütün sınavlara girmemişler.*
   'The adults at the training center did not take all the exams.'
   B: *Yetişkin-ler değil* [*çocuk-lar*]$_F$ [*bütün sınav-lar-a*]$_{DA}$
      adult-PL   not   child-PL   all   exam-PL-DAT
      [*gir-me-miş-ler*]$_{DA}$
      take-NEG-PERF-3PL
      'It is the children, not the adults, that did not take all the exams.'

neg > ∀
(203) A: *Çocuklar dershanede yapılan bütün sınavlara girmişler.*
   'The children took all the exams done at the training center.'
   B: *Yoo, hayır,*   [*çocuk-lar*]$_{AT}$ [*bütün   sınav-lar-a*]$_{DA}$
      No   child-PL   all   exam-PL-DAT
      [*gir-me-miş-ler*]$_F$
      take-NEG-PERF-3PL
      'No, the children did not take all the exams.'

Table 4 below illustrates the results for the four sets of data. The data, although limited, indicates that focus phrases take scope over negation in the absence or presence of contrastive topic phrases.

4.3 The interaction of information structural units with negation

Table 4: The Interaction of Negation with Information Structural Units.

		Focus	Contrastive topic	Aboutness topic	Discourse anaphoric
I	F_S-DA_O-DA_V	F>NEG			
	CT_S-F_O-DA_V	F>NEG			
II	CT_S-DA_O-F_V		NEG>CT		
	$CT_{S(universal)}$-F_O-DA_V		CT>NEG		
	$CT_{O(indefinite)}$-F_S-DA_V		CT>NEG		
III	AT_O-F_S-DA_V			AT>NEG	
	AT_S-F_O-DA_V			NEG>AT	
	AT_S-DA_O-F_V			NEG>AT	
IV	CT_S-DA_O-F_V				NEG>DA
	F_S-DA_O-DA_V				NEG>DA
	AT_S-DA_O-F_V				NEG>DA

A second point that the data shows is that contrastive topics, which cannot surface in the absence of focus phrases, can take scope above and below negation depending on the position of the focus phrase. If it is the verb that bears focus, negation takes scope over the contrastive topic. If focus is not on the verb, contrastive topic takes scope over negation. This is expected in the sense that in the absence of a contrastive topic phrase, focus phrases take negation under their scope, as contrastive topic constituents out-scope focus phrases, negation also surfaces under the scope of contrastive topics. As for aboutness topic phrases, when they are subject phrases or when the focus is on the verb they take narrow scope with respect to negation. Otherwise, they take scope over negation. Finally, with discourse anaphoric constituents, when they follow focus phrases or when the focus is on the verb, they take narrow scope with respect to negation. The findings can be summarized as follows:
(i) Focus takes scope over negation
(ii) If it is the verb that bears focus, negation takes scope over all constituents.
(iii) When focus is not on the verb, contrastive topic takes scope over negation, object aboutness topic takes scope over negation.
(iv) Discourse anaphoric constituents surface under the scope of negation.

Based on these findings and the discussion in the preceding section, the structure in (204a) below is proposed. FocP is generated IP internally above the *v*P projection. Only transitive sentences were tested in SOV order in which discourse anaphoric constituents always surface under the scope of negation. As the discussion in section 4.3 on quantifier scope in OSV order shows, a DaP above FocP is needed.

(204) (a) (b)

[Syntactic tree (a): CP → TP, C°; TP → DaP, T'; T' → Da', T°; Da' → FocP, Da°; FocP → vP, Foc°; vP → VP, v'; v' → V', v°; V' → V°.]

[Syntactic tree (b): CP → TP, C°; TP → Neg, TP; TP → DaP, T'; T' → Da', T°; Da' → FocP, Da°; FocP → vP, Foc°; vP → Neg, vP; vP → VP, v'; v' → V', v°; V' → V°.]

Contrastive topic phrases always take scope over negation but when the verb bears focus they surface under the scope of negation. However, contrastive topics cannot surface following focus phrases. Hence, it is assumed that at LF negation can project above vP and TP (or even in the CP projection) as illustrated in (204b). This is in line with the analysis of Kelepir (2001), who suggests that negation can project above the verbal domain or the TP domain.[69]

---

[69] Based on the interaction of indefinites and negative polarity items with negation, Kelepir (2001) argues that at LF, the negation operator in Turkish can adjoin to vP or TP (even above TP). In the constructions illustrated below in (1), adapted from Kelepir (2001), the indefinite without accusative marking in (1a) remains in its base generated position and it is under the scope of negation which adjoins to the vP domain. In (1b), the indefinite subject is at Spec TP and above the scope of negation which licences the NPI object in the vP domain. In (1c), the accusative marked indefinite is bound by the existential quantifier over choice functions but is under the scope of negation which is adjoined to the TP domain. In (1c), negation above the NPI subject at Spec TP satisfies the immediate scope constraint and the indefinite cannot take

As pointed out above, if it is the verb that bears focus, negation takes scope over all constituents. It is suggested that this is due to the presence of an assertion operator higher in the structure. When the verb bears focus, the truth value of the whole proposition is judged and the speaker emphasizes the truth value of the proposition, which is an instance of verum focus. However, in addition to the semantic content of the verb, the whole proposition is focused. Hence, it is suggested that when the focused verb bears negation, the whole clause is asserted not to be true and hence the whole clause is under the scope of negation including the contrastive topic.[70]

Finally, in SOV order, the subject aboutness topic phrases and the discourse anaphoric constituents following the focus phrase always remain within the scope of negation indicating that they remain in their base generated positions.

The next section is an investigation of the target position of the contrastive topic phrases which take scope over negation.

---

wide scope since the existential quantifier over choice functions is in the scope of the negative operator.

(1) a. [TP Hasan [Neg-Op iki kitap oku-ma-dı]]]   (sadece bir kitap okudu)
       Hasan   two book read-NEG-PAST
       'Hasan didn't read two books. (He read only one book)'
    b. [TP ∃f [TP Bir arkadaş-ım   [Neg-Op kimse-yi   davet et-me-miş]]]
              a friend-1SG.POSS   anybody-ACC invite-NEG-EVID
       'A friend of mine didn't invite anybody'
    c. [Neg-Op [TP ∃f [TP Kimse [vP bir arkadaş-ım-ı   davet et-me-miş]]]
                         anybody   a friend-1SG.POSS-ACC invite-NEG-EVID
       'Nobody invited any friend of mine'

70 An assertion operator in the presence of focus on the verb is not a far-fetched proposal when the amount of information carried by the verb is taken into account. The verb introduces the argument structure; it is the attachment site of tense, aspect and mood markers. The following example from Northern Sotho (Dyakonova 2009: 168, cited from Zerbian 2006) is taken as empirical evidence for this proposal. Northern Sotho does not mark argument focus with a morphological marker or with a special intonation pattern but does so when the verb bears focus. Focus bearing verbs are marked with the morpheme *a*.

(1)   (Context: *Are you singing at the party?*)
       Aowa, ke a bina   (mo-nyanye-ng).
       No   1 A dance   CL3-party-LOC
       'No, I am DANCING (at the party).'

See section 4.5.1 for further discussion on the nature of the assertion operator and verum focus.

4.3.1 Position of contrastive topic

As the interaction of topic phrases with negation illustrates, contrastive topics take scope over negation. For the target position of the topic phrases, there are two potential landing sites (i) the left periphery (Şener 2010) or (ii) Spec TP. In both of these alternatives, contrastive topic c-commands FocP and DaP, this is also signaled by the ordering restrictions. Spec TP as the target position is in line with some current analyses in the literature which assume discourse features of the C head to be inherited by the T head (Miyagawa 2010) and Spec TP can be filled for interpretational purposes (Öztürk 2005; Jiménez-Fernandez and İşsever 2012).

Now, assume that there is a CT subject, an indefinite object, and focus is on the verb as illustrated below. The indefinite can take scope over the universal quantifier in these kinds of examples (Göksel 1998, 2013; Kelepir 2001).

∀ ∃ / ∃ ∀
(205) A: *Öğretmenler ve öğrenciler okumak için iki kitap almışlar. Öğretmenler aldıkları kitapları okumadan geri getirmişler.*
'The teachers and the students took two books to read. The teachers brought the books they took without reading them.'

B: *Valla   öğretmen-ler-i   bil-mi-yor-um   ama   her*
   well   teacher-PL-ACC   know-NEG-IMPF-1SG   but   every
   öğrenci$_{CT}$ iki   kitab-ı$_{DA}$ oku-muş$_F$.
   student   two   book-ACC   read-PERF
   'Frankly, I don't know about the teachers, but every student read two books.'

Kelepir (2001) suggests a position above TP for the existential operator over choice functions (∃f) based on the assumption that subjects move up to Spec TP for case checking purposes. So far, conclusive evidence for or against this analysis has not been suggested. Hence, two alternative positions are proposed for the existential operator over choice functions, and in turn, possible landing sites are listed for the contrastive topic phrase. The first option is that subject phrases do not move up to Spec TP for case purposes. The existential operator over choice functions surfaces above the *v*P projection and inverse scope interpretation becomes possible in (205) in that the contrastive topic phrase at the base generated position surfaces below the existential operator over choice functions. In this scenario, the surface scope becomes possible after the movement of the contrastive topic to Spec TopP above the existential

4.3 The interaction of information structural units with negation

operator over choice functions for discourse-related purposes as illustrated below.[71] It is assumed that Neg can also adjoin to the left periphery. This line of argument is also in line with the data in (195–197), as negation takes contrastive topic under its scope. Although a single projection is shown for topic phrases in (206) for ease of exposition, the assumption is that aboutness and contrastive topic phrases move to distinct projections.

(206)

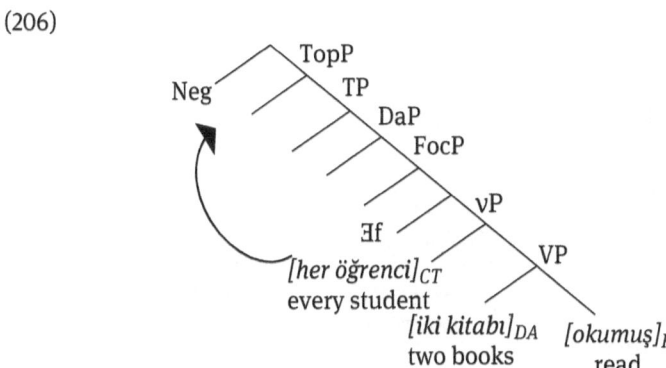

The other option is that subject phrase moves to Spec TP for case purposes. The existential quantifier over choice functions is merged at a position above TP on a par with the analysis of Kelepir (2001). Inverse scope is possible through the existential operator over choice functions projecting higher than the contrastive topic phrase and surface scope is possible only if it is assumed that contrastive topic phrase moves to Spec TopP at the left periphery.

(207)

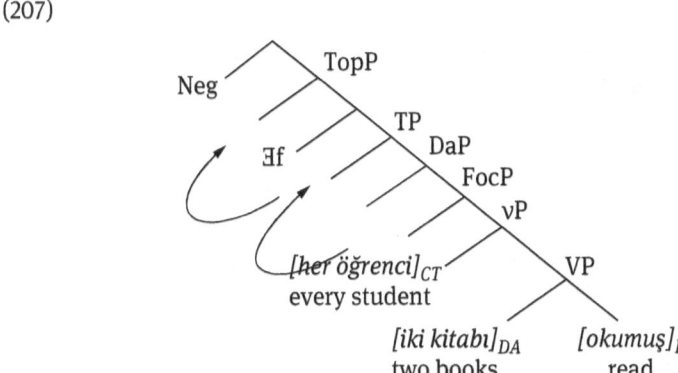

---

[71] For ease of exposition, in some of the representations the projections will be shown with their specifiers only, but note that in Turkish the head projections are on the right.

The third option is to assume that contrastive topic moves to Spec TP for discourse-related purposes. The existential quantifier over choice functions surfaces above the *v*P domain and that is how inverse scope is possible for this sentence. As for the surface scope, it can be assumed that contrastive topic moves to Spec TP where it takes the existential operator over choice functions under its scope.

(208)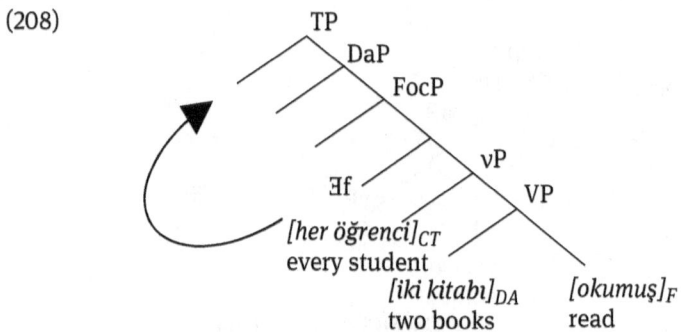

The third option is also in line with the analysis in the Turkish linguistics literature in that Spec TP is filled by constituents only for scope and discourse interpretive purposes (Öztürk 1999, 2005; Jiménez-Fernandez and İşsever 2012). However, there are a few issues for which this alternative cannot account. Firstly, aboutness topic always precedes contrastive topic and hence if they move to the same position, namely Spec TP, the triggering feature would be the same. However, as has already been discussed in Chapter 2, their semantic composition and ordering restriction are not the same. Secondly, if it is assumed that CT moves to Spec TP and the AT moves to TopP, the crucial observation that they are both utterance level constituents will be missed. The structure in (207) differs from the one in (206) with respect to the case checking mechanism and the position of the existential operator over choice functions. Remember that in SOV order, when focus is not on the verb, except for CT, all other information structural units remain in their base generated position and hence under the scope of negation. This indicates that there is no movement for case purposes which has already been suggested in the literature (Öztürk 2005; Şener 2010; Kamali 2011). Hence, the structure in (206) will be assumed for Turkish.

A further issue to be discussed in this section is the triggering feature of contrastive topic phrases to Spec TopP. There are two main lines of arguments on syntactic marking of contrastive topic phrases. Although there are slight differences within these studies, the first line of the studies labeled as the

4.3 The interaction of information structural units with negation

configurational analysis indicates that there is a single F marking strategy for both focus and contrastive topic marking (Wagner 2007, 2008; Tomioka 2010; Constant 2014). The second line of these studies assumes a CT feature for contrastive topic phrases and an F marking for focus phrases (Büring 2003; Dyakonova 2009).

The studies on contrastive topic in which a single F marking strategy is assumed for both focus and contrastive topic phrases will be reviewed first. Wagner (2007, 2008) assumes a nested foci analysis and suggests that a contrastive topic is in fact a focus phrase bound by a higher focus operator. Contrastive topic cannot surface within the scope of the lower focus phrase because this would result in an incorrect interpretation. The ordering reflects the semantic compositionality of the sentence. In English, contrastive topic can surface following the focus phrase while this is not possible in Italian or in Turkish.

Wagner (2007, 2008) suggests that different ordering restrictions are due to different scope-taking properties of these languages. In the presence of two quantifiers, English allows inverse scope but this is not possible in Italian. In English, contrastive topic takes scope over the focus phrase at LF while this has to be overt in Italian where inverse scope is not possible.

In a similar vein, for Japanese, Tomioka (2010) suggests that the lower focus phrase is bound by the lower exhaustive focus operator while the higher operator binds both the contrastive topic and the lower focus phrase as illustrated in (209) below.

(209) *Who ate what?*
    ERIKA-wa   MAME-o   tabe-ta   (kedo)
    Erika-TOP   beans-ACC   eat-PAST   (but)
    'Erika ate beans (but. ...)'
    [Op $_{1\ 2}$ [$_{Speech\ ActP}$ Assert [$_{IP}$ Exh$_3$ [$_{IP}$ ERIka-wa$_1$ [[MAME-o]$_2$]$_3$ tabeta]]]]
    (Tomioka 2010: 124, 127)

There is a single F marking strategy. The difference is that the focus value of the lower focus phrase is used up higher in the structure.

Constant (2014) suggests that contrastive topic movement can occur in syntax or at LF. He assumes a contrastive topic abstraction operator that combines the focus value of the lower focus phrase with the value of the higher focus phrase and obtains a nested focus value as illustrated in (210) below. The higher focus phrase moves to the specifier position of the topic abstraction operator. Through the abstraction operator, alternative sets of "what x brought" are obtained which then combines with the alternative sets of [Fred]$_F$ and the nested focus value is achieved.

(210) [Fred]$_{CT}$ brought [beans]$_F$

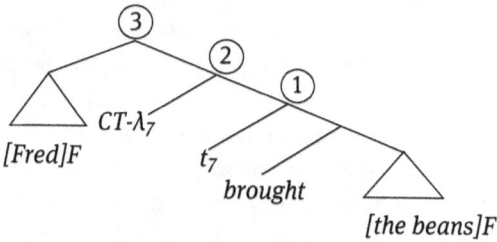

(Constant 2014: 97)

Büring (2003) also suggests that the semantic composition of contrastive topic uses the semantic value of the lower focus phrase but he assumes a CT feature independent of a focus feature. If, in line with configurational analysis, a single F feature is assumed for both contrastive topic and focus phrases, syntax would be blind to which focus phrase is attracted to the higher position. Additionally, as discussed in Chapter 2 on the semantic marking of topic and focus, the distributional properties of contrastive topic and focus phrases show variation in Turkish. While contrastive topic phrases can appear in the postverbal domain devoid of their intonational properties, this is not possible for focus phrases. This can be taken as evidence that contrastive topic and focus phrases are not nested foci even though semantic compositionality of contrastive topic is dependent on focus phrase.[72] Hence, it is suggested that what attracts contrastive topic out of its base generated position is the CT feature in line with Büring (2003).

To recap, based on the interaction of information structural units with negation it has been found that: (i) negation can surface in more than one position which is further supported by the observation that contrastive topics

---

[72] One can still argue for single F marking strategy for CT-F order. It is proposed that the lower focus phrase cannot appear in the postverbal domain as postverbal adjunction position is higher than the preverbal adjunction site. The dislocated focus phrase would end up in a higher position than the contrastive topic phrase which would result in unacceptability. However, remember that, even in the absence of a contrastive topic phrase, focus phrases cannot appear in the postverbal domain. Hence, single F marking analysis cannot account for the Turkish data.

cannot surface following the focus phrases but they surface under the scope of negation when the verb bears focus and focus phrases always take scope over negation; (ii) subject aboutness topic phrases and discourse anaphoric constituents following the focus phrase always appear within the scope of negation indicating that they remain in their base generated positions; and (iii) contrastive topic phrases undergo movement to the left periphery triggered by topic feature. In SOV order, non-movement analysis, except for contrastive topic phrases, is expected because in Turkish word order restrictions reflect a change in semantic interpretation. If the movement operation is semantically vacuous, there is no need for movement.

The next section discusses the experimental studies conducted to investigate how information structure shapes quantifier scope. The findings of these studies will further refine the phrase structure of information structural units in Turkish built up in this section based on negation data.

4.4 The interaction of information structural units with quantifier scope and binding

The interaction of information structural units with binding possibilities has been investigated by Şener (2010), the information structural units being triggered within a context. In this study, whether the match of focus, topic or discourse anaphoric constituents with the universal quantifier and the indefinite results in a special interpretation or not are examined. The findings will shed further light on the phrase structure of Turkish.

Scope interactions of the universal quantifier and the indefinite have been under discussion by various researchers (Kural 1992; Göksel 1998, 2013; Kelepir 2001; Kennelly 2003; Öztürk 2005; Özge 2010; to cite a few). A further experimental study to check scope interpretations was required because, firstly, in these studies the structures are not given in context. Although the place of focus is indicated in some of these studies, when presented out of context, the judgments may depend on how information structural units are encoded by the speaker who interprets the scope interaction in that sentence. Secondly, a general conclusion with respect to scope interpretation for universal quantifiers and indefinites cannot be extrapolated from these studies because either the judgments vary or the tense marker on the verb or the case marker on the quantifier varies.

For example, in the following pairs of examples both researchers suggest that both surface and inverse scope is possible.

                                                                                   ∀∃ / ∃∀

(211) Her   hasta-ya   bir   doktor   bak-ıyor.
every   patient-DAT   a   doctor   examine-PROG
'Every doctor is examining a patient.'
(Özge 2010: 24)

                                                                                  ∀∃ / ∃∀

(212) Her   doktor-a   bir hasta   gid-iyor.
every doctor-DAT a   patient go-PROG
'A patient goes to every doctor.'
(Göksel 1998: 4)

Göksel (1998) suggests that focus is on the preverbal subject; however, Özge (2010) does not point out the placement of focus. Özge (2010) further gives the following example, which differs from the example given in (211) with respect to the case marker on the object, and suggests that the surface scope which indicates distributive reading is not available in (213). However, he does not indicate the position of focus.

                                                                      *∀∃ / ∃∀

(213) Her   hasta-yı   bir doktor tedavi ed-iyor.
every patient-ACC a   doctor treat-PROG
'Every doctor is treating a patient.'
(Özge 2010: 25)

Finally, different inflectional markers on the verb result in confounding results. Özge (2010) suggests that the past tense marker on the verb makes wide scope for the indefinite impossible as in (214a), while this is possible when the verb bears the progressive marker as in (214b).

                                                                       ∀∃ / *∃∀

(214) a. Her   doktor bir hasta   muayene et-ti.
every doctor a   patient examine-PAST
'Every doctor examined a patient.'
(Özge 2010: 27)

                                                                         ∀∃ / ∃∀

b. Her   doktor bir hasta-yı   tedavi ed-iyor.
every doctor a   patient-ACC treat-PROG
'Every doctor is examining a patient.'
(Özge 2010: 25)

However, Göksel (1998) suggests that inverse scope is still possible when the verb bears the past marker as illustrated in (215).

∀ ∃ / ∃ ∀

(215) Her   çocuk   bir   öğretmen-e   çiçek   ver-di.
     every child   a   teacher-DAT   flower give-PAST
     'Every child gave flowers to a teacher.'
     (Göksel 1998: 1)

Note that in these examples there is either a bare indefinite object as in (214a) or the object phrases bear a different case marker as in (214b) and (215) which may have an effect on the judgments. Hence, a more systematic study is needed to determine the scope pattern and its interaction with information structural notions in Turkish.

4.4.1 First study

With the aim of investigating how information structural notions shape the scope interactions of the universal quantifier *her* 'every' and the indefinite *bir* 'a', a study restricting the data to SOV and OSV orders was conducted.

4.4.1.1 Participants and the judgment procedure

Eight informants took part in this experimental study. Five of them were male and three of them were female. All the informants were native speakers of Turkish who had been living in İstanbul for at least 3 years. All the informants were naïve to the purpose of the study and none of them was a linguist. The age span for the speakers ranged between 22 and 60 at the time of the study.

In order to make sure that the participants understood what they were expected to do, at the beginning of the session a short practice session with 3 questions was undertaken with each participant. The practice session included examples similar to the ones used in the experiment. The participants first read the context. Then, they listened to the sound file for the target sentence which was also given in written form on the computer screen. The participants could listen to the sound file as many times as they wanted. Finally, based on the context and the target sentence, they chose one and/or two of the options presented again in written form illustrated with pictures. In the presence of the researcher, the participants answered 51 questions in total. They were presented with the data on a computer and they marked the option(s) they chose. The judgments were collected in a single session in a quiet place that the participants chose. The informants took breaks whenever they needed.

4.4.1.2 The stimuli

As illustrated by the examples in section 4.4, the progressive marker can yield inverse scope which is not possible with other inflectional markers for some speakers. Hence, only the perfective marker –*mIş* was used on the verb. The inflectional marker –*DI* was not used with the aim of having a more natural dialogue with hearsay functions which –*mIş* imparts. The objects bear either dative or accusative case and hence whether case marking on the object affects scope relations or not could be readily checked.

For the SOV and OSV orders, the following possible orders were listed. The orders in Table 5 and 6 are based on the discussion in Chapter 2. The sentence initial constituents, which explicate what the rest of the sentence is about without marking contrast, are aboutness topic phrases. Contrastive topic phrases cannot follow focus phrases and focus phrases do not undergo movement and so the list in Table 5 and 6 can be extrapolated. The only possible order which is not included in the list is the order of AT-CT-F. The constituents bear a different information structural function in each case. The subject is the indefinite determiner *bir* 'a' and the object is the universal quantifier *her* 'every' in both SOV and OSV orders.

Table 5: SOV with *bir* 'a' – *her* 'every' Order.

	S	O	V
a	[indefinite]AT	F[universal]acc/dat	[mış]DA
b	[indefinite]CT	DA [universal] acc/dat	[mış]F
c	[indefinite]AT	DA [universal] acc/dat	[mış]F
d	[indefinite]CT	F[universal]acc/dat	[mış]DA
e	[indefinite]CT	F[universal] acc/dat	[mış]F[73]
f	[indefinite]F	DA [universal] acc/dat	[mış]DA
g	[indefinite]F	F[universal] acc/dat	[mış]F

The subtype of contrastive focus was used as the focus phrases in all sentences as it is easier to trigger contrastive focus in different contexts. Additionally,

---

[73] Instead of assuming two independent focus projections, it was assumed that in this word order and the order in (e) with OSV order the VP is marked with focus. The order in OSV (e) is an example of discontinuous focus projection. The discussion in section 4.6 further indicates that in Turkish the subject and the verb can form a unit excluding the object.

Table 6: OSV with *her* 'every'– *bir* 'a' Order.

	O	S	V
a	$_{CT}[\text{universal}]_{acc/dat}$	$[\text{indefinite}]_F$	$[\text{mış}]_{DA}$
b	$_{AT}[\text{universal}]_{acc/dat}$	$[\text{indefinite}]_F$	$[\text{mış}]_{DA}$
c	$_{CT}[\text{universal}]_{acc/dat}$	$[\text{indefinite}]_{DA}$	$[\text{mış}]_F$
d	$_{AT}[\text{universal}]_{acc/dat}$	$[\text{indefinite}]_{DA}$	$[\text{mış}]_F$
e	$_{CT}[\text{universal}]_{acc/dat}$	$[\text{indefinite}]_F$	$[\text{mış}]_F$

remember that in certain contexts, discourse-new constituents can be confused with contrastive topic phrases if the additional information function is not explicitly specified. Note that in the data, non-verbal focus phrases are not restricted to the immediate preverbal position in SOV order. All the participants in the study group found the structures in which non-verbal focus phrases appear in-situ to be acceptable. However, in this study, data in which focus phrases also appear in the immediate preverbal position was included. Hence, the results of the study can be generalized to the SOV and OSV data for all speakers.

For each word order possibility, three contexts were prepared. Two of these contexts were presented to the informants with two choices indicating surface and inverse scope interpretations as in (216) and (217). Each context was accompanied by pictures to make comprehension easier for the informants. The informants could choose one or both of the options. However, only surface scope could be chosen even when inverse scope was possible, as surface scope is easier to comprehend. Hence, with the third context, inverse scope interpretation was forced and the informants were asked whether the final sentence including the indefinite and universal quantifier was compatible with the context illustrated with the pictures as in (218).

In order to make sure that the informants obtained the right information structural units with the correct intonation, the target sentence was recorded. The informants listened to the target sentence after reading the context before making a choice. A few examples are given in (216–218) for OSV and SOV orders.[74]

(216) A: *Okulumuz öğretmenlerinden bazıları üç öğrenciyle birlikte ders çıkışı pikniğe gitmişler. Rüzgârı fırsat bilen öğrenciler yanlarında uçurmak için uçurtma götürmüşler. Bir de kumandayla çalışan oyuncak helikopter*

---

[74] The drawings used in examples in our experimental studies are freely available on the following websites: https://icons8.com/icons, https://www.iconfinder.com/free_icons

götürmüşler. Sen biliyor musun, piknikten sonra uçurtmaları öğretmenler mi yoksa öğrenciler mi uçurmuş?
'Some of the teachers at our school went on a picnic with three students after school. The students who took advantage of the wind brought kites with them to fly. Additionally they brought helicopters that work with remote controllers. Do you know, which ones, the students or the teachers, flew the kites?'

1.wav

universal_object$_{AT}$ indefinite_subject$_F$ verb$_{DA}$
B: Valla, duy-duğ-um   kadarıyla   her   uçurtma-yı
   well   hear-RELV-1SG.POSS   as far as   every   kite-ACC
   bir   öğrenci   uçur-muş.
   a   student   fly-PERF
   'Well, from what I heard, a student flew every kite.'

(a) Her öğrenci bir uçurtma uçurmuş.
    'Every student flew a kite.'

(b) Sadece bir öğrenci her uçurtmayı uçurmuş.
    'Only a student flew every kite.'

As illustrated in (216) above, the focus is on the preverbal subject and it is triggered by an alternative question. Within the subject phrase, it is the restriction not the quantifier that bears contrast and the students are contrasted with the teachers mentioned in the preceding sentence. Option (a) represents the surface scope interpretation, with the distributive reading. Option (b) is the inverse scope interpretation with non-distributive reading. Following the introductory text, the informants listened to the audio file. Then they read the target sentence and chose one or both of the options for the given context.

The example in (217) is similar to (216) in that both the inverse and surface scope readings are illustrated with pictures as options (a) and (b).

(217) A: *Anamurlu ve Antalyalı gruplar, yurt dışına çalışmaya gitmişti. Çalışanların iş performansına önem veren patron her işçiyi denetlemesi için amirler görevlendirmiş. Amirler işçilerin çalışmasını kontrol ediyor ve puan veriyormuş. İşçilerimiz çalıştıkları fabrikadaki Almanyalı ve Hollandalı amirlerden farklı tepkiler almışlar. Kimi amir çalışmalarını beğenmiş kimisi beğenmemiş. Sen biliyor musun, Hollandalı amirler Antalyalı mı yoksa Anamurlu işçileri mi övmüş mesela?*
'Groups of people from Anamur and Antalya went abroad to work. The boss, who considered the performance of the workers important, gave responsibility to the directors to supervise each of the workers. The directors checked the workers and gave them points. Our workers got different reactions from the directors from Germany and Holland. Some of the directors appreciated their work, some did not. Do you know which ones the Dutch directors praised, for instance, the workers from Antalya or Anamur?'

1.wav

indefinite_subject_CT universal_object_FOC verb_DA
B: *Valla Hollandalı-lar-ı bil-me-m   ama bir Almanyalı*
   well Dutch-PL-ACC know-NEG-1SG but a   German
   amir   her   Anamurlu-yu   öv-müş.
   director every person from Anamur-ACC praise-PERF
   'Well, I do not know about the Dutch people, but a German director praised every person from Anamur.'
   a. *Böylece her Almanyalı amir farklı bir Anamurlu işçiyi övmüş oldu.*
      'So in this way, every German director praised a different worker from Anamur'

   b. *Tüm Anamurlu işçileri tek bir Almanyalı amir övmüş oldu.*
      'Only one German director praised all the workers from Anamur.'

In (217), the focus phrase is triggered by an alternative question while the subject contrastive topic marks a topic shift. Within the indefinite subject phrase and the universal object phrase, it is again the restriction that bears contrast not the quantifiers. The option in (a) provides the inverse scope interpretation making distributive reading available. The option in (b) is the representation of surface scope for the indefinite determiner-universal quantifier order. Again, the informants could choose one or both of the options.

Now, consider the final context that was prepared for this study as illustrated in (218) below. The subject contrastive topic marks a shift in conversation, the object is a discourse anaphoric constituent and the verb is a corrective focus. Following the introductory text and the target sentence, the surface scope interpretation is easy to obtain. Hence, the inverse scope was forced with the pictures following the target sentence.

(218) A: *İzmir'de düzenlenecek konferans için Ankara'dan 5 bakan gelmiş. İstanbul ve Ankara'dan getirilen 10 kişilik güvenlik ekibi yoğun güvenlik önlemleri almış. Bakanların her biri kendi özel arabasını kullanmış. Güvenlik için saat tam 9'da her biri binaya farklı kapılardan giriş yapmışlar. Duyduğum kadarıyla, İstanbullu güvenlik görevlileri bakanlara hiç yardımcı olmamışlar.*

'For the conference to be held in İzmir, 5 ministers came from Ankara. The security guard crew who came from İstanbul and Ankara took security precautions. Each of the ministers used their own cars. For security purposes, they entered the building at 9 o'clock sharp but from different doors. From what I heard, the security guards from İstanbul did not help the ministers.'

1.wav

indefinite_subject$_{CT}$ universal_object$_{DA}$ verb$_{FOC}$

B: *İstanbullu güvenlik görevlilerini bilmiyorum ama saat tam 9'da*
'I do not know about the security guards from İstanbul but at 9 o'clock sharp'

bir	Ankaralı	güvenlik	görevlisi	her
a	person from Ankara	security	guard	every

bakan-a	eskortluk et-miş.
minister-DAT	escort-PERF

'a security guard from Ankara escorted every minister.'

A kapısı	B kapısı	C kapısı
'door A'	'door B'	'door C'
Savunma bakanı	Dış İşleri bakanı	Sağlık bakanı
'defense minister'	'foreign affairs minister'	health minister'

Güvenlik görevlisi:	Güvenlik görevlisi:	Güvenlik görevlisi:
'security guard'	'security guard'	'security guard'
Sadık Şen	İbrahim Mutlu	Şenol Terzi

D kapısı		E kapısı
'door D'		'door E'
Bilişim ve teknoloji bakanı		İç İşleri bakanı:
'informatics and technology minister'		'minister of internal affairs'

Güvenlik Görevlisi:		Güvenlik Görevlisi:
'security guard'		'security guard'
Mustafa Biçer		Polat Uslu
duruma uygun [ ]	duruma uygun değil [ ]	
'appropriate to the context'	'not appropriate to the context'	

The ministers enter the building at the same time but from different doors and a single security guard cannot escort each minister. As illustrated in the pictures, for each minister a different security guard should wait. The informants were asked whether the pictures were appropriate for the given context or not.

For each order indicated in Table 5 and 6, these three contexts were prepared. There were 21 contexts for SOV order and 15 contexts for OSV order. The contexts were presented in random order with additional 15 filler contexts (see Appendix C for further examples from the structures used in the first study).

4.4.1.3 Results

In SOV order, in total there were 168 contexts collected from 8 informants. It was found that in SOV order, irrespective of the position of the focus phrase, even when the inverse scope reading is forced as in (218), only surface scope was preferred in 167 contexts out of 168 contexts.

Table 7: Judgments for SOV Order When the Contrast is on the Restriction.

	S	O	V	
a	[indefinite]$_{AT}$	F[universal]acc/dat	[mış]$_{DA}$	24 surface scope
b	[indefinite]$_{CT}$	DA [universal] acc/dat	[mış]$_F$	24 surface scope
c	[indefinite]$_{AT}$	DA [universal] acc/dat	[mış]$_F$	24 surface scope
d	[indefinite]$_{CT}$	F[universal]acc/dat	[mış]$_{DA}$	24 surface scope
e	[indefinite]$_{CT}$	F[universal] acc/dat	[mış]$_F$	24 surface scope
f	[indefinite]$_F$	DA [universal] acc/dat	[mış]$_{DA}$	23 surface scope
g	[indefinite]$_F$	F[universal] acc/dat	[mış]$_F$	24 surface scope

As inverse scope interpretation is restricted to a single instance and no other informant reported inverse scope reading for any of the other structures, this single instance in (f) as inverse scope interpretation is not counted on.

In OSV order, scope can be read off the surface ordering of the quantificational elements and the universal quantifier can take scope over the indefinite. In contrast to SOV order, in addition to surface scope, inverse scope is possible with OSV order. Even with the contexts in which inverse scope is not forced, the indefinite can take scope over the universal quantifier. Out of 120 contexts, in 51 cases inverse scope was reported.[75] However, there is no coherent relationship between the position of focus and the cases in which inverse scope is possible. Each order illustrated in Table 8 below has been interpreted as allowing inverse scope without an exception.

As pointed out earlier, in all the contexts within the focus phrase the contrast is on the restriction not on the quantifier itself. With the aim of ensuring that the position of contrast within the focus phrase does not have an effect on the results, a follow up study was conducted with the same group which is explicated in the next section.

---

[75] The male speakers in the group tended to allow inverse scope more often than female speakers. In the second and third studies, however, this distinction was not observed.

Table 8: Judgments for OSV Order When the Contrast is on the Restriction.

	O	S	V	
a	CT[universal]acc/dat	[indefinite]F	[mış]DA	11 inverse scope
b	AT[universal]acc/dat	[indefinite]F	[mış]DA	12 inverse scope
c	CT[universal]acc/dat	[indefinite]DA	[mış]F	8 inverse scope
d	AT[universal]acc/dat	[indefinite]DA	[mış]F	10 inverse scope
e	CT[universal]acc/dat	[indefinite]F	[mış]F	10 inverse scope

4.4.2 Second study

For this follow up study, only the kite and worker contexts in (216) and (218) were used as the multiple choice question type. Hence, there were 14 SOV, 10 OSV, and 8 filler contexts for the second step of the study. The participants and the recording procedure were the same as those in the first study.

4.4.2.1 The stimuli

As illustrated in (219) and (220), within the focus phrase the contrast is placed on the quantifier itself rather than on the restriction. The object contrastive topic with the universal quantifier marks a shift. The subject phrase bears focus and the contrast is on the indefinite *bir* 'a', not on the restriction. The verb is discourse anaphoric, namely, given in the previous context.

(219) A: *Okulumuz öğretmenlerinden bazıları üç öğrenciyle birlikte ders çıkışı pikniğe gitmişler. Rüzgâr fırsat bilen öğrenciler yanlarında uçurmak için uçurtma götürmüşler. Bazıları da kumandayla çalışan oyuncak helikopter götürmüşler. Piknikten sonra öğretmenler de çocuklarla birlikte eğlenmişler. Helikopterleri bütün öğrenciler sırayla uçurmuşlar. Böylece helikopterlerin her birini üç öğrenci de uçurmuş.*
'Some of the teachers at our school went on a picnic with three students after school. Taking advantage of the wind, the students brought their kites with them. Some of them brought helicopters that work with remote controllers. After the picnic, the teachers also had fun with the students. The students all flew the helicopters one by one. And hence all three students flew each of the helicopters.'

1.wav

        universal_object_CT indefinite_subject_FOC verb_DA
B: *Valla helikopter-ler-i   bil-mi-yor-um   ama, her*
    well   helicopter-PL-ACC know-NEG-IMPF-1SG but   every
    uçurtma-yı   bir   öğrenci   uçur-muş.
    kite-ACC   a   student   fly-PERF
    'Well, I don't know about the helicopters, but a student flew every kite.'
(a) *Her öğrenci bir uçurtma uçurmuş.*
    'Every student flew a kite.'

(b) *Sadece bir öğrenci her uçurtmayı uçurmuş.*
    'Only a student flew every kite.'

In the following example, in the target sentence, the sentence initial constituent reveals what the rest of the sentence is about without marking a shift and hence it is an aboutness topic phrase which is discourse-given. The object focus phrase surfaces with the universal quantifier which contrasts with the indefinite *'bir'* in the preceding context.

(220) A: *Anamurlu bir grup Almanya'ya çalışmaya gitmişti. Çalışanların iş performansına önem veren patron her işçiyi denetlemesi için amirler görevlendirmiş. Amirler işçilerin çalışmasını kontrol ediyor ve puan veriyormuş. Anamurlular gece gündüz çalışmışlar. Bir Anamurlu olarak Anamurlu işçilerin övülmesini çok isterdim ama duyduğum kadarıyla bir Almanyalı amir sadece bir Anamurlu işçiyi övmüş.*
'A group of people from Anamur had gone to Germany to work. The boss, who considered the performance of the workers important, gave responsibility to the directors to supervise each of the workers. The directors checked the workers and gave them points. The people of Anamur worked day and night. As I am from Anamur, I would have liked the workers from Anamur to be praised but as far as I have heard a German director praised only one of the workers from Anamur.'

1.wav

indefinite_Subject_AT universal_Object_FOC verb_DA
B: *Yoo hayır,   bir   Almanyalı amir   her*
    no   a   German   director   every
   Anamurlu- yu   öv-müş
   person from Anamur-ACC   praise-PERF
   'No, a German director praised every person from Anamur.'
a. *Böylece her Almanyalı amir farklı bir Anamurlu işçiyi övmüş oldu.*
   'So in this way, every German director praised a different worker from Anamur'

b. *Tüm Anamurlu işçileri tek bir Almanyalı amir övmüş oldu.*
   'Only one German director praised all the workers from Anamur.'

The next section illustrates the results of this follow up study.

4.4.2.2 Results and discussion

The results of the study indicated the same results as in the first study. In SOV order, out of 112 contexts, in none of the cases is inverse scope realized and the indefinite subject takes scope over the universal object without exception.

In OSV order, the universal object takes scope over the indefinite subject yielding surface scope. In contrast to SOV order, out of 80 contexts, in 47 cases inverse scope is also realized in OSV order.

However, as illustrated in the table above, there is still no coherent mapping between the position of information structural units and the inverse scope interpretation.[76]

Each case illustrated in Table 9 has been marked as allowing inverse scope.

Table 9: Judgments for OSV Order When the Contrast is on the Quantifier.

	O	S	V	
a	CT[universal]acc/dat	[indefinite]F	[miş]DA	12 inverse scope
b	AT[universal]acc/dat	[indefinite]F	[miş]DA	10 inverse scope
c	CT[universal]acc/dat	[indefinite]DA	[miş]F	8 inverse scope
d	AT[universal]acc/dat	[indefinite]DA	[miş]F	9 inverse scope
e	CT[universal]acc/dat	[indefinite]F	[miş]F	8 inverse scope

In Turkish linguistics literature, restricting the data to SOV and OSV orders, it has been noted that scope can be read off the surface order of the quantified expressions (Kural 1992; Göksel 1998; Kelepir 2001; Özge 2010) based on which Turkish can be categorized as a scope rigid language. The findings in this study can be briefly summarized in the following way:

(221) a. *bir* 'a' > *her* 'every' : $\exists \forall / *\forall \exists$
    b. *her* 'every' > *bir* 'a'   : $\forall \exists / \exists \forall$

When the indefinite *bir* 'a' precedes the universal quantifier as in (221a) only surface scope is possible. The universal quantifier takes scope over the indefinite *bir* 'a' only when it surfaces in a preceding position in the sentence. This behavior of Turkish is in contrast to English-type languages in which the linear order of the quantified expressions does not always mark the scope possibilities as in (222) below.

(222) *Someone loved every girl.* $\exists \forall / \forall \exists$

---

[76] The two studies have shown that there is not a great difference when the contrast is placed on the quantifier or on the restriction within a focus phrase. It is suggested that this can be due to focus projection as proposed by Selkirk (1995).

(1) a. F-marking of the head of a phrase licenses F-marking of the phrase (vertical focus projection)
     b. F-marking of an internal argument of a head licenses the F-marking of the head (horizontal focus projection)

The wide scope of the indefinite over the universal quantifier is predicted based on the linear ordering of the subject and object phrases. As for the inverse scope, where the object universal quantifier takes wide scope over the subject indefinite, LF raising analysis is suggested.

The difference between Turkish and English is in line with the observation of Wurmbrand (2008: 93), who suggests that "(...) free word order entails rigid scope, rigid word order entails flexible scope." The surface scope in (221a) and (221b) is expected but wide scope interpretation of the indefinite over the universal is not expected in (221b). The question raised at this point is whether the wide scope interpretation of the indefinite over the universal can be analyzed as an instance of quantifier raising at LF in line with English-type languages or not. In the literature, indefinites have been noted to display the exceptional behavior of taking scope out of islands such as complex noun phrases (223) and conditional clauses (224), which is not possible with other quantifiers (Fodor and Sag 1982).

(223) a. *John overheard the rumor that each student of mine had been called before the dean.*
b. *John overheard the rumor that a student of mine had been called before the dean.*
(Fodor and Sag 1982: 369)

In (223a), it is not possible for the universal quantifier to take scope over the head noun and hence the interpretation cannot be that 'for each student of mine John overheard the rumor that s/he had been called before the dean.' In (223b), on the other hand, the indefinite can take scope over the head noun and the interpretation can be that there is a student of mine and John overheard that s/he had been called before the dean.

(224) a. *If each friend of mine from Texas died in the fire, I would have inherited a fortune.*
b. *If a friend of mine from Texas died in the fire, I would have inherited a fortune.*
(Fodor and Sag 1982: 369–370)

Only the indefinite in (224b) can take scope out of the antecedent of the conditional to result in the interpretation that there is a friend of mine from Texas and if he died in the fire, I would have inherited a fortune.

Reinhart (1997) suggests that this is not exceptional scope data but inverse scope interpretation is available due to the existential operator over choice functions, which is above the island domains.[77] When the operator variable chain is formed with the indefinite variable in the island domain, the indefinite is interpreted to have wide scope over the island domain. The indefinite does not move out of the island domain, the choice-function existential operator can take scope in more than one position and, due to this operator, indefinites can take scope even out of island domains.[78]

Based on this analysis, Kelepir (2001) suggests that, in Turkish, accusative marked indefinites can have wide scope over some other quantifiers because the existential operator over choice functions can project over the other operators. There is not a movement operation; instead, the operator-variable chain allows the indefinite to be interpreted higher in the structure. With non-marked indefinites on the other hand, the existential operator is projected lower in the structure and hence non-marked indefinites cannot take scope over the other quantificational elements. For accusative marked indefinites, the existential operator is proposed to be over vP or TP, and for non-marked indefinites it is proposed to be over the vP domain.

The question is whether there exists a similar case with indefinites in (221b) and whether the indefinite subject is also interpreted to have wide scope over the dislocated universal object due to existential operator over choice functions. Meltem Kelepir (p.c) suggested that, in order to ensure that inverse scope in (221b) is really not due to an operator generated high in the structure one should check the scope relations in OSV order when the dislocated object is the indefinite and the subject is the universal quantifier. If the universal subject can take scope over the indefinite object, inverse scope can also be considered for Turkish. However, if the universal quantifier cannot take wide scope, it can

---

[77] With indefinites, there is a set over which a choice is made and this creates a function. One of the members in the set is chosen and hence the name choice-function is given. There is special existential operator over choice functions as $\exists f$. In the structure where $\exists f$ can be inserted, it is flexible.

a. $\exists f$ > conditional operator = wide scope for the indefinite
b. conditional operator > $\exists f$ = narrow scope for indefinite

In (a), when the existential operator is above the conditional operator, the indefinite takes wide scope, otherwise it takes narrow scope as in (b).

[78] Kratzer (1998) and Matthewson (1999) on the other hand suggest that indefinites are ambiguous as between a choice function interpretation and a quantificational interpretation. Existential quantifier over choice functions ($\exists f$) is introduced into the structure at the top level and has wide scope over the other quantificational elements. On the other hand, the existential quantifier ($\exists$) is introduced at lower levels and hence it takes lower scope under the other quantificational elements.

be safely concluded that Turkish is a scope rigid language. A third experimental study was conducted to answer these questions.

4.4.3 Third study

4.4.3.1 The stimuli

For this last study, only the *uçurtma* 'kite' context was used as the multiple choice question type and the *güvenlik görevlisi* 'security guard' context was used to force the inverse scope. Hence, there were 10 OSV contexts for the final step of the study and 5 filler contexts. The participants and the recording procedure were the same as those in the first two studies. The order of the information structural units is given in Table 10 below.

Table 10: OSV with *bir* 'a' – *her* 'every' Order.

	O	S	V
a	CT[indefinite]acc/dat	[universal]F	[mış]DA
b	AT[indefinite]acc/dat	[universal]F	[mış]DA
c	CT[indefinite]acc/dat	[universal]DA	[mış]F
d	AT[indefinite]acc/dat	[universal]DA	[mış]F
e	CT[indefinite]acc/dat	[universal]F	[mış]F

The following examples illustrate how the contexts were presented to the informants. In (225), the contrastive topic with the indefinite *bir* 'a' marks a shift in conversation. The universal quantifier that surfaces with the focused subject phrase contrasts with the indefinite *bir* 'a' given in the preceding context.

(225) A: *Okulumuz öğretmenlerinden bazıları üç öğrenciyle birlikte ders çıkışı pikniğe gitmişler. Rüzgân fırsat bilen öğrenciler yanlarında uçurmak için uçurtma götürmüşler. Bir de kumandayla çalışan oyuncak helikopter götürmüşler. Piknikten sonra sadece bir öğrenci helikopter uçurmuş.*
'Some of the teachers at our school went on a picnic with three students after school. Taking advantage of the wind, the students brought their kites with them. They also brought helicopters that work with remote controllers. After the picnic, only one of the students flew the helicopter.'

1.wav

indefinite_object_CT universal_subject_FOC verb_DA

B: *Valla helikopter-ler-i   bil-mi-yor-um   ama,*
  well   helicopter-PL-ACC   know-NEG-IMPF-1SG   but
  bir   uçurtma-yı   her   öğrenci   uçur-muş.
  a   kite-ACC   every   student   fly-PERF
  'Well, I don't know about the helicopters but every student flew a kite.'

(a) *Her öğrenci farklı bir uçurtmayı uçurmuş.*
    'Every student flew a different kite.'

(b) *Sadece bir uçurtmayı bütün öğrenciler uçurmuş.*
    'All the students flew only one of the kites.'

In (226), the object contrastive topic marks a shift for the topic under discussion. The universal quantifier surfaces with the focused subject and again contrasts with the indefinite *'bir'* in the preceding context. In this example, the verb also bears focus. In order to force inverse scope, it was pointed out in the context that a security guard was responsible for each minister who entered the building at the same time but from different doors.

(226) A: *Başbakan konferansın yapılacağı binaya üç bakanla birlikte gelmiş. iki tane İstanbul'dan iki tane de Ankara'dan ek güvenlik görevlisi getirmişler güvenlik önlemi almak için. Başbakan makam aracıyla gelmiş ve D kapısından giriş yapmış. Bakanların her biri ise kendi özel arabasını kullanmış. Bakanların her birinden bir güvenlik görevlisi sorumluymuş. Bakanların hepsi binaya saat tam 09.00'da ve farklı kapılardan giriş yapmışlar. Başbakana bir tane bile güvenlik görevlisi eskortluk etmemiş.*
'The president came to the building in which the conference was to be held with three ministers. They had brought two additional security guards from İstanbul and two security guards from Ankara for safety. The president came with his official car and entered the building from the door D. As for the ministers, they used their private cars. A security guard was responsible for each of the ministers. All the ministers

entered the building at 9 o'clock sharp and from different doors. Not even one of the security guards escorted the president.'

1.wav

indefinite_obj_CT universal_subject_FOC verb_FOC
B: *Başbakan-ı*   *bil-me-m*   *ama bir bakan-a*
   president-ACC know-NEG-1SG but a   minister-DAT
   her   *güvenlik* *görevlisi*   *eskortluk et-miş.*
   every   security   guard   escort make-PERF
   'I do not know about the president but every security guard escorted a minister.'

A kapısı	*B kapısı*	*C kapısı*
'door A'	'door B'	'door C'
Savunma bakanı	*Dış İşleri bakanı*	*Sağlık bakanı*
'defense minister'	'foreign affairs minister'	'health minister'

Güvenlik görevlisi:	*Güvenlik görevlisi:*	*Güvenlik görevlisi:*
'security guard'	'security guard'	'security guard'
Sadık Şen	*İbrahim Mutlu*	*Şenol Terzi*

duruma uygun [ ]   *duruma uygun değil [ ]*
'appropriate to the context' 'not appropriate to the context'

The next section illustrates the results of the study.

4.4.3.2 Results

There were 16 judgments per order and 80 orders in total. Only the orders in (b), (c) and (d) in Table 11 were found to allow inverse scope interpretation. Inverse scope for the order in (c) was reported in 3 contexts with accusative marked objects and in 2 contexts with dative marked objects. The order in (d) was reported as allowing inverse scope in 2 contexts with accusative marked objects and in 3 contexts with dative marked contexts.[79] The order in (b) was reported to allow inverse scope with an accusative marked object only in 1 context. Only one of the informants found this structure to be ambiguous between distributive and non-distributive reading, and the same informant did not find

---

[79] Based on these results, it was concluded that different case markings on the object do not have an effect on scope interpretation.

Table 11: OSV *bir* 'a' > *her* 'every' order when the contrast is on the quantifier.

	O	S	V	
a	CT[indefinite]acc/dat	[universal]F	[mış]DA	16 surface scope
b	AT[indefinite]acc/dat	[universal]F	[mış]DA	1 inverse scope
c	AT[indefinite]acc/dat	[universal]DA	[mış]F	5 inverse scope
d	AT[indefinite]acc/dat	[universal]DA	[mış]F	5 inverse scope
e	CT[indefinite]acc/dat	[universal]F	[mış]F	16 surface scope

this order ambiguous in the other context. Hence, this single instance was not taken as an ambiguous form similar to the single ambiguous form in the first study. Note that there are not as many inverse scope judgments as in Table 8 and 9. Additionally, inverse scope interpretation is restricted to two of the orders only.

In the next section, a syntactic account that will capture not only the scope data in the current study but also the anaphor-binding data in Şener (2010) will be illustrated. Each experimental study will be discussed in detail.

4.5 The syntactic mechanism

4.5.1 Quantifier scope and binding in SOV with indefinite-universal quantifier order

Taking the discussion on negation which led to the structure given in (206) as the background, an attempt will be made to explain the syntactic representation of information structural units in Turkish. The binding data proposed by Şener (2010: 97–99) is taken as the starting point as illustrated in (227a), (227b) and (227c) with our addition of (227d).

(227) a. *[[...vbl...]$_{subj}$]$_{AT}$ >> [QP$_{obj}$]$_F$ >> V
    A: *Dünkü partide yalnızca Pelin'in annesi öpmüş Pelin'i. Doğru mu?*
    'I hear that at the party yesterday only Pelin's mother kissed Pelin. Is that right?'
    B: *Valla   bil-diğ-im   kadarıyla   *[pro$_i$ anne-si]*
       frankly   know-RELV-1SG.POSS as far as   mother-3SG.POSS
       herkes-i$_i$ öp-tü
       everybody-ACC kiss-PERF
       Literally: 'Frankly, as far as I know everyone, his/her mother kissed.'

b. *[[...vbl...]$_{subj}$]$_{CT}$ >> [QP$_{obj}$]$_{DA}$ >> [V]$_F$
   A: *Dünkü törende öğretmenler her öğrenciyi azarlamış. Doğru mu?*
   'I hear that at the ceremony yesterday, the teachers scolded every student. Is that right?'
   B: *Valla   öğretmen-ler-den   haber-im   yok   ama*
      frankly   teacher-PL-ABL   news-1SG.POSS   absent   but
      [pro$_i$ danışman-ı]   herkes-i$_i$ tebrik   et-ti
      mentor-3SG.POSS   everybody-ACC   congratulate   do-PERF
      tören-de
      ceremony-LOC
   Literally: 'Frankly I do not know about the teachers but everyone$_i$ was congratulated by his/her mentor$_i$ at the ceremony.'

c. [[...vbl...]$_{subj}$]$_{AT}$ >> [QP$_{obj}$]$_{DA}$ >> [V]$_F$
   A: *Dünkü törende öğretmenler her öğrenciyi azarlamış. Doğru mu?*
   'I hear that at the ceremony yesterday, the teachers scolded every student. Is that right?'
   B: *Hayır   azarla-ma-dı.   Tam tersine   [pro$_i$ öğretmen-i]*
      no   scold-NEG-PERF   On the contrary   teacher-3SG.POSS
      her   öğrenci-yi$_i$ tebrik   et-ti   tören-de
      every   student-ACC   congratulate   do-PERF   ceremony-LOC
   Literally: 'No they did not. On the contrary every student$_i$ was congratulated by his/her teacher$_i$ at the ceremony.'

d. * [[...vbl...]$_{subj}$]$_{CT}$ >> [QP$_{obj}$]$_F$ >> V
   A: *Dünkü törende öğretmenler sadece bazı öğrencileri tebrik etmişler. Doğru mu?*
   'I hear that at the ceremony yesterday, the teachers congratulated only some of the students. Is that right?'
   B: *Valla   öğretmen-ler-den   haber-im   yok   ama*
      frankly   teacher-PL-ABL   news-1SG.POSS   absent   but
      [pro$_i$ danışman-ı]   herkes-i$_i$ tebrik   et-ti
      mentor-3SG.POSS   everybody-ACC   congratulate   do-PERF
   Literally: 'Frankly I do not know about the teachers but everyone$_i$ was congratulated by his/her mentor$_i$.'

Out of four possibilities, only (227c) yields a grammatical output and the object antecedent can bind the subject variable.

Firstly, based on the findings of negation data, it is proposed that in SOV order, except for the movement of contrastive topic phrases, the constituents do not move up to higher projections. These movements will be semantically vacuous, giving the same word order with no semantic import. It is suggested that movement applies when it is not otherwise possible to convey a semantic interpretation. Information structural units form a relation with the relevant heads through long distance Agree. The interaction of information structural units with negation also gives support to this analysis in that subject aboutness topic phrases and the discourse anaphoric constituents following the focus phrase always remain within the scope of negation.

In (227a), the discourse-given constituent *annesi* 'mother.poss' remains in-situ. In Şener's analysis, the sentence initial constituent is taken as discourse anaphoric but in this study, it is taken as an aboutness topic phrase as this constituent does not mark contrast and it surfaces in sentence initial position. The aboutness topic phrase and the focus phrase *herkesi* 'everybody' Agree with the At° and Foc° respectively and check the uninterpretable features of these heads. As the constituents remain in-situ, binding is impossible.

(227a) * [[vbl]subj]AT >> [QPobj]F >> V   (227b) *[[vbl]subj]CT >> [QPobj]DA >> [V]F

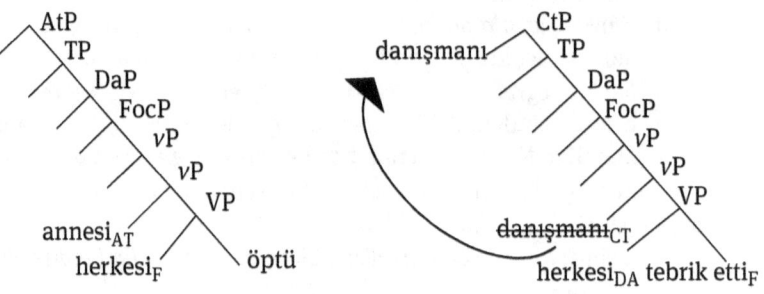

(227c) [[vbl]subj]AT >> [QPobj]DA >> [V]F   (227d) * [[vbl]subj]CT >> [QPobj]F >> V

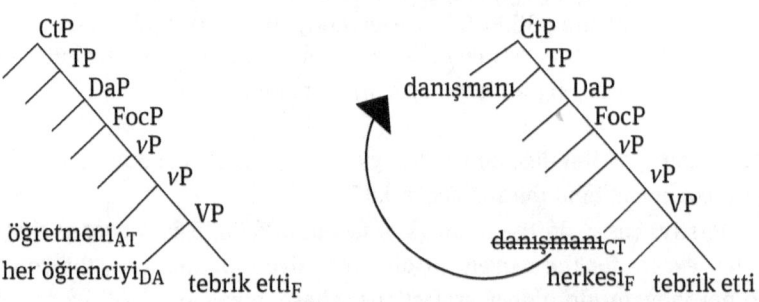

In (227b) and (227d), the contrastive topic phrase *danışmanı* 'mentor.poss' Agrees with the Ct° and checks its uninterpretable topic and contrast features

and moves to Spec CtP in one fell swoop. The discourse anaphoric and focus constituents check the uninterpretable features of the Da° and Foc° via Agree and they remain in-situ. Hence, the binders namely the discourse anaphoric constituent in (227b) and the focus constituent in (227d) cannot bind the contrastive topic phrase *danışmanı* 'mentor.poss' as they are under the c-command domain of the contrastive topic. Note that this is the same even if reconstruction is assumed for the contrastive topic phrase. The grammatical structure in (227c) then poses a problem for this analysis. If an aboutness topic phrase and discourse anaphoric constituent check uninterpretable features of the higher projections via Agree and remain in-situ, how is the subject anaphor *öğretmeni* 'teacher.poss' bound by the object antecedent *her öğrenciyi* 'every student'?

Now, another alternative derivation will be attempted. Assume that except for focus phrases, all the information structural units, contrastive topic, aboutness topic phrases and discourse anaphoric phrases, move to related functional projections even in SOV order. Note that this is in clear contrast with the findings on interaction of information structuring and negation in the current study but still whether this option captures Turkish data will be checked. Although a different internal structure is proposed, this line of a movement analysis is similar to the analysis of Şener (2010) and it can capture the data in (227c). The aboutness topic phrase *öğretmeni* 'teacher.poss' moves to Spec AtP from where it can reconstruct back to its base generated position. The discourse anaphoric constituent *her öğrenciyi* 'every student' also moves to Spec DaP and from this position it can c-command the lowest copy of the subject. Hence, binding is possible.

(227c) [[vbl]$_{subj}$]$_{AT}$ >> [QP$_{obj}$]$_{DA}$ >> [V]$_F$

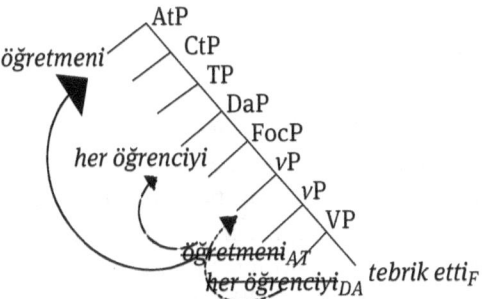

The advantage of this analysis is that it can account for the entire variable binding data. In (227b), both the contrastive topic and the discourse anaphoric constituent move to the relevant functional projections. However, binding is not possible, which indicates that contrastive topic cannot reconstruct back to its base generated position as already noted by Şener (2010). In (227a) and (227d), the focus phrase, which does not move to FocP following the feature checking mechanism, cannot take the dislocated aboutness topic *annesi* 'mother.poss' and the contrastive topic phrase *danışmanı* 'mentor.poss' under it is c-command domain.

However, this analysis runs into problems with scope data as illustrated in (228c) below. In their base generated positions and with the existential quantifier over choice functions surfacing above *v*P, the indefinite subject can take scope over the universal object giving the surface order. As is the case in (227c), the aboutness topic *bir öğrenci* 'every student' moves to Spec AtP. The discourse anaphoric constituent *her uçurtmayı* 'every kite' moves to Spec DaP as illustrated in the first representation. From this position, the universal quantifier can take the existential quantifier over choice functions under its scope. However, inverse scope is still not possible in (228c).

(228c) Bir   öğrenci$_{AT}$ her   uçurtma-yı$_{DA}$ uçur-muş$_F$
       a   student   every   kite-ACC   fly-PERF
       'A student flew every kite.'

To solve this problem it is necessary to turn to the first suggestion. There is no movement in SOV order except for contrastive topic movement. Remember that this analysis is based on an empirical test on the interaction of negation and information structuring. However, the same problem remains. Compare (227c) binding data and (228c) quantifier scope data. With quantifier scope data in (228c), there is an additional existential operator over choice functions above the *v*P projection. Note that in both cases it is the verb that bears focus. It is suggested that when the verb is focused, the utterance is actually an instance of verum focus and the truth value of the whole proposition is emphasized.[80] In these structures, there is an operator that takes the whole proposition under its scope and this operator is labeled as an assertion operator as the truth of the whole proposition is emphasized.[81] Remember that in (227c), when the verb bears focus binding is possible in the absence of movement. It is suggested that through the assertion operator there is a flattening effect in the vP domain as indicated with the lines in (228c) below. The flattening effect makes it possible for the constituents in this domain to have mutual c-command over each other. Hence, binding becomes possible.[82] Note that this domain is also within the scope of Focus.[83]

The following question is raised at this point: Why does the same flattening effect not occur with quantifier scope data? Note that in quantifier scope data in (228c), in contrast to binding data in (227c), there is an existential quantifier over choice functions. It would appear that the existential operator is below the assertion operator and creates an intervention effect for the assertion operator. Hence, the same flattening effect is not observed and only surface scope is possible.

---

[80] Höhle (1988, 1992) suggests that verum focus surfaces in German when (i) the fronted finite verb is focused, (ii) the complementiser is focused. Lohnstein & Stommel (2009) further suggest a syntactic verum feature in the left periphery.

[81] One of the reviewers suggests that assertion is a property of declarative clauses and hence assuming an assertion operator only for those structures in which the verb bears focus is problematic. (See Emonds 1969; Ross 1970; Hooper & Thompson 1973; Haegeman 2012; among many others for a detailed discussion of assertion operator in root clauses) However, the term "assertion" is used for the operator to indicate that the whole proposition is emphasized to be true. This is due to verum focus and bearing verum focus is not a property of all declarative clauses. It would have been possible to use verum as an operator but as the discussion will show Turkish focus phrases do not behave like operators in that they can have scope over other constituents only when they surface with another quantificational element. Hence, the use of the assertion has been adopted in this study.

[82] Kiss (2008) makes a similar analysis for Hungarian postverbal constituents. Although the word order is fixed in the preverbal domain it is not so in the postverbal domain. Binding and scope interpretations which are not possible in the preverbal domain are licit in the postverbal domain in Hungarian.

[83] The assertion operator surfaces when focus is on the verb and has a flattening effect on the vP domain. Hence, one can suggest vP not CP as the attachment site for this operator. This operator does not have a direct effect on the CP domain but the interpretation of the constituents is also based on the situational TP domain and hence CP is proposed as the attachment site of this operator.

(228c) *Bir öğrenci$_{AT}$ her uçurtma-yı$_{DA}$ uçur-muş$_F$*
     a   student   every kite-ACC   fly-PERF
     'A student flew every kite.'

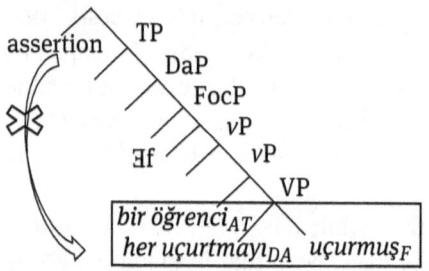

Now, consider the remaining scope and binding data together to determine whether this account can capture these structures in a parsimonious way. In both of the representations below, the aboutness topic and the focus phrases remain in-situ. The aboutness topic phrases check the uninterpretable topic feature of At° and the focus phrase checks the [F] feature of Foc° via Agree. In (228a), the indefinite is also bound by the existential operator above the At projection. Binding is not possible in (227a) even when movement and reconstruction to the base generated position is assumed for the aboutness topic phrase as focus constituent *herkesi* 'everybody' cannot take the aboutness topic *annesi* 'mother.poss' under its c-command domain.

In (228a), only the indefinite takes wide scope over the universal quantifier because the universal focus quantifier *her uçurtmayı* 'every kite' cannot take the existential operator over *v*P under its scope.

(227a) * [[vbl]$_{subj}$]$_{AT}$ >> [QP$_{obj}$]$_F$ >> V

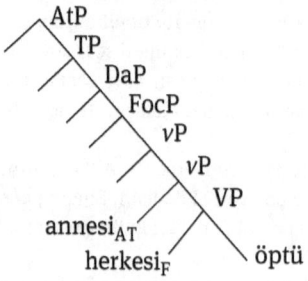

(228a) *bir öğrenci*$_{AT}$ *her   uçurtma-yı*$_F$ *uçur-muş*$_{DA}$
a   student   every kite-ACC   fly-PERF
'A student flew every kite.'

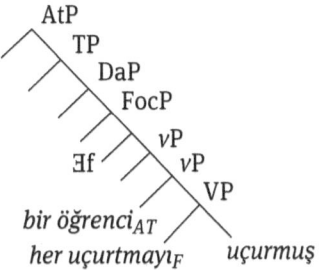

In derivations (227b) and (228b) below, the contrastive topic moves out of the scope of focus in one fell swoop to the Spec CtP projection. Note that there is an assertion operator and hence within the domain of *v*P a flattening effect is predicted. A natural question is raised at this point concerning how movement is possible in the presence of a flattening effect. Recall from Chapter 2 that the semantic compositionality of contrastive topic is dependent on focus phrases. Hence, the movement of contrastive topic over focus phrase is an obligatory scope taking operation with a semantic import. As binding is not possible in (227b), the data further indicate that contrastive topic cannot move back to its base generated position and hence mutual c-command is not possible due to the flattening effect. In a sense, scope-taking movement of the contrastive topic obviates the flattening effect.

In (228b), the existential operator creates an intervention effect for the assertion operator and the flattening effect is not observed. The only option is surface scope which is within the predictions of this analysis.

(227b)   *[[vbl]$_{subj}$]$_{CT}$ >>[QP$_{obj}$]$_{DA}$ >>[V]$_F$

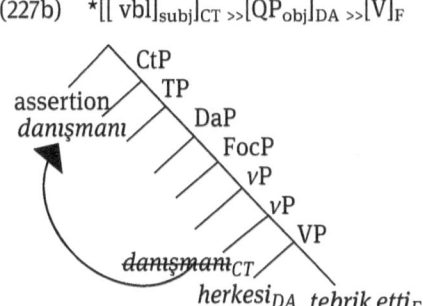

(228b) bir öğrenci$_{CT}$ her uçurtma-yı$_{DA}$ uçur-muş$_F$
a student every kite-ACC fly-PERF
'A student flew every kite.

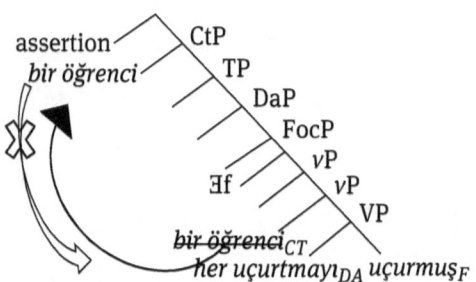

The derivation of (227c) and (228c) was discussed above and hence the discussion of (227d) and (228d) is considered. In both of the representations, attracted by the edge feature of CtP, the contrastive topic moves to Spec CtP following the feature checking mechanism. The focus phrase agrees with the FocP in-situ and hence binding is not possible in (227d). In (228d), contrastive topic is bound further by the existential operator. As the lower focus phrase agrees with the FocP in-situ, there is no way for it to take the existential operator under its c-command domain and hence inverse scope is not possible.

(227d) *[[vbl]$_{subj}$]$_{CT}$ >> [QP$_{obj}$]$_{FOC}$ >> V

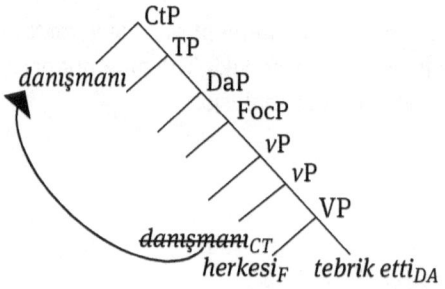

(228d) bir öğrenci$_{CT}$ her uçurtma-yı$_F$ uçur-muş$_{DA}$
a student every kite-ACC fly-PERF
'A student flew every kite.'

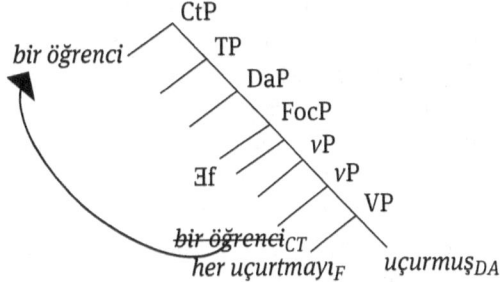

Up to this point, the derivation of both quantifier scope and binding data can be accounted for, assuming no movement in SOV order for the information structural units except for contrastive topic phrases. Now, consider the remaining quantifier scope data.

(228e) *bir öğrenci*$_{CT}$ *her   uçurtma-yı*$_F$ *uçur-muş*$_F$
       a   student   every kite-ACC   fly-PERF
       'A student flew every kite.'

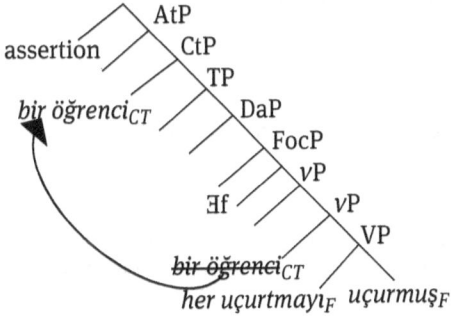

(228f) *Bir öğrenci*$_F$ *her   uçurtma-yı*$_{DA}$ *uçur-muş*$_{DA}$
       a   student   every kite-ACC   fly-PERF
       'A student flew every kite.'

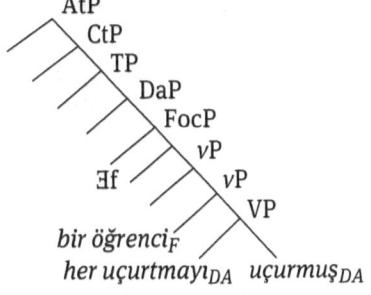

In (228e), the contrastive topic *bir öğrenci* 'a student' moves out of the base generated position to Spec CtP. Although there is an assertion operator that can yield a flattening effect in the *v*P domain, movement of the contrastive topic rules out the flattening effect and only surface scope is possible. The other factor that rules out the flattening effect of the assertion operator is the presence of the existential operator that surfaces over *v*P.[84] In (228f), the focus phrase *bir öğrenci* 'a student' agrees with FocP in-situ and it is further bound by the existential operator. The discourse anaphoric constituent *her uçurtmayı* 'every kite' also agrees with Da° in-situ and checks its uninterpretable discourse anaphoric features. Hence, only surface scope is observed in (228f).

To recap, (i) in SOV order, only contrastive topic undergoes movement for scope purposes, (ii) aboutness topic, discourse anaphoric and focus phrases remain in-situ and form long distance Agree with the relevant heads which is also in line with the findings of the data on the interaction of negation with these constituents, (iii) when the verb bears focus, there is an assertion operator that yields a flattening effect in the *v*P domain which is also within the c-command domain of focus, (iv) existential operator over choice functions creates an intervention effect for the assertion operator. The next section focuses on the derivation of binding and scope data in OSV order.

4.5.2 Quantifier scope and binding in OSV with universal-indefinite quantifier order

The derivation of the binding and scope data with the same information structural ordering will now be discussed. The examples below illustrate the OSV binding data of Şener (2010: 85–87).

(229) a. *[[…vbl…]$_{obj}$]$_{CT}$ >> [QP$_{subj}$]$_F$ >> V
    A: *Dünkü mezuniyet töreninden sonra bazı çocuklar önce babalarını öptü.*
    'After the graduation ceremony yesterday some kids kissed their fathers first.'
    B: ?*[pro$_i$ anne-si]-ni-yse   herkes$_i$ t$_{[pro\ anne\text{-}si]\text{-}ni\text{-}yse}$ öp-tü.
    mother-3SG.POSS-ACC-as for everybody   kiss-PERF
    Literally: 'His/her mother everyone kissed.'

---

84 Remember that in the absence of movement in (228c), the existential operator over choice functions creates an intervention effect for the flattening effect of the assertion operator.

b. [[...vbl...]$_{obj}$]$_{AT}$ >> [QP$_{subj}$]$_F$ >> V
   A: *Mezuniyet töreninden sonra kim annesini öptü, haberin var mı?*
   'Do you know who kissed his mother after the graduation ceremony? Do you know anything about that?'
   B: *Duy-duğ-um   kadarıyla   [pro$_i$ anne-si]-ni*
      hear-RELV-1SG.POSS   as far as   mother-3SG.POSS-ACC
      herkes$_i$ t[pro anne--si-ni]   öp-müş.
      everybody   kiss-PERF
   Literally: 'As far as I have heard his/her mother everyone kissed.'
c. [[...vbl...]$_{obj}$]$_{CT}$ >> [QP$_{subj}$]$_{DA}$ >> [V]$_F$
   A: *Dünkü törende her öğretmen bir öğrencisini tebrik etmiş. Doğru mu?*
   'I hear that at the ceremony yesterday every teacher congratulated a student of hers. Is that right?'
   B: *Valla,   öğrenci-ler-den   haber-im   yok   ama*
      frankly   student-PL-ABL   news-1SG.POSS   absent   but
      [pro$_i$ bir arkadaş-ı]-nı   her öğretmen$_i$
      a   friend-3SG.POSS-ACC   every teacher
      t[pro bir arkadaş-ı-nı]   azarla-dı   sert bir şekilde.
                                scold-PERF   in a harsh way
   'Frankly, I do not know about the students but every teacher scolded a friend of hers in a harsh way.'
d. [[...vbl...]$_{obj}$]$_{AT}$ >> [QP$_{subj}$]$_{DA}$ >> [V]$_F$
   A: *Dünkü törende her öğretmen bir öğrencisini tebrik etmiş. Doğru mu?*
   'I hear that at the ceremony yesterday every teacher congratulated a student of hers. Is that right?'
   B: *Valla,   tebrik-ten   haber-im   yok*
      frankly   congratulatation-ABL   news-1SG.POSS   absent
      ama [pro$_i$ bir öğrenci-si]-ni   her öğretmen$_i$
      but   a   student-3SG.POSS-ACC   every teacher
      t[pro bir öğrenci-si-ni]   azarla-dı   sert bir şekilde.
                                 scold-PERF   in a harsh manner
   'Frankly, I do not know about the congratulations but every teacher scolded a student of hers in a harsh way.'

In (229a), the object contrastive topic *annesiniyse* 'mother.poss' moves from its base generated position to the outmost Spec vP to Spec CtP. Remember that edge positions of phases serve as an escape hatch. The focus phrase *herkes* 'everybody' Agrees with the FocP and remains in-situ. Hence, the in-situ subject antecedent cannot bind the dislocated object anaphor. This example again shows that CT cannot reconstruct back to its base generated position.

(229a) *[[vbl]_{obj}]_{CT} >> [QP_{subj}]_F >> V

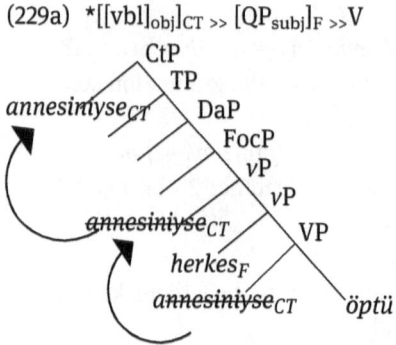

(230a) her   uçurtma-yı_{CT} bir öğrenci_F uçur-muş_{DA}
       every   kite-ACC   a   student   fly-PERF
       'A student flew every kite.'

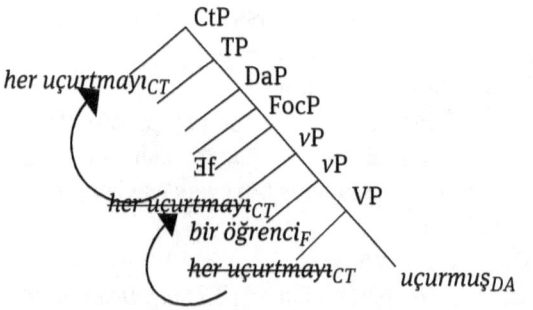

In (230a), the existential operator over choice functions takes the universal quantifier in its base generated position under its scope and hence inverse scope is possible.[85] The other option is that the CT phrase reconstructs back to the outmost specifier of *v*P and the existential operator over choice functions above *v*P can take scope over it making inverse scope possible.[86] As for the surface scope interpretation, the contrastive topic moves from its base generated position to the outmost Spec *v*P to Spec CtP. From this position, the universal quantifier can take the existential quantifier over choice functions, which surfaces above Spec *v*P under its scope.

---

[85] As the discussion on semantic properties of information structural units in Chapter 2 has shown, focus phrases have quantificational properties in that they denote a relationship between two sets. Note that focus phrases in Turkish can take scope over other constituents only when they are accompanied by another quantificational element. That is how Turkish focus phrases differ from focus phrases with quantificational force in other languages such as Hungarian.

[86] The discussion in section 4.5.3 shows that inverse scope is possible just based on the intermediary reconstruction sites.

In (229b) and (230b), the sentence initial constituent, aboutness topic checks the uninterpretable topic feature of AT° and it is attracted to Spec AT. The subject focus phrases remain in-situ. Note that binding is possible in (229b). This indicates that the aboutness topic phrases can move back to their base generated positions as their movement to Spec AT is not a scope taking operation. This is a significant difference between CT and AT phrases.

(229b) [[vbl]$_{obj}$]$_{AT}$ >> [QP$_{subj}$]$_F$ >> V

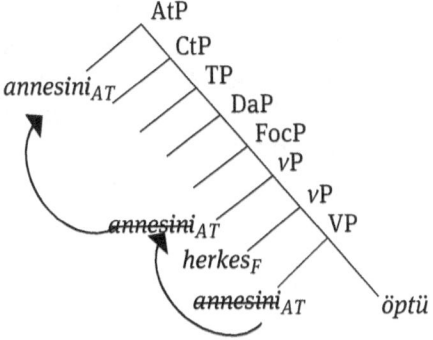

(230b) her   uçurtma-yı$_{AT}$ bir öğrenci$_F$ uçur-muş$_{DA}$
       every kite-ACC   a   student   fly-PERF
       'A student flew every kite.'

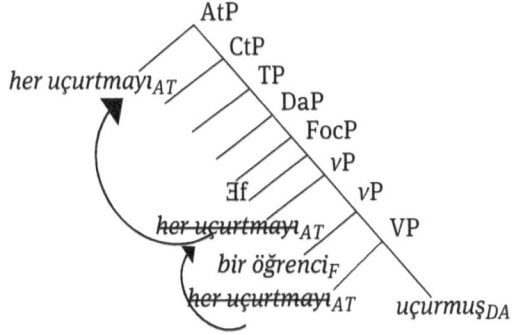

In (230b), the inverse scope interpretation is available as the existential operator surfaces above vP and hence over the universal quantifier. Note that inverse scope is also possible as AT phrase reconstructs back to its base generated position. As for the surface scope interpretation in (230b), it is suggested that the dislocated universal quantifier at Spec AtP takes scope over the existential operator over choice functions above vP which yields surface scope interpretation.

As illustrated in (229c) and (230c) below, contrastive topic object phrases move from the outmost Spec vP to Spec CtP. In (229a) and (229b), the subject phrases were focus phrases which do not move in Turkish. In (229c), there is a discourse anaphoric constituent as the subject. Either the discourse anaphoric constituent moves to Spec DaP or it remains in-situ similar to SOV order. Compare the derivation in (229c) with the one in (229a). Note that in (229c), binding is possible. The derivation in (229a) has shown that binding is not possible as the contrastive topic cannot reconstruct back to its base generated position. The fact that the DA constituent can bind the dislocated CT constituent clearly shows that the DA constituent also moves to Spec DA position as indicated with a broken line. However, from Spec DA, the DA constituent cannot bind the variable at Spec CtP which clearly indicates that the CT can reconstruct back to the intermediary position of the outmost Spec vP that serves as an escape hatch and that is how binding becomes possible.

(229c) [[vbl]$_{obj}$]$_{CT}$ >>[QP$_{subj}$]$_{DA}$ > [V]$_F$

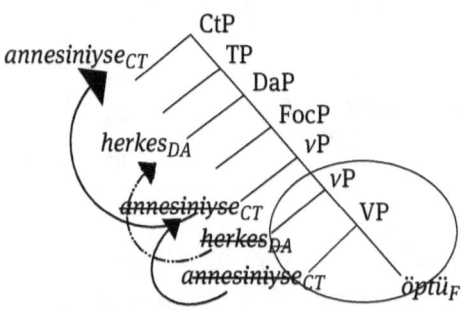

(230c) *her   uçurtma-yı$_{CT}$ bir   öğrenci$_{DA}$ uçur-muş$_F$*
       every kite-ACC   a   student   fly-PERF
      'A student flew every kite.'

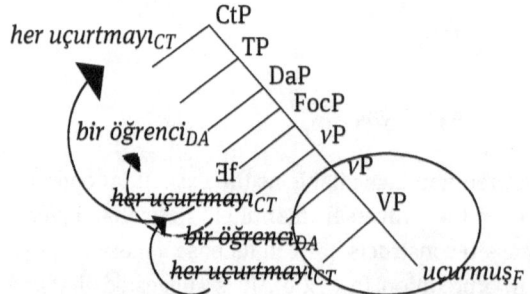

Up to this point, it has been argued that a CT phrase does not move back to its base generated position which has been labeled as the complement domain of *v*P phase. Note that the edge position that serves as an escape hatch to which reconstruction is possible does not strictly overlap with the edges of a phase, escape hatches, as discussed in the first chapter. The Turkish data shows that it is only the outmost specifier position that serves as a reconstruction site, while the lower domain is forbidden for the contrastive topic. Now, it is time to reconsider the nature of this domain which is shown with a circle in (229c) and (230c). Remember that contrastive topic phrases in Turkish cannot surface following focus phrases and their semantic compositionality is dependent on alternative propositions of focus phrases. Based on these facts, this domain is labeled as the scope domain of focus, as contrastive topic phrases cannot surface following the focus phrases. In the remaining tree structures, this domain will be indicated with a circle.

Now it is time to focus on the derivation of (230c) above. The universal quantifier takes scope over the indefinite following its movement to Spec CT for discourse related purposes; the universal quantifier surfaces above the existential operator at Spec *v*P. For the same structure, inverse scope interpretation is available as the CT phrase reconstructs back to the outmost specifier of *v*P and binding becomes possible. Additionally, inverse scope is possible in base generated positions as the existential quantifier over choice functions takes the CT constituent under its scope. Finally, note that in both (229c) and (230c), there is an assertion operator above the existential operator. However, the movements of the constituents to higher projections in (229c) and the presence of the existential operator in (230c) obviate flattening effects in the lower focus domain.

Now, consider the derivations of (229d) and (230d). The derivation of (229d) and (230d) is similar to the derivation of (229c) and (230c). The sentence initial aboutness topic moves from outmost Spec *v*P to Spec AtP. The AT phrase reconstructs back to the outmost specifier position of *v*P or its base generated position as already shown in (229b). Hence, binding is possible. In (230d), surface scope is possible, as the dislocated universal quantifier can take scope over the existential quantifier above *v*P. As for inverse scope interpretation, the reconstruction of the object phrase back to its base generated position yields inverse scope interpretation. Additionally, inverse scope is possible in base generated positions as the existential quantifier over choice functions takes the aboutness topic under its scope. The flattening effect of the assertion operator is not possible as the constituents move out of the scope domain of the focus phrase. Additionally, in (230d) the existential operator creates an intervention effect.

(229d) [[vbl]_obj]_AT >> [QP_subj]_DA >> [V]_F

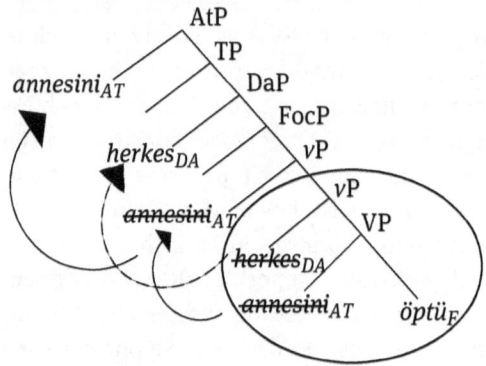

(230d) her   uçurtma-yı_AT bir öğrenci_DA uçur-muş_F
       every kite-ACC   a   student   fly-PERF
       'A student flew every kite.'

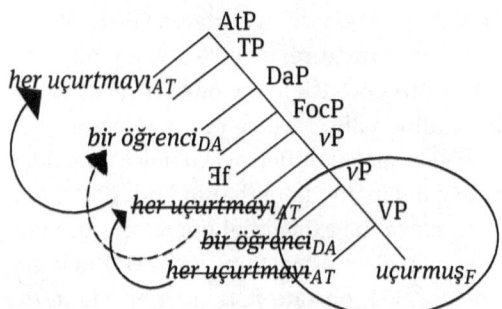

Finally, consider the derivation of the final OSV scope data.

(230e) her   uçurtma-yı_CT bir öğrenci_F uçur-muş_F
       every kite-ACC   a   student   fly-PERF
       'A student flew every kite.'

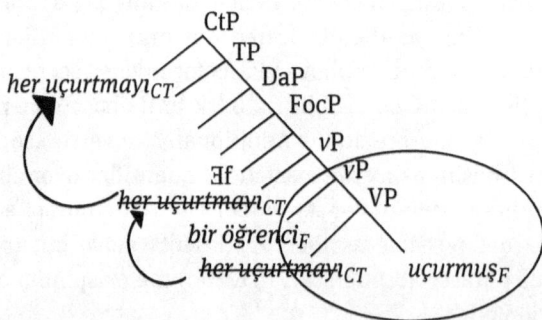

The CT object phrase *her uçurtmayı* 'every kite' moves out of the scope domain of the F phrase to Spec CT attracted by the edge feature. The indefinite F phrase *bir öğrenci* 'a student' agrees with the FocP checks its feature and remains in-situ. The indefinite F phrase is interpreted to have wide scope over the dislocated CT by way of the existential operator over choice functions above the *v*P projection in its base generated position. The other possibility is that the CT phrase moves back to the outmost specifier of *v*P which makes the phrase within the scope of the existential quantifier over choice functions above *v*P. As for the surface scope interpretation, the CT at Spec CtP takes the existential operator under its scope and this yields surface scope. The next section focuses on OSV order with the indefinite-universal quantifier order.

4.5.3 Quantifier scope in OSV with indefinite-universal quantifier order

In this section, the focus is on the derivation of OSV order when the object is indefinite and the subject is the universal quantifier. The examples in this section show whether inverse scope interpretation is possible in Turkish independent of the existential operator over choice functions.

As illustrated in (231a), the CT object *bir uçurtmayı* 'a kite' moves from outmost Spec *v*P to Spec CtP. The universal focused subject *her öğrenci* 'every student' agrees with the FocP and checks its features in-situ. As CT cannot reconstruct back to the scope domain of focus, there is no way for the in-situ F phrase to take the existential operator and the indefinite CT under its scope. Hence, inverse scope is not possible.

(231a) *bir uçurtma-yı*$_{CT}$ *her öğrenci*$_F$ *uçur-muş*$_{DA}$
       a   kite-ACC   every student   fly-PERF
       'A student flew every kite.'

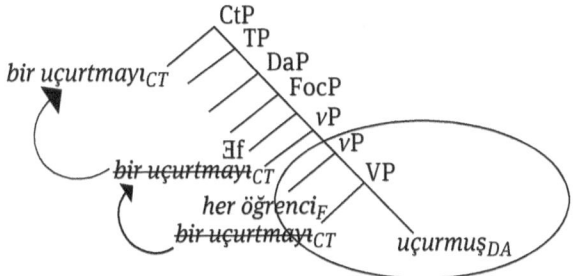

Now, consider the derivation in (231b) below. Remember that there were two contexts for this order. In this order, only one speaker found the order ambiguous in only one context. As the same informant did not find the same order acceptable in the other context and there are no other informants finding this order as ambiguous, on this single instance inverse scope interpretation is not counted on in line with the decision in section 4.4.1.3.

(231b) *bir uçurtma-yı*$_{AT}$ *her öğrenci*$_F$ *uçur-muş*$_{DA}$
     a   kite-ACC   every student fly-PERF
    'A student flew every kite.'

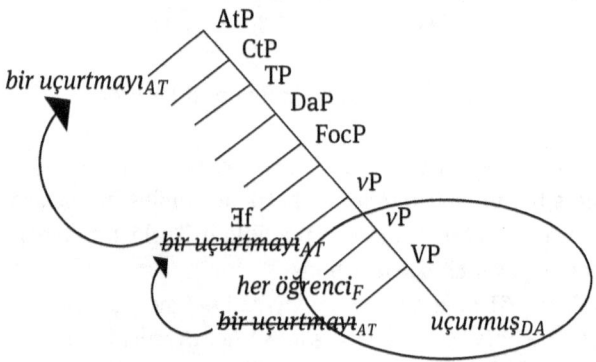

The AT phrase *bir uçurtmayı* 'a kite' moves from outmost Spec *v*P to Spec AT. The F phrase *her öğrenci* 'every student' remains in-situ and agrees with the FocP and checks its features. The AT can surface within the scope domain of focus. However, there is no way for the F phrase to take the existential operator above *v*P under its scope. Hence, inverse scope is not possible.

In (231c) below, the CT indefinite object *bir uçurtmayı* 'a kite' moves from outer Spec *v*P to Spec CtP. The DA universal quantifier subject *her öğrenci* 'every student' moves from its base generated position to Spec DaP. As indicated in Table 11, this order is found to be ambiguous in 5 of the 16 contexts, without being restricted to a certain context or speaker.

(231c) *bir uçurtma-yı*$_{CT}$ *her öğrenci*$_{DA}$ *uçur-muş*$_F$
     a   kite-ACC   every student fly-PERF
    'A student flew every kite.'

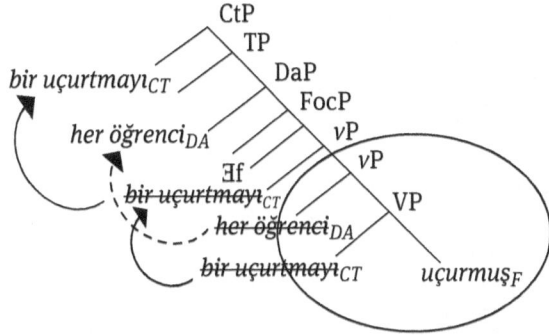

The flattening effect is not observed due to the movement operations and the intervention effect of the existential operator. The indefinite takes scope over the universal quantifier via the existential operator above vP, yielding surface scope. As for the inverse scope interpretation, it is suggested that the dislocated DA universal quantifier takes scope over the existential quantifier over choice functions above vP, yielding inverse scope interpretation.

Now, consider the following ordering which is found to be ambiguous in 5 of the structures without being restricted to a certain context or speaker.

(231d) *bir uçurtma-yı*$_{AT}$ *her öğrenci*$_{DA}$ *uçur-muş*$_F$
    a kite-ACC   every student fly-PERF
    'A student flew every kite.'

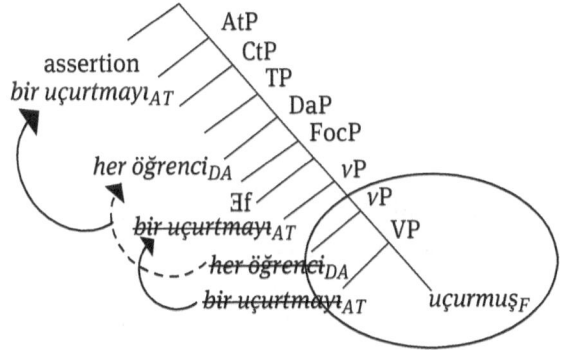

The indefinite AT *bir uçurtmayı* 'a kite' moves out of the base generated position to outmost Spec vP to Spec AT. The DA constituent *her öğrenci* 'every student' moves from its base generated position to Spec DaP. The existential quantifier over choice functions can take scope over the DA universal quantifier in its base generated position but also as a result of its reconstruction to its base generated position. The inverse scope interpretation is also possible as a result of the DA constituent's movement to Spec DaP above the *vP* domain, taking the existential quantifier over choice functions under its scope.

The examples in (231c) and (231d) show that, in Turkish, inverse scope is possible in OSV sentences with indefinite-universal quantifier order which cannot be reduced to the presence of the existential operator over choice functions as in OSV sentences with universal-indefinite quantifie order. However, the inverse scope interpretations in OSV sentences with indefinite-universal quantifier order are not as readily available as is the case in OSV sentences with universal-indefinite quantifier order.

Finally, consider the derivation of CT-F-F order for which inverse scope judgment has not been reported. The indefinite CT object phrase moves from outmost Spec *vP* to Spec CT. Additionally, the existential operator below assertion operator creates an intervention effect and the flattening effect is ruled out.

(231e) bir uçurtma-yı$_{CT}$ her   öğrenci$_F$ uçur-muş$_F$
        a   kite-ACC   every student   fly-PERF
        'A student flew every kite.'

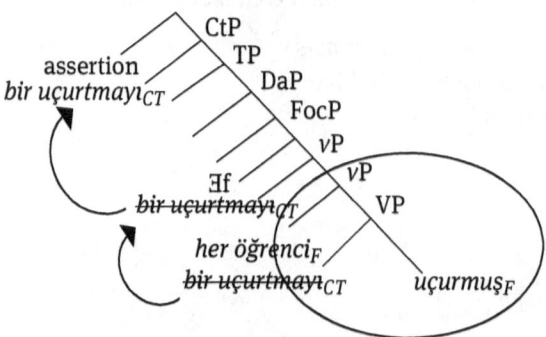

The CT cannot reconstruct back to the scope domain of the F phrase. The universal quantifier focused subject being in-situ cannot take the existential quantifier and the indefinite under its scope and hence inverse scope is not possible.

As the discussion illustrates, with the IP internal functional projections, Spec AtP and CtP as the target position of topic phrases and scope domain of focus, not only is it possible to account for the binding data but it is also possible to account for the quantifier scope data in SOV and OSV orders.

To sum up, the interaction of the quantifier scope and binding data with information structural units in OSV order shows that: (i) except for focus phrases all information structural constituents undergo movement; (ii) contrastive topic cannot reconstruct back to the scope domain of focus which maps on to vP domain excluding the specifier of vP which serves as the escape hatch for the object phrases; (iii) aboutness topic phrases and discourse anaphoric constituents can reconstruct back to the scope domain of focus, as these movements are not scope taking operations; (iv) although restricted, inverse scope is possible in Turkish, independent of the exceptional scope taking properties of the existential operator over choice functions;[87] and (v) focus does not have a direct effect on scope interpretation and inverse scope cases can be explained by restrictions on movement operations.[88] In the next section, the scope domain of focus is discussed.

---

[87] Remember that in (230a), (230b), (230c), (230d) and (230e) inverse scope interpretation is possible not only due to intermediary reconstructions sites but also due to existential quantifier over choice functions. In OSV indefinite-universal quantifier order, inverse scope is rather restricted but it is possible due to movement operations.

[88] This analysis can also account for the data already discussed in Turkish linguistics literature.

(1) *Bir kitab-ı   her   çocuk dün$_F$ oku-du*
     one book-ACC every child yesterday read-PAST

   i. 'Every child read a specific book yesterday.'
   ii. 'Every child read a different book out of a definite set yesterday.'
   (Öztürk 2005: 182)

In the presence of focus phrase, the dislocated constituents are either topic or discourse anaphoric constituents. Even if it is assumed that the indefinite object phrase is the contrastive topic, as reconstruction to the outer specifier of vP is possible, the universal subject quantifier can take scope over the existential operator and the indefinite object.

As for the following structure, it is suggested that the structure is found to be unacceptable when the dislocated constituent is interpreted as contrastive topic. This contrast can also be seen with the binding contrast in (229a) vs. (229b).

(2) *[Kendi$_i$ komşu-sun-u]$_j$ [Işık $_i$]$_F$ t$_j$ gör-dü.
      self   neighbor-POSS-ACC   Işık   see-PAST
     'Her neighbor was seen by Işık'
     (Jiménez-Fernandez and İşsever 2012: 9)

When given in a context that would render an aboutness topic interpretation to the object the sentence is predicted to be acceptable. With some modifications when the sentence is placed in context, an acceptable sentence is achieved.

(3) A: *Işık törende çok heyecanlıydı. Kimseyle ilgilenmedi. Kendi komşusuyla bile ilgilenmedi. Arkadaşları komşusuyla ilgilendi.*
       'Işık was very anxious at the ceremony. She didn't take notice of her neighbor. Her friends took notice of her neighbor.'
     B: *Olur mu öyle şey? Kendi komşusuyla Işık ilgilendi.*
       'Come on! Işık took notice of her neighbor.'

4.6 Scope domain of focus

In this section, the scope domain of focus, which is illicit for the reconstruction of the contrastive topic phrases as illustrated in the preceding section, is dealt with in more detail. Remember that this domain is a possible reconstruction site for aboutness topic phrases and discourse anaphoric constituents but not for contrastive topic phrases although they are all base generated in this domain. From a semantic point of view, the alternative set of the focus phrase is determined based on the constituents in this domain as all the constituents are base generated in this domain.

(232) a. A: *Balonu kim uçurmuş?*
'Who flew the balloon?'
B: *Balon-u   bil-mi-yor-um   ama [uçurtma-yı]$_{CT}$*
balloon-ACC know-NEG-IMPF-1SG but kite-ACC
[Ayşe]$_F$ [uçur-muş]$_{DA}$
Ayşe   fly-PERF
'I don't know about the balloon but Ayşe flew the kite.'

b.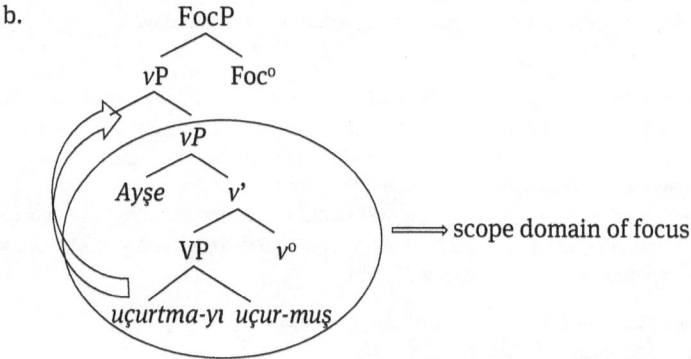

Contrastive topic phrases differ from discourse anaphoric constituents and aboutness topic phrases with respect to triggering alternatives. Remember that the alternative propositions of the focus phrase also form part of the alternative set of the contrastive topic phrase. Hence, for the contrastive topic to evoke alternative sets in (232), it has to move out of the scope domain of the focus phrase otherwise it will act as a discourse anaphoric constituent or an aboutness topic, which cannot evoke alternatives and form part of an alternative set of the focus phrase. In a sense, the alternative set of focus phrases within the scope domain of focus becomes a referential unit to be used as part of the alternative set of sets of propositions evoked by contrastive topic. Hence, contrastive topic moves out of the focus domain, from the *v*P domain, for scope taking purposes. It is suggested that the information structural unit evoking alternatives cannot surface in this domain and that is why aboutness topic phrases and discourse anaphoric constituents can surface in this domain. In this study, this domain is labeled as the scope domain of the focus phrase. The derivation of binding and scope data has further shown that the scope domain of focus includes the whole *v*P domain excluding the outer specifier position of the *v*P which serves as the escape hatch for the movement of the object phrase to the higher projections. Now, the exact function of this domain will be investigated.

The first hypothesis is that movement to this domain is restricted due to the phase impenetrability condition, namely, once the higher phase is introduced, the complement domain of the *v*P phase is no longer accessible for further operations. However, this analysis leads to some other problems. Firstly, discourse anaphoric and aboutness topic phrases can reconstruct back to this domain but contrastive topic phrases cannot. According to this hypothesis, the same domain is accessible to one information structural unit but not to the other which is contradictory.

The other problem with this hypothesis is that this scope domain of focus does not directly map on to the complement domain of the *v*P phase, namely the spell-out domain. The base position of the external argument is expected to be accessible to further operations according to the phase impenetrability condition. However, the binding and scope data have shown that this position is not accessible. Actually, in the literature, the same effect is observed in many different languages for movement and binding operations. Bošković (2016) suggests that if a phase XP has more than one edge (specifier), only the highest edge serves as an escape hatch for XP and movement is possible only from this position. Now, consider the following relevant examples of movement and binding. In (233a) and (233b) in a Serbo-Croatian noun phrase, there are two phrases at the specifier positions. The movement of the lower phrase over the higher phrase results in unacceptability and that phrase can only move if it is at the highest specifier of the NP phrase as in (233c).

(233) a. *Na tebe$_i$ sam vidio [$_{NP}$ Jovanovog [$_{NP}$ [ponosnog t$_i$] [$_{NP}$ oca]]]
　　　 of　 you　 am　 seen　　 Jovan's　　　　　 proud　　　　 father
　　b. *Na tebe$_i$ sam vidio [$_{NP}$ tog [$_{NP}$ [ponosnog t$_i$] [$_{NP}$ oca]]]
　　　 of　 you　 am　 seen　 that　　　 proud　　　　 father
　　c. Na tebe$_i$ sam vidio [$_{NP}$ [ponosnog t$_i$] [$_{NP}$ oca]]]
　　　 of　 you　 am　 seen　 proud　　　　 father
　　　 (Bošković 2016: 13)

In Serbo-Croatian again, in (234a), the anaphor in the NP is bound by the matrix subject as it is at the highest specifier of the phrase. However, this is not possible in (234b) as the anaphor is not at the accessible specifier position, as it is not the highest specifier.

(234) a. *Marija je prodala svoju omiljenu knjigu.*
       Marija is sold her-anaphor favorite book
       'Marija sold her favorite book.'
   b. **Marija je prodala omiljenu svoju knjigu.*
      (Bošković 2016: 20)

Note that in (232b), there is a similar restriction in the sense that it is the highest specifier of *v*P that is a possible site for movement and reconstruction. In a sense, the lower scope domain of focus indicated in a circle serves as the spell-out domain excluding the highest specifier position.

Note that this line of argument requires amendments to the phase theory (Chomsky 2000, 2001). Remember that in Chapter 3, the discussion on IP level stress assignment has further shown that taking the *v*P phase as a stress assignment domain for Turkish also results in problems for the stress assignment in unaccusative and unergative sentences. These facts make the status of *v*P as a phase in Turkish untenable in the way that it is defined in the literature.

Öztürk (2005) further notes that *v*P and VP partitioning is not observed in Turkish which is expected if VP is the complement domain of the *v*P phase. The empirical evidence arises from restrictions on idiom formation. The idiom test is a conclusive test because if an argument is close to the lexical verb in the syntactic structure, it is easier to find idioms containing the verb and that argument (Marantz 1984). The object argument is merged immediately adjacent to the verb while the external argument is merged at the specifier position of the phase edge. Hence, idiom formation is expected to be found with the verb and the internal argument. Öztürk (2005) shows that in Turkish, the verb not only forms an idiom with the object to the exclusion of the subject (235a) but also with the subject to the exclusion of the direct object (235b). If there were a partitioning between *v*P and VP, VP being the complement domain of the *v*P phase, (235b) could not be possible.

(235) a. *Ali surat as-tı.*   (theme)
       Ali face hang-PAST
       'Ali made a sour face.'

b. *Ali-yi   kurt kap-tı.*   (agent)
   Ali-ACC wolf snatch-PAST
   'Ali got hurt'
   (Öztürk 2005: 54)

This is in line with the findings, in that the lower specifier position of *v*P seems to be a part of the spell-out domain. Hence, there is no difference between an internal argument and an external argument with respect to idiom formation. Based on these properties, it is suggested that the spell-out domain of *v*P in Turkish does not show the same properties as defined in the literature.

Now, it is time to reveal the function of this domain. Note that the scope domain of focus includes not only the internal argument but also the external argument. It is suggested that this is the event structure domain proposed by Ramchand and Svenonius (2013), which is defined as the domain where all the arguments of the verb are introduced. Ramchand and Svenonius (2013) decompose the clause structure into three domains that have semantic grounds. The first domain is the timeless, eventual zone of VP in which the relation between individuals and events are formed. The TP domain, the situational domain, is the time-anchored zone, which is taken as an elaboration of the eventuality domain. Finally, the CP domain, the propositional domain anchored to a discourse context, is an elaboration of the situational zone. The empirical evidence comes from (i) the perfect and progressive participles and (ii) adverb placement.

(236) a. *There could have been a truck being loaded.*
      b. **There could have a truck been being loaded.*

(237) a. *If Mary says that the cakes will have been being eaten, then...*
         ....   *[being eaten], they will have been.*
      b. *....   [been being eaten], they will have.*

(238) a. *John has left and Mary has done also.*
      b. **John is leaving and Mary is (*doing) also.*
         (adapted from Ramchand and Svenonius 2013: 156–157)

The thematic subject of the clause can never surface to the left of the perfect participle but it can appear to the left of the progressive participle (236). VP fronting is possible only when the progressive is not accompanied by the perfect participle (237). Finally, do substitution is possible only with the perfect participle but not with the progressive participle (238).

Based on the data given above, Ramchand and Svenonius (2013) suggest that the differences between perfect and progressive participles is due to different attachment domains of these participles. The progressive participle attaches to the timeless, eventual zone of VP as temporal information is irrelevant for the progressive. The perfect participle, for which temporal information is relevant, attaches to the temporally anchored situational TP domain. The positions these aspectual markers attach to serve as a cut-off point for different domains.

If this analysis is correct and what has been described as the scope domain of focus is, in fact, the eventual zone of VP, differences with respect to scope interactions of focus, are expected to be found based on the progressive and perfective marking on the verb. As the contrast below in (239) and (240) indicates, scope interpretations in Turkish differ depending on the aspectual marker on the verb.

(239) *Bir öğrenci her uçurtma-yı uçur-muş*   *∀∃ / ∃∀
     a student every kite-ACC fly-PERF
     'One student flew every kite.'

(240) a. *Bir doktor her hasta-ya bak-ıyor.*   ?∀∃ / ∃∀
       a doctor every patient-DAT examine-PROG
       'A doctor is examining every patient'
    b. *Bir doktor her hasta-yı tedavi ed-iyor*   ∀∃ / ∃∀
       a doctor every patient-ACC treat-PROG
       'A doctor is treating every patient'
    (Özge 2010: 25)

The placement of focus is not indicated but the structures in (239) and (240b) differ only with respect to the perfect or progressive markers on the verb. Hence, the inverse scope in (240b) can only be due to the interaction of focus with the progressive marker. The progressive is in the VP domain while the perfect is in the situational TP domain. The perfective participle is in the TP domain and hence it does not interact with FocP above *v*P, while the progressive is within the c-command domain of FocP and has an effect on scope interpretations. This difference also provides further empirical evidence for the Focus projection above the *v*P domain in the IP internal structure. Otherwise, FocP in the left periphery is predicted to take both progressive and perfective projections under its c-command domain.[89]

---

[89] Cinque (2001: 51) notes the following order of Aspectual heads for Turkish which is also in line with this analysis.

$$\text{Fut} > \text{Mod}_{\text{Alethic}} > \text{Asp}_{\text{Perfect}} > \text{Asp}_{\text{Progressive}} > \text{Neg} > \text{Mod}_{\text{Ability}} (> V)$$
$$\text{Asp}_{\text{Resultative}}$$

The other prediction of this line of argument is that event modifying adverbs will be restricted to the eventuality domain while situation modifying adverbs will be restricted to the situational domain. If an adverb is licit in both domains, either (i) additional interpretation is available or (ii) another extrinsic factor is at play (Ramchand and Svenonius 2013).

The adverb placement has in fact been used in the Turkish linguistics literature to mark the edge of VP through manner adverbs and the edge of TP through sentential adverbs. Aygen (1999) investigates the subject and object positions with the following examples.

(241) a. *Ben   hızlı   kitab-ı   oku-du-m
        I   fast   book-ACC   read-PAST-1SG
        'I read the book fast'
     b. Ben   kitab-ı   hızlı   oku-du-m.
        I   book-ACC   fast   read-PAST-1SG
        'I read the book fast'

(242) a. Çok şükür   bu   fare-ler   bozuk   peynir-i   ye-di.
        fortunately   this   mouse-PL   spoiled   cheese-ACC   eat-PAST
        'Fortunately these mice ate the spoiled cheese'
     b. Bu   fare-ler   çok şükür   bozuk   peynir-i   yedi.
        this   mouse-PL   fortunately   spoiled   cheese-ACC   eat-PAST
        Fortunately, these mice ate the spoiled cheese.
        Fortunately, these mice ate the spoiled cheese not the nice cake, etc.
        (Aygen 1999: 1)

Aygen (1999) suggests that in (241b), the object moves to the case checking position for the objects, while lack of this movement yields ungrammaticality in (241a) as the VP edge marking adverb indicates. The subject, on the other hand, can remain in-situ or move to Spec TP as the TP edge marking adverb indicates in (242). Aygen (2002b), in a footnote, suggests that Turkish being a free word order language, adverb placement is not a conclusive test and the unacceptability of (241a) above can be due to the ambiguity of *hızlı* 'fast' being interpreted

---

Based on the following example noted by Kornfilt (1997), Cinque suggests that $Asp_{Resultative}$ is lower than $Asp_{Perfect}$ and $Asp_{Progressive}$.

(1) Hasan   böylelikle   yarış-ı   kazan-mış   ol-uyor-du
    Hasan   thus   competititon-ACC   win-PERF   be-PROG-PAST
    'Hasan was thus being the winner of the competition.'
    (Kornfilt 1997: 363)

as an adjective or an adverb. In the immediate preverbal focus position, reduplication yields the adverb interpretation.

(243) *Ben   hızlı   hızlı   kitab-ı   oku-r-um*
       I   fast   fast   book-ACC   read-AOR-1SG
    'I read the book fast'
    (Aygen 2002b: 3)

Note that, even without reduplication, the structure in (241a) becomes more acceptable when focus is placed on another constituent.

(244) *Ben   hızlı   bir tek   kitab-ı   oku-r-um,   dergi-ler-i*
       I   fast   only   book-ACC   read-AOR-1SG   magazine-PL-ACC
    değil.
    not
    'I only read books in a fast way not magazines.'

Hence, adverb placement in Turkish is closely related to focus. In the following examples, *neyseki* 'fortunately' and *henüz* 'yet' are used as situational domain adverbs and *gizlice* 'secretly' and *doğru düzgün* 'properly' as eventual domain adverbs.

(245) A: *Ne var ne yok?*
         'How is it going?'
      B: *Ali   henüz   doğru düzgün   ödev-ler-in-i*
         Ali   yet   properly   homework-PL-3SG.POSS-ACC
         yap-ma-mış.
         do-NEG-PERF
         'Ali hasn't done his homework properly yet.'
         Biz de dışarı çıkmak için onu bekliyoruz.
         'We are waiting for him to go out.'
      B': (?) *Ali   doğru düzgün   henüz   ödev-ler-in-i*
              Ali   properly   yet   homework-PL-3SG.POSS-ACC
         yap-ma-mış.
         do-NEG-PERF
         Biz de dışarı çıkmak için onu bekliyoruz.
         'We are waiting for him to go out.'

As illustrated in (245), the situational domain adverb *henüz* 'yet' and the eventual domain adverb *doğru düzgün* 'properly' can occur in either order. These adverbs do not provide clear-cut results. Now, the situational domain adverb *neyseki* 'fortunately' and the eventual domain adverb *gizlice* 'secretly' will be tested.

(246) A: *Soygunla ilgili bir gelişme var mı?*
'Is there anything new about the robbery?'
B: *Neyseki   Ali gizlice$_F$ gir-miş   içeri.*
fortunately Ali secretly enter-PERF inside
'Fortunately, Ali sneaked (into the building).'
Herkes Hakan'dan şüpheleniyor.
'Everybody suspects Hakan of the robbery'
B': *Neyseki$_F$ Ali gizlice   gir-miş   içeri.*
fortunately Ali secretly enter-PERF inside
'Fortunately, Ali sneaked (into the building).'
Herkes Hakan'dan şüpheleniyor.
'Everybody suspects Hakan of the robbery'

(247) A: *Soygunla ilgili bir gelişme var mı?*
'Is there anything new about the robbery?'
B: (??) *Gizlice$_F$ Ali   neyseki   girmiş   içeri.*
        secretly   Ali   fortunately enter-PERF inside
'Fortunately, Ali sneaked (into the building).'
Herkes Hakan'dan şüpheleniyor.
'Everybody suspects Hakan of the robbery'
B': (??) *Gizlice$_F$ Ali   neyseki   girmiş   içeri.*
        secretly   Ali   fortunately enter-PERF inside
'Fortunately, Ali sneaked (into the building).'
Ya biri görseydi onu?
'What if someone had seen him?'

Although not completely ungrammatical, the sentences are judged to be better when the eventual domain adverb follows the situational domain adverb.[90]

Based on these examples, it can be concluded that the domain which the contrastive topic leaves is, in fact, the event structure domain where all the

---

90 In Turkish the placement of adverbs needs further research which is beyond the scope of this study. Ramchand and Svenonius (2013) give the following example as an example of ordering restriction which is unacceptable due to pragmatic anomaly.

(1) a. *John was probably once married.* b. **John was once probably married.*

However, the equivalents of these sentences are acceptable in Turkish.

(2) a. *John belki   bir zamanlar evliydi.*
        John probably   once   married
     b. *John bir zamanlar belki   evliydi.*
        John once   probably   married
     'John was probably once married'

arguments of the verb are realized.[91] It is suggested that the movement of the contrastive topic is a scope taking operation as the semantic value of the focus phrase is used up by the semantic composition of the contrastive topic phrase.

The final issue to be discussed in this section is the restriction on the reconstruction of contrastive topics. As the discussion so far indicates, this property has been analyzed as a restriction on reconstruction to the eventual domain/scope domain of focus phrases. In line with Wagner (2007, 2008), it is suggested that the movement of the contrastive topic is a scope taking operation. The semantic composition of the contrastive topic is dependent on the lower focus phrase and hence they cannot surface within the same domain. Aboutness topics are omitted from the discussion as they can reconstruct back to the scope domain of focus, since this is not a scope taking movement operation. Şener (2010), on the other hand, suggests that this restriction is due to the requirement that topic phrases cannot reconstruct back to their base generated positions, labeled as no-reconstruction-to-base-position. He gives the following example with a focused time adverbial as evidence for this suggestion. Şener (2010) suggests that no-reconstruction-below-focus analysis cannot account for this example even if the adverb is proposed to be generated at vP or TP levels. The object with the variable is the contrastive topic while the antecedent subject is discourse anaphoric and finally the adverbial bears focus.

---

[91] The other alternative is to assume a tripartite domain analysis similar to the prolific domain account of Grohmann (2003). Within the assumptions of this analysis, the phrase structure is composed of three domains as theta domain (VP domain), agreement domain (TP) domain and discourse-information domain (CP). In the first domain, thematic relations are formed between the predicate and base generated arguments; in the second domain, agreement relations are formed; and in the final domain, discourse relations are formed. Grohmann (2003) further defines a lower bound for movement stating that movement must not be too local namely; movement within the same domain is not licit. The outer specifier of the vP domain is problematic for this line of argument as the internal argument is predicted to undergo movement within the same prolific domain for case checking purposes. The same position which results in problems for the phase theory poses some further problems for the prolific domain approach. Grohmann (2003) suggests that there is only a unique specifier position for the maximal projections and the landing site of the internal argument is AgrOP in the next prolific domain and hence there is no need for the outer specifier of vP. Note that this line of argument cannot account for Turkish data. Firstly, within the current account there is no movement for case checking purposes, all movement operations are driven by discourse interpretational purposes. Additionally, removing the outer specifier of Spec vP leaves no tools for an escape hatch and the peculiar reconstruction properties of informational structural units cannot be explained with respect to scope and binding as discussed in section 4.6.

(248) A: Herkes babasını mezuniyet töreninden sonra$_F$ öptü.
'Everyone kissed their father after the graduation ceremony.'
B: [pro^i anne-si-ni-yse]$_{CT}$ [herkes^i]$_{DA}$ [tören-den önce]$_F$
mother-3SG.POSS-as for everybody ceremony-ABL before
öp-müş.
kiss-PAST
Literally: 'As for his/her mother, reportedly, everyone kissed her before the ceremony.'
(Şener 2010: 95)

Now, consider the derivation of this structure in (249) within the assumptions of the current analysis. The contrastive topic moves to Spec vP and then moves up to Spec CtP. The discourse anaphoric constituent moves to Spec Da. Assume that the adverbial is base generated at Spec FocP or vP. Then movement of the contrastive topic to the specifier of the vP is not a problem, as the eventual domain/scope domain of focus indicated with an ellipse is still lower than the intermediary copy of the contrastive topic phrase.

(249)
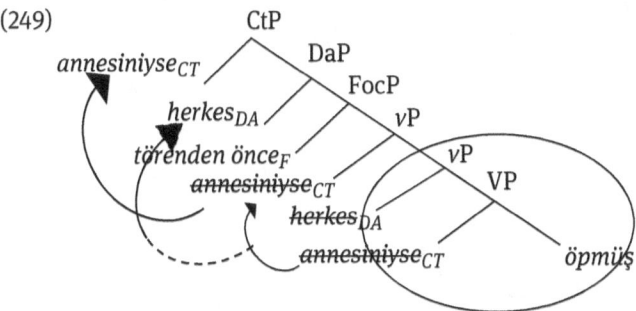

Hence, this restriction can be labeled as no-reconstruction-to-scope-domain-of-focus. The other issue is that if this restriction on movement is taken as a general ban on movements of topics to their base generated positions, the binding data with sentence initial aboutness topic phrases poses a problem. Şener (2010) analyzes these phrases as discourse anaphoric constituents but if they are taken as aboutness topics moving to the left periphery, then they are not expected to reconstruct back to their base generated position. This poses a problem as illustrated in (250) below.

(250) pro anne-sin-i$_{DA}$ herkes$_F$ öp-müş$_{DA}$
mother-3SG.POSS-ACC everybody kiss-PERF
Literally: 'His/her mother, everyone kissed.'

If the sentence initial discourse anaphoric constituent is taken as aboutness topic that moves to a higher projection, with the no-reconstruction-to-the-base restriction as Şener (2010) suggests, the binding possibility in (250) remains unsolved. Hence, the restriction is labeled as no-reconstruction-to-scope-domain-of-focus.

4.7 Derivation of information structural units at LF

Bobaljik and Wurmbrand (2012) and Neeleman and Van de Koot (2012) suggest that the distribution of contrastive topic and focus can be captured by restrictions at the LF domain. Within this line of argument, there is no designated position at the left periphery for the information structural units. Movement operations of these units are derived through other restrictions on movement such as quantifier movement.

Neeleman and Van de Koot (2012) suggest that contrastive topic and focus are quantificational in nature in that they mark contrast and they can be analyzed similarly to quantifiers. Quantifiers give information about the relationship between two sets in the universe of discourse. Contrast also gives information about the relationship between two sets as illustrated in (251) below with the examples.

(251)   Quantifier
    a.   Most students read books.

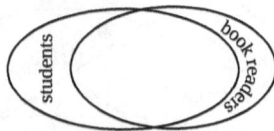

                Contrastive Focus
    b.   A: *John read The Magus.*
          B: *No, John read The Collector.*

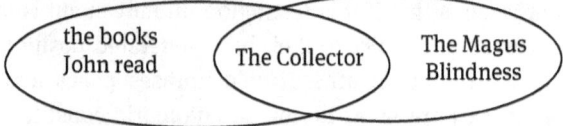

                Contrastive Topic
    c.   A: *Did John read The Magus, The Collector and Blindness?*
          B: *He read The Collector.*

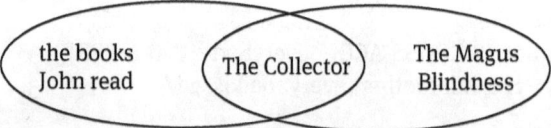

In (251a), the quantifier expresses the overlapping part of the two sets; in (251b), the focused phrase is the overlapping part and the rest of the set of the books are excluded. Finally, in (251c), the speaker B mentions only the overlapping part of the two sets; however, it is not exhaustively identified as the correct answer. The speaker does not make an assertion about the other members of the set of books.

Based on these similarities, Neeleman and Van de Koot (2012) suggest that the derivation of contrastive topic and focus is on a par with quantifier scope. They further suggest that quantifier movement applies only when a quantifier must take scope over another quantifier c-commanding it. Hence, a topic phrase can move over a focus phrase that is in a c-commanding position only when the topic phrase must take scope over the focus phrase. Topics are utterance level constituents while focus phrases are propositional level. Based on the assumption that this is a universal restriction which requires topics to be interpreted outside the scope domain of focus phrases, they try to capture the possible orderings of topic-focus constructions through restrictions on movements. They do not appeal to fixed hierarchical functional projections. Neeleman and Van de Koot (2012: 43) propose the following rules:

(i) Condition on Scope Shift (CSS): no node may inherit two indices.
(ii) Scope Extension: If a Q percolates its index to a dominating node, then its scope coincides with that node minus the Q itself.
(iii) Economy: Scope extension must give rise to an otherwise unavailable interpretation.
(iv) Default Scope Rule: If a Q doesn't percolate its index, it takes scope over its scope domain.

These rules can be explained by the following representations.

(252) a.   b.

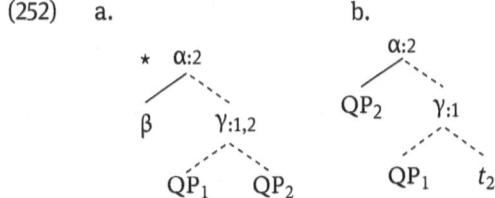

(Neeleman and Van de Koot 2012: 44)

If the QP$_1$ percolates its index to a dominating node [γ], the rule CSS rules out the indexation of the same node by QP$_2$ as in (252a). The scope domain of QP2 can extend over QP1 through overt movement as in (252b). However, in (252b), QP$_1$ cannot further extend its indexation to the node [α] as both [γ] and [α] would bear two indices which leads to the violation of the CSS. These two representations indicate that if there is no movement, surface scope is observed and in (252), QP_1 takes scope over QP_2 without movement or scope extension.

From four possible LF and PF matches, based on topic and focus order variations in Dutch, Neeleman and Van de Koot (2012) propose the following orderings in Table 12. Remember that topic phrases cannot surface within the c-command domain of focus phrases. Only option B is unacceptable because topic phrases cannot surface following the focus phrase but the CSS does not allow scope extension of the topic phrase over the dislocated focus phrase.

Table 12: Possible LF and PF Orderings.

	LF	PF		
A	A[TOP]>B[FOC]	A[TOP]>B[FOC]	+	LF represents surface scope, no index percolation
B	A[TOP]>B[FOC]	B[FOC]>A[TOP]	*	Violation of CSS, the index of topic cannot be carried by the node which also bears the index of focus which has undergone movement
C	B[TOP]>A[FOC]	A[FOC]>B[TOP]	+	Index percolation is possible
D	B[TOP]>A[FOC]	B[TOP]>A[FOC]	+	Via overt movement topic takes scope over focus

In a similar vein, Bobaljik and Wurmbrand (2012) suggest that LF determines PF, which is labeled as scope transparency (ScoT). ScoT is respected when LF and PF match, violation of ScoT is allowed when it is not otherwise possible for the word order to reflect the scope relation. Bobaljik and Wurmbrand (2012) suggest that if the order of two elements at LF is A>B, the order at PF is A>B, if the order is B>A at LF, PF can be B>A or A>B. Similar to Neeleman and Van de Koot (2012), they suggest that there is a universal restriction which requires topics to precede focus phrases because topics are utterance level constituents while focus phrases are propositional level. From four possible orders given in Table 13, the unacceptability of (B) is predicted as LF and PF do not match, violating ScoT. Additionally, overt movement in syntax is a costly operation and hence movement of the focus phrase violates Move.

As is the case in Table 12, except for the order in B, the other three orders are found to be acceptable as they satisfy either ScoT or Move.

Now, it is time to turn to Turkish data to determine how this line of argument captures the Turkish data. As the discussion so far has shown, from four possible LF and PF orders only (A) and (D) are observed in Turkish while the orders in

4.7 Derivation of information structural units at LF — 211

Table 13: Possible LF and PF Orderings.

	LF	PF	ScoT	Move	
A	A[TOP]>B[FOC]	A[TOP]>B[FOC]	+	+	LF and PF match
B	A[TOP]>B[FOC]	B[FOC]>A[TOP]	*	*	Movement is costly, LF and PF do not match
C	B[TOP]>A[FOC]	A[FOC]>B[TOP]	*	+	No overt movement but LF and PF do not match
D	B[TOP]>A[FOC]	B[TOP]>A[FOC]	+	*	LF and PF match but overt movement is costly

(B) and (C) are not possible, in that, contrastive topic cannot follow focus. It can be concluded that Turkish is much more restrictive than the sets given above. The unacceptability of (B) is universal and it is predictable. The unavailability of the order in (C) indicates that to a large extent Turkish is a scope rigid language, although exceptions can be found as illustrated in section 4.6 with OSV indefinite-universal order, namely, in the presence of another quantificational element.

When the order is *bir* 'a' > *her* 'every' in SOV order and, as the topic precedes focus phrases, only surface scope is possible. Within the assumptions of the analysis of Neeleman and Van de Koot (2012), it is predicted that no quantifier raising will apply when surface scope is observed. If scope extension does not result in an otherwise unavailable scope relation, quantifiers do not percolate their index or move at LF. In the data in this study, the indefinite quantifier takes scope over its scope domain as there is no scope index percolation. For the same order, the analysis of Bobaljik and Wurmbrand (2012) predict that for the CT>CF LF order, the only possible PF realization is CT>CF because the CF>CT order violates both ScoT and Move. It violates ScoT because there is a mismatch between the PF and LF representations. It violates Move because overt movement is a costly operation.

Now, consider the predictions of the two analyses for OSV order. Remember that in Turkish OSV order, two patterns are observed. For the OSV order with the *her* 'every' > *bir* 'a' pattern, both surface and inverse scope is possible due to the high attachment site of the existential operator that binds the indefinite quantifier. An additional rule must be added that allows contrastive focus to be interpreted to take scope over the contrastive topic in the presence of the existential operator.[92]

---

[92] This is important in the sense that focus phrases in Turkish can take scope over contrastive topic only in the presence of another quantifier. In base generated orders, this is not possible and hence CF-CT order is not found in Turkish.

Additionally, for the OSV order with *bir* 'a' > *her* 'every' order inverse scope is restricted to a few cases in which it is the discourse anaphoric constituent and not the contrastive focus, which takes scope over the contrastive topic. Discourse anaphoric constituents do not form part of either of the analyses. However, based on the data discussion in section 3, it can be concluded that, similar to contrastive topic and contrastive focus order only contrastive topic can precede discourse anaphoric constituents at PF given that only topic phrases are utterance level constituents. Discourse anaphoric constituents can take scope over contrastive topic phrases in *bir* 'a' > *her* 'every' order by way of the existential operator and in *her* 'every' > *bir* 'a' order due to intermediary reconstruction sites.

This appears to solve the problem with discourse anaphoric constituents but some of the binding data discussed in section 3 gives contradictory results for SOV and OSV orders.

(253) * [[...vbl...]$_{subj}$]$_{CT}$ >> [QP$_{obj}$]$_{DA}$ >> [V]$_F$
    A: *Dünkü törende öğretmenler her öğrenciyi azarlamış. Doğru mu?*
       'I hear that at the ceremony yesterday, the teachers scolded every student. Is that right?'
    B: *Valla   öğretmen-ler-den   haber-im   yok   ama*
       frankly   teacher-PL-ABL   news-1SG.POSS   absent   but
       *[pro$_i$ danışman-ı]   herkes-i$_i$ tebrik   et-ti
       mentor-3SG.POSS   everybody-ACC   congratulate   do-PAST
       tören-de
       ceremony-LOC
       Literally: 'Frankly I do not know about the teachers but everyone$_i$ was congratulated by his/her mentor$_i$ at the ceremony.'
       (Şener 2010: 98)

As illustrated in (253), when the order is SOV, LF and PF do not match. The LF and PF ordering is indicated in Table 14 above as the B option. This ordering violates ScoT, however Move is not violated as there is not an overt movement. It would be expected that this order will be acceptable but it is not. The discourse anaphoric constituent can extend its index without violating CSS; however, the structure is unacceptable. Now, consider the same information structural order in OSV.

Table 14: Possible LF and PF Orderings for CT and DA Constituents.

	LF	PF	ScoT	Move	
A	A[TOP]>B[DA]	A[TOP]>B[DA]	+	+	LF and PF match
B	B[DA]>A[TOP]	A[TOP]>B[DA]	*	+	LF and PF do not match
C	B[TOP]>A[DA]	B[TOP]>A[DA]	+	*	overt movement but LF and PF match

(254) [[...vbl...]$_{obj}$]$_{CT}$ >> [QP$_{subj}$]$_{DA}$ >> [V]$_F$
   A: *Dünkü törende her öğretmen bir öğrencisini tebrik etmiş. Doğru mu?*
       'I hear that at the ceremony yesterday every teacher congratulated a student of her. Is that right?'
   B: *Valla,   öğrenci-ler-den   haber-im   yok   ama*
       frankly   student-PL-ABL   news-1SG.POSS   absent   but
       [pro$_i$ bir arkadaş-ı]-nı   her   öğretmen$_i$
              a   friend-3SG.POSS-ACC   every   teacher
       t[$_{pro\ bir\ arkadaşını}$] azarla-dı   sert bir şekilde.
                               scold-PAST   in a harsh manner
       'Frankly, I do not know about the students but every teacher scolded a friend of her in a harsh way.'
       (Şener 2010: 86)

The LF representation of this acceptable structure is A[DA] > B[CT] and the PF representation is B[CT] > A[DA]. In the assumptions of Bobaljik and Wurmbrand (2012), both ScoT and Move are violated as LF and PF do not match and there is overt movement of the contrastive topic over the discourse anaphoric constituent. In the assumptions of Neeleman and Van de Koot (2012), the scope extension of the discourse anaphoric constituent violates CSS as the index of this constituent moves to the node, which also carries the index of the dislocated contrastive topic. However, the structure is fully acceptable. If the unacceptability proposed in (253) is due to another well formedness condition which states that discourse anaphoric constituents cannot take contrastive topics under their scope, then the structure in (254) still remains a puzzle. These contradictory results show that the quantificational LF analysis falls short of explaining the scope and binding data of information structural units in Turkish.

The syntactic analysis proposed in this study captures binding and scope data not only for the binary distinction of topic and focus but also the ternary distinction of topic, focus and discourse anaphoric constituents.

4.8 Multiple focus projections

The syntactic analysis pursued in this study assumes an IP internal FocP. The quantifier scope and binding data has shown that there is no need for an additional FocP at the left periphery. In Turkish linguistics literature, an IP internal and a CP level FocP have been proposed to account for the distribution of the question particle and the negation marker (Kahnemuyipour and Kornfilt 2011), or the question particle and multiple foci constructions (Su 2012). In this section, these analyses will be considered to see whether the data discussed in these studies can be captured within the syntactic mechanism applied in this study.

Kahnemuyipour and Kornfilt (2011) suggest the phrase structure in (256) for the structure given below.

(255) köpeğ-i   gez-dir-me-di-niz-mi?
      dog-ACC walk-CAUSE-NEG-PAST-2PL-QP
      'Didn't you walk the dog?'

The stress domain maps onto the syntactic domain containing the Tense/Aspect/Modality projection and FocP is above this projection. Hence, in (256), there are two FocP projections, the head projections of which are filled by negation and the question particle.

Kamali and Samuels (2008) and Kamali (2011) argue against the analysis of taking NegP as FocP based on the distinctions between negation and the question particle in that (i) only the question particle follows the constituent bearing focus while negation always attracts stress to the verb, and (ii) the position of focus is important for the question particle but irrelevant for negation.

(256)

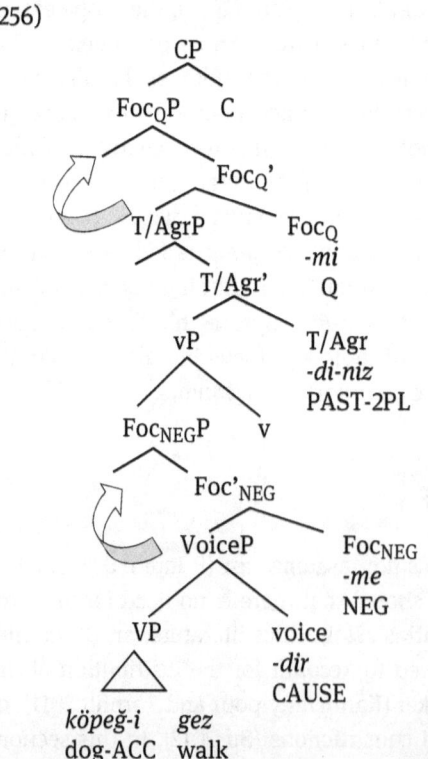

(Kahnemuyipour and Kornfilt 2011: 215)

The data with yes/no questions in sections 2.3.1.2 and 2.3.2.2 has also shown that although yes/no questions can trigger both contrastive focus and topic phrases, the question particle *–mI* always follows the focus phrase. The other distinction is that every constituent in a sentence can bear focus and can be followed by the *–mI* question particle. However, only verbal predicates can bear the negation marker *–mA*.

The following examples also support the analysis that negation and the question particle are not of the same nature. In the presence of a contrastive topic phrase, the verb bears focus in (257), and note that the verb is followed by the question particle.

(257) A: *Almanya ve Hollanda'ya çalışmaya giden Alanyalılar büyük beğeni toplamışlar. Hollandalılar da onları öven bir konuşma yapıyor.*
'One of the groups that went from Alanya to Holland and Germany won recognition with their work. Now the Dutch people give a vote of thanks.'

B: [Almanyalı-lar]$_{CT}$ Alanyalı-lar-ı   [öv-üyor]$_F$ mu?
German-PL   people of A.-PL-ACC   praise-IMPF   QP
'Do the German people praise the people from Alanya?'

It is not possible to add another focus constituent to this sentence as the following example illustrates.

(258) A: *Almanya ve Hollanda'ya çalışmaya giden Alanyalılar ve Anamurlular büyük beğeni toplamışlar. Hollandalılar da onları öven bir konuşma yapıyor.*
'One of the groups that went from Alanya to Holland and Germany won recognition with their work. Now the Dutch people give a vote of thanks.'

B: # [Almanyalı-lar]$_{CT}$ [sadece   Alanyalı-lar-ı]$_F$
German-PL   only   people of A.-PL-ACC
[öv-üyor]$_F$ mu?
praise-IMPF   QP
Intended reading: 'Do the German people praise only the people from Alanya?'

However, negation on the verb can surface in a similar context.

(259) A: *Alanyalılar ve Anamurlular Almanya ve Hollanda'ya çalışmaya gitmişti. Hollandalılar iki grubu da beğenmemiş. Konuşmalarında iki grubu da övmediler.*
'People from Alanya and Anamur went to Germany and Holland to work. The Dutch did not like either of the two groups. They did not praise the two groups in their speech.'

B: [*Almanyalı-lar*]$_{CT}$ *ise*   [*sadece*   *Alanyalı-lar-ı*]$_F$
    German-PL   as for   only   people of Alanya-PL-ACC
    öv-mü-yor
    praise-NEG-IMPF
'The German people, on the other hand, do not praise only the people from Alanya.'

In the presence of a focus phrase in (258), an additional focus phrase with an overt particle is not licit. However, this restriction is not observed with negation as illustrated in (259).[93] Hence, there appears to be no clear reason to take negation as focus projection. With the current analysis, in (255) it is the verb that bears focus and it agrees with the FocP in-situ. Whether the question particle is the head of the FocP or not, as the negation is clearly not, the current analysis can still account for the data with a single FocP.

Su (2012) also suggest an IP internal and a CP level FocP. However, based on the arguments of Kamali and Samuels (2008) and Kamali (2011), Su (2012) also suggests that negation does not project a FocP. Su (2012) argues for an inner and an outer FocP based on the following examples.

(260) a. *Kim   ney-i   gör-müş?*
       who   what-ACC   see-PAST
       'Who saw what?'

---

93 Recall that with contrastive topic phrases, it is possible to interpret the discourse-given verb as the focus phrase although none of the inflectional markers contrast with another marker given in the previous context. The relevant example is repeated below for ease of explication.

(1)   A: *Parti-ye   kaç   kişi   gel-ecek?*
              party-DAT   how many   person   come-FUT
              'How many people will come to the party?'
     B: *Bildiğim kadarıyla,   üç   kişi*$_{CT}$ *gel-ecek,   diğer-ler-in-den*
              As far as I know   three   person   come-FUT   other-PL-POSS-ABL
              haber-im   yok
              news-1SG.POSS   absent
              'As far as I know, three people will come; I don't know anything about the others.'

b. *Okul-a   ne zaman gid-ecek-sin?*
   school-DAT when   go-FUT-2SG
   'When will you go to school?'
   (Su 2012: 136–137)

Su (2012) suggests the following structure for these constructions but notes that the question particle can also attach to the outer FocP. In (261) below, the F feature of inner FocP is valued by the focused phrase in its Spec position. The outer FocP Agrees with the inner FocP and the F feature is valued. The interrogative feature is valued with the C head through long distance Agree. This is similar to a nested-foci analysis.

(261)

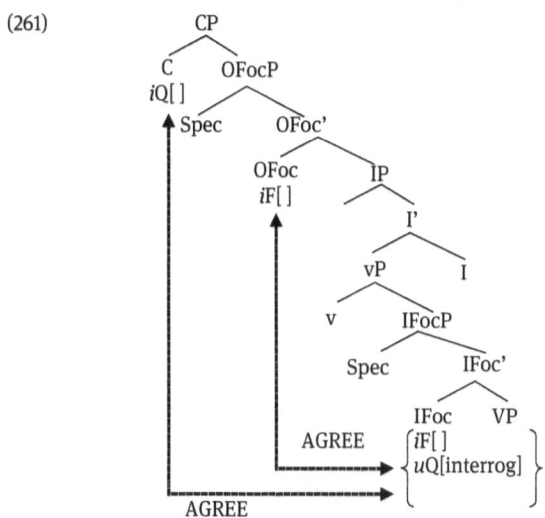

(Su 2012: 138)

Now, it is time to determine whether the current analysis can account for this set of data without appealing to an additional FocP projection at the left periphery. Remember from Chapter 3, negation can surface above the *v*P and TP domains and hence an additional FocP for negation is not required in contrast to the analysis of Kahnemuyipour and Kornfilt (2011).[94] As for the multiple focus phrases given in (260) above, recall that in section 2.3.2.2, it has already been

---

[94] Remember that in the presence of focus on the verb, contrastive topic phrases remain within the scope of negation; otherwise contrastive topic phrases take wide scope over negation. Within the current analysis, negation can project above *v*P or CT and hence different scope interpretations can be obtained. If it is assumed that negation occupies Foc°, then either the lower or the higher Foc° hosts negation and contrastive topic remains within the scope of negation.

suggested that the initial constituent is not a focus phrase but a contrastive topic phrase occupying Spec CtP position above FocP. Additionally, focus phrases in Turkish do not undergo movement.

Now, consider the question particle. In the phrase structure, Foc° position can be taken as the projection site of this particle. The other option is that the question particle heads its own projection above FocP. Based on the distribution of the particle in relation to the focus phrases, it is plausible to take the question particle as occupying Foc°. However, some of the properties of this particle cast doubt on this line of argument. It is not possible to attach *–mI* to the embedded verb with the following intended reading.

(262) **Ayşe-nin   ekmeğ-i   al-dığ-ın-ı   mı*
      Ayşe-GEN   bread-ACC   buy-NOML-3SG.POSS-ACC   QP
      bil-iyor-um.
      know-IMPF-1SG
      Intended reading: 'I know whether Ayşe bought the bread.'

However, a focus bearing verb can be found in the embedded clause.

(263) *Ayşe-nin   ekmeğ-i   al-dığ-ın-ı*
      Ayşe-GEN   bread-ACC   buy-NOML-3SG.POSS-ACC
      bil-iyor-um,   ver-diğ-in-i   değil.
      know-IMPF-1SG   give-NOML-3SG.POSS-ACC   not
      'I know that Ayşe bought the bread not that she gave the bread.'

It is possible to find a wh-question that is [F] marked in the same context.

(264) *Ayşe-nin   ekmeğ-i   ne zaman   al-dığ-ın-ı*
      Ayşe-GEN   bread-ACC   when   buy-NOML-3SG.POSS-ACC
      bil-iyor-um.
      know-IMPF-1SG
      'I know when Ayşe bought the bread.'

Kamali (2014) notes a difference in the intonation pattern of wh-phrases and yes/no questions in that there is always a final rise with wh-phrases but not with yes/no questions. The restriction for the yes/no question to appear in

---

However, the data has shown that in Turkish, contrastive topic phrases cannot remain within the scope domain of focus. Hence, negation cannot be taken as a focus projection.

embedded clauses as in (262) can be due to this distinctive prosodic property. As neither hypothesis makes any significant change to this analysis, and based on the dependency between focus phrases and the question particle, it is suggested that *-mI* is the head of FocP in this study.

4.8.1 Focus and wh-features

The discussion in the previous section has shown that there is no need to assume two FocP positions for multiple wh-questions as one is a contrastive topic and the other is a focus phrase. In this section, whether a single feature [F] can be applied for both focus and wh-phrases is now investigated. Actually, wh-feature and focus feature are closely related. They show similar semantic, syntactic, morphological, prosodic properties in some languages.

From a semantic point of view, both focus and wh-phrases trigger alternative propositions. Truckenbrodt (2013a) suggests that the difference between a focus and a wh-phrase is that focus phrases have an additional ordinary semantic value while wh-questions do not.

(265) *Who ate the cake?*
focus semantic value
{John ate the cake, Mary ate the cake, Sue ate the cake...}

(266) *[John]$_F$ ate the cake.*
ordinary semantic value
{John ate the cake}
focus semantic value
{John ate the cake, Mary ate the cake, Sue ate the cake...}

In Gungbe, focus phrases and wh-phrases are marked with the same marker (Aboh 2007). The focus marker is found immediately to the left adjacent to the focus or wh-phrase.

(267) a. *Sésínù wè dà Àsíàbá*
Sessinou Foc marry Asiaba
'Sessinou married Asiaba.'
  b. *Ménù wè dà Àsíàbá?*
who Foc marry Asiaba
'Who married Asiaba?'
(adapted from Aboh 2007: 289)

In Japanese, focus (268) and wh-phrases (269) trigger focus intonation patterns, namely, a focal boost followed by a post focal reduction (Ishihara 2003).

(268) *Aóyama-ga   aníyome-ni$_F$ erímaki-o   ánda*
    Aoyama-NOM sister-in-law-DAT scarf-ACC knitted
    'Aoyama knitted a scarf for his sister-in-law.'

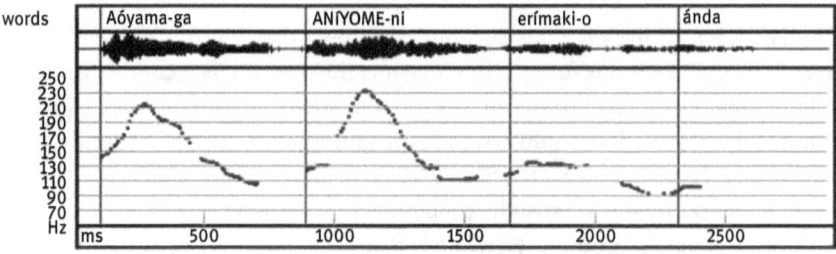

Figure 36: Pitch contour of an utterance with a focus phrase. (Ishihara 2003: 30–31).

(269) *Náoya-ga   náni-o   nomíya-de   nónda no?*
    Naoya-NOM what-ACC bar-LOC   drank Q
    'What$_i$ did Naoya drink t$_i$?'

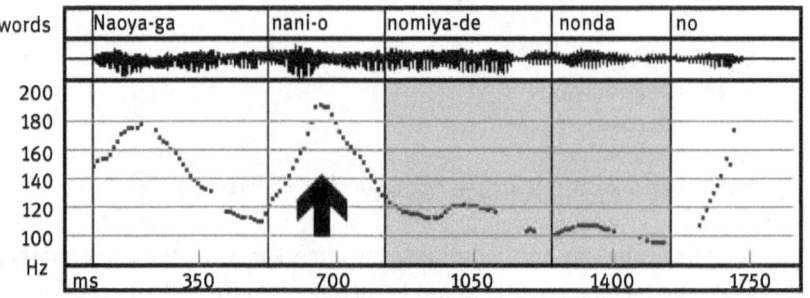

Figure 37: Pitch contour of an utterance with a wh-phrase. (Ishihara 2003: 52–53).

In Italian, focus and wh-phrases are mutually exclusive in matrix clauses (Rizzi 2001) which is taken as an indication that they move to the same position in the left periphery.

(270) a. *A   chi   questo$_F$ hanno   detto   (non qualcos'altro)?
       'To   whom   this   they   said   (not something else)?

b. * Questo_F   a   chi   hanno   detto   (non qualcos'altro)?
   'This   to   whom   they   said   (not something else)?'
   (Rizzi 2001: 290)

As discussed in Chapter 2, in Turkish, focus phrases do not undergo movement and they cannot appear in the postverbal domain. The discussion in Chapter 3 has further shown that focus phrases attract IP level prominence. Wh-phrases are similar to focus phrases in that: (i) they do not undergo movement (271a); (ii) they cannot appear in the postverbal domain (271b); and (iii) there is a rise with wh-phrases in wh-questions Göksel and Kerslake (2005: 36).

(271) a. *Nere-ye   Ahmet   gid-iyor?
         where-DAT   Ahmet   go-IMPF
         'Where is Ahmet going?'
         *Ahmet   gid-iyor nere-ye?

Göksel et al. (2009) and Kamali (2014) indicate that interrogatives have a distinctive intonational pattern having a final rise, prefocal compression and postfocal deaccentuation. Kamali (2014) further notes a higher pitch height with wh-phrases.

(272) Yüzyirmi   arayan-ı   hangi   memura   bağlı-yo
      120   caller-ACC   which   employee-DAT   connect-PROG
      'Which employee does 120 connects a caller to?'

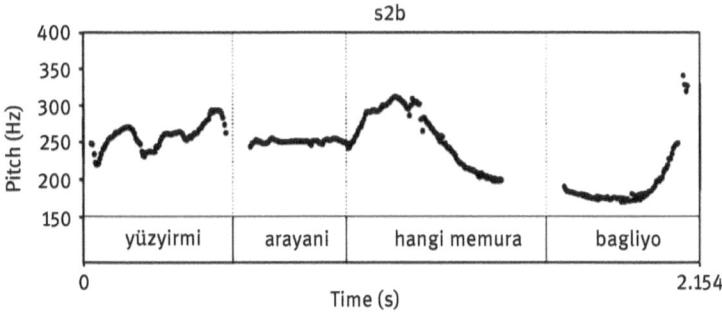

Figure 38: Pitch track of a sentence with a wh-phrase (Kamali 2014: 199).

Based on these parallelisms between focus and wh-phrases cross linguistically, one can suggest that there is a single feature triggering all these effects and it is [F] feature. Actually, Ishihara (2003: 92) suggests that "(...) it may be plausible to consider that what we have been calling the FOCUS feature in this thesis is a phonological property of alternative-inducing elements in general, not just of focus."

However, a closer look at wh-phrases reveals that not all wh-phrases are similar to focus phrases. In Turkish, some wh-phrases can undergo movement, and these are labeled as discourse-linked. (Şener 2010).

(273) *Mete and Pelin are invited to Suna's wedding, and they see that Suna has kissed at least 20 well-wishers so far. Suna has not been the only kisser; her husband, Selim, has kissed as many people as Suna has. Mete and Pelin have noticed that the people Suna kisses, Selim does not kiss, and vice versa, obviously to minimize the amount of kissing as there are still many guests in line.*
Selim-in   öp-tük-ler-in-i   gör-dü-m.
Selim-GEN   kiss-RELV-PL-3SG.POSS-ACC   see-PAST-1SG
Peki,   kim-ler-i$_i$ Suna   t$_i$ öp-tü?
OK   who-PL-ACC   Suna   kiss-PAST
'I saw those people Selim kissed, but who did Suna kiss?'
(Şener 2010: 160)

Drawing on the context preceding the question, it is proposed that the wh-word is a contrastive topic. The big question of "Who kissed whom?" is narrowed down to sub-questions. As the wh-phrase is not a focus phrase, [F] feature is not part of this phrase. The other difference concerns the intonation patterns of interrogatives. As is clear in Figure 38, in addition to attracting main prominence, the contour of wh-phrases involves an additional rise at the end of the utterance as well as prefocal compression neither of which are observed with focus phrases.[95] Hence, it is suggested that wh- and focus features are not one and the same thing. It can be concluded that a focus feature may form part of some wh-questions but an additional Q feature is required to account for the distinctive properties of questions.

4.9 Conclusion

In this chapter, information packaging within syntax domain has been investigated. The data show that: (i) IP internal FocP, DaP and Spec AtP and CtP as

---

[95] Kamali (2014) does not take final rise as a marker of question intonation as it does not necessarily surface with yes/no questions with the question particle *–mI*.

the target position of topic phrases account for facts in Turkish; (ii) an additional FocP at the left periphery (Kahnemuyipour and Kornfilt 2011; Su 2012) is not necessary; analyzing multiple focus phrases as contrastive topic-focus phrases makes the left peripheral FocP redundant; (iii) in Turkish, edge positions of vP do not have the status of phase edges in that only the outer specifier of vP serves as an escape hatch and the complement domain of vP does not allow reconstruction for contrastive topic phrases but reconstruction is licit for aboutness topics and discourse anaphoric constituents; (iv) the scope domain of focus does not map onto the spell-out domain of the vP phase but it maps onto the eventual domain (Ramchand and Svenonius 2013); (v) in SOV order, only the contrastive topic moves out of the eventual domain but in OSV order, except for the focus phrase, the subject and the object move out of their base generated positions; and (vi) in both SOV and OSV orders, the information structural status of the constituents does not directly shape the quantifier scope interpretations and the inverse scope interpretations can be accounted for by way of the exceptional scope taking properties of the existential operator over choice functions and different restrictions on reconstructions sites for the information structural units.

The next chapter discusses the implications of these findings for the phrase structure of Turkish.

Chapter 5
Revisiting the phrase structure of Turkish

5.1 Introduction

In this chapter, based on the findings in the previous chapters, a number of possibilities regarding the phrase structure of Turkish will be examined. The quantifier scope and binding data indicated that the spell-out domain of *v*P in Turkish does not map precisely onto the one indicated in the literature (Chomsky 2000, 2001). Restrictions on reconstruction led us to the scope domain of focus which includes the domain except for the outmost specifier position of *v*P. The phasehood status of *v*P will be further tested based on long distance binding to determine whether it serves as a barrier for operations.

As for the representation of information structural units, IP internal FocP and DaP and CP level AtP and CtP projections can capture the Turkish SOV and OSV data. The untenable status of *v*P as a phase raised questions concerning the inventory of functional projections of Turkish. Turkish is interesting in that the existence of DP has also been questioned. Based on the assumption that there is CP/DP parallelism (Abney 1987; Svenonius 2004; Hiraiwa 2005) the first question under investigation in this chapter is whether conclusive evidence exists for the phase status of *v*P and CP in Turkish. Turkish does not have overt definite articles and complementizers, with the exception of *–ki* borrowed from Persian and the subordinator *diye*.[96] There are two possible alternatives: (i) DP and CP projections are part of the functional inventory of Turkish but they are not realized phonologically; or (ii) the absence of overt determiners and complementizers indicate the absence of these projections for Turkish. It has been observed that there are structural similarities between CP/DP and TP/PossP (Hiraiwa 2005). Despić (2011) shows that in the absence of PossP, DP loses its phasehood properties. Bošković (2012) and Kang (2014) also argue that the absence of DP in a language signals the absence of TP. With these studies, focus shifts to TP/DP parallelism. Hence, the second issue investigated in this chapter is the presence or absence of TP in Turkish in the absence of DP, which is expected to have an effect on the phasehood properties of CP. The discussion of the data on (i) subject reflexives, (ii) ECM clauses,

---

96 Göksel and Kerslake (2005: 462) list the functions of *diye* as expressing "(...) reason, purpose, precaution or understanding (...)"

(iii) bounding nodes, (iii) subject-object extraction, (iv) the absence of expletives, (v) sequence of tense, and (vi) suspended affixation (Zanon 2014) show that, in addition to *v*P, CP also lacks phasehood properties which can be taken as an indication of the absence of TP. The discussion on the T(ense)/A (spect)/M(ood) markers of Turkish reveal that temporal interpretation in Turkish is dependent on Mood markers and a Tense projection is not needed. In the next section, the parallelisms between the CP and the DP projections will be discussed.

5.2 CP/DP parallelism

The discussion in the previous chapter reveals that, in Turkish, *v*P does not show phasehood properties in the sense that the escape hatch positions are more restricted. This observation raises a question about the phasehood status of CP in Turkish. This issue will be investigated in this chapter focusing on CP and DP.

CP and DP projections are parallel in structure. These projections bear similar properties not only with respect to their external syntax but also regarding their internal structure (Abney 1987; Svenonius 2004; Hiraiwa 2005; Despić 2011). This is illustrated below for English.

(274) a. *John destroyed the spaceship*
    b. *John's destruction of the spaceship*
       (Abney 1987: 15)

In Turkish, nominalized complement clauses and genitive-possessive constructions surface with the same morphology.

(275) a. [Sen-in   Ankara-ya   git-tiğ-in]-i
      you-GEN Ankara-DAT go-NOML-2SG.POSS-ACC
      bil-iyor-um.
      know-IMPF-1SG
      'I know that you went to Ankara.'
    b. [Sen-in   ev-in]-i   bil-iyor-um.
      you-GEN house-2SG.POSS-ACC know-IMPF-1SG
      'I know your house.'

The embedded subject in (275a) and the possessor in (275b) bear genitive case. The embedded verb in (275a) and the head noun in (275b) bear a possessive agreement marker that agrees in person and number with the genitive case marked constituent.

Recall that bare nominals in Turkish tend to surface in the immediate preverbal position, pseudo-incorporated into the verb. As passivization is still possible for these constituents, it is suggested that they preserve their syntactic argument status. Aygen (2002b) shows that similar restrictions hold for complement clauses without a case maker. Embedded finite complement clauses (276) and factive nominalized clauses (277) cannot surface as the subject of the matrix clause, but these clauses can be passivized.

(276) a. *[Kürşat gel-di]   biz-i   şaşırt-tı
          Kürşat come-PAST we-ACC surprise-PAST
          Intended reading: 'That Kürşat came surprised us.'
     b. [Kürşat gel-di]   san-ıl-ıyor
          Kürşat come-PAST think-PASS-PROG
          'It is thought that Kürşat came.'

(277) a. *[Kürşat-ın gel-diğ-i]   biz-i   şaşırt-tı
          Kürşat-GEN come-NOML-AGR we-ACC surprise-PAST
          Intended reading: 'That Kürşat came surprised us.'
     b. [Kürşat-ın gel-diğ-i]   bil-in-iyor
          Kürşat-GEN come-NOML-AGR know-PASS-PROG
          'That Kürşat came is known.'
          (Aygen 2002b: 99–100)

The data indicates that, in Turkish, bare nominals and bare complement clauses have similar internal and external syntactic properties.

Hiraiwa (2005: 19) takes a further step and suggests that CP and DP are surface variations of the same underlying structure, as illustrated in (278) below, and argues that both CP and DP are phases. C_3 is the ForceP while D_3 is the demonstrative phrase. C_2 corresponds to Finiteness, D_2 is the definite determiner. TP in the CP projection corresponds to PossP in the DP projection. What is important with this proposal is that the absence of one in the inventory can be taken as an indication of the absence of the other if they are really surface realizations of the same structure. Indeed, in the literature the absence of DP is taken as an indication of the absence of TP in a language (Despić 2011; Bošković 2012; Kang 2014). Within the minimalist program, $C°$ is the locus of all features and percolates its features down to T°. Hence, in the absence of T°, CP is not expected to show phasehood properties.

(278)

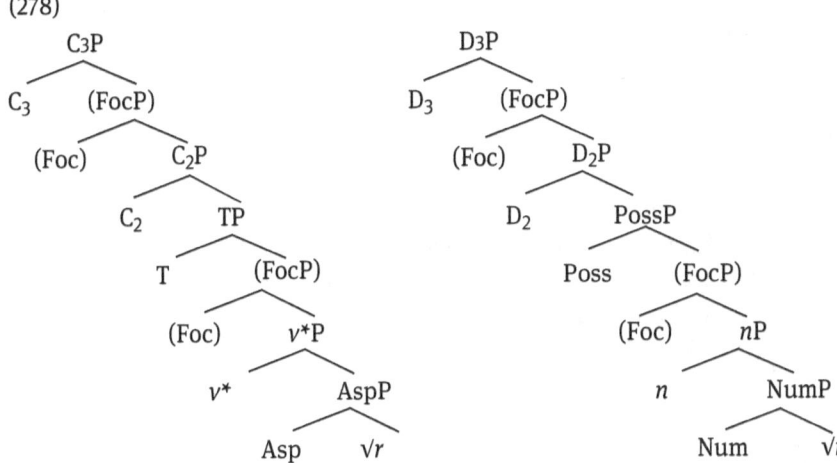

In the next section, the investigation is pursued within this line of argument. Firstly, the status of DP in Turkish is discussed based on the data presented in the previous studies, followed by the status of CP drawing on new data in Turkish.

5.3 Determiner phrase in Turkish

D head assigns referentiality to an NP and type shifts it into an argument (Longobardi 1994). In English, NPs are predicative in nature and when they are merged under DP projection, they are type shifted into arguments. The fact that Turkish lacks overt definite determiners brings the nature of referentiality assignment for Turkish NPs into question.

5.3.1 Arguments against DP

Öztürk (2005) suggests that there is a strict correlation between referentiality and case assignment in that the same functional head is responsible for these functions. The subject is merged at Spec AgentP and obtains its referentiality and checks its case feature in the same position, making movement to Spec TP redundant. ThemeP checks referentiality and the case feature of the object phrase.

Nominals surfacing without overt case morphology serves as the testing ground for this analysis. Öztürk (2005) shows that non-case marked nominals are non-referential.[97]

(279) a. *Ali kitap oku-du.   Reng-i   kırmızı-ydı.
         Ali book read-PAST color-3SG.POSS red-PAST
         'Ali did book reading. It was red.'
     b. Ali kitab-ı oku-du.   Reng-i   kırmızı-ydı.
         Ali book-ACC read-PAST color-3SG.POSS red-PAST
         'Ali read the book. It was red.'
         (Öztürk 2005: 60)

---

[97] Öztürk (2005) suggests that bare nominals are pseudo-incorporated to the verb and, as they are part of the verbal complex, they are predicative in nature. Hence, these nominals do not show properties of syntactic arguments. For example, under passivization, in contrast to a case marked nominal (1a), only an impersonal passive reading is possible with bare nominals (1b).

(1) a. Kitap oda-da   oku-n-du.
         book room-LOC read-PASS-PAST
         'The book was read in the room.'
     b. Oda-da   kitap oku-n-du.
         room-LOC book   read-PASS-PAST
         'Book-reading was done in the room.'
         (Öztürk 2005: 47)

Bare nominals surface with idioms (2a) and with the light verb –et (2b) and in all these cases they form [NP+V] complex predicate structure with the verb. The NP forms are not head incorporated into the verb as some particles can surface between the NP and the verb (Öztürk 2005). This is indicated in the following examples with the insertion of question particle.

(2) a. Ali bu problem-e   kafa mı patlat-tı?
         Ali this problem-DAT head QP burst-PAST
         'Did Ali spend mental energy on this problem?'
         Literally: to burst the head
     b. Meclis   yasa-yı   [NPredd] mi et-ti?
         assembly law-ACC reject   QP do-PAST
         'Did the assembly reject the law?'
         (Öztürk 2005: 54–56)

In (279a), the immediate preverbal object is non-case marked and hence referentiality is not possible. Case assignment type shifts predicative NPs into arguments and leads to kinds, generic or definite readings as illustrated below.

(280) a. *Ali kitab-ı oku-du.* (definite)
Ali book-ACC read-PAST
'Ali read the book.'
b. *Edison ampül-ü icat et-ti* (kind)
Edison light bulb-ACC invent-PAST
'Edison invented the light bulb.'
c. *Ali köpek-ler-i/dondurma-yı sev-er.* (generic)
Ali dog-PL-ACC/ice-cream-ACC like-AOR
'Ali likes dogs/ice-cream'
(Öztürk 2005: 64)

Öztürk (2005) concludes that there is no overt definite determiner that is the equivalent of "the" in English. It is case assignment that type shifts predicative NPs into arguments.

Bošković and Şener (2014) also suggest that Turkish is similar to traditional NP languages not DP languages based on the following set of syntactic and semantic diagnostics applicable only to NP languages.[98] In Turkish:
i. negative raising is disallowed,
ii. transitive nominals with two lexical genitives are disallowed,
iii. scrambling is possible,
iv. radical pro-drop is possible,
v. double negation reading is absent,
vi. possessors do not induce an exhaustivity presupposition,
vii. left branch extraction is possible,
viii. majority superlative reading is not possible,
ix. inverse scope is restricted,
x. number morphology is not obligatory.

---

[98] See Bošković and Şener (2014) for the relevant examples. The observation that a language does not have a phonologically realized definite determiner may not necessarily indicate the absence of the DP projection. These tests have been found to be closely related to the presence of an article. For instance, in literary Finnish there is no phonologically realized definite determiner and left branch extraction is disallowed. In colloquial Finnish, in which a definite article has developed, left branch extraction is possible. Readers are referred to Bošković (2008, 2010) for further arguments and Kornfilt (2018) for counter arguments for Turkish.

Based on these diagnostics, the following representation is suggested for Turkish NPs.[99] The possessor and the demonstrative are adjoined to the NP while the adjective and the numerical occupy specifier positions.[100]

(281)

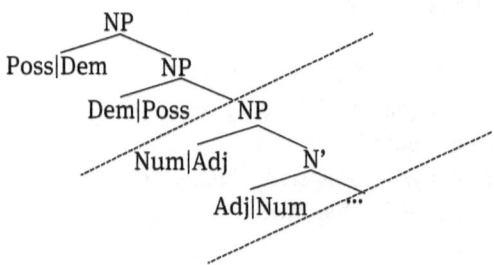

(Bošković and Şener 2014: 11)

They further propose the following example to indicate that in Turkish DP level is missing.

(282) a. *[Şu Özpetek[j]-in   film-i]   o-nu[i]
         that Özpetek-GEN film-3SG.POSS he-ACC
         hayal kırıklığına uğrat-tı.
         disappoint-PAST
         'That movie of Özpetek's disappointed him.'
     b. *[Şu o-nun[i]   film-i]   Özpetek[j]-i
         that he-GEN film-3SG.POSS Özpetek-ACC
         hayal kırıklığına uğrat-tı.
         disappoint-PAST
         'That movie of him disappointed Özpetek.'
         (Bošković and Şener 2014: 11)

---

99 Ellipsis and stranding are possible with phrases but not with segments and bar level constituents. Bošković and Şener (2014) further show that: (i) possessor stranding is not possible; (i) ellipsis inside bare nominals with adjectives and numerals is not possible; and (iii) numerals inside bare numerals can be stranded only in the presence of classifier-like elements. This indicates that numerals, possessors, and adjectives are not phrases.
100 Bošković and Şener (2014) then modify this phrase structure adding a further possessor projection below NumP.

Both the demonstrative and the possessor are an adjunct to the NP projection and they can c-command out of the subject NP. In the absence of a DP projection to close off the binding domain, co-indexation is possible yielding the condition B and C violations in (282a) and (282b).

While discussing the presence of DP projection in a language, Bošković (2008, 2010) bases his arguments on the presence/absence of definite determiners. In the following section, what is suggested for indefinite noun phrases in Turkish will be briefly reviewed. It is suggested that in the absence of a definite article in a language, an indefinite article is not expected (Crisma 1997; Longobardi 2001). The discussion in the next section will show whether Turkish is an exception to this observation.

5.3.1.1 Indefinite noun phrases

Indefinite noun phrases in Turkish can surface as accusative marked or without a case marker. Accusative case marked forms are referred to as specific indefinites (283a), while the zero marked ones are referred to as non-specific indefinites (283b).

(283) a. *Ali bir kitab-ı oku-du.*
Ali a book-ACC read-PERF
'Ali read a book'
b. *Ali bir kitap oku-du.*
Ali a book read-PERF
'Ali read a book'

Specificity has been used to denote partitivity, referentiality, presuppositionality. Kelepir (2001) suggests that in the contexts where accusative marked indefinites appear, the semantic property that captures all the data is not partitivity or referentiality but presuppositionality. General presuppositionality means that the set denoted by the restrictor is not empty. The following examples illustrate the difference between accusative and zero marked indefinites. In an intensional context, only an accusative marked indefinite has a de re reading, while this reading with the zero marked indefinite is illicit in the same context as shown in (284b).

(284) *Hasan bugünlerde ne yapıyor?*
'What is Hasan doing these days?'
a. *Hasan Cambridge-de bir sokağ-ı arı-yor*
Hasan Cambridge-LOC a street-ACC look for-PROG
'Hasan is looking for a street in Cambridge.'

b. #/*Hasan Cambridge-de   bir sokak ar-ıyor
   Hasan   Cambridge-LOC a   street look for-PROG
   'Hasan is looking for a street in Cambridge.'
   (Kelepir 2001: 79)

In (285), the context does not trigger existential presupposition; hence only the zero marked indefinite is possible within this context.

(285) *Bu yazı kontrol edildi mi bilmiyorum.*
   'I don't know whether this text has been edited.'
   a. #*Bir hata-yı   bul-ur-sa-n   bana haber ver.*
        a   mistake-ACC find-AOR-COND-2SG let me know
      'If you find one of the mistakes, let me know.'
   b. *Bir hata   bul-ur-sa-n   bana haber ver.*
        a   mistake find-AOR-COND-2SG let me know
      'If you find a mistake, let me know.'
      (Kelepir 2001: 70)

Finally, in (286), only the accusative marked indefinite can take scope over the negation operator.

(286) a. *Hasan Ali-ye   bir hediye   al-ma-dı.*
         Hasan Ali-DAT a   present buy-NEG-PAST
         'Hasan did not buy Ali a present.'
     b. *Hasan bir ödev-i   yap-ma-dı*
         Hasan a   homework-ACC do-NEG-PAST
         'Hasan didn't do a homework.'
         ('Hasan didn't do one of the homeworks.)
         (Kelepir 2001: 85)

Now, consider how case as referentiality assignor analysis works for Turkish indefinites. Öztürk (2005) takes zero marked indefinites in line with pseudo-incorporated bare nominals. She bases her arguments on scope data and suggests that zero marked constructions always take narrow scope, as is the case with bare nominals.[101]

---

[101] Öztürk (2005) makes a further distinction for zero marked indefinites as stressed *bir* 'a' and stress-less *bir*. Stressed *bir* is an adverbial modifying the whole event. Similar to an adverbial, *bir* measures out the event.

(287) a. *Her   çocuk   bir   kitab-ı   oku-du*   ∀∃ / ∃∀
every child one book-ACC read-PAST
'Every child read a book.'
b. *Her   çocuk   bir   kitap   oku-du*   ∀∃ / *∃∀
every child one book read-PAST
'Every child read a book.'
c. *Her   çocuk   kitap   oku-du*   ∀∃ / *∃∀[102]
every child book read-PAST
'Every child did book-reading.'
(Öztürk 2005: 67–68)

Furthermore, the indefinite is not a functional projection in that it cannot close a projection (288) and it does not obey the head final properties of other functional projections in Turkish (289).

(288) a. *kırmızı bir kitap* b. *bir kırmızı kitap*
red   one book   one book
'a/one red book.'

(289) a. *bu   kitap*   b. **kitap   bu*
this book   book   this
(Öztürk 2005: 20–21)

---

(1) a. *Ali [BİR [CompPred [kırmızı kitap aldı]]*
Ali one   red   book   bought
'Ali bought one red book.'
b. *Ali [bir tane [CompPred [kırmızı kitap okudu]]*
Ali one CL   red   book   read
'Ali did book reading for one unit of red book.'
(Öztürk 2005: 70)

Stress-less *bir* is a predicate modifier and similar to an adjective, modifies the pseudo-incorporated NP.

(2)   *Ali [CompPred bir kitap okudu]*
Ali   one book read
'Ali read a book.'

[102] Although wide scope is not possible with zero marked indefinites, scope interpretation with bare nominals appears not to be possible either. Hence, they cannot be compared in terms of scope interpretation.

Recall that Öztürk (2005) suggests that case type-shifts predicative NPs into arguments and leads to generic, kind or definite readings. As for case marked indefinites, the analysis of Öztürk (2005) predicts them to be referential as they are marked for case. Specific indefinites have neither a kind nor definite reading.

Kelepir (2001) notes that accusative marked indefinites are not always referential as they do not take the widest scope in all cases. Öztürk (2005) adapts the analysis of Schwarzschild (2002) according to whom indefinites encode existential quantification but wide scope reading is available when its domain is a singleton, as indicated with the example in (290) from Schwarzschild (2002).

(290) a. *Everyone at the party voted to watch a movie that Phil liked.*
b. *A movie that Phil liked was such that everyone at the party voted to watch it.*

The specific indefinite is interpreted to be referential because it has a singleton domain and the indefinite has an 'almost definite' reading. However, the following example cannot be analyzed within a singleton domain.

(291) *Kitap-lar-ın   iki-sin-i   al   geri-sin-i*
      book-PL-GEN two-3SG.POSS-ACC take remainder-3SG.POSS-ACC
      kutu-da   bırak.
      box-LOC   leave
      'Take (any) two of the books and leave the remainder (of the books) in the box.'
      (Kornfilt 2000, cited in Kelepir 2001: 82)

In this context, a partitive reading or presuppositionality is easier to obtain than a referentiality reading. An almost definite reading is not possible as the example refers to any two of the books. Hence, it it suggested that if it is case that type shifts predicative NPs into arguments leading to definite, kind or generic reading as indicated by Öztürk (2005), then the existential presupposition reading should also be included in this list. With the addition of presuppositionality, all the semantic instances of accusative marked indefinites can be captured.

However, there are some exceptions to these generalizations. In certain contexts, zero marked indefinites can also trigger existential presuppositionality which is not expected in the absence of overt case marking.

(292) *Bir sokak arıyorum. Adres kağıtta yazılı. Yardımcı olur musunuz?*
      'I am looking for a street. The address is written on the paper. Can you help me?'

(293) *Bir çocuk arıyorum. 5 yaşlarında. Kırmızı mont giyinmiş. Gördünüz mü?*
'I am looking for a child. He is around 5. He had a red coat. Did you see him?'

In these contexts, zero-marked indefinites have the same interpretation as the accusative marked indefinites. Thus, it is not always accusative marking that causes a constituent to have an existential presupposition reading. Drawing on similar examples, Zidani-Eroğlu (2017) questions whether the Turkish indefinite marker is grammaticalized to an indefinite article based on the following scale of grammaticalization process for indefinite markers (Geist 2013: 7).

Table 15: Grammaticalization Process for Indefinite Markers.

1 the numeral	2 the presentative marker	3 the specificity marker	4 the non-specific marker	5 the generalized article
I numeral	II indefinite determiner		III indefinite article	

The numeral *bir* 'a' is stressed and it can surface with focus particles and in contrastive focus structure (294a) and (294b), while the indefinite *bir* does not bear stress and it cannot surface with focus particles or in contrastive focus structures (295a) and (295b). Hence, the first stage is over in that the indefinite determiner can be differentiated from the numeral.

(294) a. *Ali sadece bir film izle-di*
Ali only one film watch-PAST
'Ali watched only one film.'
b. *Ali bir kitap oku-du beş değil*
Ali one book read-PAST five not
'Ali read one book, not five.'

(295) a. #*Ali-nin sadece bir kardeş-i var*
Ali-GEN only a sibling-3SG.POSS exist
'Ali has only one sibling.'
b. #*Ali bir kitap oku-du, beş değil*
Ali a book read-PAST five not
'Ali read a book, not five.'

As for the intermediary stage of being an indefinite determiner, Zidani-Eroğlu (2017) concludes that *bir* can surface as presentative marker, namely it can introduce a new referent to the discourse (296), and mark specificity (297).

(296) a. *İstanbulda gezerken bir hediye aldım. (Eve varınca) onu arkadaşıma vereceğim. Ama önce (onu) paketlemeliyim.*
'When I was visiting İstanbul, I bought a gift. (When I get home) I am going to give it to my friend. But first I have to wrap it.'
b. *İstanbulda gezerken (bir) hediye aldım. Otele döndükten sonra da biraz dinlendim ve akşam konsere gittim.*
'When I was visiting İstanbul, I bought a gift. After I returned to the hotel, I relaxed a bit and then went to the concert in the evening.'

(297) *Ali bir doktor-la evlen-mek isti-yor.*
Ali one doctor-COM marry-INF want-PROG
'Ali wants to marry a doctor.'
a. *Ailesi de onu çok beğeniyor.*
'His family likes her a lot, too.'
b. *Ama ne yazık ki (hiç) doktor adayı yok*
'But unfortunately, there are no candidates of doctors.'
c. *Doktor kim olursa olsun...*
'It doesn't matter which doctor.'

The indefinite marker can mark existential presupposition as (297a) indicates. However, *bir* as presentative marker does not have to be discourse persistent (296b) which indicates that this function has not stabilized.

In the final stage, much more instability is observed. First, if *bir* is an article it is predicted to encode non-referential reading in predicative position. However, as the following examples indicate in predicative position *bir* is used a referential unit (298b), not as a non-referential predicational copula sentence (298a).

(298) a. A: *Ali ne iş yap-ar?*
Ali what job do-AOR
'What does Ali do for a living?'
B: *Ali (*bir) öğretmen.*
Ali teacher
'Ali is a teacher.'
b. A: *Ali kim?*
Ali who
'Who is Ali?'

B: *Ali   geçen yıl   kongre-de   tanış-tığ-ım*
   Ali   last   year   conference-LOC   meet -NOML-1SG.POSS
   bir öğretmen-(dir)
   a   teacher-(FACT)
   'Ali is a teacher I met at a conference last year.'

Finally, if *bir* is an article it must surface with generic subjects. However, as the following example indicates it is optional in these contexts.

(299) *Bir   çocuk (dediğin) anne   baba   laf-ı   dinle-meli*[103]
      one child   mother   father word-CM   listen-NEC
      'A child should listen to mom and dad.'

Based on these diagnostics Zidani-Eroğlu (2017) concludes that *bir* has not as yet reached Stage III and it is not grammaticalized to an indefinite article.

The discussion in this sub-section shows that the distinction between accusative case marked and non-case marked indefinites is not as clear cut as the previous studies have suggested. Case cannot be taken as the sole indicator of referentiality as non-case marked indefinites can also encode existential presupposition. However, one cannot also argue that the indefinite marker has gained the status of an article. Hence, a DP like projection cannot be suggested for indefinite phrases.

5.3.2 Arguments for DP

Arslan-Kechriotis (2006a) argues for the presence of a DP projection. Arslan-Kechriotis (2006a) bases her arguments on distinctions between zero marked indefinite noun phrases and bare nominals. Contra Öztürk (2005), Arslan-Kechriotis (2006a) suggests that in contrast to bare nominals, zero marked indefinites in Turkish are referential. This is similar to the referentiality interpretation of Fodor and Sag (1982) in that there is a referent in mind that exists in the real or imaginary world. Hence, it is not case that assigns referentiality to noun phrases but DP projection.

Aydemir (2004) and Arslan-Kechriotis (2006a) further argue against analyzing zero marked indefinites similarly to bare nominals based on the following tests.

---

[103] This sentence is even better when the indefinite marker is omitted.

(300)a. *Ali kitap oku-du.   Reng-i   kırmızı-ydı
       Ali book read-PAST color-3SG.POSS red-PAST
       'Ali did book reading. It was red.'
       (Öztürk 2005: 60)
   b. *Ali bir kitap oku-du.   Reng-i   kırmızı-ydı
       Ali one book read-PAST color-3SG.POSS red-PAST
       'Ali read the book. It was red.
       (Arslan-Kechriotis 2006a: 30)

(301) a. Bütün gün kitap oku-du-m,   *san-a da
         all   day book read-PAST-1SG you-DAT too
         oku-ma-n-ı   tavsiye ed-er-im
         read-NOML-2SG.POSS-ACC   recommend-AOR-1SG
         Intended reading: 'I did book reading the whole day. I recommend
         you to read (it) too.'
    b. Dün   bir kitap oku-du-m,   san-a   da
       yesterday one book read-PAST-1SG you-DAT too
       oku-ma-n-ı   tavsiye ed-er-im
       read-NOML-2SG.POSS-ACC   recommend-AOR-1SG
       'I read a book yesterday. I recommend you to read (it) too.'
       (Aydemir 2004: 468)

In (300a), the bare nominal cannot be referential but referential interpretation is possible in (300b). Elliptical constructions are possible with zero marked indefinites (301b) but not with bare nominals (301a).

Öztürk (2005) suggests that an elliptical clause is not possible with bare nominals because *pro* in the second clause needs a referential antecedent with number specification but this is not possible with bare nominals. The grammaticality of (301b) is not due to the referential status of the zero marked indefinite. It is the number interpretation of *bir* that makes ellipsis possible. This analysis can be extended to (300a) in that *pro* in the second clause needs an antecedent with number specification and this is not possible with pseudo-incorporated bare nominals.

This is not the only test that Arslan-Kechriotis (2006a) uses to base her arguments. Arslan-Kechriotis (2006a) further argues that zero marked indefinites and bare nominals do not behave in the same way with respect to adverbial modification and relativization as shown in the following examples.

(302) a. *Mehmet kötü araba kullan-ıyor*
Mehmet bad car use-IMPF
'Mehmet drives badly.'
b. *Mehmet kötü bir araba kullan-ıyor*
Mehmet bad one car use-IMPF
'Mehmet drives a bad car.'
(Aydemir 2004: 467)

Öztürk (2005), on the other hand, suggests that adverbial modification is possible in (302b) when the zero marked indefinite is contrastively focused.

(303) *Mehmet hızlı kırmızı bir araba kullan-ıyor,*
Mehmet fast red one car use-IMPF
(yeşil bir motosiklet değil)
green one motorcycle not
'Mehmet drives a red car fast, (not a green motorcycle).'
(Öztürk 2005: 74)

Aydemir (2004) notes another difference between zero marked indefinites and bare nominals as illustrated below with different telic expressions.

(304) a. *Ali bir saat boyunca/*bir saat-te çay iç-ti*
Ali one hour long one hour-LOC tea drink-PAST
'Ali drank tea for an hour/*in an hour'
b. *Ali bir saat-te bir (bardak) çay iç-ti*
Ali one hour-LOC one (glass) tea drink-PAST
'Ali drank (a glass of) tea in an hour'
(Aydemir 2004: 469)

In the following example, Öztürk (2005) suggests that telicity cannot be due only to the presence of an event measuring object. Zero marked indefinites can also be used with telic expressions.

(305) *Ali (bir saat boyunca) bir (bardak) çay iç-ti.*
Ali one hour long one (glass of) tea drink-PAST
'Ali drank a (glass of) tea in an hour'

Arslan-Kechriotis (2006a) further notes that zero marked indefinites and bare nominals also differ with respect to passivization. As illustrated in (306), only impersonal passivization is possible with bare nominals but this is not the case with zero marked indefinites.

(306) a. *Hasan tarafından bir pasta ye-n-di.*
Hasan by one cake eat-PASS-PAST
'A cake was eaten by Hasan.'
b. *Hasan tarafından pasta ye-n-di.*
Hasan by cake eat-PASS-PAST
Intended reading: 'cake was eaten by Hasan.'
(Kornfilt 1984: 250)

The shortcoming of this test is that in (306a), it is uncertain whether it is the passive form of a zero marked indefinite or an accusative marked indefinite. Hence, this test is also inconclusive.

It is observed that languages without DP do not show island effects in scrambling (Boeckx 2003, as cited in Arslan-Kechriotis 2006a). Arslan-Kechriotis (2006a: 38) suggests that Turkish exhibits island effects with wh-scrambling in (i) complex noun phrases, (ii) wh-islands, and (iii) sentential subjects, and hence one cannot propose that DP is missing in Turkish.

(307) a. *Sen [kim-in yaz-dığ-ı kitab]-ı*
you who-GEN write-NOML-3SG.POSS book-ACC
beğen-di-n?
like-PAST-2SG
'Who (x) is it such that you liked the book x wrote?'
b. **Kim-in$_i$ [sen [t$_i$ yaz-dığ-ı kitab]-ı beğen-di-n?*

(308) a. *Aylin kim-e [Zeynep-in kim-i*
Aylin who-DAT Zeynep-GEN who-ACC
gör-düğ-ün]-ü sor-du?
see-NOML-3SG.POSS-ACC ask-PAST
'Whom$_i$ did Aylin ask t$_i$ whom$_j$ Zeynep saw t$_j$?'
b. **[Kim-i$_i$ [Aylin kim-e [Zeynep-in t$_i$ gör-düğ-ün]-ü sor-du]]?*

(309) a. *[Zeynep-in ne-yi oku-ma-sı]*
Zeynep-GEN what-ACC read-NOML-3SG.POSS
herkes-i şaşırt-tı?
everyone-ACC astonish-PAST
'What (x) is it such that [Zeynep's reading x] astonished everyone?'

b. *?Ne-yi_i [Zeynep-in t_i oku-ma-sı] herkes-i şaşırt-tı?
(Arslan-Kechriotis 2006a: 38, 40)

However, this is not a conclusive test either. The unacceptability of the structures in (307b), (308b) and (309b) has to do with the information structural status of the wh-phrases. Remember that wh-phrases can be contrastive topics or focus phrases and focus movement yields unacceptability. In (308), while the first wh- phrase is a contrastive topic the second wh-phrase is a contrastive focus. Hence, the unacceptability of (308b), in which the focus wh-phrase moves and takes contrastive topic under its scope, has already been predicted in the current study. In the following examples, contexts were provided to the remaining examples to show that these constructions are acceptable when wh-phrases are interpreted as contrastive topic phrases.

(310) A: *Ayşe, Melis ve Hale bu yaz evlenecekti. Annen birinin evlendiği haberini duymuş. Bir sor bakalım.*
'Ayşe, Melis and Hale were going to get married this summer. Your mother heard that one of them got married. Ask away.'
B: *(?)Kim-in   dün   anne-n   evlen-diğ-i*
who-GEN   yesterday   mother-2SG.POSS   marry-NOML-3SG.POSS
haber-in-i   duy-muş?[104]
news-3SG.POSS-ACC   hear-PERF
'Who (x) is it such that your mother heard the news that x got married?'

(311) A: *Zeynep'e okuması için bir dergi ve roman bırakmıştım. İkisini de okumuş. Herkes buna çok şaşırmış.*
'I had left a magazine and a novel for Zeynep to read. She read them both. This astonished everyone.'
B: *Ne-yi_i   [Zeynep-in   t_i   oku-ma-sı]*
what-ACC   Zeynep-GEN   read- NOML-3SG.POSS
herkes-i   en çok şaşırt-tı?
everyone-ACC   most   astonish-PERF
'What (x) is it such that [Zeynep's reading x] astonished everyone the most?'

As the examples above indicate, island effects are obviated when wh-phrases are interpreted as discourse-linked, non-focused phrases. The discussion in the

---

[104] The target sentence has been changed in this way to ensure that the head noun and the wh-phrase are not judged as a semantic unit.

previous section has shown that case cannot be the sole assigner of referentiality as non-case marked indefinites can also be interpreted as referential. However, this cannot be taken as a valid argument for the presence of DP in Turkish.[105] The discussion in this section clearly indicate that Turkish shows the properties of languages without DP projection and hence in line with Öztürk (2005) and Bošković and Şener (2014), it can be concluded that Turkish does not have a DP projection.

5.4 Complementizer phrase in Turkish

There are no conclusive tests showing that Turkish has DP projection. Building on the parallelism between DP and CP, now the status of CP in Turkish will be investigated. The overt complementizers in Turkish are *–ki* which is borrowed from Persian (Kornfilt 1997, Göksel and Kerslake 2005) and *diye* (Göksel and Kerslake 2005). The clause following the complementizer *–ki* displays the syntactic properties of a root clause.

(312) a. *San-ıyor-um   [ki   iş-in-i   bırak-mak*
       think-IMPF-1SG that job-3SG.POSS-ACC leave-NOML
       isti-yor]
       want-IMPF
       'I think [s/he wants to leave his/her job].'
       (Göksel and Kerslake 2005: 409)
   b. *Sen iş-in-i   bırak-mak   isti-yor-sun*
       you job-2SG.POSS-ACC leave-NOML want-IMPF-2SG
       diye bil-iyor-um.
       C   know-IMPF-1SG
       'I know that you want to leave your job.'

In contrast to other functional projections in Turkish, note that the verb head is not final with the borrowed form *–ki*. Kural (1993) suggests that *–k* in

---

105 The discussion in section 5.3.1.1 shows that the indefinite marker has not gained the status of an article. Additionally, it is argued that indefinite articles are not hosted by DP projection (Bowers 1987; Stowell 1989; Chomsky 1995; Bošković 2007). Arslan-Kechriotis (2006a) also argues that the indefinite marker in Turkish is not an article but it is a determiner at Spec DP position. In the absence of DP and problems with case as in the referentiality assigner analysis, what licenses NPs in Turkish remains in question. As this issue is beyond the scope of this study, the question is left for further research.

nominalizer –*DIK* and –*EcEK* is also of C° category, –*DI* and –*EcEK* being past and future tense morphology, respectively. Kural (1993) takes the following binding data as evidence for –*k* being the complementizer. In (313a), the CP creates the binding domain for pronouns, while the lack of a CP level in (313b) yields binding violations.

(313) a. *[Ahmet$_i$ [pro$_i$ Ankara-ya   git-ti-ğ-in-i]*
       Ahmet   3SG   Ankara-DAT   go-PAST-COMPL-AGR-ACC
       san-ıyor]
       think-PROG
       'Ahmet thinks he went to Ankara.'
   b. **[Ahmet$_i$ [pro$_i$ Ankara-ya   git-ti]   san-ıyor]*
       Ahmet   3SG   Ankara-DAT   go-PAST   think-PROG
       'Ahmet thinks he went to Ankara.'
       (Kural 1993: 34)

The following data indicates that –*k*, if it is taken as the complementizer, does not always create an opaque domain.

(314) a. *[Ahmet [kimse-nin   Ankara-ya   git-tiğ-in-i]*
       Ahmet   no one-GEN   Ankara-DAT   go-NOML-3SG.POSS-ACC
       san-mı-yor]
       think-NEG-IMPF
       'Ahmet does not think that anyone went to Ankara.'
   b. **[Ahmet [kimse   Ankara-ya   git-ti]   san-mı-yor]*
       Ahmet   no one   Ankara-DAT   go-PERF   think-NEG-IMPF
       'Ahmet does not think that anyone went to Ankara.'

In (314a), matrix negation can license the negative polarity item in the embedded clause but it cannot license the negative polarity item in (314b). If it is the presence of –*k* that creates an opaque domain, the opposite pattern would be expected. Hence, taking –*k* as the complementizer is problematic.

The other alternative is that the CP domain headed by –*k* is not opaque but defective. Actually, there are some studies which follow this line of argument. Kelepir (2007) classifies the studies on Turkish nominalized clauses into three categories: (i) VP selected by a nominalizer (Kornfilt 1984); (ii) nominalizers as tense markers and –*k* as the complementizer (Kural 1994; Göksel 1997); and (iii) nominalizers as aspectual markers with no TP and CP levels (Aygen 2002a). Kelepir (2007) also takes –*k* of –*DIK* and –*EcEK* as complementizer suggesting that tense is defective in nominalized clauses. Hence, the question of whether there is an overt complementizer in nominal clauses and the nature of its status (defective or not) has not yet been resolved. The following section investigates binding, ECM clauses and bounding nodes that will help to shed light on the status of CP.

5.4.1 Binding data and the CP domain

In the literature, the absence of DP is also explicated as a signal of the defective nature of CP in the absence of TP (Bošković 2008, 2010, 2012; Despić 2011). For Serbo-Croatian (SC), Despić (2011) suggests that DP is missing and CP is not a phase due to the absence of a TP projection.

Consider why the defective nature of CP is taken as an indication of the absence of TP. Within the minimalist program C is the locus of all (agreement, case) features and with the percolation of these features to T head, the C-T amalgamation agrees with a goal in the search domain of T. Despić (2011) suggests that CP can be a phase if there is a T head for the features to percolate and argues that in DP-less languages there is also no TP projection. This argument, in turn, is based on CP-DP and TP-PossP parallelism. When PossP is missing in the structure DP is defective, then the prediction is that when CP is defective in nature, it is due to the absence of TP projection in the structure. Now, consider the empirical evidence for these suggestions. In the absence of an overt possessor in the structure, binding relations change.[106]

(315) a. $John_i$ saw $[_{DP}[_{PossP}$ $Bill_j$'s picture of $himself_{*i/j}]]$
b. $John_i$ saw $[_{DP}$ the picture of $himself_i]$
(Despić 2011: 163)

Principle A requires anaphors to be bound in their domain. In the presence of a PossP, DP is not defective and serves as the binding domain. The matrix subject cannot bind an anaphor in the DP domain. In (315b), in the absence of PossP, DP is defective and hence the binding domain moves a step further and the matrix subject binds the anaphor.

Despić (2011) illustrates the absence of DP projection in SC with the following example.

---

106 Despić (2011) takes DP as a phase and defines the application domain of binding requirements as the phase domain.

(316) *[$_{NP}$ Ovaj [$_{NP}$ Kusturicin$_i$ [$_{NP}$ najnoviji [$_{NP}$ film]]]] ga$_i$ je
　　　　this　　　Kusturica's　　latest　　　　film　　　him　is
zaista　　razocarao.
really　　disappointed
'This latest film of Kustirica$_i$ really disappointed him$_i$.'
(Despić 2011: 34)

If the subject NP were a real DP projection, co-indexation with the pronoun would not be possible. However, in SC, there is not a DP projection and the demonstrative and the possessor are NP adjuncts which enable them to bind the anaphor and yield Principle B violation. Recall that the same binding violation has been exemplified for Turkish in (282) by Bošković and Şener (2014).

Despić (2011) argues that if DP without PossP becomes transparent for binding, then the prediction is that CP without TP is also transparent for binding. Note that the prediction is also in line with the suggested parallelism in (278) between TP and PossP proposed by Hiraiwa (2005).

Despić (2011) cites the following example from Aikawa (1994) for Japanese. The reflexive *zibun-zisin* 'self', which is a local subject oriented anaphor, can occur in subject position and can be co-indexed with the matrix subject.

(317) *John$_i$-wa [$_{CP}$ [$_{IP}$ zibun-zisin$_i$-ga　　Mary-o　　korosita] to] omotteiru.*
　　　　TOP　　　　self　　　　NOM　　ACC　killed　　that think
'John$_i$ thinks that zibun-zisin$_i$ killed Mary.'
(Despić 2011: 167)

In the absence of a TP projection, CP is no longer a phase. There is no local subject in the embedded clause and, in the presence of a defective CP, the matrix subject becomes a potential antecedent. Despić (2011) notes that this is only relevant for a single CP projection and binding is not possible across two CP projections as cited from Progovac (1998).

(318) *John$_i$-ga　　Peter$_j$-ga　　kare*$_{*i/j}$-zisin-ga　Bill-o　　hihansita-to*
　　　John-NOM　Peter-NOM　self-NOM　　　　Bill-ACC　criticized-COMP
　　　ommotteiru　koto-o　　sitteiru
　　　think　　　　comp-ACC　knows
'John$_i$ knows that Peter$_j$ thinks that self*$_{*i/j}$ criticized Bill.'
(Despić 2011: 169)

The reflexive *karezisin*, which is not strictly a subject oriented reflexive, can be bound only by the embedded subject one clause up. The CP phase of the most embedded clause is defective due to the absence of TP and the quest for a possible binder continues with the higher clause. The external argument of the next vP phase, which is not defective, binds the anaphor. Hence, the matrix subject cannot bind the anaphor.

Now, it is time to investigate the Turkish data. In Turkish, there are two reflexive forms *kendi* and its inflected form with possessive marker *kendisi*.[107] The Turkish reflexive is not strictly subject oriented.

(319) Ahmet$_i$ Ayşe-ye$_j$ kendi$_{i/j}$ ile ilgili soru-lar sor-du.
Ahmet Ayşe-DAT self COM about question-PL ask-PERF
'Ahmet asked Ayşe questions about himself/herself.'

Göksel and Kerslake (2005) note that of the two forms *kendi* is more local than *kendisi* in that the antecedent of *kendi* is more likely to be in the same clausal domain with the reflexive. Hence, for the tests in Turkish, *kendi* will be used but the inflected form is also possible with the same interpretation. As is the case in (320), Turkish reflexives can occur in subject positions and can be bound by the matrix subject when the embedded clause is a finite clause (320a) or a nominalized clause with the nominalizer –*DIK* (320b), or –*mA* (320c).

(320) a. Ayşe$_i$ [kendi$_{i/*j}$ Ahmet-i$_j$ vur-du] san-ıyor.
Ayşe self Ahmet-ACC shoot-PERF think-IMPF
'Ayşe$_i$ thinks that self$_{i/*j}$ shoot Ahmet$_j$.'
b. Ayşe$_i$ Ahmet-e$_j$ [kendi$_{i/?j}$-nin yarış-ı
Ayşe Ahmet-DAT self-GEN competition-ACC
kazan-dığ-ın] -ı söyle-di
win-NOML-3SG.POSS-ACC tell-PERF
'Ayşe$_i$ told Ahmet$_j$ that self$_{i/?j}$ won the competition.'

---

107 Göksel and Kerslake (2005) suggest that *kendi* can be used as an adjectival modifier, while *kendisi* can be a marker for (i) emphatic, (ii) reflexive, (iii) pronominal, (iv) resumptive usages. Meral (2010: 196) lists the following usage domains for the two forms:

	Anaphor	Pronominal	Resumptive	Emphatic	Logophoric	Adjectival
Kendi	Yes	Yes	No	Yes	No	Yes
Kendisi	Yes	Yes	Yes	Yes	Yes	No

In a grammaticality judgement test, Özbek and Kahraman (2016: 88) find out that variations in judgments exist but "(...) while Turkish speakers interpret *kendi* as referring to either the local or non-local subject, *kendisi* is seen as more likely to refer to the non-local subject."

c. *Ayşe$_i$ [Ahmet$_j$-in   kendi$_{i/j}$-ni   mutlu   et-me-sin]-i*
   Ayşe Ahmet-GEN self-ACC happy make-NOML-3SG.POSS-ACC
   isti-yor
   want-IMPF
   'Ayşe wants Ahmet to make self$_{i/j}$ happy.'

This property of reflexives has already been noted by Meral (2010) for nominalized clauses, ECM clauses and adjunct clauses.

(321) a. *Ali$_i$ [kendi$_i$-ni İstanbul-a   gid-iyor] san-ıyor*
        Ali   self-ACC   İstanbul-DAT go-PROG   think-PROG
        'Ali considers himself going to İstanbul.'
     b. *Ali$_i$ [kendi$_i$-ni ayna-da   gör-ünce]   şaşır-dı*
        Ali   self-ACC   mirror-LOC see-when   surprise-PAST
        'Ali was surprised when he saw himself in the mirror.'
        (Meral 2010: 170)

This test shows that, in Turkish, not only DP but also TP can be missing, which makes CP defective. Defective CP makes exceptional binding possible. Note that in (320c) the matrix subject can bind the reflexive in the presence of a potential antecedent in the embedded clause. Hence, binding of the reflexive with the matrix antecedent is not due to the absence of another local antecedent.

Now, it is time to test whether binding is possible across two CP boundaries, which is not possible in Japanese as illustrated in (318). Recall that in the previous chapter, the scope data indicated that *v*P in Turkish does not display the properties of a phase with respect to reconstruction sites. This is taken as an indication of the defective nature of *v*P in Turkish. If this analysis is correct, then it would be expected that binding is possible across two CP boundaries because for Japanese what blocks co-indexation in the intermediate CP is suggested to be the presence of a *v*P phase. If *v*P is defective, as proposed, then binding should be possible with the matrix subject as well.

(322) *[Ahmet$_i$ [Ayşe-nin$_j$ [boş yere   kendi$_{i/j/*k}$-nin Mete-yi$_k$*
       Ahmet   Ayşe-GEN   without a reason self-GEN   Mete-ACC
       eleştir-diğ-in-i]$_{CP1}$ düşün-düğ-ün-ü]$_{CP2}$
       criticize-NOML-3SG.POSS-ACC   think-NOML-3SG.POSS-ACC
       bil-iyor]$_{CP3}$
       know-IMPF
       'Ahmet$_i$ knows that Ayşe$_j$ thinks that self$_{i/j/*k}$ criticized Mete$_k$ without a reason.'

Note that the hypothesis is supported by the data. In contrast to Japanese, binding across two CP boundaries is possible in Turkish. The CP in the most embedded clause is defective and the binding domain moves a step further to the intermediary embedded clause. If the vP in the intermediate embedded clause were not defective, it would have blocked binding of the reflexive by the matrix clause. However, it does not. These findings amount to saying that the phase status of vP and CP in Turkish is untenable as they do not create boundaries for binding.

The question raised at this point is whether this exceptional anaphor binding data can be taken as pronominal. One of the usage domains of reflexives has already been suggested to be pronominalization (Göksel and Kerslake 2005; Meral 2010). However, the following example of Meral (2010) rules out this possibility.[108]

(323) [Ali$_i$ [Ahmet$_k$-in kendi$_{i/k}$-ne gül-düğ-ün-ü]
  Ali Ahmet-GEN self-DAT laugh-NOML-3SG.POSS-ACC
  san-dı]
  think-PAST
  'Ali thought that Ali laughed at himself.'
  (Meral 2010: 254)

If the reflexive is taken as a pronominal, then binding with the embedded subject is problematic. However, if *kendi* is taken as an anaphor, the binding possibility of the matrix subject by way of a defective CP projection follows as a natural consequence. The embedded subject is already a potential binder for the reflexive.

As the principles for the anaphors and the pronouns are in complementary distribution, the acceptable structures above are expected to be unacceptable with pronouns. Now, it is time to check this prediction. As illustrated in (324), defective CP and vP violate the binding requirement of pronouns to be free in

---

108 Meral (2010) explains the exceptional behavior of reflexives via operator-variable chains in line with Boeckx (2003). The reflexive is merged in the structure with the operator. The operator moves to CP domain successive cyclically and relates the reflexive to a lexical antecedent as illustrated below.

(1) Ali [kendin-e bir takım elbise al-ma-m] -ı   isti-yor
   Ali self-DAT a   suit   buy-NOML-1SG.POSS-ACC want-PROG
   'Ali wants me to buy himself a suit.'

   [$_{C\ Domain1}$ OP$_i$ [$_{T\ Domain1}$ Ahmet$_i$... [$_{C\ Domain2}$ t$_i$ [$_{T\ Domain2}$ [t$_i$ + kendin−e$_i$]]]

their domain. In complement and adjunct clauses, binding of the pronominal results in unacceptability.

(324) a. *Ayşe$_i$ [o$_{*i/m}$ Ahmet-i$_j$ vur-du]   san-ıyor.*
   Ayşe s/he Ahmet-ACC shoot-PERF think-IMPF
   'Ayşe$_i$ thinks that s/he$_{*i/m}$ shot Ahmet$_j$.'
   b. *Ayşe$_i$ [o$_{*i/m}$-nun yarış-ı   kazan-dığ-ın]-ı*
      Ayşe s/he-GEN competition-ACC win-NOML-3SG.POSS-ACC
      söyle-di
      tell-PERF
      'Ayşe$_i$ told Ahmet$_j$ that s/he$_{?i/j/m}$ won the competition.'
   c. *Ali$_i$ [o$_{*i/m}$-nu İstanbul-a   gid-iyor] san-ıyor*
      Ali s/he-ACC İstanbul-DAT go-IMPF think-IMPF
      'Ali considers him/her going to İstanbul.'
   d. *Ali$_i$ [o$_{*i/m}$-nu ayna-da   gör-ünce] şaşır-dı*
      Ali self-ACC mirror-LOC see-when surprise-PERF
      'Ali was surprised when he saw him/her in the mirror.'

This is in line with the predictions in this argument in the sense that the embedded clauses lack a T projection which takes away the phasehood of the embedded CP and the matrix clause becomes the binding domain of the pronoun. Binding with a local antecedent in this domain results in violation of Principle B.

There is another set of data that is suggested to be acceptable with reflexive *kendi*. In (325a), there is a comparative construction, and in (325b) there is a post-positional phrase and they form their own projections. The analysis in this study predicts binding with the matrix subject to be unacceptable but it is not.

(325) a. *Ali$_i$ [Veli$_k$-yi [kendin$_i$-den daha başarılı]] san-ıyor.*
      Ali Veli-ACC self-ABL   more successful think-PROG
      'Ali considers Veli more successful than him.'
   b. *Ali$_i$ [pro$_k$ [kendi$_i$-ne bağlı] ol-ma-mız]-ı*
      Ali   self-DAT loyal be-NOML-1PL.POSS-ACC
      isti-yor.
      want-PROG
      'Ali wants us to be loyal to him.'
      (Meral 2010: 174)

These forms are also acceptable with pronouns as illustrated below, which, in a sense, sheds light on the acceptability of the examples in (325).

(326) a. Ali$_i$ [Veli$_k$-yi [o$_i$-ndan daha başarılı]] san-ıyor.
Ali Veli-ACC s/he-ABL more successful think-IMPF
'Ali considers Veli more successful than him.'
b. Ali$_i$ [pro$_k$ [o$_i$-na bağlı] ol-ma-mız]-ı
Ali s/he-DAT loyal be-NOML-1PL.POSS-ACC
isti-yor
want-IMPF
'Ali wants us to be loyal to him.'

Remember that one of the usage domains of reflexives is pronominals (see footnote 106). We suggest that the reflexives are used as pronominals in (325). If it is assumed that an independent projection for comparative and post-positional phrases, the acceptability of (325) and (326) becomes apparent. The pronouns are bound by antecedents that do not surface in their local domain.

However, there is another problem noted by Meral (2010) for which CP as a defective phase analysis has to find an answer. In the following examples, the pronominal elements are in the same domain with their antecedents but the structures are fully acceptable.

(327) a. Ben ben-i sev-er-im
I I-ACC love-AOR-1SG
'I love me.'
b. Sen-i san-a emanet ed-iyor-um.
you-ACC you-DAT entrust-PROG-1SG
'I entrust you to you.'
(Meral 2010: 242)

Meral (2010) suggests that Turkish pronouns cannot occur in the subject position of the embedded clauses if they are co-indexed with the matrix subject as in (324), leaving the above mentioned structures for further research. Examples similar to the ones above are judged to be degraded or unacceptable when used with the third person singular.

(328) a. *O$_i$ o$_i$-nu sev-er
s/he s/he-ACC love-AOR
'S/he loves him/her.'
b. ?O$_i$-nu o$_i$-na emanet ed-iyor-um.
s/he-ACC s/he-DAT entrust-IMPF-1SG
'I entrust her/him to herself/himself.'

(329) a. *Biz biz-i sev-er-iz.*
we we-ACC love-AOR-1PL
'We love ourselves.'
b. *Biz-i biz-e emanet et-ti.*
we-ACC we-DAT entrust-PERF
'S/he entrusted us to ourselves.'

The structures in (328) and (329) differ from the ones given in (324) in which the antecedent is a referential expression in that the antecedent is a pronominal expression. Note that this usage of the pronominals is similar to reflexives as the translation of the structures in (326) and (327) indicates. It is suggested that, similar to reflexives with pronominal usages, pronominals may have reflexive usages. Hence, the grammatical binding data in (327) and (329) is merely reflexive usage of the pronominals in Turkish. The unacceptability of (328) with the third person pronouns can be due to the fact that the referents of the third person pronouns are not as explicit as the first and second person pronouns. Hence, the degradation is pragmatically conditioned, independent of the reflexive usage of the pronominals.

The binding data in this section has further shown that the defective projection is CP not TP as the defective nature of CP appears to be due to the absence of TP in the structure (Bošković 2008, 2010; Despić 2011; Kang 2014). Remember that the binding data is based on the assumption that TP in the CP domain and PossP in the DP domain are parallel in nature. The absence of PossP in the DP domain makes DP defective and the prediction is that in the absence of TP, CP becomes a defective phase. The Turkish data indicates that CP is defective with respect to binding data which signals the absence of TP.

One can still suggest that the grammaticality of (322) can be due to the logophoric nature of the reflexive in Turkish and the ungrammaticality of (324) can be due to redundant overt pronoun usage violating the Avoid Pronoun Principle. Hence, the next section presents further arguments for the defective nature of CP.

5.4.2 ECM clauses and the CP domain

In addition to the binding data, ECM clauses can also offer ideas regarding the status of TP and CP in the structure. If CP is defective in nature, it can be predicted that the embedded subject receives its theta role from the embedded verb but can surface with the accusative case. The accusative case is taken as an indication of a case checking relation between the embedded subject and the matrix verb. The following example indicates that this is the case in Turkish.

(330) *Ben sen-i okul-a git-ti-(n) san-dı-m*
I you-ACC school-DAT go-PERF-(2SG) think-PERF-1SG
'I thought you went to school.'

The appearance of the agreement marker on the verb is subject to variation in that for some speakers it is optional, for others its appearance is obligatory and for others its appearance yields unacceptability.

The position of the accusative marked embedded subject has been analyzed to be: (i) the embedded clause (Aygen 2002a; Öztürk 2005; Oded 2006; Şener 2008; Meral 2010); (ii) the matrix clause (Zidani-Eroğlu 1997; Özsoy 2001; Arslan-Kechriotis 2006a); and (iii) base generation in the matrix clause (Ince 2006). Whether the embedded subject moves to the matrix clause or remains in-situ, accusative marking on the subject indicates the defective nature of the embedded CP projection.

Based on adverb modification, NPI licensing and word order restrictions, Zidani-Eroğlu (1997) suggests that the accusative marked subject is in the matrix clause.

(331) a. *(Siz) Ali-yi sabah-tan beri öp-ül-dü*
you Ali-ACC morning-ABL since kiss-PASS-PAST
san-ıyor-sunuz
think-PROG-2PL
'You believe Ali to have been kissed since this morning.'
b. **Siz kimse-yi bu kitab-ı oku-ma-dı*
you anybody-ACC this book-ACC read-NEG-PAST
san-ıyor-sunuz
believe-PROG-2PL
'You believe nobody to have read this book.'
c. **Ali bu kitab-ı Banu-yu oku-du san-ıyor*
Ali this book-ACC Banu-ACC read-PAST believe-PROG
'Ali believes Banu to have read this book.'
(Zidani-Eroğlu 1997: 222, 226, 228)

In (331a), the adverb which is compatible with an imperfective interpretation is compatible with the matrix predicate. In (331b), negation in the embedded clause cannot license the accusative marked NPI. Finally, in (331c), scrambling of the embedded object to a position preceding the accusative marked subject is unacceptable. Zidani-Eroğlu (1997) argues that these tests indicate that the accusative marked subject is in the matrix clause.[109] Özsoy (2001) also suggests that T is defective in ECM clauses and hence the case of the embedded subject is checked in the matrix clause.[110]

Aygen (2002a), on the other hand, suggests that the accusative marked subject is in fact at the edge of the CP domain but not in the matrix clause based on the following adverbial test.

(332) *Ben Kürşat-ı   her zaman geç kal-ıyor   san-ıyor-du-m*
      I   Kürşat-ACC always   be late-PROG   think-PROG-PAST-1SG
      'I thought Kürşat was always being late.'
      (Aygen 2002a: 224)

Aygen (2002a) and Öztürk (2005) suggest that the adverbial modifies only the embedded verb not the matrix verb indicating that the accusative marked subject is in the embedded clause. Aygen (2002a) also assumes that the embedded clause is defective in that it is an AspP.

In a similar vein, Şener (2008) suggests that movement of the accusative case marked subject is to Spec TopP at the left periphery of the embedded clause, for discourse-related purposes and hence is optional. The derivation of an ECM clause (333) with overt agreement markers on the verb is illustrated in (334).

(333) *Pelin sen-i   Timbuktu-ya   git-ti-n   diye*
      Pelin you-ACC Timbuktu-DAT   go-PAST-2SG   C
      bil-iyor-muş.
      know-PROG-EVID
      'Pelin thought that you went to Timbuktu.'

---

109 See Şener (2008) for an alternative analysis for the same set of data.
110 Özsoy (2001) makes a further distinction for ECM clauses as (i) VP/AP and (ii) DP/PP. When the phrase following the accusative case marked subject is VP/AP, the ECM clause is like a small clause. When the phrase following the accusative case marked subject is DP/PP, the ECM clause is similar to a complex predicate construction.

(334) ...[TP T_{AGR} [vP   SU   [v' v⁰[VP ... V⁰]]]]
           [uφ]   [iφ]-NOM
            ↦ AGREE ↤
                              MOVE
                   ↓
       ...[vP v⁰ [VP ... [TopP SU Top⁰ ... [TP T_{AGR} [vPtSU[[v' v⁰[VP... V⁰]]]]]]]
           [uφ]   [iφ]-ACC
            ↦   AGREE   ↤

(Şener 2008: 32)

T° forms an Agree relation with the subject in its base generated position and checks nominative case on the subject. The subject then undergoes movement to Spec TopP for discourse-related purposes. Case rewriting applies and another Agree relation is formed with the dislocated constituent and the matrix v° through which accusative case is checked on this constituent. As for ECM clauses with no overt agreement markers on the embedded predicate, Şener (2008) proposes that T° is a non-agreeing head and cannot assign nominative case to the embedded subject.

(335) *Pelin sen-i   Timbuktu-ya   git-ti-Ø   diye bil-iyor-muş.*
       Pelin you-ACC Timbuktu-DAT go-PAST C   know-PROG-EVID
       'Pelin thought that you went to Timbuktu.'

(336)   MOVE

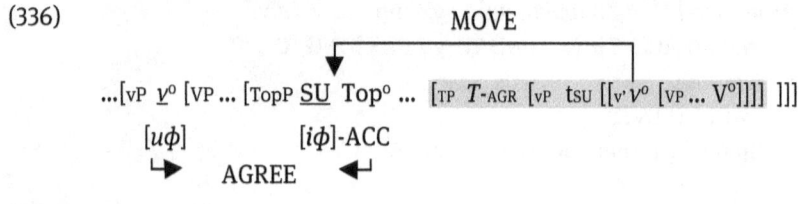

       ...[vP v⁰ [VP ... [TopP SU Top⁰ ... [TP T-AGR [vP tsu [[v' v⁰ [VP ... V⁰]]]]]]]
           [uφ]   [iφ]-ACC
            ↦   AGREE   ↤

(Şener 2008: 32–33)

The embedded subject again moves to the left periphery for discourse interpretational purposes and has its case checked by the matrix $v°$.[111]

---

[111] Şener (2008) further suggests that for accusative case to be assigned to the dislocated topic constituent, it must surface in the highest specifier position of the embedded CP based on the following example.

(1) *Pelin Mert-i   kim-e   vur-du   diye sor-du/merak et-ti.
      Pelin Mert-ACC who-DAT   hit-PAST C   ask-PAST/wonder do-PAST
      Intended reading: 'Pelin asked/wondered who Mert hit.'

WhP, being a phase head at the highest position in the embedded CP, makes the accusative case marked topic phrase at Spec TopP inaccessible for the matrix $v°$. The dislocated topic phrase surfacing at Spec TopP lower than the WhP is sent to spell-out when the matrix $v°$ is merged into the structure.

Note that this restriction itself also indicates that the phase impenetrability condition given in Chapter 1 repeated below for ease of exposition should undergo refinement.

(2)
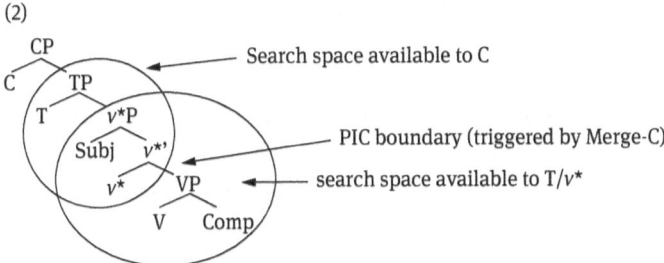

Within this representation, not only the head positions but also the specifier positions of the lower phase are a search space for the higher phase. Remember that in contrast to this representation, Turkish data show that for the contrastive topic phrases only the highest specifier position of vP serves as an escape hatch. It is interesting that a similar restriction holds for ECM clauses. Bošković (2016) suggests that in contrast to the Phase Impenetrability Condition (Chomsky 2000, 2001) what counts as a phase edge is in fact only the outmost specifier of the phase. At this point one may question whether we can account for the Turkish data preserving the phasehood status of vP and CP by taking only the outmost specifier of these phases as an escape hatch in line with Bošković (2016). This line of argument will not be pursued in this study because as already pointed out: (i) vP/VP partitioning is also not observed in Turkish as the idiom formation test of Öztürk (2005) indicates; (ii) the so-called complement domain of the vP phase allows reconstruction of the aboutness topic and discourse anaphoric constituents but not the contrastive topic phrases; and (iii) binding is possible even across two CP boundaries.

Arslan-Kechriotis (2006a) argues against the analysis that the accusative case marked subject is in the embedded clause based on the following test.

(337) *Ben sen-i hep Ankara-da doğ-du*
I you-ACC always Ankara-DAT get-born-PAST
san-ıyor-du-m
think-PROG-PAST-1SG
'I always thought you were born in Ankara.'
'*I thought you were always born in Ankara.'
(Arslan-Kechriotis 2006a: 57)

The adverb *hep* 'always' cannot modify the embedded verb which indicates that the accusative case marked subject is in the matrix clause. The third line of analysis, namely, base generation in the matrix clause (Ince 2005), is based on the tests on idiom interpretation. Ince (2006) suggests that under passivization, the idiomatic reading is preserved but in ECM clauses idioms cannot preserve their idiomatic interpretation.

(338) a. *pro₁ [[Hasan-ın defter-i]-Ø dür-ül-dü-Ø]*
Hasan-GEN notebook-3SG.POSS prepare-PASS-PERF
san-ıyor-du-m.
assume-PROG-PAST-1SG
Intended reading: 'I thought that Hasan's number's up.'
b. *pro₁ [[Hasan-ın defter-in]-i dür-ül-dü-Ø]*
Hasan-GEN notebook-3SG.POSS-ACC prepare-PASS-PERF
san-ıyor-du-m.
assume-PROG-PAST-1SG
Intended reading: 'I thought that Hasan's notebook was closed.'

Ince (2006) suggests that the accusative case marked constituent is base generated in the matrix clause, otherwise the movement would be A-movement and under A-movement idiomatic interpretation is preserved. However, in (338) theta role assignment remains unsolved. Additionally, Şener (2008) suggests that the base generation analysis cannot capture the fact that accusative case marking is optional in the sense that the constituent can also appear in the nominative case.[112]

---

[112] See Arslan-Kechriotis (2006a) for further arguments against base generation in the matrix clause analysis for ECM subjects.

Based on this discussion, it is proposed that, whether no-movement to the matrix clause or movement to the matrix clause analyses are pursued, defective CP analysis would account for the data. In the no-movement to the matrix clause analysis, CP is a transparent domain in that accusative case on the subject is checked by Agree with the relevant projection in the matrix clause. Defective CP does not block this case checking relation. In the movement to the matrix clause analysis, embedded CP is a transparent domain in that movement to the matrix clause is not blocked. To recap, binding and ECM data support the hypothesis in this study that CP is defective in Turkish.

5.4.3 Bounding nodes and the CP domain

As is well known, relative clauses and complex noun phrases are analyzed as islands out of which movement yields unacceptability (Ross 1967). For Turkish, Kornfilt (1984) argues that NP, S and PP are bounding nodes creating islands. Remember that Arslan-Kechriotis (2006a) also suggests that islands effects can be observed in Turkish with the examples (307–309). However, in Turkish, constraints on movement are observed when the movement is in the right direction in which, in any event, focus phrases cannot appear anyway. As the discussion in Chapters 2 and 4 have shown and as noted by Şener (2010) and Bošković and Şener (2014), leftward movement in Turkish can be the movement of contrastive topics, aboutness topics or discourse anaphoric constituents. Rightward movement is restricted to discourse anaphoric constituents and to contrastive topics in certain instances.

Now, consider the following structure. As the movement of the focus phrase is not allowed, in (339b) the rightward movement of the wh-phrase yields unacceptability. However, the leftward movement of the genitive phrase is totally acceptable as in (340).

(339) a. *[[[[kim-e   [ver-eceğ-im-i   [tahmin et-tiğ-in-i*
       who-DAT   give-NOML-1SG.POSS-ACC   guess-NOML-2SG.POSS-ACC
       [bil-diğ-im]   bu   yüzük] çok   değerli
       know-NOML-1SG.POSS   this ring   very   precious
       'This ring, which I know you guess to whom I will give it, is very precious.'
   b. *[[[[----[ver-eceğ-im-i [tahmin et-tiğ-in-i kim-e [bil-diğ-im]
       bu yüzük] çok değerli*

(340) *[[[[Ahmet-in [gizlice fotoğraf-ım-ı çek-en]*
Ahmet-GEN secretly photo-1SG.POSS-ACC take-REL
gazeteci-ler-e] ----- bağır-dığ-ı] kulüp]
journalist-PL-DAT shout-NOML-3SG.POSS club
'The club at which Ahmet shouted at the journalists who took my photos secretly.'

Balkız Öztürk (p.c) suggests that relative clauses in Turkish can still be analyzed as island domains based on the following example.

(341) *(?)Fotoğraf-ı ben [[Ali-nin --------koy-duğ-u] albüm-ü]*
photo-ACC I Ali-GEN put-NOML-3SG.POSS album-ACC
gör-dü-m
see-PERF-1SG
'I saw the album in which Ali put the photo.'

Adapting the analysis of Karimi (1999), Aygen (2000) accounts for extraction out of embedded clauses through the restriction that a constituent bearing the same case marking with the highest head cannot move out of that domain. This can explain the degradation of the construction in (341) in that the head noun bears accusative case. Hence, degradation is not related to the island domains. This is further supported with the following example. Note that in (342), the topicalized dative marked constituent moves out of its base generated position to the left of the matrix subject but the construction is grammatical.[113]

(342) a. *Ben_F [[Ahmet-in Ayşe-ye evlenme teklif-i*
I Ahmet-GEN Ayşe-DAT marriage proposal-CM
et-tiğ-i] söylenti-sin-e
make-NOML-3SG.POSS rumor-3SG.POSS-DAT
inan-ma-dı-m]
believe-NEG-PERF-1SG
'I didn't believe in the rumor that Ahmet made a proposal of marriage to Ayşe.'
b. *[Ayşe-ye ben_F [[Ahmet-in --- evlenme teklif-i et-tiğ-i]*
söylenti-sin-e] inan-ma-dı-m]

---

[113] This sentence is ungrammatical for some of the speakers which indicates that for these speakers CP is an opaque domain out of which a constituent cannot move, especially if it is not the highest constituent in the CP domain.

Based on this set of data, it is suggested that relative clauses and complex noun phrase constructions are not strong island domains in Turkish and CP as a defective projection can account for this property.

To recap, the data on (i) binding, (ii) ECM clauses, (iii) bounding nodes have shown that CP in Turkish does not show phasehood properties in that C does not create an opaque domain with respect to binding or movement operations. An objection to this proposal would be the nature of the empirical evidence that has been used. The data discussed in section 5.4 is based on complement clauses of various types and hence one can suggest that the defective nature of CP might be restricted to embedded clauses and not generalizable to root clauses. Embedded clauses may have some missing projections making CP defective. Aygen (2002a), for instance, suggests that in contrast to root clauses, in finite complement clauses, indicative, subjunctive mood, epistemic modality, deontic modality is allowed but obligation is not licit. With the aim of determining the status of CP in Turkish, and in line with the discussions in sections 5.5 and 5.5.1, TP in Turkish will be investigated. Remember that the defective nature of CP is based on the absence of TP projection (Despić 2011; Bošković 2012; Kang 2014). Hence, if it is shown that TP is missing in Turkish, it can be safely argued that CP is defective in the absence of TP even in matrix clauses. The next section investigates the status of TP in Turkish which will shed light on the status of CP in matrix clauses.

5.5 Tense phrase in Turkish

The role of TP for case checking has already been questioned in Turkish linguistics literature (George and Kornfilt 1981, Aygen 2002, Öztürk 2005). The presence of TP for temporal interpretation will also be questioned. The next section is a brief summary of alternative projections for case checking and temporal interpretation suggested in the literature for Turkish.

5.5.1 Alternative heads for case checking and temporal interpretation

In the following example, the embedded subject can move leftward to the matrix clause. George and Kornfilt (1981) suggest that, in Turkish, tense does not create an opaque domain for movement.[114]

---

[114] Tense is the "grammaticalized expression of location in time" (Comrie 1985: 9). Aspects are "different ways of viewing the internal temporal constituency of a situation" (Comrie 1976: 3).

(343) Biz$_i$ san-a   [t$_i$ içki-yi   iç-ti-(k)]   gibi
     we   you-DAT   alcoholic drink-ACC drink-PERF-1PL like
     görün-dü-k.
     appear-PERF-1PL
     'We appeared to you to have drunk alcohol.'

They further suggest that in Turkish it is not the T head but Agreement that defines finiteness and assigns case. As pointed out in section 5.4.2, the presence of agreement markers on the verb is subject to variation. George and Kornfilt (1981) suggest the obligatory absence of agreement markers on the verb with accusative case marked subjects of ECM clauses. Hence, ECM clauses serve as their empirical evidence for positing not T but Agr head as the case licenser. Aygen (2002a) shows that, contrary to George and Kornfilt (1981), Agreement is not the case assigner in Turkish. She bases her arguments on ECM constructions with an overt agreement marker on the verb with accusative case on the subject.

(344) Ben sen-i   gel-di-n   san-dı-m
     I   you-ACC come-PERF-2SG think-PERF-1SG
     'I thought you came/have come.'

Aygen (2002a) further notes that it is neither tense nor agreement that licenses nominative case. It is a combination of epistemic modality from the inflectional domain and mood from the complementizer domain that checks nominative case.[115] She takes tense as a kind of epistemic modality in line with Lyons (1977). As for agreement, which is suggested to be a case licenser by George and Kornfilt (1981), Aygen (2002a) suggests that agreement is the manifestation

---

Mood/modality expresses the speakers' attitude towards an utterance or event. Moods "are expressed inflectionally, generally in distinct sets of verbal paradigms, e.g. indicative, subjunctive, optative, imperative, conditional etc., which vary from one language to another with respect to number as well as to the semantic distinctions they mark. Modality, on the other hand, is the semantic domain pertaining to elements of meaning that languages express. It covers a broad range of semantic nuances –jussive, desiderative, intentive, hypothetical, potential, obligative, dubitative, hortatory, exclamative etc." (Bybee and Fleischman 1995: 2).

[115] Halliday (1970: 349) defines epistemic modality as "(...) the speaker's assessment of probability and predictability. It is external to the content, being a part of the attitude taken up by the speaker: his attitude in this case, towards his own speech role as 'declarer'."

of Mood on C. She bases her arguments on ECM constructions, in which mood is present but not the epistemic modality. The structure in (345b) is unacceptable, as epistemic modality is illicit with ECM constructions but it is acceptable with a deontic modality marker.[116]

(345) a. *Ben Kürşat-ı   gel-di/iyor/miş/ir/meli/ebilir (D)*
       I   Kürşat-ACC   come-ASP/DEON
       san-dı-m
       think-PAST/PERF-1SG
       'I thought Kürşat to have come/to be coming/to have (to be required) to come/to be able to come.'
   b. **Ben Kürşat-ı   gel-ebil-ir-di   san-dı-m*
       I   Kürşat-ACC come-able-AOR-PAST think-PAST/PERF-1SG
       (Aygen 2002a: 159)

The agreement marker on the verb is optional but this is not a problem because agreement by itself cannot check nominative case in the absence of epistemic modality. The following is a representation of a structure that can check nominative case on the subject within this analysis.

(346)

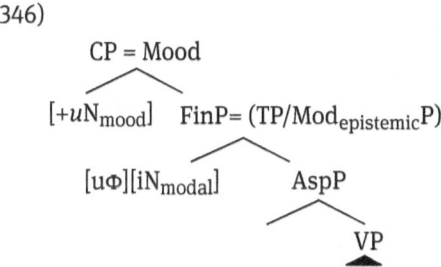

Öztürk (2005) suggests the following phrase structure for Turkish. It is not TP that checks the case feature of the external argument but the AgentP.

---

[116] Deontic modality expresses the speaker's will or desire according to some normative background. Simpson (1993) relates deontic modality with obligation, duty, and commitment.

(347)

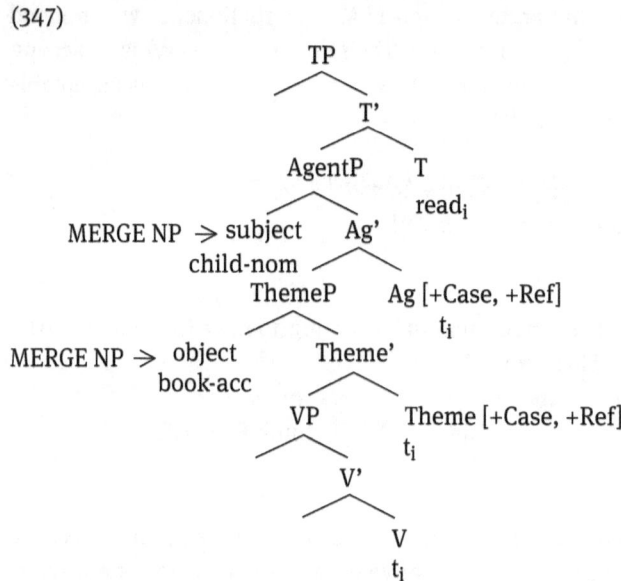

Based on this discussion, it can be safely concluded that case checking is not dependent on TP in Turkish. The discussion of case checking head for the external argument will be maintained to the end of the chapter.

Now, the next issue, namely, temporal interpretation in the absence of TP will be investigated. If the defective nature of CP is taken as an indication of the absence of TP, how is temporal interpretation realized in Turkish? In fact, for nominalized embedded clauses, it has already been suggested that the nominalizers, which share the same morphology with *–DI* past marker and *–EcEK* future marker, are modality markers. Taylan (1988) points out that *–DIK/–(y) AcAK* express modality based on adverbial tests. *–DIK* can co-occur with past, present and future adverbials as the following examples indicate.

(348) *Sen-in   dün   gel-diğ-in-i   bil-iyor-um.*
      you-GEN yesterday come-DIK-3SG.POSS-ACC know-IMPF-1SG
      'I know that you came yesterday.'

(349) *Hasan sen-in   şimdi uyu-duğ-un-u   düşün-ecek.*
      Hasan you-GEN now   sleep-DIK-2SG.POSS-ACC think-FUT
      'Hasan will think that you are sleeping now.'

(350) *Sen-in   yarın   git-tiğ-in-e*
you-GEN tomorrow go-DIK-2SG.POSS-DAT
inan-a-mı-yor-um.
believe-ABIL-NEG-IMPF-1SG
'I can't believe you are going tomorrow.'

–(y)AcAK also expresses modality as it is possible to use it with a past adverbial.

(351) *Hasan-ın   dün   gel-eceğ-in-i*
Hasan-GEN yesterday come-AcAK-3SG.POSS-ACC
bil-iyor-du-m.
know-IMPF-PAST-1SG
'You knew Hasan was going to come yesterday.'

(352) *Engin-in   dün   televizyon-da konuş-acağ-ın-ı*
Engin-GEN yesterday TV-LOC   talk-AcAK-3SG.POSS-ACC
ban-a   söyle-me-di-ler.
I-DAT   tell-NEG-PAST-3PL
'They didn't tell me that Engin was speaking on TV yesterday.'

If they were real tense markers, they would not be compatible with these adverbials.[117] The question raised at this point is whether the same argument can be proposed for matrix clauses. Is TP required to encode temporal information in Turkish? The next section deals with this question.

5.5.2 Verbal inflectional morphology and the status of TP

Verbal inflectional morphology of Turkish has been investigated in great detail (Lewis 1967; Underhill 1976; Yavaş 1980a; Slobin and Aksu 1982; Taylan 1988, 1996; Aksu-Koç 1988; Kornfilt 1997; Kelepir 2001; Sezer 2001; Cinque 2001; Aygen 2002a; Göksel and Kerslake 2005; Sağ 2013; among many others). A detailed discussion of tense, aspect and modality marking in Turkish is beyond the scope of this study; hence only a cursory look will be given to the Turkish facts in this section.

---

117 Kelepir (2007) also suggests that, in nominalized clauses, T is defective with no tense interpretation.

Tense, aspect and modality express "(....) the temporal placement of the event relative to the speech act, the temporal contour of the event, and the attitude of the speaker towards the event" respectively (Slobin and Aksu 1982: 186). While modality is a semantic notion, mood is taken as its morphological realization on the verb. For Turkish, Kornfilt (1997) makes a three way distinction for tense interpretation as past, present and future. Göksel and Kerslake (2005) make a primary tense categorization as past and non-past and add that future is a relative tense. Kornfilt (1997) analyzes aspect as perfective, imperfective, habitual, continuous, progressive, ingressive, terminative, iterative, semelfactive, punctual and simultaneous aspects. Göksel and Kerslake (2005) classify aspect as perfective and imperfective and imperfective is further divided into habitual and progressive. Kornfilt (1997) lists indicative, conditional, imperative, optative, intentional, debitive, potential (ability), degree of certainty, authority for assertion, hortatory, monitory, consecutive, narrative as mood types in Turkish. Göksel and Kerslake (2005) list the modalized utterances in the following way: (i) a generalization, general rule, or statement of principle; (ii) an assumption or hypothesis; (iii) a statement concerning the possibility or necessity of the occurrence of an event or state; (iv) a statement based upon knowledge acquired indirectly; and (v) an expression of desire or willingness for an event or state to occur: imperative, optative, conditional, and aorist forms.[118]

Cinque (1999, 2001) argues for a universal order for the functional structure of the clause as Mood >Tense >Aspect. Not only mood, tense and aspect but also subtypes of these categories are also suggested to be rigidly ordered. Based on the Mirror Principle of Baker (1985), the other assumption of this cartographic approach is that an outer suffix surfaces in the structure higher than the suffixes that are near the root. However, in Turkish, a verbal inflectional

---

[118] The following illustrates the modal system proposed by Palmer (2001).

Propositional Modality		Event Modality	
Epistemic	Evidential	Deontic	Dynamic
Speculative	Reported	Permissive	Abilitive
Deductive	Sensory	Obligative	Volitive
Assumptive		Commissive	

Corcu (2003) indicates that in studies on Turkish modality, epistemic modality is used as the indicative mood making a judgment or statement about the truth value of the proposition. Deontic modality on the other hand reflects the speaker's attitude towards the proposition of the utterance.

morphology can be used to encode mood, tense or aspect and this makes the categorization of the affixes challenging. As indicated above, a three-way classification is suggested for tense in Turkish as: (i) past, (ii) non-past, and (iii) future. Firstly, whether the morphological markers used for these functions have additional aspectual or modal functions will be investigated.[119]

Sezer (2001) suggests that *–DI* serves as a past tense (353a), perfective (353b) and present (353c) marker in the following examples. For the same inflectional suffix Kornfilt (1997) suggests that in addition to past tense marking, it functions as a mood marker expressing authority for assertion as in (354). Göksel and Kerslake (2005) suggest that it is ambiguous as between past tense and a perfective interpretation in (355).

(353) a. *Dün saat beş-te gel-di-m.*
yesterday clock five-LOC come-PAST-1SG
'I arrived home at five o'clock yesterday.'
b. *Yeni gel-di-m.*
just arrive-PAST-1SG
'I have just arrived.'
c. *Şimdi çok üzül-dü-m.*
now very sadden-PAST-1SG
'I am very saddened now.'
(Sezer 2001: 10)

---

[119] Sezer (2001) categorizes the inflectional morphemes in the following way:
Tense 1: *–DI* definite witnessed past; *–sE* subjunctive conditional; *–mIş* inferential past/present perfect; *–Iyor* continuous; *–EcEG* future; *–Ir/–Er* aorist; *–yE* opt/subj; *–mEll* necessitative;
–mEktE continuous
Tense 2: *i-DI/–(y)DI* definite witnessed past; *i-sE/–(y)sE* indicative conditional; *–mIş/–(y)mIş* inferential.
Tense 3: *i-sE/–(y)sE* indicative conditional; *i-mIş/–(y)mIş* inferential.
Enç (2004) divides the inflectional morphemes into three zones.

V < Zone 1	< Zone 2	< Zone3
–A (perm./abil.)	–Ir/–Er (aorist)	–DI (past)
–mA (negation)	–AcAk (future)	–mIş (evidential)
–AbIl (possib.)	–Iyor (progressive)	
[+verbal]	–mAll (necessity)	
	–mIş (perfect)	
	[-verbal]	

(354) *Hasan dün akşam sinema-ya git-ti.*
Hasan yesterday night cinema-DAT go-PAST
'Hasan went to the cinema last night.'
(Kornfilt 1997: 1310)

(355) *Ev-i sat-tı-nız mı?*
house-ACC sell-PERF-2PL QP
'Did/have you sold the house?'
(Göksel and Kerslake 2005: 327)

The same ambiguity holds for *–mIş*, to which past tense, inference, hearsay, perfect, narrative and evidential mood functions have been attributed (Johanson 1971; Banguoğlu 1974; Underhill 1976; Yavaş 1980b; Slobin and Aksu 1982; Aksu-Koç 1988; Taylan 1996, 2001; Kornfilt 1997; Kelepir 2000; Johanson 2000; Göksel and Kerslake 2005; Arslan-Kechriotis 2006b; among many others). Note that this suffix is compatible with adverbials with different temporal anchoring properties.

(356) *Ali dün/şu anda/yarın ev-de-ymiş.*
Ali yesterday/this moment/tomorrow home-LOC-INF.PAST
'It turns out that Ali was/is/will be at home yesterday/now/tomorrow.'
(adapted from Sezer 2001: 11)

The data indicates that *–DI* and *–mIş* are ambiguous as between aspect, mood and tense interpretation. This amounts to saying that *–DI* and *–mIş* cannot be suggested to be pure tense markers. As for the future tense marker *–EcEk*, Yavaş (1980b) suggests that this marker in fact expresses presumptive modality. Underhill (1976) argues that when *–EcEk* is attached to the copula *ol* 'be' following *–mIş*, it has a future perfect interpretation.[120] Yavaş (1980b) argues against this view with the following examples.

---

120 Kelepir (2007) classifies the copula markers in Turkish in the following way:

'Be'	Properties	
i–	With past tense marker & evidentiality marker (zone 3)	"High copula"
Ø	In present tense (zone 3?)	"High copula"
Ol–	All tense, aspect, modality markers (zone 1 & 2)	"Low copula"

(357) a. *John-a   telefon   et-me   şimdi   uyu-yor*
John-DAT telephone make-NEG now sleep-PROG
ol-acak
be
'Don't call John, he will be sleeping now.'
b. *John   dün-kü   sınav-ı   geç-miş   ol-acak*
John yesterday-REL exam-ACC pass-PERF be
ki   yüz-ü   gül-üyor
COMPL face-3SG.POSS smile-PROG
'John must have passed yesterday's exam, that is why he looks happy.'
(Yavaş 1980b: 140)

In these examples, instead of a future temporal interpretation, *–EcEK* marks a presumption that the situation expressed in the utterance holds. This function of *–EcEK* is similar to epistemic modality in that the speaker makes a speculative or deductive judgment on the truth value of the proposition. The same marker can be used to give orders or commands (Yavaş 1980b) expressing volitional modality (Göksel and Kerslake 2005).

(358) *Şimdi   doğru   yatağ-a   gid-ecek-sin*
now straight bed-DAT go-EcEK-2SG
'Now you will go straight to bed.'
(Yavaş 1980b: 146)

Yavaş (1980b) suggests that *–EcEk* is a marker of epistemic modality and encodes presumptive mood. By using the marker *–EcEk,* the speaker makes a presumption that the situation which is uncertain holds true. Gale (1968) (cited in Yavaş 1980b: 139) suggests that "since past events have become present, they have already won their ontological diplomas, unlike future events which still exist in a limbo of mere possibility." The utterances with *–EcEk* are interpreted as future tense because presumptive judgments are, in general, made about future events which have not taken place.

Now, it is time to investigate present tense markers. Kornfilt (1997) suggests the aorist marker *–Ir/Er* as the present tense marker. Göksel and Kerslake (2005) suggest that present tense is indicated by *–(I)yor,* less commonly by *–mAktA* or by absence of the copula *–(y)DI.* As is the case with past and future tense markers, aspectual functions have been suggested for these markers as well. The markers *–(I)yor* and *–mAktA* express progressive (359a) and habitual aspect

(359b) (Göksel and Kerslake 2005). The marker *–Ir/Er* expresses habitual aspect (Kornfilt 1997) as in (360).

(359) a. *Şu sıralarda   konferans-ım-ı   hazırla-makta-yım.*
          at the moment conference-1SG.POSS-ACC prepare-mAktA-1SG
          'At the moment I am preparing my lecture.'
    b. *Cumartesileri Ahmet futbol   oynu-yor-(du).*
       Saturdays   Ahmet football play-Iyor-PAST.COP
       'On Saturdays, Ahmet plays (used to play) football.'
       (adapted from Göksel and Kerslake 2005: 542)

(360) *Hasan piyano çal-ar*
     Hasan piano play-AOR
     'Hasan plays the piano.'
     (Kornfilt 1997: 1232)

The discussion so far indicates that the markers for non-past and future tense can readily be analyzed as aspect and mood markers.

Now, consider the copula forms of *–(y)DI*, *–(y)mIş* and *–(y)sE*. Of these three forms *–(y)mIş* and *–(y)sE* are suggested to express evidential mood and conditional mood respectively.

(361) *Her   yaz   Amerika-ya   gid-iyor-lar-mış.*
     every summer America-DAT go-PROG-3PL-EVID
     'It seems they go/went to America every summer.'
     (Göksel and Kerslake 2005: 545)

(362) *kitab-ı   oku-yor-sa-m*
     book-ACC read-PROG-COND-1SG
     'If I am reading the book'
     (Kornfilt 1997: 1267)

The translation of the sentence in (361) clearly indicates that *–(y)mIş* does not necessarily indicate past interpretation. A judgment is made on the truth value of a proposition based on sensory or reported information.

As for the marker *–(y)DI*, Göksel and Kerslake (2005) suggest that it marks past tense. Zanon (2014) suggests indicative mood function for the same marker in that the listener is making a statement referring to the real world.

(363) *Hasan böylelikle yarış-ı   kazan-mış-tı.*
    Hasan thus   competition-ACC win-PERF-PAST
    'Hasan had thus won the competition.'
    (Kornfilt 1997: 1257)

Zanon (2014: 184) suggests that the past temporal interpretation with the markers *–(y)DI* and *–(y)mIş* can be due to parasitic tense on mood markers or that the marker itself is specified as [past]. This analysis is problematic in that tense is still preserved as a parasitic feature on mood.

In the current analysis, for the past temporal interpretation of *–(y)DI* and *–(y)mIş*, the analysis of Yavaş (1980b) for the marker *–EcEk* is extended to these markers. It is suggested that *–(y)DI* marks indicative mood and the speakers make a judgment about the truth value of a proposal as authority for an assertion. The speaker makes a presumption that the situation holds true based on direct experience. The marker *–(y)mIş*, on the other hand, marks evidential mood and the speakers make a judgment about the truth value of a proposition based on reported data or sensory information. As direct experience or reported, sensory information is generally on events that have become present, with these markers past tense interpretation becomes readily available. Within this analysis, past and future tense interpretations are only secondary effects of the nature of the propositions.[121] That is why it is possible to find these markers with non-past interpretations with some time adverbials as in (353) for *–DI* and (356) and (361) for *–mIş*.

To conclude, MoodP and AspP are sufficient to encode verbal inflectional morphology for Turkish and tense interpretation is only a secondary effect of Mood and Aspect. In section 5.5.2.1, suspended affixation data will be reviewed that will provide further evidence for this line of argument.

5.5.2.1 Suspended affixation

In this section, a study that captures suspended affixation in Turkish in the absence of TP will be briefly reviewed. Suspended affixation is a widely discussed

---

[121] This analysis is further supported by the fact that *–DI* cannot be followed by *–DIR* which turns factual statements into non-factual statements.

(1)   a. *Ali çoktan geldi bile.*
         'Ali has already come.'
      b. **Ali çoktan geldiDİR bile.*
         (Sansa 1986: 151)

issue in Turkish linguistics literature (Lewis 1967; Kornfilt 1996; Good and Yu 2000; Kelepir 2001; Kabak 2007). Zanon (2014) investigates suspended affixation in Turkish to reveal whether T head exists in Turkish or not. Zanon (2014) analyzes the verbal inflectional suffixes as (i) mood/modality: –*DI* and –Ø (indicative), –*mIş* (inferential), –*sA* (conditional), and (ii) aspectual: –*Iyor* (progressive), –*AcAk* (inceptive), –*mIş* (perfective), –*Ir* (habitual). The first group surfaces at MoodP above AspP and does not allow suspended affixation (364b), while the second group occupies AspP and allows suspended affixation (364a).

(364) a. *gel-iyor   ve   gid-iyor-um*
come-PROG and go-PROG-1SG
'I am coming and going.'
b. **(kitab-ı)   oku-du   ve   anla-dı-n*
book-ACC read-PAST and understand-PAST-2SG
'You read and understood the book.'
(Kornfilt 1996: 110)

The markers of –*Iyor* (progressive), –*AcAk* (inceptive), –*mIş* (perfective), –*Ir* (habitual) can precede any of –*DI* (+indicative, -inferential), –*sA* (conditional), –*mIş* (inferential) suffixes but not vice versa. Based on the universal order of Mood >Tense >Aspect (Cinque 1999) and these ordering restrictions, Zanon (2014) analyzes –*DI*, –*mIş*, and –*sA* as mood/modality markers from which –*k* agreement suffixes cannot separate.[122] This accords with the analysis of Aygen (2002a) who takes agreement markers as realization of MoodP at the C domain. The markers of –*Iyor* (progressive), –*AcAk* (inceptive)[123], –*mIş* (perfective), –*Ir* (habitual) are taken as aspectual markers. Now, consider the data within these assumptions.

---

122 Agreement markers in Turkish can be divided into two as –k and –z paradigms based on the first person plural agreement marker.

	1SG	2SG	3SG	1PL	2PL	3PL
–k	–m	–n	–	–k	–nIz	–lEr
–z	–(y)Im	–sIn	–	–Iz	–sInIz	–lEr

123 Inceptive aspectual markers are used to express the beginning of an action.

(365) a. *çalış-tı   ve   başar-dı-k
       work-PAST   and   succeed-PAST-1PL
       Intended reading: 'We worked and succeeded.'

b.
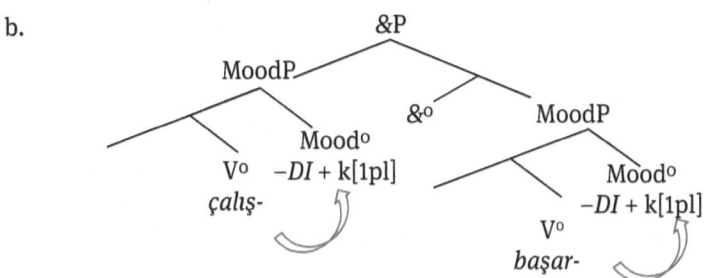

(Zanon 2014: 182)

In (365b) above, two Mood phrases are coordinated. The mood marker -*DI* heads a MoodP with agreement markers attached to it. The verb moves to MoodP. However, as the agreement markers are not separable from the Mood head, suspended affixation is unacceptable.

(366) a. çalış-acak ve   başar-acak-ø-tı-k   / başar-acak
        work-FUT and succeed-FUT-Ø-PAST-1PL   succeed-FUT
        i-di-k
        COP-PAST-1PL
        'We were going to work and succeed.'

b.
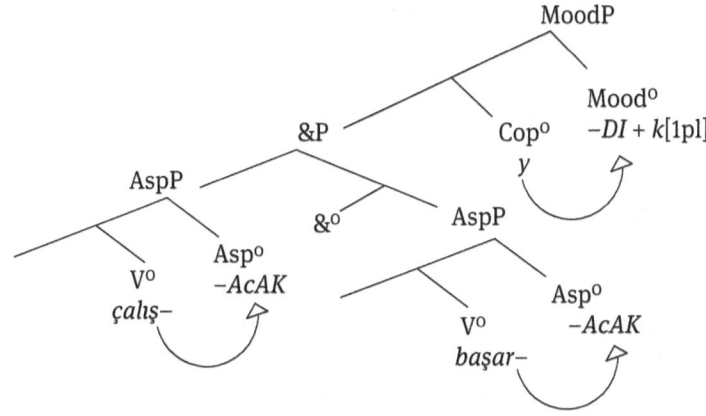

(Zanon 2014: 182)

As illustrated in (366b) above, the aspectual markers surface at Asp°. The verb moves to Asp° and as this composite head is [-verbal] in nature, there is no need for further movement. There is a copula between the MoodP and AspP that carries the remaining inflectional morphology. In (366b) above, the copula moves to MoodP and in the phonological component it is realized overtly or covertly.

Zanon (2014) suggests that this analysis easily accounts for the observation that when the question particle is attached to these forms, the two groups behave differently with regard to the placement of agreement markers. The question particle surfaces between the AspP and the MoodP in (367) but it follows the MoodP, as agreement is inseparable from the mood marker in (368).

(367) a. *gid-ecek-mi-siniz?*
go-FUT-QP-2PL
'Will you go?'
b. **/??gid-ecek-siniz-mi?*

(368) a. *git-ti-niz-mi?*
go-PAST-2PL-QP
'Did you go?'
b. **git-ti-mi-niz?*
(Kornfilt 1996: 106)

The question particle cannot intervene between the agreement marker and the mood marker in (368b).

To recap, the discussion so far has shown that in the absence of TP, temporal information can be encoded by MoodP, AspP and adverbials in Turkish. The suspended affixation data also support this proposal. The next section analyzes the diagnostics, the syntactic properties of languages without DP and TP projections, proposed by Bošković (2012).

5.5.3 No DP no TP

Bošković (2012) argues that in languages without a definite determiner, TP projection is also absent. He lists the following generalizations for languages without a TP projection: (a) in article-less languages there seem to be no subject expletives; (b) article-less languages do not exhibit subject-object asymmetries in extraction; (c) nominative case is either default case or some contextual case; (d) article-less languages do not exhibit sequence of tense; and (e) only article-less languages may have subject reflexive constructions (Despić 2011). The subject reflexive constructions have been discussed in section 5.4.1. Hence, the remaining diagnostics for Turkish will be elaborated upon in the following sub-sections.

5.5.3.1 Subject expletives
Expletives are semantically vacuous constituents that occupy the subject position. This property is closely related to the TP projection because in some languages the subject position is filled with expletives to satisfy the EPP requirement as in (369).

(369) a. *It seems that the fly is in my soup.*
b. *There seems to be a fly in my soup.*

If there is no TP projection then there is no need for the subjects to move to satisfy EPP. In Turkish, there is no expletive and the requirement of EPP has been under discussion in the literature. Öztürk (2005); İşsever (2008); Şener (2010); Kamali (2011) argue against the EPP requirement for Turkish. Öztürk (2005) suggests that Spec TP is not always projected and V to T movement satisfies the EPP requirement of TP. Spec TP is filled only for discourse-related purposes. Gürer (2010), on the other hand, suggests that the EPP requirement exists in Turkish independent of case and agreement. The following examples are given to support this suggestion. The ungrammaticality of (370a) is suggested to be due to a restriction on reconstruction in that the target position of the dislocated constituent is to an A position from which reconstruction is not possible.

(370) a. *Kimse$_i$ ban-a [t$_i$ kitab-ı oku-ma-mış] gibi
 nobody I-DAT book-ACC read-NEG-PERF like
 görün-üyor
 appear-IMPF
 'Nobody seems to me to have read the book.'
b. Ayşe$_i$ ban-a [t$_i$ kitab-ı oku-ma-mış] gibi
 nobody I-DAT book-ACC read-NEG-PERF like
 görün-üyor
 appear-IMPF
 'It seems to me that Ayşe has not read the book.'
 (Gürer 2010: 184)

As the discussion in Chapter 4 has shown, in Turkish, all movement operations are for discourse-related purposes, and hence the information structural status of the dislocated constituents must be considered. The sentence initial dislocated constituent can be a contrastive topic, as in SOV order, aboutness topics do not move. The ungrammaticality of (370a) can be due to the fact that the negative polarity item cannot be a contrastive topic in that it resolves the issue fully. Note that the structure is fully acceptable in the following context.

(371) A: *Sanırım Ahmet dergiyi okumamış.*
'I think Ahmet has read the magazine.'
B: *Valla Ahmet'i bilmiyorum ama Ayşe bana kitabı okumamış gibi görünüyor.*
'Well, I don't know about Ahmet but it seems to me that Ayşe has not read the book.'

The referential expression is a contrastive topic and it marks a shift for the question under discussion. The comparison of the two constructions in (370a) and (370b) is not conclusive, as they do not have the same information structural statuses, and hence they do not undergo the same restrictions on movement. The data shows that it is not possible to generalize a property of a construction to another construction if they do not have the same information structural constituents.[124]

In addition, the controversial status of EPP in Turkish might be due to the discussion of different sets of data. There is no topic movement in all sentences, hence subjects in Turkish do not move to a position to fulfill the EPP requirement. In some other constructions, contrastive topic obligatorily moves out of its base generated position for scope taking purposes. As every movement is for discourse-related purposes, the movement operations can be accounted for without appealing to EPP.

---

[124] Kelepir (2001: 100) also gives a similar example with a question mark. If the focus is on the object, the subject is either the aboutness topic or the contrastive topic.

(1) ?*Kimse bir arkadaş-ım-ı davet et-me-miş.*
Anybody a friend-1SG.POSS-ACC invite-NEG-EVID
Only reading: 'Nobody invited any friend of mine.'
*'A friend of mine is s.t nobody invited him/her.'

5.5.3.2 Subject-object extraction

In English, extraction out of subject and object positions shows asymmetry in that only object extraction is possible as in (372).

(372) a. *Who$_i$ do you think that John saw t$_i$?*
b. **Who$_i$ do you think that t$_i$ saw John?*
(Bošković 2012: 30)

Bošković (2012) suggests that in languages without TP projection, the subject-object extraction asymmetry that is observed in English does not occur. In Turkish, wh-focus phrases do not move for interpretational purposes, only discourse-linked wh-phrases can optionally move (Şener 2010). Hence, it is not easy to test subject-object extraction with wh-phrases. For Turkish, Aygen (2000) investigates subject and object extraction out of (i) nominalized complement clauses, (ii) finite complement clauses, and (iii) ECM clauses and comes up with the following results.

(373) (i) Nominalized Complement   ✓sbj ✓obj; sbj+gen; obj+acc.
          Clauses:
     (ii) Finite Complement Clauses: * sbj ✓obj; sbj+nom; obj+acc.
     (iii) ECM Clauses: ✓sbj * obj; sbj+acc; obj+acc.

In nominalized complement clauses, both the subject and the object can be extracted out of the complement domain. In finite complement clauses, the subject cannot be extracted and in ECM clauses the object cannot be extracted. Aygen (2000) suggests that this is related to the case marker of the constituent over which the dislocated constituent moves. Finite complement clauses do not bear a case marker and hence nominative subjects having the same morphology cannot move out of this domain. In ECM clauses, the accusative case marked constituents cannot move over the accusative case marked subject. As the extraction constraints are not the same as indicated in (373), it is suggested that subject-object extraction difference is not observed in Turkish.

5.4.3.3 Nominative case

Bošković (2010) argues that in the absence of TP projection, nominative case is licensed by another projection or it is licensed as a default case. In line with George and Kornfilt (1981), he suggests that Agr can be the case licenser in Turkish. However, as illustrated in section 5.5.1, with ECM clauses Agr cannot be the case licensing head in Turkish, so this is not an option.

The other possibility is that nominative case is the default case licensed in the absence of a probe. Nominative case has already been suggested to be the default case (Kornfilt 2003b). However, this line of argument runs into problems in Turkish for which it has also been suggested in this study that *v*P has non-phasehood properties. Being defective in nature, if *v*P cannot license accusative case, accusative case is also a default case. However, both accusative and nominative case cannot be default case markings in Turkish.

The other alternative is to assume different functional projections for the nominative and accusative case. Consider first the accusative case. In line with Öztürk (2005), it can be assumed that object phrases are base generated in ThemeP and get accusative case in this position.

(374)

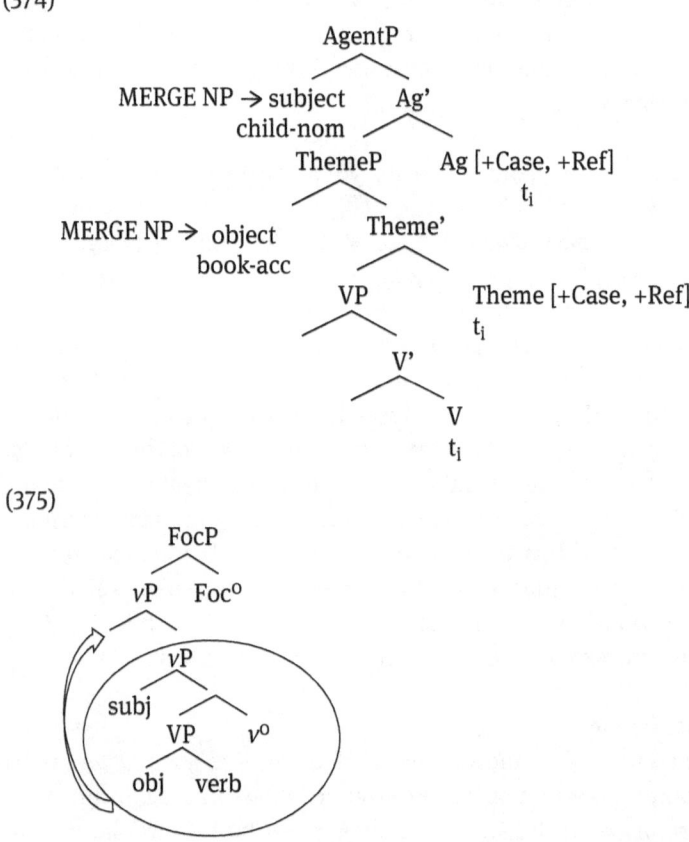

(375)

As the discussion in the previous chapter has shown, the specifier position of *v*P above the external argument is used as a reconstruction site by contrastive topics but this is not the case for the specifier position of the subject. Additionally, a contrastive topic cannot reconstruct back to the event structure domain indicated with the ellipse in (375) above. In (374) with an AgentP above ThemeP this position is missing which makes reconstruction of the contrastive topic unexplained. Hence, *v*P will be retained as the case checking site of object phrases.[125]

As for nominative case checking, within the assumptions of the minimalist program, C is the locus of all features which percolate down to T head. In the absence of T head, we propose FinP/MoodP to be the nominative case checking heads for the external arguments in line with Aygen (2002a).[126] CP does not have the general properties of a phase and hence instead of feature percolation we can also suggest that the heads enter the derivation with the relevant features. However, *v*P is also defective but it can check accusative case of the object and hence it is suggested that CP can also percolate its features down to FinP/MoodP. CP becomes defective in the absence of TP, not being able to form CP/TP amalgam.

5.5.3.4 Sequence of tense

Sequence of Tense (SOT) refers to the ambiguity in the interpretation of tenses in embedded clauses with attitude verbs. The possible interpretation shows variation from language to language. In English, the example in (376) is ambiguous in that the temporal interpretation of the embedded clause can be dependent on the matrix verb, yielding simultaneous reading, or the past tense interpretation of the embedded clause can precede the matrix verb, yielding anteriority reading.

(376) *John believed that Mary was ill.*
    Non-past/simultaneous reading: John's belief: Mary is ill (time of the alleged illness overlaps John's now)
    Anteriority reading: John's belief: Mary was ill (the time of the alleged illness precedes John's now)
    (Bošković 2012: 35)

---

[125] In Turkish, the phasehood status of *v*P as a barrier for long-distance binding and its complement domain as a reconstruction site is untenable. However, remember that the phase impenetrability condition for reconstruction operations can still be captured by the scope domain of focus.

[126] As the discussion so far indicates, in the absence of TP, MoodP is proposed as the case checking head for nominative case marked subjects and the source of temporary information as a secondary effect. However, MoodP is not proposed as an alternative to TP in the sense that in the presence of TP, MoodP would also be expected to be found in the structure. Hence, in the absence of TP, it cannot be suggested that MoodP makes CP phase defective.

In Japanese, on the other hand, the temporal interpretation of the embedded verb is dependent on the matrix speech act. Hence, in Japanese only the simultaneous reading is possible.

(377) *Taroo-wa   Hanako-ga   byooki-da   to   iu-ta*
       TOP   NOM   be.sick-PRES   that   say-PAST
   'Taroo said that Mary was sick' (simultaneous reading only)
   (Ogihara 1994: 252)

As illustrated in (378a) below, in Turkish also, only a simultaneous reading is possible. An anteriority reading is available only when *–mIş* is attached to the embedded verb. This is predictable as *–mIş* can be interpreted as a perfective marker.

(378) a. *Ahmet Ayşe-nin   hasta ol-duğ-un-u   söyle-di.*
         Ahmet Ayşe-GEN   ill   be-NOML-3SG.POSS-ACC   say-PERF
         'Ahmet said that Ayşe was ill.'
     b. *Ahmet Ayşe git-miş   de-di.*
         Ahmet Ayşe go-PERF   say-PERF
         'Ahmet said that Ayşe was ill.'

The discussion in these subsections has shown that the properties of no DP and hence no TP analysis proposed by Bošković (2012) holds in Turkish. Based on the discussion so far the following phrase structure in (379) for Turkish can be derived.

In the previous chapter it was suggested that Spec CtP and AtP are the target position of contrastive and aboutness topic phrases respectively. One might alternatively suggest that it is the nominative case checking head, FinP/MoodP, that hosts the topic phrases. But then there would be the problem of assuming an edge feature as trigger, for instance, an accusative or dative case marked topic constituent to this position. However, if TopP projections are assumed, the relevant feature would be [top] feature and this would strengthen the argument that in Turkish all the movements are triggered by discourse-related purposes.

It is MoodP and not TP projection that checks Nominative case for the subjects. Accusative case is checked by *v*P projection. As case checking is done in-situ, if there is a movement operation, it is triggered by interpretational purposes and it cannot be semantically vacuous. The spell-out domain of *v*P maps onto the scope domain of focus. How spell-out domains are determined may change between discourse-configurational and non-discourse-configurational languages. However, a firm conclusion cannot be drawn on this issue without further research.

(379)

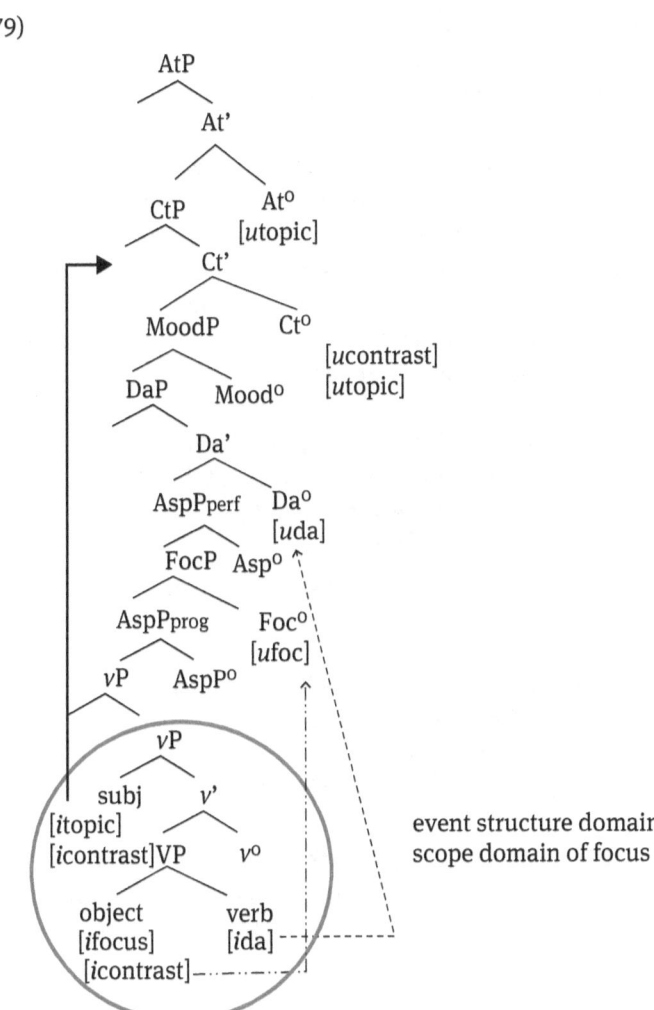

event structure domain
scope domain of focus

Finally, the TP domain of Ramchand and Svenonius (2013), defined as the time anchored situational domain would correspond to AspP and MoodP projections, as temporal interpretation is made possible with the markers that surface with these projections. Specifier positions for AspP and MoodP have not been proposed as these projections are in fact a reflection of morphology in syntax, and in morphological representations the structure is reduced in that either complement or adjunct positions are allowed but not both (Di Sciullo 2002). In addition, in the absence of TP projection, it is also not possible to talk about IP internal FocP and DaP in that there is no an intermediary TP projection between vP and the CP domain.

As the interaction of focus with progressive aspect and perfective aspect has shown in section 4.2.2, the aspectual projections have an effect on focus. While the progressive aspect marker changes scope readings, the perfective aspect marker does not. This difference has been reflected in the representation above by positing the Asp$_{perf}$ above FocP and the Asp$_{prog}$ below FocP.

However, in Turkish the verb is more dependent on aspect, indicating that aspect can in fact be even closer to the verb. As illustrated below, it is possible to elide (i) the verb with aspectual marker (380a), (ii) the verb and the object (380b), but it is not possible to negate the verb in the second conjunct and elide the verb (380c). The equivalent of this sentence with the intended reading in English illustrates that this is possible in English.

(380) a. *Ayşe piyano çal-ıyor   Mete de   flüt   (çal-ıyor)*
       Ayşe piano   play-IMPF Mete as for flute (play-IMPF)
       'Ayşe plays the piano and Mete does the flute.'
   b. *Ayşe piyano çal-ıyor   Mete de   (piyano çal-ıyor) /*
       Ayşe piano   play-IMPF Mete too   (piano play-IMPF) /
       öyle
       as such
       'Ayşe plays the piano and Mete (plays the piano) too/ so does'
   c. **Ayşe   piyano   çal-ıyor   ama   Mete   değil.*
       Ayşe   piano   play-IMPF   but   Mete   not
       Intended reading: 'Ayşe plays the piano but Mete does not.'

It is suggested that this can be due to the fact that aspectual markers and negation are bound morphemes in Turkish and they cannot surface in the absence of verb. However, the following example is not acceptable in Turkish, which is fully grammatical in English.

(381) a. *John wants to eat ice-cream and eat ice-cream he will.*
   b. **Mete dondurma ye-mek   isti-yor   ve*
       Mete ice cream eat-NOML want-IMPF and
       dondurma   ye   yap-acak.
       ice cream   eat   make-FUT
       Intended reading: 'Mete wants to eat ice-cream and eat ice-cream he will.'

In English it is possible to use the bare form of the verb as in (381a) but this is not possible in Turkish (381b). The verb in Turkish cannot be used in its bare form without an overt or zero aspectual or a modal marker. Note that the verb following the bare verb in (381b) bears an aspectual marker but even this does not save the structure. The representation of aspect with which the verb is closely related needs detailed investigation, which is left for further research.

5.6 Concluding Remarks

In this chapter, relying on the previous studies on the functional structure of Turkish, the inventory of Turkish functional projections has been investigated. The main proposals of the chapter can be listed in the following way: (i) Turkish is an NP language and DP does not exist (Öztürk 2005; Bošković and Şener 2014); (ii) as binding, subject reflexives, ECM clauses, bounding nodes, subject-object extraction, the absence of expletives, sequence of tense diagnostics and the data on suspended affixation indicate, TP is missing in Turkish; (iii) in the absence of TP, EPP becomes redundant and all movement operations are triggered by discourse-related purposes; (iv) in the absence of TP, CP does not show the phasehood properties in that binding is possible across two CP boundaries and this gives support to the claim in this study that CP and *v*P in Turkish do not display phasehood properties as indicated in the literature; and (v) TP is not required to encode temporal interpretation and the markers that are proposed to indicate tense in Turkish can be analyzed as Aspect and Mood markers.

Appendix A
Samples from the first study on the prosody of focus phrases

I Given-Contrastive Focus-Given Order with Lexically Stressed Words

(1) A: *Alanya ve Anamur'dan Almanya'ya giden gurbetçilerden bir grup Almanya'da çalışmalarıyla büyük beğeni toplamış. Her iki grup da elinden geleni yapmaya çalışıyor, şimdi de Almanyalılar onları öven bir konuşma yapıyor.*
'One of the guest worker groups who went from Alanya and Anamur to Germany won recognition with their work. Both of the groups try to do their best and now the German people make a speech that praises them.'

B: *Peki Almanyalılar Alanyalıları mı yoksa Anamurluları mı övüyorlar?*
'Do the German people praise the people from Anamur or Alanya?'

A: *Almanyalılar Anamurluları övüyorlar.*
'The German people praise the people from Anamur.'

II Given-Discourse New-Given Order with Finally Stressed Words

(2) A: *Eskiden elemanlar maaşları yüksekken ne bulurlarsa alır ve yerlerdi çünkü alacak paraları vardı. Sence bu kadar az maaş zammından sonra elemanlar neye yumulurlar?*
'In the past when the wages of the personnel were high they would buy and eat whatever they find because they had enough money. With so little increase in salary what do you think they will eat?'

B: *Elemanlar menemene yumulurlar. Domates en ucuz sebze.*
'The personnel will eat menemen. Tomato is the cheapest vegetable.'

III Contrastive Focus-Given-Given Order with Finally Stressed Words

(3) A: *Bu bina artık kullanılamaz hale geldi. Bazı değişiklikler yapmak şart oldu ben de mimarları çağırdım. İşe avludan başlarlar ve mermerleri yenilerler.*
'This building became unusable. It became inevitable to make some changes and I called the architects. They will start from the yard and change the marbles.'

B: *İyi de bu mimarların işi değil ki. Ameleler mermerleri yenilerler.*
'But that is not the job of architects. Workers change the marbles.'

IV All-Given

(4) A: *Sınav öncesi şu notların üzerinden geçelim. Ticaret yaptıkları için diğer medeniyetlerle etkileşim içinde bulunan İyonyalılar Menemen'e yayılıyorlar.*
'Let's go over the notes before the exam. The Ionians, who kept in touch with other civilizations as they traded, moved towards Menemen.'

B: *Bu notları okudum. İyonyalılar Menemen'e yayılıyorlar. Bu bölümü hatırlıyorum başka bölüme geçelim.*
'I read those notes. The Ionians move towards Menemen. I remember that part. Let's move onto another part.'

V All-New

(5) A: *Ne izliyorsun, ne var televizyonda?*
'What are you watching, what is on TV?'

B: *Almanyalılar Anamurluları övüyorlar. Belli ki Anamurlular iyi çalışıyorlar.*
'The German people praise the people from Anamur. Apparently, the people from Anamur work hard.'

VI Filler with Finally Stressed Words

(6) A: *Uzun zamandır haberleri izleyemiyorum. Neler oluyor dünyada anlatsana?*
'I haven't been watching the news for a long time. What is going on in the world?'

B: *Son haberler Almanya'dan. Amiraller mayınları yolluyorlar.*
'The latest news is from Germany. The admirals send the mines.'

Appendix B
Samples from the second study on the prosody of focus phrases

I Given-Contrastive Focus-Given Order

(1) A: *Bazı sebzelerde GDO'lu tohum kullanıldığı ortaya çıkmış. Sağlık bakanlığı duruma el koymuş ve sebzelerin yetiştirenler tarafından imha edilmesine karar vermiş. Alanyalılar börülce yoluyorlar.*
'It was found out that genetically modified seeds were used in some vegetables. The ministry of health took the issue in hand and decided that the growers would annihilate the vegetables. The people of Alanya pull up peas.'

B: *Alanyalılar barbunya yoluyorlar.*
'The people of Alanya pull up kidney beans.'

II Given-Discourse New-Given Order

(2) A: *Ümraniyeliler çevre düzenlemesi yapıyorlar. İlçeyi çiçeklerle donattılar. Solmuş çiçekleri çıkarıp yeni çiçek dikiyorlar. Papatyaları yenilediler.*
'The people of Ümraniye make environment planning. They decorate the town with flowers. They take out the wilted flowers and plant new flowers. They renewed the daisies.'

B: *Ümraniyeliler başka neyi yeniliyorlar?*
'What else do the people of Ümraniye renew?'

A: *Ümraniyeliler manolyaları yeniliyorlar.*
'The people of Ümraniye renew the magnolias.'

III All-New

(3) A: *Haberlerde ne var?*
'What is on the news?'

B: *Memurlara zam geliyor.*
'There is an increase for the wages of the officers.'

A: *Başka?*
'What else?'
B: *Romanyalılar uranyuma yöneliyorlar.*
'The Rumanians tend towards uranium.'

IV Fillers

(4) A: *Dün maymunlarla ilgili bir filme başladım ama filmin sonunu göremeden uyuyakaldım. Sen izledin mi o filmi, nasıl bitiyor film?*
'Yesterday I watched a film on monkeys but I fell asleep before watching the end of the film. Did you watch that film, how does it end?'
B: *Maymunlar ormanı buluyorlar.*
'The monkeys find the forest.'

(5) A: *Kasabamızda yapılacak işlere belediye yetişemeyince görev paylaşımı yaptık.*
'As the municipality couldn't do all the things for our town on its own, we tried job sharing.'
B: *Peki bu elemanlar neden burada bekliyor?*
'Well, why do the personnel wait in here?'
A: *Elemanlar yolları yenileyecekler.*
'The personnel will renew the roads.'

(6) A: *Korsanlar tarafından kaçırılan gemi mürettebatıyla birlikte ülkemize döndü.*
'The ship which was abducted by the pirates has returned to our country with its crew.'
B: *Bundan sonra ne gibi gelişmeler olur?*
'What kind of developments will happen from now on?'
A: *Amiraller anılarını yayınlarlar.*
'The admirals will publish their memories.'

Appendix C
Samples from the study on the interaction of information structural units with quantifier scope

I First Study

(1) A: *İstanbul'da düzenlenecek konferans için Ankara'dan 5 tane bakan gelmiş. Ankara'dan getirilen 2 kişilik güvenlik ekibi yoğun güvenlik önlemleri almış. Bakanların her biri kendi özel arabasını kullanmış. Hepsi binaya aynı anda ve B kapısından giriş yapmış ama bakanlara Ankaralı güvenlik görevlileri hiç yardımcı olmamışlar.*
'For the conference to be held in İstanbul, 5 ministers came from Ankara. Two security guards who came from Ankara took safety precautions. Each of the ministers used their own cars. They all entered the building at the same time and from door B. But the security guards from Ankara did not help the ministers.'
Universal_Object$_{DA}$ Indefinite_Subject$_{DA}$ verb$_F$

B: Yo, hayır.   Her   bakan-a   bir   Ankaralı
   No.   each   minister-DAT   a   person from Ankara
   güvenlik görevlisi eskortluk et-miş.
   security guard   escort   make-PERF
   'No, a security guard from Ankara escorted each minister.'

B kapısı
'Door B'

Savunma bakanı
'minister of defence'

Sağlık bakanı
'minister of health'

Dış İşleri bakanı
'minister of foreign affairs'

İç İşleri bakanı
'minister of internal affairs'

https://doi.org/10.1515/9781501505584-008

Bilişim ve teknoloji bakanı
'minister of information and techonology'

duruma uygun [ ]   duruma uygun değil [ ]
'appropriate to the context'   'not appropriate to the context'

(2) A: *Anamur ve Antalyalı gruplar Almanya'ya çalışmaya gitmişti. Çalışanların iş performansına önem veren patron her işçiyi denetlemesi için bir amir görevlendirmiş. Her amir sorumlu olduğu işçinin çalışmasını kontrol ediyor ve ona puan veriyormuş. Bir Antalyalı olarak Antalyalı işçilerin övülmesini çok isterim. Sen biliyor musun, Almanyalı amirler Anamurlu işçileri mi yoksa Antalyalı işçileri mi övmüşler?*

'Groups of people from Anamur and Antalya went to Germany to work. The boss, who considered the performance of the workers important, gave responsibilities to the directors to supervise each of the workers. The directors checked the workers and gave them points. As I am from Antalya, I really want workers from Antalya to be praised. Do you know, which ones, the German directors praised, the workers from Anamur or Antalya?'

                 Indefinite_subject_DA universal_object_FOC verb_DA

B: Üzgün-üm ama, bir Almanyalı amir   her
     sorry-1SG but   a   German   director   every
     Anamurlu-yu   öv-müş.
     person from Anamur-ACC   praise-PERF
     'I am sorry but, a German director praised every worker from Anamur.'

a. *Böylece her Almanyalı amir farklı bir Anamurlu işçiyi övmüş oldu.*
'So in this way, every German director praised a different worker from Anamur'

b. *Tüm Anamurlu işçileri tek bir Almanyalı amir övmüş oldu.*
   'Only one German director praised all the workers from Anamur.'

(3) A: *Okulumuz öğretmenlerinden bazıları üç öğrenciyle birlikte ders çıkışı pikniğe gitmişler. Rüzgârı fırsat bilen öğrenciler yanlarında uçurmak için uçurtma götürmüşler. Bir de kumandayla çalışan oyuncak helikopter götürmüşler. Piknikten sonra öğretmenler de çocuklarla birlikte eğlenmişler. Sen bilirsin, helikopterleri öğretmenler mi yoksa öğrenciler mi uçurmuşlar?*
   'Some of the teachers from our school went on a picnic with three of the students after school. The students who took advantage of the wind took kites with them. Additionally, they brought helicopters that worked with remote controllers. After the picnic, the teachers also had fun with the students. Do you know, which ones, the teachers or the students flew the helicopters?'

	universal_object_CT		indefinite_subject_FOC	verb_DA
B: *Valla*	*helikopter-ler-i*		*bil-mi-yor-um*	*ama,*
frankly	helicopter-PL-ACC		know-NEG-IMPF-1SG	but
her	*uçurtma-yı*	*bir*	*öğrenci*	*uçur-muş.*
every	kite-ACC	a	student	fly-PERF

   'Well, I do not know about the helicopters but a student flew every kite.'

(a) *Her öğrenci bir uçurtma uçurmuş.*
   'Every student flew a kite.'

(b) *Sadece bir öğrenci her uçurtmayı uçurmuş.*
   'Only a student flew every kite.'

II Second Study

(1) A: *Okulumuz öğretmenlerinden bazıları 3 öğrenciyle birlikte ders çıkışı pikniğe gitmişler. Rüzgârı fırsat bilen öğrenciler yanlarında uçurmak için uçurtma götürmüşler. Duyduğum kadarıyla bir öğrenci sadece bir uçurtmayı uçurtmuş.*

'Some of the teachers from our school went on a picnic with three of the students after school. The students who took advantage of the wind took kites with them. As far as I have heard, a student flew only one of the kites.'

indefinite_subject_{AT} universal_object_F verb_{-DA}

B: *Yoo hayır, bir öğrenci her uçurtma-yı uçur-muş.*
   no   a   student every kite-ACC   fly-PERF
   'No, a student flew every kite.'

(a) *Her öğrenci bir uçurtma uçurmuş.*
    'Every student flew a kite.'

(b) *Sadece bir öğrenci her uçurtmayı uçurmuş.*
    'Only a student flew every kite.'

(2) A: *Antalya ve Anamur'dan bir grup işçi Türkiye'den yurt dışına çalışmaya gitmiş. Patron işçileri denetlemesi için amirler görevlendirmiş. Almanyalı amirler işçilerimizin çalışmasını ay sonunda değerlendirecekmiş. Övülen her işçi ek maaş alacakmış. Sen bilirsin, Antalyalı işçilerimizi Almanyalı amirler övmüş mü yoksa eleştirmiş mi?*

'A group of workers from Anamur and Antalya went abroad to work. The boss gave responsibilities to the directors to check the workers. At the end of the month, the directors were going to evaluate the workers and the ones who were praised would get extra salary. Do you know, did the German directors praise or criticize the workers from Antalya?'

Universal_object_CT indefinite_subject_DA verb_FOC

B: *Antalyalı   işçi-ler-i   bil-me-m   ama*
   person from Antalya worker-PL-ACC know-NEG-1SG but
   her   Anamurlu   işçi-yi   bir   Almanyalı
   every   person from Anamur   worker-ACC   a   German
   amir   öv-müş.
   director   praise-PERF
   'I do not know about the workers from Antalya, but a German director praised every worker from Anamur.'

a. *Böylece her Almanyalı amir farklı bir Anamurlu işçiyi övmüş oldu.*
   'So in this way, every German director praised a different worker from Anamur'

b. *Tüm Anamurlu işçileri tek bir Almanyalı amir övmüş oldu.*
   'Only one German director praised all the workers from Anamur.'

III Third Study

(1) A: *Başbakan konferansın yapılacağı binaya üç bakanla birlikte gelmiş. 2 tane İstanbul'dan 2 tane de Ankara'dan ek güvenlik görevlisi getirmişler güvenlik önlemi almak için. Başbakan makam aracıyla gelmiş ve A kapısından giriş yapmış. Bakanların her biri kendi özel arabasını kullanmış. Bakanların her birinden bir güvenlik görevlisi sorumluymuş. Bakanların hepsi binaya saat tam 09.00'da ve farklı farklı kapılardan giriş yapmışlar. Duyduğum kadarıyla güvenlik görevlilerinin hepsi başka işlerle uğraşmış başbakana da eskortluk etmemişler.*

'The prime minister came with three ministers to the building where the conference was to be held. Additionally, two security guards from İstanbul and two security guards from Ankara came for safety precautions. The prime minister came with his official car and entered the building from door A. The ministers used their own cars. A different security guard was responsible for each of the ministers. The ministers entered the building from different doors at 9:00 o'clock sharp. As far as I have heard, the security guards did other things and did not escort the prime minister.'

       indefinite_object$_{CT}$ universal_subject$_{DA}$ verb$_F$

B: *Başbakan-ı*   *bil-me-m*   *ama bir bakan-a* *her*
  prime minister-ACC know-NEG-1SG but a minister-DAT every
  güvenlik görevlisi eskortluk et-miş.
  security guard escort make-PERF
  'I do not know about the prime minister but every security guard escorted a minister.'

A kapısı   *B kapısı*   *C kapısı*
'door A'   'door B'   'door C'
Savunma bakanı *Dış İşleri bakanı* *Sağlık bakanı*
'defense minister' 'foreign affairs minister' health minister'

Güvenlik görevlisi: *Güvenlik görevlisi:* *Güvenlik görevlisi:*
'security guard' 'security guard' 'security guard'
Sadık Şen   *İbrahim Mutlu* *Şenol Terzi*

duruma uygun [ ] *duruma uygun değil [ ]*
'appropriate to the context' 'not appropriate to the context'

(2) A: *Okulumuz öğretmenlerinden bazıları üç öğrenciyle birlikte ders çıkışı pikniğe gitmişler. Rüzgârı fırsat bilen öğrenciler yanlarında uçurmak için uçurtma götürmüşler. Piknikten sonra sadece bir öğrenci uçurtma uçurmuş.*
   'Some of the teachers from our school went on a picnic with three of the students after school. The students who took advantage of the wind took kites with them. After the picnic, only one of the students flew kites.'

      Indefinite_Object$_{DA}$ universal_Subject$_{FOC}$ verb$_{DA}$

 B: *Yoo hayır, bir uçurtma-yı her öğrenci uçur-muş.*
   no a kite-ACC every student fly-PERF
   'No, every student flew a kite.'

(a) *Her öğrenci farklı bir uçurtmayı uçurmuş.*
    'Every student flew a different kite.'

(b) *Sadece bir uçurtmayı bütün öğrenciler uçurmuş.*
    'All the students flew only one of the kites.'

IV Fillers

(1) A: *Okul çıkışı öğretmenler 4 öğrenciyle birlikte piknik yapacaktı. Hava çok sıcak olduğu için öğretmenler çocuklardan güneş çarpmasın diye şapka takmalarını istemişti.*
'After school, the teachers were going on a picnic with four students. As it was very hot, the teachers told the students to wear hats against sunstroke.'

B: *Anlaşılan bazı çocuklar bu uyarıyı göz ardı etmişler. Hepsi şapka takmamış.*
'Apparently, some of the kids did not take heed of this warning. Not all the kids wore hats.'

duruma uygun [   ]   duruma uygun değil [   ]
'appropriate to the context' 'not appropriate to the context'

(2) A: *Tatile çıkmadan önce çiçeklerimi sulaması için komşuma emanet etmiştim. Gitmeden önce sulamayı unutmayacağını söylemişti ama maalesef sözünde durmamış.*

'Before going on holiday, I left my flowers to my neighbor. She told me that she would water them but unfortunately she did not keep her promise.'

B: *Abartma ya, çiçeklerin hepsi solmamış.*
'Do not exaggerate, all the flowers did not wilt.'

a) *Bütün çiçekler sağlam, solan çiçek yok.*
'None of the flowers wilted'
b) *Bazı çiçekler solmuş, bazıları solmamış.*
'Some of the flowers wilted, some did not.'

Bibliography

Abney, Steven Paul. 1987. *The English noun phrase in its sentential aspect*. Cambridge, Massachusetts Institute of Technology dissertation.
Aboh, Enoch Oláde. 2007. Focused versus non-focused wh-phrases. In Enoch Oláde Aboh, Katharina Hartmann & Malte Zimmermann (eds.), *Focus strategies in Niger Congo and Afro-Asiatic*, 287–315. Berlin & New York: Mouton de Gruyter.
Abusch, Dorit. 2010. Presupposition triggering from alternatives. *Journal of Semantics* 27 (1). 37–80.
Aikawa, Takako. 1994. Logophoric use of the Japanese reflexive zibun-zisin 'selfself'. In Masatoshi Koizumi & Hiroyuki Ura (eds.), *Formal approaches to Japanese linguistics 1: MIT working papers in linguistics* 24, 1–22. Cambridge, Massachusetts Institute of Technology.
Aksu-Koç, Ayhan. 1988. *The acquisition of aspect and modality*. Cambridge: Cambridge University Press.
Arslan-Kechriotis, Ceyda. 2006a. *Case as an uninterpretable feature*. Boğaziçi University dissertation.
Arslan-Kechriotis, Ceyda. 2006b. Perfect in Turkish. *Turkic Languages* 10. 246–270.
Aydemir, Yasemin. 2004. Are Turkish preverbal bare nouns syntactic arguments? *Linguistic Inquiry* 35 (3). 465–474.
Aygen, Gülşat. 1999. *Specificity and subject-object positions/scope interactions in Turkish* (unpublished manuscript). Harvard University.
Aygen, Gülşat. 2000. T-to-C: extractable subjects and EPP. In Vida Samiian (ed.), *Proceedings of the Western Conference on Linguistics*, 65–81. California State University, California.
Aygen, Gülşat. 2002a. *Finiteness, case and clausal architecture*. Harvard University dissertation.
Aygen, Gülşat. 2002b. *The interpretational and word order properties of case in Turkish* (unpublished manuscript). Harvard University.
Baker, Mark. 1985. The mirror principle and morphosyntactic explanation. *Linguistic Inquiry* 16 (3). 373–416.
Banguoğlu, Tahsin. 1974. *Türkçe'nin grameri*. İstanbul: Baha Publications.
Belletti, Adriana. 2003. Aspects of the low IP area. In Luigi Rizzi (ed.), *The structure of IP and CP: The cartography of syntactic structures*, 2, 16–51. Oxford: Oxford University Press.
Bobaljik, Jonathan David & Susi Wurmbrand. 2012. Word order and scope: Transparent interfaces and the 3/4 signature. *Linguistic Inquiry*, 43 (3). 371–421.
Boeckx, Cedric. 2003. *Islands and Chains*. Amsterdam: John Benjamins.
Boersma, Paul & David Weenink. 1992–2018. *Praat, doing phonetics by computer* [Computer program]. http://www.praat.org/ (Version 6.0.40, accessed on 6 July 2019)
Bolinger, Dwight. 1986. *Intonation and its parts: Melody in spoken English*. Stanford, CA: Stanford University Press.
Bošković, Željko. 2007. On the locality and motivation of Move and Agree: An even more minimal theory. *Linguistic Inquiry* 38. 589–644.
Bošković, Željko. 2008. On the clausal and NP structure of Serbo-Croatian. In Richard Compton, Magdalena Goledzinowska & Ulyana Savchenko (eds), *Proceedings of FASL 15*, 42–75. Michigan Slavic Publications.

Bošković, Željko. 2010. Conjunct-sensitive agreement: Serbo-Croatian vs. Russian. In Gerhild Zybatow, Philip Dudchuk, Serge Minor & Ekaterina Pschehotskaya (eds.), *Proceedings of FDSL* 7.5, 31–48. Frankfurt am main: P. Lang.

Bošković, Željko. 2012. On NPs and clauses. In Günther Grewendorf & Thomas Ede Zimmermann (eds.), *Discourse and grammar: From sentence types to lexical categories*, 179–242. Berlin & New York: Mouton de Gruyter.

Bošković, Željko. 2016. Getting really edgy: On the edge of the edge. *Linguistic Inquiry* 47. 1–33.

Bošković, Željko & Serkan Şener. 2014. The Turkish NP. In Patricia Cabredo Hofherr & Anne Zribi-Hertz (eds.), *Crosslinguistic studies on nominal reference: With and without articles*, 102–140. Leiden: Brill.

Bowers, John. 1987. Extended X-bar theory, the ECP, and the left branch condition. In Megan Crowhurst (ed.), *Proceedings of WCCFL* 6, 47–62. Stanford CA: Stanford Linguistics Association.

Burton-Roberts, Noel. 1989. *The limits to debate: A revised theory of semantic presupposition*. Cambridge: Cambridge University Press.

Butler, Jonny. 2004. *Phase structure, phrase structure and quantification*. University of York dissertation.

Büring, Daniel. 2003. On D-trees, beans and B-accents. *Linguistic and Philosophy* 26 (5). 511–545.

Büring, Daniel. 2009. Towards a typology of focus realization. In Malte Zimmermann & Caroline Féry (eds.), *Information structure*, 177–205. Oxford: Oxford University Press.

Büring, Daniel. 2013. Givenness, contrast and topic, prosody and information status. Paper presented at 35th Annual Conference of the German Linguistic Society (DGfS), Potsdam University, 13–14 March.

Bybee, Joan & Suzanne Fleishcman. 1995. *Modality in grammar and discourse*. Amsterdam/Philadelphia: Benjamins; Typological Studies in Language 32.

Chafe, Wallace L. 1976. Givenness, contrastiveness, definiteness, subjects, topics and point of view. In Charles N. Li (ed.), *Subject and topic*, 27–55. New York, Academic Press.

Charette, Monik, Aslı Göksel & Serkan Şener. 2007. *Initial stress in morphologically complex words in Turkish: the interface of prosodic structure and 'phrase' structure*. Manuscript.

Chomsky, Noam. 1995. *The minimalist program*. Cambridge, MA: MIT Press.

Chomsky, Noam. 2000. Minimalist inquiries: The framework. In Roger Martin, David Michaels & Juan Urigereka (eds.), *Step by step: Essays on minimalist syntax in honor of Howard Lasnik*, 89–155. Cambridge, MA: MIT Press.

Chomsky, Noam. 2001. Derivation by phase. In Michael Kenstowicz (ed.), *Ken Hale: A Life in Language*, 1–52. Cambridge, MA: MIT Press.

Chomsky, Noam. 2008. On phases. In Robert Freidin, Carlos P. Otero & Maria Luisa Zubizarreta (eds.), *Foundational issues in linguistic theory. Essays in honor of Jean-Roger Vergnaud*, 133–166. MIT Press, Cambridge, Massachusetts.

Cinque, Guglielmo. 1999. *Adverbs and functional heads: A cross-linguistic perspective*. Oxford: Oxford University Press.

Cinque, Guglielmo. 2001. A note on mood, modality, tense and aspect affixes in Turkish. In Emine Eser Taylan (ed.), *The verb in Turkish*, 47–59. Amsterdam: John Benjamins.

Comrie, Bernard. 1976. *Aspect*. Cambridge: Cambridge University Press.

Comrie, Bernard. 1985. *Tense*. Cambridge: Cambridge University Press.

Constant, Noah. 2014. *Contrastive topic: Meanings and realizations*. University of Massachusetts Amherst dissertation.
Corcu, Demet. 2003. The scope of epistemic modal adverbs as discourse particles on root necessity in Turkish and English. In Henk Zeevat & Manfred Setede (eds.), *Proceedings of ESSLLI 2003 Workshop on the meaning and implementation of discourse particles*, 65–72.
Crisma, Paola. 1997. *L'articolo nella prosa inglese antica e la teoria degli articoli nulli* [The article in Old English prose and the theory of null articles]. Università di Padova dissertation.
Demircan, Ömer. 1996. The rules of inversion in Turkish. In Bengisu Rona (ed.), *Current issues in Turkish linguistics*, 33–46. Ankara: Hitit Yayınevi.
Despić, Miloje. 2011. *Syntax in the absence of determiner phrase*. University of Connecticut dissertation.
Di Sciullo, Anne-Marie. 2002. The asymmetry of morphology. In Paul Boucher (ed.), *Many morphologies*, 1–28. New York: Cascadilla Press.
Dyakonova, Marina. 2009. *A phase based approach to Russian free word order*. University of Amsterdam dissertation.
Emonds, Joseph E. 1969. *Roots and structure-preserving transformations*. MIT dissertation.
Emre, Ahmet Cevat. 1931. *Yeni bir gramer metodu hakkında layıha* [A report about a new grammar method]. İstanbul: Devlet Matbaası.
Enç, Mürvet. 2004. Functional categories in Turkish. In Aniko Csirmaz, Youngjoo Lee & Mary Ann Walter (eds.), *Proceedings of the Workshop on Altaic Formal Linguistics I*, 208–226. MIT Working Papers in Linguistics.
Erguvanlı, Eser. 1984. *The function of word order in Turkish grammar*. Berkeley: University of California Press.
Erkü, Feride. 1982. Topic, comment and word order in Turkish. *Minnesota Papers in Linguistics and Philosophy of Language* 8. 30–38.
Ertheschik-Shir Nomi. 1997. *The dynamics of focus structure*. Cambridge: Cambridge University Press.
Féry, Caroline & Vieri Samek-Lodovici. 2006. Focus projection and prosodic prominence in nested foci. *Language* 82 (1). 131–150.
Féry, Caroline & Frank Kügler. 2008. Pitch accent scaling on given, new and focused constituents in German. *Journal of Phonetics* 36. 680–703.
Féry, Caroline & Shinichiro Ishihara. 2009. How focus and givenness shape prosody. In Malte Zimmermann & Caroline Féry (eds.), *Information structure from different perspectives*, 36–63. Oxford: Oxford University Press.
Fodor, Janet Dean & Ivan A. Sag. 1982. Referential and quantificational indefinites. *Linguistics and Philosophy* (5). 355–398.
Frascarelli, Mara. 1997. The phonology of focus and topic in Italian. *The Linguistic Review* 14. 221–248.
Frascarelli, Mara. 2000. *The syntax-phonology interface in focus and topic constructions in Italian*. Dordrecht: Kluwer.
Frascarelli, Mara. 2012. The interpretation of discourse categories. Cartography for a crash-proof syntax. In Valentina Bianchi & Cristiano Chesi (eds.), *Enjoy Linguistics! Papers offered to Luigi Rizzi's on the occasion of his 60th birthday*. CISCL, Siena. http://www.ciscl.unisi.it/gg60/papers/frascarelli.pdf

Frascarelli, Mara & Roland Hinterhölzl. 2007. Types of topics in German and Italian. In Susanne Winkler & Kerstin Schwabe (eds.), *On information structure, meaning and form*, 87–116. Amsterdam/Philadelphia: John Benjamins.
Geist, Ljudmila. 2013. Bulgarian edin: The rise of an indefinite article. In Uwe Junghanns, Dorothee Fehrmann, Denisa Lenertová & Hagen Pitsch (eds.), *Formal description of Slavic languages: The ninth conference* [Linguistik International 18], 125–148. Frankfurt: Peter Lang.
Genzel, Susanne, Shinichiro Ishihara & Balázs Surányi. 2014. The prosodic expression of focus, contrast and givenness: A production study of Hungarian. *Lingua* 165. 183–204.
George, Leland & Jaklin Kornfilt. 1981. Finiteness and boundedness in Turkish. In Frank Heny (ed.), *Binding and filtering*, 105–127. Cambridge, MA: MIT Press.
Good, Jeff & Alan Yu. 2000. Affix placement variation in Turkish. In Jeff Good & Alan Yu (eds.), *Proceedings of 25th Annual Meeting of Berkeley Linguistics Society*, 63–74. Berkeley: Berkeley Linguistics Society.
Göksel, Aslı. 1997. Morphological asymmetries between Turkish and Yakut. In Kamile İmer & Nadir Engin Uzun (eds.), *Proceedings of the 8th International Conference on Turkish Linguistics*, 69–76. Ankara: Ankara Üniversitesi Basımevi.
Göksel, Aslı. 1998. Linearity, focus and the post verbal position in Turkish. In Lars Johanson, Éva Ágnes Csató, Vanessa Locke, Astrid Menz & Deborah Winterling (eds.), *The Mainz Meeting*, 85–106. Wiesbaden: Otto Harrossowitz Verlag.
Göksel, Aslı. 2010. Focus in words with truth values. *Iberia* 2 (1). 89–112.
Göksel, Aslı. 2013. Free word order and anchors of the clause. *SOAS Working Papers in Linguistics* 16. 3–25.
Göksel, Aslı & Celia Kerslake. 2005. *Turkish: A comprehensive grammar*. London-New York: Routledge.
Göksel, Aslı & Ayşe Sumru Özsoy. 2000. Is there a focus position in Turkish? In Aslı Göksel & Celia Kerslake (eds.), *Studies on Turkish and Turkic Languages; Proceedings of the ninth international conference on Turkish linguistics*, 219–228. Wiesbaden: Harrassowitz.
Göksel, Aslı & Ayşe Sumru Özsoy. 2003. dA as a focus/topic associated clitic in Turkish. In Ayşe Sumru Özsoy & Aslı Göksel (guest editors), *Lingua, Special edition on Focus in Turkish*, 1143–1167.
Göksel, Aslı, Meltem Kelepir & Aslı Üntak-Tarhan. 2009. Decomposition of question intonation: The structure of response seeking utterances. In Janet Grijzenhout & Barış Kabak (eds.), *Phonological domains; Universals and deviations*, 249–286. Interface Explorations, Berlin & New York: Mouton de Gruyter.
Götze Michael, Thomas Weskott, Cornelia Endriss, Ines Fiedler, Stefan Hinterwimmer, Svetlana Petrova, Anne Schwarz, Stavros Skopeteas & Ruben Stoel. 2007. Information structure. In Stefanie Dipper, Michael Götze & Stavros Skopeteas (eds.), *Information structure in cross-linguistic corpora: Annotation guidelines for phonology*, morphology, syntax, semantics, *and information structure*, 147–187. Working Papers of the SFB632, Interdisciplinary Studies on Information Structure (ISIS) 7. Potsdam: Universitätsverlag Potsdam.
Gracanin-Yüksek, Martina & Selçuk İşsever. 2011. Movement of bare objects in Turkish. *Dilbilim Arastirmalari Dergisi* [Journal of Linguistics Research] 1. 33–49.
Grohmann K. Kleanthes. 2003. *Prolific domains: On the anti-locality of movement dependencies* (Linguistik Aktuell 66). Amsterdam: John Benjamins Publishing Company.
Gussenhoven, Carlos. 2004. *The phonology of tone and intonation*. Cambridge: Cambridge University Press.

Güneş, G. 2013. On the role of prosodic constituency in Turkish. In Umut Özge (ed.), *Proceedings of workshop on Altaic formal linguistics 8*, 115–128. Cambridge: MITWPL.
Güneş, Güliz & Aslı Göksel. 2016. M-word vs. ω-word: Top down prosody vs. bottom up syntax. Paper presented at the Workshop: The word and the morpheme. Humboldt Universität zu Berlin, 22–24 September.
Gürer, Aslı. 2010. *Subject positions, case checking and EPP in complex noun phrase constructions in Turkish*. Boğaziçi University MA thesis.
Gürer, Aslı. 2014. Prosody of contrastive focus and discourse new constituents in Turkish. *Dilbilim Araştırmaları Dergisi* [Journal of Linguistics Research] 1. 31–58.
Gürer, Aslı & Aslı Göksel. 2018. (Prosodic-) structural constraints on gapping in Turkish. In Ayşe Sumru Özsoy (ed.), *Word order in Turkish*, 219–259. Springer.
Haegeman, Liliane. 2012. *Adverbial clauses, main clause phenomena, and the composition of the left periphery*. Oxford: Oxford University Press.
Halliday, Michael Alexander Kirkwood. 1970. Functional diversity in language, as seen from a consideration of modality and mood in English. *Foundations of Language*, 6. 322–361.
Heim, Irene. 1982. *The semantics of definite and indefinite noun phrases*. Amherst, MA: University of Massachusetts dissertation.
Hiraiwa, Ken. 2005. *Dimensions of symmetries in syntax: Agreement and clausal architecture*. MIT dissertation.
Hoffman, Beryl. 1995. *The computational analysis of the syntax and interpretation of 'free' word order in Turkish*. University of Pennsylvania dissertation.
Hooper Joan & Sandra Thompson. 1973. On the applicability of root transformations. *Linguistic Inquiry*. 465–497.
Horn, Laurence. 1996. Exclusive company: Only and the dynamics of vertical inference. *Journal of Semantics* 13. 1–40.
Horvath, Julia. 2005. Is 'focus movement' driven by stress? In Christopher Piñón & Péter Siptár (eds.), *Approaches to Hungarian 9*, 131–158. Budapest: Akadémiai Kiadó.
Horvath, Julia. 2010. Discourse features, syntactic displacement and the status of contrast. *Lingua* 120. 1346–1369.
Höhle, Tilman. 1988. Vorwort und nachwort zu *verum-fokus*. *Sprache und Pragmatik 5*. 1–7.
Höhle, Tilman. 1992. Über *verum-fokus* im Deutschen. In Joachim Jacobs (ed.), *Informationsstruktur und Grammatik*. 112–141.
Ince, Atakan. 2006. ECMs as object control structures in Turkish. In Erin Bainbridge & Brian Agbayani (eds.), *Proceedings of WECOL: 17*, 208–221.
Inkelas, Sharon. 1989. *Prosodic constituency in the lexicon*. Stanford University dissertation.
Ipek, Canan. 2011. Phonetic realization of focus with on-focus pitch range expansion in Turkish. In Wai-Sum Lee & Eric Zee (eds.), *Proceedings of the 17th international congress of phonetic sciences*, 140–143. Hong Kong : City University of Hong Kong.
Ipek, Canan & Sun-Ah Jun. 2013. Towards a model of intonational phonology of Turkish: Neutral intonation. *Proceedings of meetings on acoustics*, Montreal 19, 060230.
Ishihara, Shinichiro. 2003. *Intonation and interface conditions*. Massachusetts Institute of Technology dissertation.
İkizoğlu, Didem. 2010. *Direct reported speech: Positioning and relational work*. Boğaziçi University MA thesis.
İkizoğlu, Didem & Beste Kamali. 2015. Compound stress in Turkish is phrase stress. In Deniz Zeyrek, Çiğdem Sağın Şimşek, Ufuk Ataş & Jochen Rehbein (eds.), *Proceedings of the 16th International Conference on Turkish Linguistics*, 40–52. Harrassowitz Verlag.

İşsever, Selçuk. 2003. Information structure in Turkish: The word order–prosody interface. *Lingua* 113. 1025–1053.
İşsever, Selçuk. 2008. EPP-driven scrambling and Turkish. In Tokusu Kurebito (ed.), *Ambiguity of morphological and syntactic analyses*, 27–41. Tokyo: Tokyo University of Foreign Studies Press.
İvoşeviç, Senka & İpek Pınar Bekâr. 2015. Acoustic correlates of focus in Turkish. In Deniz Zeyrek, Çiğdem Sağın Şimşek, Ufuk Ataş & Jochen Rehbein (eds.), *Proceedings of the 16th international conference on Turkish linguistics*, 20–27. Harrassowitz Verlag.
Jayaseelan, Karattuparambil A. 2001. IP internal topic and focus phrases. *Studia Linguistica* 55. 39–75.
Jackendoff, Ray S. 1972. *Semantic interpretation in generative grammar*. Cambridge, MA: MIT Press.
Jimenez-Fernandez Ángel & Selçuk İşsever. 2012. Deriving A/A'-effects in topic fronting: Intervention of focus and binding. In Joanna Błaszczak, Bozena Rozwadowska & Wojciech Witkowski (eds.), *Current issues in generative linguistics*, 8–25. Wroclaw: Center for General and Comparative Linguistics.
Johanson, Lars. 1971. *Aspekt im Türkischen* [Aspect in Turkish]. Uppsala: Almqvist & Wiksell.
Johanson, Lars. 2000. Viewpoint operators in European languages. In Östen Dahl (ed.), *Tense and aspect in the languages of Europe*, 27–187. Berlin & New York: Mouton de Gruyter.
Kabagema-Bilan, Elena, Beatriz López-Jiménez & Hubert Truckenbrodt. 2011. Multiple focus in Mandarin Chinese. In Nicole Dehe, Ingo Feldhausen & Shinichiro Ishihara (eds.), *Lingua* 121 (13). 1890–1905.
Kabak, Barış & Irene Vogel. (2001). The phonological word and stress assignment in Turkish. *Phonology* 18. 315–360.
Kabak, Barış. 2007. Turkish suspended affixation. *Linguistics* 45 (2). 311–347.
Kahnemuyipour, Arsalan. 2004. *The syntax of sentential stress*. University of Toronto dissertation.
Kahnemuyipour, Arsalan & Jaklin Kornfilt. 2011. The syntax and prosody of Turkish 'pre-stressing' suffixes. In Raffaella Folli & Christiane Ulbrich (eds.), *Interfaces in linguistics: New research perspectives*, 205–221. Oxford, Oxford University Press.
Kaisse, Ellen M. 1985. *Connected speech: The interaction of syntax and phonology*. San Diego, Academic Press.
Kamali, Beste. 2011. *Topics at the PF interface of Turkish*. Harvard University dissertation.
Kamali, Beste. 2014. Beyond morphosyntax: Interrogative intonation and its role in Turkish. *Turkic Languages* 18. 189–206.
Kamali, Beste & Bridget Samuels. 2008. The syntax of Turkish pre-stressing suffixes. *TIE 3*, Lisbon. http://ling.umd.edu/~bridget/pdfs/TIE3.pdf
Kamali, Beste & Daniel Büring. 2011. Topics in questions. Paper presented at GLOW 34, University of Vienna, 28–30 April. https://homepage.univie.ac.at/glow34.linguistics/kamali.pdf
Kan, Seda. 2009. *Prosodic domains and the syntax-prosody mapping in Turkish*. Boğaziçi University MA thesis.
Kang, Jungmin. 2014. *On the absence of TP and its consequences: Evidence from Korean*. University of Connecticut dissertation.
Karimi, Simin. 1999. Is scrambling as strange as we think? In Karlos Arregi, Benjamin Bruening, Cornelia Krause & Vivian Lin (eds.), *Papers on syntax and morphology, cycle 1*, 159–189. MIT Working Papers in Linguistics.

Karttunen, Lauri. 1974. Presupposition and linguistic context. *Theoretical Linguistics* 1. 181–193.

Katz, Jonah & Elisabeth Selkirk. 2011. Contrastive focus vs. discourse-new: Evidence from phonetic prominence in English. *Language* 87 (4). 771–816.

Kawahara, Shigeto & Takahito Shinya. 2008. The intonation of gapping and coordination in Japanese: Evidence for intonational phrase and utterance. *Phonetica* 65 (1–2). 62–105.

Kelepir, Meltem. 2000. *Perfect constructions in Turkish*. MIT unpublished manuscript.

Kelepir, Meltem. 2001. *Topics in Turkish syntax: Clausal structure and scope*. Massachusetts Institute of Technology dissertation.

Kelepir, Meltem. 2007. Copular forms in Turkish, Turkmen and Nogay. In Meltem Kelepir & Balkız Öztürk (eds.), *Proceedings of the 2nd workshop on Altaic formal linguistics*, 83–100. MIT Working Papers in Linguistics.

Kennelly, Sarah D. 1999. The syntax of the P-focus position in Turkish. In Georges Rebuschi & Laurice Tuller (eds.), *The grammar of focus*, 179–211. Amsterdam, Benjamins.

Kennelly, Sarah D. 2003. The implications of quantification on the role of focus in discourse structure. *Lingua* 114. 367–388.

Kerslake, Celia. 1992. The role of connectives in discourse construction in Turkish. In Ahmet Konrot (ed.), *Proceedings of the 6th international conference on Turkish linguistics*, 77–104. Eskişehir, Turkey: Anadolu University.

Kesen, Yasemin. 2010. *Intervention effects in simple wh-questions in Turkish*. Boğaziçi University MA thesis.

Kılıçaslan, Yılmaz. 2004. Syntax of information structure in Turkish. *Linguistics* 42 (4). 717–765.

Kiss, Katalin É. 1998. Identificational focus versus information focus. *Language* 74. 245–273.

Kiss, Katalin É. 2002. *The syntactic structure of Hungarian*. Cambridge: Cambridge University Press.

Kiss, Katalin É. 2008. Free word order, (non)configurationality, and phases. *Linguistic Inquiry* 39 (3). 411–475.

Kornfilt, Jaklin. 1984. *Case marking, agreement and empty categories in Turkish*. Harvard University dissertation.

Kornfilt, Jaklin. 1996. On copular clitics in Turkish. In Artemis Alexiadou, Nanna Fuhrhop, Paul Law, Sylvia Loehken (eds.), *ZAS papers in linguistics*, 96–114. Berlin: ZAS 6.

Kornfilt, Jaklin. 1997. *Turkish*. Routledge, London.

Kornfilt, Jaklin. 2000. Local and long distance reflexives in Turkish. In Peter Cole, Gabriella Hermon and James Huang (eds.), *Long distance reflexives*, 197–226. San Diego: Academic Press.

Kornfilt, Jaklin. 2001. Functional projections and their subjects in Turkish clauses. In Emine Eser Taylan (ed.), *The verb in Turkish*, 183–212. Amsterdam: John Benjamins.

Kornfilt, Jaklin. 2003a. Scrambling, subscrambling, and case in Turkish. In Simon Karimi (ed.), *Word order and scrambling*, 125–155. Oxford: Blackwell.

Kornfilt, Jaklin. 2003b. Subject case in Turkish nominalized clauses. In Uwe Junghanns and Luka Szucsich (eds.), *Syntactic structures and morphological information*, 129–215. Berlin & New York: Mouton de Gruyter.

Kornfilt, Jaklin. 2018. NP versus DP: Which one fits Turkish nominal phrases better? *Turkic Languages* 22 (2). 155–167.

Kratzer, Angelika. 1998. Scope or pseudo-scope? Are there wide scope indefinites? In Susan Rothstein (ed.), *Events in grammar*, 163–196. Kluwer Academic Publishers, Dordrecht.

Krifka, Manfred. 2006. Association with focus phrases. In Valerie Molnar & Susanne Winkler (eds.), *The architecture of focus*, 105–136. Berlin & New York: Mouton de Gruyter.
Krifka, Manfred. 2008. Basic notions of information structure. In Caroline Féry & Manfred Krifka (eds.), *Interdisciplinary studies on information structure 6*, 13–56. Potsdam: Universitätsverlag.
Kural, Murat. 1992. *Properties of scrambling in Turkish*. UCLA unpublished manuscript.
Kural, Murat. 1993. V-to-I-to-C in Turkish. In Felipo Beghelli & Murat Kural (eds.), *UCLA occasional papers in linguistics*, 1–37. University of California Los Angeles, Los Angeles.
Ladd, Robert. 1996. *Intonational phonology*. Cambridge Studies in Linguistics. Cambridge University Press.
Ladefoged, Peter. 2010. *A course in phonetics*. Thomson, Wadsworth.
Legate, Julie Anne. 2003. Some interface properties of the phase. *Linguistic Inquiry* 34. 506–516.
Levi, Susannah. 2005. Acoustic correlates of lexical accent in Turkish. *Journal of the International Phonetic Association* 35. 73–97.
Lewis, Geoffrey L. 1967. *Turkish grammar*. Oxford: Oxford University Press.
Lohnstein, Horst & Hildegard, Stommel. 2009. Verum focus and phases. In Kleanthes Grohman & Phoevos Panageotidis (eds.), *Linguistic Analysis. Volume 35, 1–4 Special Issue: Phase Edge Investigations*, 109–140.
Longobardi, Giuseppe. 1994. Reference and proper names: A theory of N-movement in syntax and logical form. *Linguistic Inquiry* 25. 609–665.
Longobardi, Giuseppe. 2001. The structure of DPs: Some principles, parameters and problems. In Mark Baltin & Chris Collins (eds.), *The handbook of contemporary syntactic theory*, 562–603. Oxford: Blackwell.
Lyons, John. 1977. *Semantics 2*. Cambridge, Cambridge University Press.
Marantz, Alec. 1984. *On the nature of grammatical relations*. MIT Press, Cambridge.
Matthewson, Lisa. 1999. On the interpretation of wide-scope indefinites. *Natural Language Semantics* 7. 79–134.
Meral, Hasan Mesut. 2010. *Resumption, A'- chains and implications on clausal architecture*. Boğaziçi University dissertation.
Miyagawa, Shigeru. 2010. *Why agree? Why move? Unifying agreement-based and discourse configurational languages. Linguistic Inquiry Monograph 54*. MIT Press.
Nakipoğlu, Mine. 2009. The semantics of the Turkish accusative marked definites and the relation between prosodic structure and information structure. *Lingua* 119 (9). 1253–1280.
Neeleman, Ad & Tanya Reinhart. 1998. Scrambling and the PF interface. In Miriam Butt and Wilhelm Gueder (eds.), *The projection of arguments*, 309–353. Stanford: CSLI.
Neeleman, Ad & Reiko Vermeulen. 2012. *The syntax of topic, focus and contrast: An interface based approach*. Berlin & New York: Mouton de Gruyter.
Neeleman, Ad & Hans van de Koot. 2012. Towards a unified encoding of contrast and scope. In Ad Neeleman & Reiko Vermeulen (eds.), *The syntax of topic, focus and contrast: An interface based approach*, 39–76. Berlin & New York: Mouton de Gruyter.
Odden, David. 1995. Phonology at the phrasal level in Bantu. In Francis Katamba (ed.), *Bantu phonology and morphology*, 40–68. München-Newcastle, LINCOM EUROPA.
Oded, İlknur. 2006. *Control in Turkish*. Boğaziçi University MA thesis.
Ogihara, Toshiyuki. 1994. Adverbs of quantification and sequence-of-tense phenomena. In Mandy Harvey & Lynn Santelman (eds.), *Proceedings of the 4th semantics and linguistic theory*, 251–267. CLC Publications, Cornell University.

Özbek, Aydın & Barış Kahraman. 2016. Interpretations of Turkish reflexive pronouns kendi and kendisi. *Mersin University Journal of Linguistics & Literature* 13 (1). 73–96.
Özge, Umut. 2003. *A tune based account of Turkish information structure.* Middle East Technical University MA thesis.
Özge, Umut. 2010. *Grammar and information: A study of Turkish indefinites.* Middle East Technical University dissertation.
Özge, Umut & Cem Bozşahin. 2010. Intonation in the grammar of Turkish. *Lingua* 120. 132–175.
Özsoy, Ayşe Sumru. 2001. On 'small' clauses, other 'bare' verbal complements and feature checking in Turkish. In Emine Eser Taylan (ed.), *The verb in Turkish*, 213–237. Amsterdam: John Benjamins.
Öztürk, Balkız. 1999. *Turkish as a non-pro drop language.* Boğaziçi University MA thesis.
Öztürk, Balkız. 2005. *Case, referentiality and phrase structure.* Linguistik Aktuell, Amsterdam: John Benjamins.
Öztürk, Balkız. 2009. Incorporating agents. *Lingua* 119. 334–358.
Palmer, Frank Robert. 2001. *Mood and modality.* Cambridge: Cambridge University Press.
Pesetsky, David. 1987. Wh-in-situ, movement and unselective binding. In Eric Reuland & Alice ter Meulen (eds.), *The representation of (in)definiteness*, 98–129. Cambridge, MA, MIT Press.
Pierrehumbert, Janet. 1980. *The phonology and phonetics of English intonation.* Massachusetts Institute of Technology dissertation.
Progovac, Ljiljana. 1998. Determiner phrase in language without determiners. *Journal of Linguistics* 34. 165–179.
Ramchand, Gillian & Peter Svenonius. 2013. Deriving the functional hierarchy. *Language Sciences* 46. 152–174.
Reinhart, Tanya. 1981. Pragmatics and linguistics: An analysis of sentence topics. *Philosophica* 27. 53–94.
Reinhart, Tanya. 1997. Quantifier scope: How labor is divided between QR and choice functions. *Linguistics and Philosophy* 20. 335–397.
Richards, Marc. 2012. Probing the past: On reconciling long-distance agreement with the PIC. In Artemis Alexiadou, Tibor Kiss & Gereon Müller (eds.), *Local modelling of nonlocal dependencies in syntax*, 135–154. Berlin & New York: Mouton de Gruyter.
Richards, Norvin. 2016. *Contiguity theory.* Cambridge: The MIT Press.
Rizzi, Luigi. 1997. The fine structure of the left periphery. In Liliane Haegeman (ed.), *Elements of grammar*, 281–337. Kluwer, Dordrecht.
Rizzi, Luigi. 2001. On the position 'Int(errogative)' in the left periphery of the clause. In Guglielmo Cinque & Giampaolo Salvi (eds.), *Current studies in Italian syntax: Essays offered to Lorenzo Renzi*, 287–296. New York: Elsevier.
Roberts, Craige. 1996. Informative structure in discourse: Towards an integrated formal theory of pragmatics. In Jae Hak Yoon & Andreas Kathol (eds.), *OSU working papers in linguistics 49; Paper in semantics*, 91–136. Columbus OH: Ohio State University.
Rooth, Mats. 1985. *Association with focus.* University of Massachusetts dissertation.
Rooth, Mats. 1992. A theory of focus interpretation. *Natural Language Semantics* 1. 75–116.
Rooth, Mats. 1996. Focus. In Shalom Lappin (ed.), *The handbook of contemporary semantic theory*, 271–298. Oxford: Blackwell.
Ross, John. 1967. *Constraints on variables in syntax.* MIT dissertation.

Ross John R. 1970. On declarative sentences. In Roderick A. Jacobs & Peter S. Rosenbaumn (eds), *Readings in English transformational grammar*, 222–272. Waltham, Mass: Ginn & Co.
Sağ, Yağmur. 2013. Copula in Turkish. In Umut Özge (ed.), *Proceedings of workshop on Altaic formal linguistics 8*, 293–298. Cambridge: MITWPL.
Sansa, Sabahat. 1986. –Dir in modern Turkish. In Ayhan Aksu Koç & Eser Erguvanlı Taylan (Eds.), *Modern studies in Turkish linguistics: Proceeding of the second international conference on Turkish linguistics*. 145–159. İstanbul: Boğaziçi University Press.
Schwarzschild, Roger. 2002. The grammar of measurement. In Brendan Jackson (ed.), *Proceedings of SALT XII*, 225–245. Ithaca, NY: CLC Publications.
Selkirk, Elisabeth. 1983. The syntax of rhythm and intonation in English. In John F. Richardson, Mitchell Marks & Amy Chukerman (eds.) *Papers from the parasession on the interplay of phonology, morphology, and syntax*, 238–258. Chicago: Chicago Linguistic Society.
Selkirk, Elisabeth. 1995. Sentence prosody: intonation, stress, and phrasing. In John A. Goldsmith (ed.), *The handbook of phonological theory*, 550–569. Cambridge, MA, and Oxford, UK: Blackwell.
Selkirk, Elisabeth. 2002. Contrastive focus vs. presentational focus: Prosodic evidence from right node raising in English. In Bernard Bel & Isabelle Marlien (eds.), *Speech Prosody 2002: Proceedings of the 1st international conference on speech prosody*, 643–646. Aix-en-Provence, France.
Selkirk, Elisabeth. 2005. Comments on intonational phrasing. In Sónia Frota, Marina Vigário, and Maria João Freitas (eds.), *Prosodies*, 11–58. Berlin & New York: Mouton de Gruyter.
Selkirk, Elisabeth & Koichi Tateishi. 1991. Syntax and downstep in Japanese. In Carol Georgopoulos & Roberta Ishihara (eds.), *Interdisciplinary approaches to language: Essays in honor of S.-Y. Kuroda*, 519–543. Dordrecht: Kluwer Academic Publishers.
Sezer, Ayhan. 1996. Türkçede sözdizimsel kısıtlamalar. *Proceedings of the 9th linguistics conference*, 236–263. Bolu: Abant İzzet Baysal Üniversitesi Yayınları.
Sezer, Engin. 2001. Finite Inflection in Turkish. In Emine Eser Taylan (ed.), *The verb in Turkish*, 1–47. Amsterdam: John Benjamins.
Simpson, Paul. 1993. *Language, ideology and point of view*. London: Routledge.
Slioussar, Natalia. 2007. *Grammar and information structure: A study with reference to Russian*. Utrecht Institute of Linguistics OTS dissertation.
Slobin, Dan Isaac & Ayhan A. Aksu. 1982. Tense, aspect, and modality in the use of the Turkish evidential. In Paul J. Hopper (ed.), *Tense-aspect: Between syntax and pragmatics*, 185–200. John Benjamins, Amsterdam.
Slobin, Dan Isaac & Thomas G. Bever. 1982. Children use canonical sentence schemas: A crosslinguistic study of word order and inflections. *Cognition*, 12. 229–265.
Stalnaker, Robert. 1974. Pragmatic presuppositions. In Milton Munitz & Peter Unger (eds.), *Semantics and philosophy*, 197–213. New York: New York University Press.
Stalnaker, Robert. 2002. Common ground. *Linguistics and Philosophy* 25. 701–721.
Steedman, Mark. 2014. The surface compositional semantics of English intonation. *Language* 90 (1). 2–57.
Stowell, Timothy. 1989. Subjects, specifiers, and X-bar theory. In Mark Baltin & Anthony Kroch (eds.), *Alternative conceptions of phrase structure*, 232–262. Chicago: University of Chicago Press.
Su, Julia Yu-Ying. 2012. *The syntax of functional projections in the vP periphery*. University of Toronto dissertation.

Szabolcsi, Anna. 1981. The semantics of topic-focus articulation. In Jan Groenendijk, Theo Janssen & Martin Stokhof (eds.), *Formal methods in the study of language*, 513–540. Amsterdam: Matematisch Centrum.
Svenonius, Peter. 2004. On the edge. In David Adger, Cécile de Cat & George Tsoulas (eds.), *Peripheries: Syntactic edges and their effects*, 261–287. Kluwer, Dordrecht.
Şener, Serkan. 2008. *Non-canonical case licensing is canonical: Accusative subjects of CPs in Turkish*. University of Connecticut unpublished manuscript.
Şener, Serkan. 2010. *Non- peripheral matters in Turkish syntax*. University of Connecticut dissertation.
Taylan, Eser. 1988. On the expression of temporal reference in subordinate clauses in Turkish. In Sabri Koç (ed.), *Studies on Turkish linguistics*, 333–351. Ankara: ODTÜ Yayınları.
Taylan, Eser. 1996. On the parameter of aspect in Turkish. In Ahmet Konrot (ed.), *Modern studies in Turkish linguistics: Proceedings of the 6th international conference on Turkish linguistics*, 153–168. Eskişehir, Turkey: Anadolu University.
Taylan, Eser. 2001. On the relation between temporal/aspectual adverbs and the verb form in Turkish. In Eser Erguvanlı-Taylan (ed.), *The verb in Turkish*, 97–128. Amsterdam: John Benjamins.
Tomioka, Satoshi. 2010. A scope theory of contrastive topics. *Iberia* 2 (1). 113–130.
Truckenbrodt, Hubert. 1995. *Phonological phrases: Their relation to syntax, focus, and prominence*. Massachusetts Institute of Technology dissertation.
Truckenbrodt, Hubert. 2009. On rises and falls in interrogatives. In Hiyon Y. Yoo & Élisabeth Delais-Russarie (eds.) *Proceedings from IDP*, 33–46. Paris.
Truckenbrodt, Hubert. 2013a. An analysis of prosodic F-effects in interrogatives: prosody, syntax and semantics. *Lingua* 124. 131–175.
Truckenbrodt, Hubert. 2013b. *Information structure and tonal height in intonation*. ZAS unpublished manuscript.
Underhill, Robert. 1976. *Turkish grammar*. Cambridge: MIT Press.
Uygun, Dilek. 2006. Scrambling bare singular nominal objects in Turkish. Paper presented at ICTL 13, Uppsala University, Sweden, 16–20 August.
Uygun, Dilek. 2009. *A split model for category specification: Lexical categories in Turkish*. Boğaziçi University dissertation.
Üntak-Tarhan, Aslı. 2006. *Topics in syntax-phonology interface in Turkish: Sentential stress and phases*. Boğaziçi University MA thesis.
Vallduví, Enric. 1990. *The information component*. University of Pennsylvania dissertation.
Vallduví, Enric & Elisabet Engdahl. 1996. The linguistic realization of information packaging. *Linguistics* 34. 459–519.
Vallduví, Enric & Maria Vilkuna. 1998. On rheme and kontrast. In Peter W. Culicover & Louise McNally (eds.), *The limits of syntax (Syntax & Semantics 29)*, 79–108. San Diego: Academic Press.
Wagner, Michael. 2007. Focus, topic and word order: A compositional view. In Jeroen van Craenenbroeck (ed.), *Alternatives to cartography*, 53–86. Berlin & New York: Mouton de Gruyter.
Wagner, Michael. 2008. A compositional analysis of contrastive topic. In Muhammad Abdurrahman, Anisa Schardl & Martin Walkow (eds.), *Proceedings of the north east linguistics society (NELS)* 38, 455–468. Amherst, MA: University of Massachusetts, Graduate Linguistics Student Association.

Wurmbrand, Susi. 2008. Word order and scope in German. *Groninger Arbeiten zur Germanischen Linguistik 46*. 89–110.
Yavaş, Feryal. 1980a. The Turkish future marker. *Kansas working papers in linguistics* 5 (1). 139–149.
Yavaş, Feryal. 1980b. *On the meaning of the tense and aspect markers in Turkish*. University of Kansas dissertation.
Xu, Yi. 1999. Effects of tone and focus on the formation and alignment of f0 contours. *Journal of Phonetics* 27. 55–105.
Xu, Yi. 2013. ProsodyPro — A tool for large-scale systematic prosody analysis. In *Proceedings of tools and resources for the analysis of speech prosody* (TRASP 2013). Aix-en-Provence, France.
Zanon, Ksenia. 2014. On the status of TP in Turkish. *Studies on Polish Linguistics* 9 (3). 163–201.
Zidani-Eroğlu, Leyla. 1997. Exceptionally case marked NPs as matrix objects. *Linguistic Inquiry* 28. 219–230.
Zidani-Eroğlu, Leyla. 2017. Grammaticalization of Turkish numeral 'bir' as an indefiniteness marker. Paper presented at the International Conference on Turkish Linguistics, Çukurova University, 24–26 February.
Zimmermann, Malte. 2008. Contrastive focus and emphasis. *Acta Linguistica Hungarica* 55. 347–360.
Zimmermann, Malte. 2011. The grammatical expression of focus in West Chadic: Variation and uniformity in and across languages. *Linguistics* 49 (5). 1161–1211.
Zimmermann, Malte & Edgar Onea. 2011. Focus marking and focus interpretation. *Lingua* 121. 1651–1670.
Zubizarreta, Maria Luisa. 1998. Prosody, focus, and word order. *Linguistic Inquiry Monograph 33*. MIT Press.

Index

Adverb 201, 203–207, 238–239, 252–253, 256, 262–263, 266
Aboutness topic 1, 3, 9, 15, 39, 41–44, 55, 69, 73, 76–77, 79, 140, 145, 147, 149, 151, 154, 157, 160, 168, 178–180, 182, 189, 191, 197–199, 206–208, 274, 278
All-given 97, 99, 103–105
All-new 11, 13, 85–86, 90, 97, 103–105, 125, 133
Aspect 18–19, 140, 142, 202, 214, 243, 259, 263–272, 280–281,
Alternative semantics 26–27, 33, 48
Assertion operator 151, 181, 183, 186, 191, 196

Binding 4–6, 140–141, 157, 176, 178–191, 196–197, 199, 207–208, 212–213, 243–245, 247–249, 251, 259, 277, 281
Broad focus 2, 4, 11–13, 84–85, 88, 90, 95–97, 99–115, 117–120, 125–127, 130, 138
Bounding nodes 257–259, 281
Büring, D. 1, 7, 12–13, 45, 47–48, 52, 155–156

Cartographic approach 4, 6, 44, 140–141, 264
Chomsky, N. 5–6, 22, 133, 200, 224, 242, 255
Complementizer phrase 242–259
Contrast 3, 11, 32–33, 37, 44, 52–55, 66, 68–72, 81, 106, 146, 160, 162, 164, 166–168, 170, 176, 178, 208
Contrastive focus 1–4, 8, 11, 13, 16, 27–28, 30–37, 45, 47–48, 52–53, 56, 58, 60, 62–63, 65–67, 69–72, 83, 87–88, 91–92, 95–98, 101, 103, 105–107, 110, 114–117, 120, 124–126, 136, 160, 208, 211–212, 215, 235, 241
Contrastive topic 1, 3–4, 8–9, 12–13, 15, 29, 37, 44–53, 56, 59–60, 66–69, 72–79, 81, 92, 124, 140, 144, 146, 149–157, 160–161, 164, 167, 173–174, 177–180, 183–188, 190–191, 196–199, 205–213, 215–219, 222–223, 241, 255, 257, 274, 277

Default scope rule 209
Deontic modality 259, 261, 264
Determiner phrase 227–242
Direct reference hypothesis 121, 123
Discourse anaphora rule 131–133
Discourse anaphoric 1, 3, 7, 9, 13, 15, 24, 41, 43–44, 53–56, 62–63, 72, 77–82, 140, 142, 145, 148–149, 151, 157, 164, 167, 178–180, 186, 190, 197–199, 206–208, 212–213, 223, 255, 257
Discourse-new focus 1–4, 8, 11, 13, 27–30, 32–37, 44, 52–53, 55, 58, 60, 63–66, 68–73, 83–84, 87, 95–97, 99–100, 103, 105–107, 110, 114–115, 118–120, 124–126, 138, 161
Discourse configurational 7, 14, 278
Discourse features 7–9, 152
Discourse linked 13, 29, 222, 241, 275
Discourse tree 48–49, 52
Domain of focus 83, 120, 122, 126, 138
Dutch 37, 73–74, 210

ECM 224, 247, 251–257, 259–261, 275–276
English 1, 28, 37, 74, 83, 87, 114, 125, 141, 155, 170–171, 225, 227, 275, 277, 280
Erguvanlı-Taylan, E. 3, 15–16, 22–24, 39, 41, 58–60, 69, 79, 84, 140
Epistemic modality 259–261, 264, 267
EPP 17, 143, 273–274
Event structure domain 18, 201, 205, 277, 279
(Extended) indirect reference hypothesis 121–125
External merge 5
Exhaustive identification 3, 33, 35–37, 56, 72, 117
Existential presupposition 25–27, 105, 232, 234–237
Existential quantifier 150–151, 153–154, 172, 180–181, 188, 191, 193, 195–197

Flattening effect 181, 183, 186, 191, 195–196
Focus 1–4, 7–11, 15–16, 18, 20–27
Focus prominence 4, 19, 79, 83–84, 120, 125–126, 128, 130, 138
Focus semantic value 10–11, 26–30, 32, 34, 36, 48, 56, 63, 219
Frascarelli, M. 1–3, 7–8, 83, 85–86
Frascarelli, M & R. Hinterhölzl 2, 13, 44, 54, 141

Göksel, A. 7, 14, 79, 136–138, 140, 152, 157–159, 170, 243
Göksel, A. & C. Kerslake 3, 14, 221, 224, 242, 246, 248, 263–268
Göksel, A. & S. Özsoy 16, 24, 34, 35, 49–50, 58, 61, 63, 70, 78, 84, 140
Gungbe 1–2, 7, 219
Ground 11, 22–23, 25

Hungarian 2, 33, 58, 61, 83–84, 88, 114, 120, 181, 188

Identificational focus 2, 11, 27, 58, 61, 71
Information(al) focus 11, 28, 33–34, 58, 61, 95–96
Information packaging 1–3, 10, 15–17, 20–21, 23–24, 39, 41, 78
In-situ 1, 3, 16, 33, 41, 61, 63–65, 69, 71–73, 80, 129, 161, 178–179, 182, 184, 186–187, 189–190, 193–194, 196, 203, 216, 252
Internal merge 5, 7
Intonation(al)phrase 84–85, 89, 122–125, 128
Inverse scope 140, 152–155, 157, 159–162, 164, 166–167, 169–176, 180, 184, 188–189, 191, 193–197, 202, 211–212, 223, 229
Island (effects/domains) 171–172, 240–241, 257–259
Italian 2, 83, 85–86, 121, 141, 155, 220

Japanese 2, 83–84, 86–87, 128, 155, 220, 245, 247–248, 278

Katz, J. & E. Selkirk 2, 11, 13, 22, 28, 83, 87, 97, 114, 120, 124–125
Kiss, K. 2, 11, 33, 36, 58, 71–72, 181
Kontrast 11, 71

Merge 5–7, 255, 262, 276
Mood 19, 151, 259–261, 264–272, 277–279, 281

Narrow Focus 2, 11–12, 84, 88, 96–97, 100–101, 114, 117–120, 122, 125–128, 130
Neeleman, A. & H. van de Koot 73–74, 140, 208–211, 213
Neeleman, A. & R. Vermeulen 11-13, 32-33, 37, 44, 47, 52-53, 141
Neeleman, A. & T. Reinhart 131
Negation 4, 19, 32–33, 37, 74, 140, 142–145, 147–157, 213–218, 229, 232, 243, 252, 265, 280
Nominative case 254, 256, 260–261, 272, 275–278
Nuclear domain 76, 93–94, 100–101, 110–111, 114–117

Ordinary semantic value 26–30, 34, 36, 48, 63, 219

Particle 8, 51, 56–60, 70, 228, 235
Phase 4–7, 19, 83–84, 131–136, 140, 187, 191, 199–200, 206, 223–225, 244–251, 255, 276–277
Phase impenetrability condition 5–6, 199, 255, 277
Phonological phrase 2, 4, 9, 79, 84–86, 88, 90, 122–125, 129, 133, 135–136
Post-focal compression 87, 101, 110, 114, 120–121, 128
Postnuclear domain 76, 94–95, 100–101, 103, 105, 110–113, 115, 117, 119
Postverbal 2, 4, 15, 23, 43, 55, 69–70, 77–80, 124, 156, 181, 221
Prenuclear domain 76, 93, 97, 100–101, 103, 105, 110–115, 117, 119, 129
Presentational focus 11, 16, 27, 32, 60, 63, 83, 91–92, 96
Presupposition 22, 25–27, 105, 231–237

Prosodic domains 3, 84, 88–89, 121
Prosodic word 84, 129, 131, 137–138

Question particle 31, 47–48, 213–219, 222, 228, 272
Quantifier 4–5, 19, 37, 46–47, 208–209, 211

Reflexive 245–251, 273
Reinhart, T. 12, 21–22, 38, 44, 131, 171
Rheme 11, 13, 22, 71, 91
Rooth, M. 10, 25–27, 48, 56, 122
Russian 2, 141–142,

Scope domain of focus 18, 73, 122, 140, 191, 193–194, 196–209, 224, 277–279
Scope transparency 210
Selkirk, E. 84, 170
Sentential stress 130–136
Sentential stress rule 131, 133–134
Serbo-Croatian 199–200, 244
Somali 1–2, 7
Structured meaning approach 25
Surface scope 152–154, 158, 161–162, 164, 166, 169–171, 176, 181, 183, 186, 188–191, 193, 195, 210–211
Suspended affixation 225, 269–272

Tense phrase 224–227, 224–251, 259–281
Theme 11, 13, 22–23, 91
Topic 1–3, 7–8, 12–13, 21–23, 37–39
Truckenbrodt, H. 31, 83–85, 120–122, 125, 128, 219

Universal Quantifier 144–148, 152, 157, 159–161, 164, 166–168, 170–174, 176, 180, 182, 188–191, 193–197
Utterance 84

vP 4–6, 131–135, 140–142, 149–150, 152, 154, 172, 180–181, 198–208, 224, 246–248, 255, 277–278

Wagner, M. 4, 12, 47, 52, 72, 78, 124, 155, 206
Wh-feature 7, 19, 219–222
Wh-phrase 8, 27, 29, 50–52, 64–66, 141, 218–222, 241, 257, 275
Wh-question 7, 28–29, 56, 59, 67–68, 87, 99, 106–107, 123, 218–219, 221–222

Yes/no questions 31–32, 47, 74–75, 215, 218, 222

www.ingramcontent.com/pod-product-compliance
Lightning Source LLC
Chambersburg PA
CBHW031326230426
43670CB00006B/249